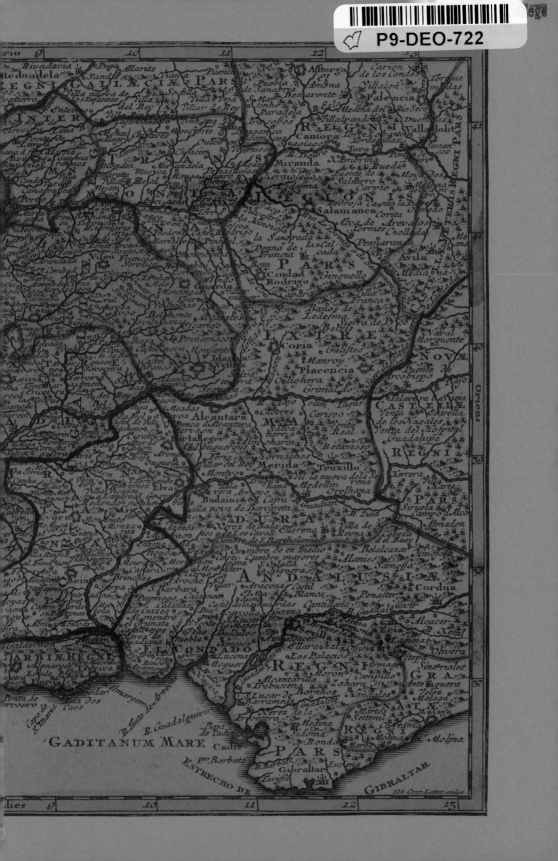

THE PORTUGUESE LANGUAGE

THE HISTORY AND STRUCTURE OF LANGUAGES
General Editor, Eric Hamp

THE JAPANESE LANGUAGE, by Roy Andrew Miller (1967)

JAPANESE AND THE OTHER ALTAIC LANGUAGES, by Roy Andrew Miller (1971)

THE PORTUGUESE LANGUAGE, by J. Mattoso Camara, Jr. (1972)

In preparation:

THE ITALIAN LANGUAGE, by Giacomo Devoto

THE GREEK LANGUAGE, by André Mirambel and Michel Lejeune

History and Structure of Languages

The
Portuguese Language

J. MATTOSO CAMARA, JR.

Translated by Anthony J. Naro

*With an Analytical Bibliography of the
Writings of Joaquim Mattoso Camara, Jr., compiled by
Anthony J. Naro and John Reighard*

THE UNIVERSITY OF CHICAGO PRESS
Chicago & London

THE UNIVERSITY OF CHICAGO PRESS, CHICAGO 60637
The University of Chicago Press, Ltd., London

© 1972 by The University of Chicago
All rights reserved.
Published 1972
Printed in the United States of America

International Standard Book Number: 0-226-51121-9
Library of Congress Catalog Card Number: 79-167939

Contents

Translator's Preface

The culmination of a lifetime of scholarly activity concentrated in the field of Portuguese linguistics, *The Portuguese Language*, by Joaquim Mattoso Camara, sadly must now appear as a posthumous publication. The news of Professor Camara's untimely death on 4 March 1970 was received with shock and dismay by scholars around the world, but the loss was nowhere more acutely felt than in his native Brazil, which must now carry on its linguistic work without the expert guidance of the *Mestre*.

The path that led Mattoso Camara to become Brazil's most outstanding linguist was a rather indirect one. The son of Dr. Joaquim Mattoso Duque Estrada Camara, an expert on financial affairs and the author of a book and several other works on that subject, Joaquim

Mattoso Camara, Jr., was born in Rio de Janeiro in 1904. His early formal education was mainly in architecture and law, and he did not entirely give up the practice of the former profession until 1937. Quite soon, however, Mattoso's interest in linguistic matters, especially poetry, became evident. In 1928 he began his long career in secondary education, a field to which he contributed several textbooks on Portuguese, English, and French. Among these are the *Curso da Língua Pátria* (in collaboration with Carlos Henrique da Rocha Lima) and *Páginas Inglêsas* (in collaboration with Carlos Ramos). His interest in higher level linguistics, stimulated by the discovery of the first volume of the *Travaux du Cercle Linguistique de Prague* (1929), dates from the same period. It was not until 1937, however, when the French scholar Georges Millardet served as visiting professor at the Universidade do Distrito Federal in Rio, that he was able to pursue formal university level studies in his chosen field.

Millardet and Sousa da Silveira, the professor of Portuguese, recognized in Mattoso a brilliant scholar. He was invited to give the course on general linguistics in 1938 and 1939, but the demise of the municipal university caused an unfortunate interruption in Mattoso's university teaching career until 1950, when he joined the staff of the Faculdade Nacional de Filosofia. Nonetheless, Mattoso did give higher level courses at the Museu Nacional beginning in 1943. His lectures at the university were, at the insistence of Sousa da Silveira, published serially in the *Revista de Cultura* and later appeared in book form (see the bibliography of the author's works that follows the text, items no. 114–18). His first published scholarly articles also date from this period, as does his translation of Sapir's *Language* (completed in 1938 but not published until 1954; item no. 124 in the bibliography).

Perhaps the most notable single event in Mattoso's formative years was his stay in the United States from September 1943 until April 1944. Despite, or rather, because of the war this was a particularly exciting period for linguistics in North America. The leading figure in the United States at the time was Leonard Bloomfield, and many enthusiastic younger scholars (Robert A. Hall, Morris Swadesh, Zellig Harris, and others) were working in the field. But most important of all, from Mattoso's point of view, was the establishment in New York of Roman Jakobson and with him a branch of the Prague school of thought. In fact, during his stay in the States Mattoso chose to work mainly, although not exclusively, within the European-oriented group led by Jakobson at Columbia University and the École Libre des Hautes Études. His work in general linguistics with Americans was, for the most part, limited to an older generation of scholars. The American who most impressed Mattoso during this period was unquestionably Professor Louis Gray of Columbia, who had already retired at the time. In addition to Jakobson and Gray, Mattoso also studied under Professors Anthony Paura (Sanskrit) and George Herzog (African languages) of Columbia, as well as under Professor Clarence Parmenter of the University of Chicago (experimental phonetics). At Chicago he also had some contact with Professor Carl Buck (classical philology).

Upon his return to Rio, Mattoso resumed his activities at the Museu Nacional but it was not until 1958 that a *Setor Lingüístico* was formally established there. In 1957 he began his association with the Faculdade de Filosofia, Ciências e Letras of the Catholic University of Petrópolis in the state of Rio de Janeiro, and also served as a visiting professor at the University of Paraná. On other occasions he was visiting professor at the University of Lisbon, Georgetown University (Washington, D.C.), El Colegio de México, and at the summer linguistic institutes of the Linguistic Society of America.

In 1949, four years after his return from the United States, Mattoso was awarded the *doutorado em letras clássicas* by the Faculdade Nacional de Filosofia. His thesis *Para o estudo da fonêmica portuguêsa*, one of the first written in Brazil, was approved with highest honors by a committee headed by Sousa da Silveira and was later published both in the journal *Boletim de Filologia* and in book form (item no. 1; see also item no. 63). As Mattoso himself has stated, this thesis was very much influenced by Jakobson (item no. 57, p. 232).

The task of introducing modern linguistics into Brazil, implicitly entrusted to Mattoso as early as 1938, was not an easy one. Although he received the support of such leading figures as Sousa da Silveira, Mattoso had to fight against a tremendous backlog of incompetence on the lower levels cast in the form of pedantically normative school grammarians (see item no. 70, pp. 3–5; cf. also items 71 and 80). After four years at the Instituto de Educação, a teacher's college, he gave up the effort because of lack of support from his colleagues (see item no. 58, p. 62). The official *Nomenclatura gramatical brasileira* shows few signs of any progress, despite the fact that it was issued in 1958, precisely twenty years after Mattoso's first course. Furthermore, linguistics was not even represented as a course at the university in Rio for a decade. Surely, the fact that Mattoso continued to teach in the face of such obstacles is in itself an impressive testimony for his dedication to the science of language.

Mattoso's interest in language was not in any sense restricted to the domain of grammar. As early as 1941, in one of his first scholarly works, Mattoso published a brilliant stylistic study on Machado de Assis's use of the terms *cão* and *cachorro* 'dog' in the *Quincas Borba*. This was soon followed by a series of further studies on Machado de Assis that at times reach a pinnacle of such astounding insight as to leave the attentive reader nearly breathless.

Speaking in very general terms, it would be correct to say that Mattoso's over-all outlook on language was established very early in his career, in fact before his visit to the United States. His dedication to the Prague school can, as we have seen, be traced back to the first volume of its *Travaux* (1929). His interest in the teachings of Sapir had led to the translation of *Language* by 1938. Combining these two influences with the earlier work of Saussure, one can only agree wholeheartedly with Mattoso himself when he states that his 'connections are chiefly with the Prague Circle, the Saussurian orientation, and the linguistic philosophy of Sapir' (item no. 57, p. 232). His aversion to what he considered the excessively mechanistic orientation of Bloomfield emerges clearly from his choice of teachers during his stay in the United States in 1943–44, and even more clearly from his later works. Hampejs was precisely correct when he named these three influences (plus Millardet) and observed that Mattoso 'has remained faithful to the teachings of this school until the present day and writes all of his linguistic works in accord with its guiding spirit' (Zdenek Hampejs, 'Filólogos Brasileiros', *Boletín de Filología*, Universidad de Chile, 13 (1961):165–234; see p. 225). On the other hand, Leodegário de Azevedo Filho missed the mark to a certain extent when he wrote that Mattoso's work is 'connected in a fundamental way with American linguistics' (review of item no. 114, p. 145). Mattoso's biggest debt is directly to the Prague Circle through Roman Jakobson; the only American who exercised a strong influence on him was Sapir, and this influence was of necessity indirect. In fact, Mattoso's works have not been well received in reviews by American linguists for about twenty years. The last passable review by an American structuralist was

Garvin's commentary in 1950 (review of item no. 3) on part of
Mattoso's thesis. Thereafter American reviewers tended to show im-
patience at his obvious rejection of their doctrines.

Mattoso's harking back to Sapir is of particular interest since it
brings up the whole question of 'psychological reality', and in general
the relevance of intuition to linguistic analysis. From a cursory examination of almost any of his works one could easily gain the impression that Mattoso was totally opposed to psychologizing of any sort
in linguistics, but this impression would be only halfway correct. He
did, indeed, consider intuition to be out of place in synchronic analysis,
but at the same time his own diachronic analysis of the Portuguese
verbal form in -*ria* depends very heavily on psychological ideas (see the
comments on item no. 12 in the bibliography). Thus, Mattoso adopted
the position that psychology is irrelevant and misleading in synchronic
analysis, but necessary for a satisfactory understanding of linguistic
history.

It is perhaps to the distinction noted above that one may trace a
certain subtle difference in tone between Mattoso's writings in the
two fields. His synchronic work is always very methodical and shows
the qualities of a fine workman, but it fails to awaken a feeling of
intellectual excitement in the reader. The diachronic works, on the
other hand, are more like the studies on Machado de Assis in that a
sense of awareness of the nonobvious is communicated to the reader.

The present work covers both diachrony and synchrony, but the
tone associated with the latter prevails. The first draft was written at
the request of the University of Chicago Press between 1963 and 1965.
A series of revisions, amounting to no more than ten pages, was
received in 1967. Sections of the translation were sent to Professor
Camara for final revision as they became available and he had re-
turned the corrected manuscript up to Chapter 9. The final section
was in his hands at the time of his death, but as he did not make any
important substantive changes in the earlier sections we can be rea-
sonably sure that this final part is representative of his thought. Only
the difficulties of communication with author, translator, readers, and
editors spread out over five continents can explain the delays involved
in getting the book, which appears with a 1972 imprint, to press.

The generative linguist of 1972, like his descriptive predecessors,
will probably not receive Mattoso's work kindly since its orientation is
essentially that adopted by the author as early as the twenties and

thirties. This is not to say that Mattoso was out of touch with the latest works of such scholars as André Martinet or that he had not read Chomsky; it does mean that American linguistics, from the bygone days of neo-Bloomfieldian descriptivism to the present reawakening of an interest in generalization, explanation, and linguistic insight, is little represented in his work, if at all. In fact, from the present point of view Mattoso's older positions seem more appropriate. Particularly interesting in this respect is a comparison of his definition of linguistics in 1942 with that of 1956 (reprinted unchanged in 1967):

> 1942:   I must persist in my view that the goal of linguistics is merely to observe and to generalize on the basis of observed phenomena (item no. 83, p. 60).
>
> 1956:   The goal of all linguistic study is much more to discern and to distinguish, rather than to associate and to generalize (item no. 12, p. 12).

Similarly, the linguist of 1972 may be surprised to find the word *theoretical* used to mean both 'systematic phonemic' and 'fake' (see the comments on item no. 11), and he will probably look askance at the rather consistent use of ironic quotation marks around the word *regular*. But *The Portuguese Language* was not intended as a contribution to general linguistics, or for that matter, as a contribution to any particular theory of grammar. It is above all an explicit and masterful exposition of the facts of the Portuguese language that will be of use to scholars of all theoretical persuasions, Praguean or otherwise.

In closing, it is interesting to note that Mattoso himself has stated that 'current trends of linguistic studies in Brazil are somewhat outdated in the face of current linguistic trends in the United States of America and Europe' (item no. 57, p. 245). If we count Mattoso and his followers as the first generation of Brazilian linguists, the second generation of Bloomfieldian and neo-Bloomfieldian descriptivists is devoid of a leader of Mattoso's stature and is, in fact, nearly nonexistent. But, there are today in Brazil very encouraging signs of a third generation devoted to the goal of explanation in synchronic linguistics. At the Museu Nacional, the very same institution that provided Mattoso with academic facilities during the decade in which linguistics was barred from the universities, Professor Miriam Lemle has been carrying out a series of excellent research projects and giving expert instruction in that institution's graduate program in linguistics.

Also worthy of note are the programs at the Pontifical Catholic University of São Paulo, the University of Rio Grande do Sul, and the University of Bahia. Perhaps the lack of a significant mechanistically inclined descriptivist school in Brazil will give these new programs clear ground on which to work. In any event, their task would be completely impossible if it were not for the pioneering work of Joaquim Mattoso Camara.

ANTHONY J. NARO

Luanda, Angola

Chapter 1

The Portuguese Language

The Concept of Language

In ordinary speech the word *language*, which is used to refer to that
which is uttered or written, has an unclear, impressionistic meaning.
Even though the man-in-the-street can use the term without any
hesitation or doubt, he does so in an unstudied, intuitive way and is
therefore quite unable to explain the reason for the use of this particular word rather than some other. Similarly, linguists have found the
exact definition of the concept of language to be elusive. The principal
cause of this difficulty is the countless number of variations of infi-
nitely small degrees of differentiation that human languages exhibit.
Such variations may occur either horizontally, along a geographical
axis, or vertically, along a social axis, according to social classes and

their interactions. Horizontal, or spatial, variation has created the necessity to distinguish between *language* and geographical *dialect*, a problem that even linguists have been unable to resolve in a uniform, coherent, and generally acceptable way.

Language, viewed as a whole, is an ideal structure that contains within itself those basic features that are common to all its realizations. It is a virtual, abstract invariant that underlies a mosaic of concrete, realized versions.

In societies that have a developed culture (often called 'civilization') the concept of language reduces to what is called 'common language' or 'national language'. This, in turn, is the basis both of the written language, that is, the 'literary language', *lato sensu*,[1] and also of the 'spoken' language of the so-called upper classes, the latter used only in more or less strictly determined conditions. Situations of this type lead to the establishment of a rigid norm that reduces acceptable variation to a minimum and serves as an ideal model for linguistic communication. The observance of the norm eventually comes to constitute so-called correctness.

Although the norm cannot eliminate either the multiple variety of regional and social dialects or their numerous and complex interactions, it does create an area of relative stability that can be treated as language itself. Concentrating primarily on this zone of invariance, we have something more connected to deal with when we speak of specific languages such as Portuguese, English, or Arabic, and we can distinguish any norm from any other, even when two norms occur in contiguous territories, as in the case of Portuguese and Spanish. Furthermore, the norm, considered as an entity itself, can be taught to foreigners as the 'usual' or model language and one can trace its history and describe its structure, even though one is often dealing with a structure that is not real. Let us not forget, however, that the linguistic norm merely reduces allowable variation to a minimum, without eliminating it entirely.

1. The term 'literary language *stricto sensu*' refers to the language used in literary art. In general it is based on the written language, or the literary language *lato sensu*, although its general mode of organization and some of its characteristic features are determined by the circumstance that it is primarily an aesthetic language. In some cases a literary language *stricto sensu* can be based on a regional or social dialect, but the writer's purpose must always be primarily aesthetic.

Language in More than One Country

Although the above reservation is important for any language at all, it is even more significant for one that, like Portuguese or English, belongs to politically and culturally distinct societies that also happen to be separated geographically. In this case linguistic variation, which is intrinsic and everpresent, tends to become polarized in subnorms for the different countries in which the language occurs. Thus, we find American and British English or Brazilian and European Portuguese.

The man-in-the-street, whom we mentioned at the outset, may become a bit perplexed at this state of affairs. The essentially impressionistic sense that he gives to the word *language* does not permit him to decide if such subnorms constitute separate languages. Sometimes the evidence of the differences absorbs him and he thinks of two different languages; sometimes he summarily puts these differences aside and sees only one language that he would like to think of as uniform. The linguist must be more objective and cautious. In general, the problem of linguistic variation can be resolved only within the framework of a hierarchy of differences.

In the case of a common language that occurs in more than one country, the basic unity of the situation may justify talking about a single language. One must take account, however, of possible variations within this fundamental unity and must never fall into the old trap of mistaking a subnorm for a norm and then establishing a concept of correctness based on the subnorm. Description must proceed from fundamental shared features and must be based primarily on them. Differences are of secondary importance to general linguistic structure.

The Geographical Distribution of Portuguese

Portuguese occurs as a national language in two countries: Portugal, in Europe,[2] and, in South America, Brazil. In both countries, it is surrounded by Spanish, a language to which it has a great over-all similarity but from which it is distinguished by several fundamental structural features. The two languages differ in phonological structure,

2. Today the European variety of Portuguese is found in certain centers of Portuguese civilization in Africa, such as Angola and Mozambique.

in grammatical forms and syntactic patterns, and in the lexicon as a whole, as well as in the distribution of individual entries.

In the form of creole dialects, Portuguese is also found in various places in Africa and Asia, where the language was carried during the period of overseas expansion (fifteenth and sixteenth century). Here one is not dealing with a national language, but with *sui generis* dialects that resulted from the adoption of Portuguese as a language of communication by various ethnic and cultural groups that also retained their native languages. Examples of this type are the dialects of Diu, Damão, and Goa in India, Macau in China, and the Cabo Verde archipelago and the islands of São Tomé and Príncipe in Africa.

Within the territories of Portugal and Brazil there are various dialects alongside of the two established sub-norms, but in both countries the study and classification of dialects has been carried out with little technical precision. The rigorous methodology of linguistic geography has only recently been introduced in Portugal, and these studies are still in a developmental stage (cf. Boléo 1942, Cintra 1954). In Brazil a first preliminary attempt to carry out a geographic study of dialects was confined to the state of Bahia (Rossi 1964). Early work in Portugal, beginning especially with that of Leite de Vasconcelos at the end of the nineteenth and the beginning of the twentieth century (1901), was carried out with impressive devotion, coherence, and continuity, but the methodology employed was always somewhat impressionistic.

It is generally agreed that within Portugal there are two main dialect areas, the north and the south. To these one may add a central dialect (the province of Beira), which is in reality transitional between the first two. The general divisions encompass lesser regional dialectal differences that, lacking a precise linguistic criterion, are usually considered to coincide with the political division of the provinces: in the north, Minho, Douro, and Trás-os-Montes; in the south, Portuguese Estremadura, Ribatejo, Alentejo, and the Algarve. The dialects of the island of Madeira and of the archipelago of the Azores show more extreme variation.

The most generally accepted classification of Brazilian dialects is that of Antenor Nascentes. One must, however, keep in mind that these results were organized primarily on the basis of impressions gathered while traveling through the country. According to Nascentes, Brazil is divided into two major dialect areas, the north and the south.

The line of separation that he suggested begins at the coast between the states of Espírito Santo and Bahia, continuing to the city of Mato Grosso and through the state of the same name, after also having cut across the states of Minas Gerais and Goiás. In the north there are two major subdivisions: Amazonian (Pará, Amazonas, Acre, and the northwest of Goiás) and northeastern (Maranhão, Piauí, Ceará, Rio Grande do Norte, Paraíba, Pernambuco, Alagoas, and the northeast of Goiás). In the south there are four subdivisions: Bahian (including Bahia itself, Sergipe, the north of Minas Gerais, and the center of Goiás), Fluminense (Espírito Santo, Rio de Janeiro, part of the east of Minas), Mineiro (most of the state of Minas Gerais), and southern (São Paulo, Paraná, Santa Catarina, Rio Grande do Sul, in addition to the south of Minas, the south of Goiás and Mato Grosso). (Nascentes 1953, 18–26).

Dialects: Causes

Dialectal distinctions can always be explained in part by political and cultural factors (including population movements) and in part by the centrifugal forces of human language itself. The latter generate dialect differentiation in any relatively large territory through crystallization of variant structures. The extent to which this process can occur is, of course, directly proportional to the degree of isolation of the region in question from a center of linguistic radiation.

The dialectal division between the north and south of Portugal is a result of the historical circumstance that Portugal was carved out of a strip of territory along the northern coast of the Atlantic at a time when the southern part of the coast was occupied by the Moors. Similarly, historical circumstances are also responsible for the division of Brazil into dialect areas. In this case the division was first established in the early colonial period and was reinforced by subsequent economic and cultural developments.

Portuguese dialectology will not be treated in this book. As has been already stated, our object of study will be the general language and its ideal norm, with only marginal consideration of the European and Brazilian subnorms. Our first topic will be the origins of Portuguese and its territorial expansion. This will provide the necessary background for our studies of the historical changes that the language has undergone, without losing in the process its structural identity as a single language, chronologically differentiated into successive phases.

HISTORY

The Romance Languages

Portuguese, like several other modern languages of the West, belongs to a group of languages, called 'Romance' or 'Neo-Latin', that evolved from Latin, the language of Latium in ancient Italy or, more specifically, of the city of Rome. The number of languages included in this group by different authors varies noticeably for at least two reasons. First, there is the problem of distinguishing languages proper from dialects. Second, many such languages have either died out or are of little significance in the modern world in spite of their unquestionable importance in the Middle Ages.

Among the national or literary languages (*lato sensu*), one finds from east to west in Europe: Rumanian (Rumania, in the Balkans), Italian (Italy), French (France), and in the Iberian or Hispanic (Spanish) Peninsula, Castilian or Spanish (Spain), and Portuguese (Portugal). Of these the following occur as literary languages *lato sensu* in the New World: French (Canada), in an appreciable part of that country, and, as national languages, Spanish (the whole of Central America and a large part of South America) and Portuguese (the vast area encompassed by the Republic of Brazil). Mention should also be made of two other languages. Catalan, the language of the north-eastern Spanish province of Catalonia, was an important national and literary language in the Middle Ages and is still maintained today in certain regions as a literary language under the official hegemony of Spanish. In medieval France there was in addition to French, which was found only in the central and northern regions, another literary language (*lato* and *stricto sensu*), Provençal, in the south, of which some dialectal remnants still exist.

In addition to the national and literary languages, one must also consider as a 'virtual, abstract invariant that underlies a mosaic of concrete, realized versions', as we have just defined 'language', Rhaeto-Romanic or Ladin, which is found in an area including the far south of Switzerland and the far north of Italy. Sardinian, a language whose fundamental structural features are quite unique and distinguish it clearly from an Italian dialect, is found under similar conditions on the island of Sardinia. Until the nineteenth century there was also a Dalmatian group, including Vegliote, along the eastern shore of the Adriatic Sea, facing Italy.

The Territorial Expansion of Latin

All of the languages mentioned above evolved from Latin, which, as we shall see, was implanted in a large part of Europe as a result of the military victories of the Romans and their subsequent political and cultural hegemony. Latin first became the language of the whole of ancient Italy itself when the Romans, beginning in the third century B.C., conquered the entire Italic Peninsula, causing the other languages of the area to weaken and, finally, disappear. Among these languages was Etruscan, a language both structurally and historically unrelated to Latin. It was spoken in a nation of city-states located above Rome along a wide strip of the coast of the Tyrrhenian Sea, facing the island of Corsica. In earlier periods Etruscan culture, which was quite unique, had a profound influence on Rome. Two other languages of the Peninsula were Oscan and Umbrian, spoken in the regions of Samnium (which surrounded Latium) and Umbria (between Samnium and Etruria), respectively.[3] These languages closely resembled Latin, and all three are considered to have originated from a common Italic proto-language. There were also other Indo-European languages (a large family including Latin, Oscan, Umbrian, and many ancient and modern languages of Europe and Asia) that, however, were not closely related to Latin.[4] Almost all that remain of these languages are their names and a few unclear or doubtful bits of information. One exception is Celtic, an Indo-European family whose general structure is understood. This family includes, outside of Italy, such languages as Gaulish (Gaul), Irish (Ireland), and Welsh (Wales, in Great Britain). In ancient Italy itself Celtic was found, beginning in the fourth century B.C., in a region that was called *Gallia Citerior* because it was located between the Apennines and the Alps. Greek, another well-studied Indo-European language, was spoken in an area the Romans called *Magna Graecia*, which consisted of a series of

3. Some linguists (see Devoto 1944, 67) deny the existence of a prehistoric Italic group. To them, Latin and Oscan-Umbrian are originally distinct Indo-European groups that, because of geographical and cultural contact within Italy, influenced one another.

4. Some examples are: Ligurian, in the northeast, reaching to southern Gaul; Messapian, in Apulia and Calabria, probably the language of the nation called the 'Iapiges' by the Greeks; Venetian, in the eastern part of the plain of the Po; Illyrian, in the Tirol, reaching to the middle of the Danube region; and Sicilian, starting out in the far south of Italy but later extending to Sicily. All of these languages were very probably Indo-European.

colonial cities located along the southeast coast of Italy extending to Sicily.

Although Roman conquests could have led to analogous changes of language in *all* the nations of Europe, Africa, and Asia that made up the great Roman Empire, such changes were in fact limited to a smaller area. At one point the Latinized area included the whole of Italy and adjacent islands, the far south of Switzerland, the Dalmatian coast, Gaul (corresponding to what is today France and a large part of Belgium), Iberia, Libya (the Mediterranean coast of Africa), and Dacia (corresponding in part to modern Rumania). In northern Africa Latin survived only until the beginning of the Middle Ages, when it was replaced by Old Berber and Arabic dialects introduced during the Moslem invasions and the resulting Islamization (beginning in the seventh century).

Iberian Latin

We shall be concerned specifically with the history of the implantation of Latin in the Iberian Peninsula, a territory first penetrated by Rome in the second century B.C. as a result of the Second Punic War. After suffering defeat in a war that was fought mainly on the seas, the Carthaginians, under Hamilcar Barca, the father of Hannibal, established military occupation zones in Iberia and mobilized the native population in an attempt to take revenge on Rome. It was from Iberia that Hannibal started out when he attacked Italy and Rome by land, and Iberia was, in turn, the primary target of the Roman counterattack, a long and fierce battle that was finally decided in favor of the Romans in the battlefields of Africa.

The Roman occupation of the Iberian Peninsula was total and permanent. Large numbers of colonists were sent from Italy and the territory was methodically divided into administrative and military zones. Although the boundaries of these zones were changed more than once, three military and administrative centers can be easily distinguished. In the northeast, from the valley of the Ebro to the *meseta central*, was the province of *Tarraconensis* or *Hispania Citerior*. *Hispania Ulterior*, or *Baetica* understood in a broad sense, was in the southwest. *Lusitania*, which extended along the central Atlantic coast, was soon detached from this zone and thus came to be distinguished from Baetica proper.

Very little is known about the people or languages of Iberia at the time of the Roman conquest. The only thing known for sure is that there were many individual nations that had very different languages and cultures. From an ethnic point of view, there were at least two distinct levels of population: a very ancient one, called 'Iberian' proper (the adoption of this term does not preclude the possibility of this group itself being composed of subgroups of distinct origin, culture and language, as is likely), and another more recent one, the Celts, whose main strength was in Gaul but who penetrated the Hispanic Peninsula, just as they did the north of Italy. It seems that in certain regions the Celts and the native population merged into a single race that the Romans called 'Celtiberi'. Everything indicates that the Romans' tripartite administrative system was an attempt to reflect certain basic ethno-cultural features of the native population. Thus Lusitania, which included all of modern Portugal, must have had unique ethnic, cultural, and linguistic characteristics.

Gradually Latin became established in the peninsula and finally replaced the native languages. Only in a limited region in the Pyrenees did one of the pre-Celtic languages, Basque, survive. It still exists in that region today, as a sort of enclave between the Spanish of the south and the French of the north.

The Iberian Peninsula in the Middle Ages

In the area in which Romance languages eventually developed Latin was the dominant language by the time of the political and military decline of the Roman Empire. When the Germanic invasions took on force in the fifth century, Latin, which of course had developed significant regional variations, was the new native language of the Iberian Peninsula. Occupation of these territories by Germanic tribes had no significant effect on their language. Latin, along with most other aspects of Roman culture, was maintained both in the small Swabian kingdom, located along the Atlantic coast above the Tagus, and in the great empire of the Visigoths, who dominated the rest of the peninsula and eventually conquered the Swabians as well.

The language that the Moorish invaders found in the Iberian Peninsula when they occupied it at the beginning of the eighth century was therefore Latin, and this language was tolerated in the new empire under the official hegemony of Arabic. The former, already quite different from the classical language, had regional variants that continued to evolve in the mouths of the subjugated population, the so-called Mozarabs. At the same time Hispanic or Spanish Latin was isolated in the north, where a small nucleus of Christians whom the

Moors could not conquer had developed. The Hispanic and Mozarabic dialects came into contact when Christians from the north reconquered parts of the Islamic empire in the south.

Both of these dialects represent a new linguistic stage, in which one is dealing with a state of the language that is different from Latin itself. This is what is called 'Romance', a technical term used to cover many different regional types of speech that evolved from Latin during the early Middle Ages. Medieval political states served to encourage development of national languages from contiguous groups of speech types, as happened, for example, in the north of France.

In the Hispanic Peninsula, the Christians were not able to maintain political unity and even in the early periods separate kingdoms appeared. The most important of the early kingdoms were León in the west and Aragon in the east. Although the Leonese dialect was at first used in the kingdom of León, the increasing importance of the province of Castile (zone of Burgos) eventually resulted in the imposition of Castilian as the national language of the kingdom, which came to be called the kingdom of León and Castile. Similarly in the east, the county of Barcelona, in the region of Catalonia, imposed itself on the rest of Aragon, causing Catalan to become a national and literary language.

Portuguese

When the county of Portugal, with center in the Oporto (Portu Cale) region on the Atlantic coast, was separated from the kingdom of León and Castile in the eleventh century, it adopted its own particular Romance, which was essentially Portuguese, as a national language. Further to the north, the region of Galicia, in which the same Romance was spoken, remained politically subjugated to the kingdom of León and Castile, and even today Galician therefore remains a regional dialect, under the official hegemony of Spanish.

The Oporto region was the first linguistic center of Portugal, but as the country's borders advanced southward along the Atlantic coast its language came into contact with various similarly structured Mozarabic dialects and was consequently modified and enriched in its role as the national language. The linguistic center itself soon shifted to Lisbon, a city on the banks of the river Tagus that was taken from the Moors and made the capital of the kingdom by the first king of Portugal, Afonso Henriques.

The present borders of Portugal were established in the second half of the thirteenth century when the far south of the Atlantic coast, the Algarve, was reconquered. By this time a rich school of lyric poetry, similar in technique and thematic content to the Provençal school of southern France, had developed in Portuguese, which thus joined Castilian and Catalan in the list of literary languages *stricto sensu*.[5] Written prose, both ordinary and literary, made its appearance somewhat later since it was necessary first to break the habit of writing in Latin. This written 'Latin', incidentally, suffered somewhat from the influence of spoken Portuguese, and not infrequently one can discover certain features of Portuguese in it.

On the assumption that the written language reflects in a general way the state of the national language and changes along with it, it is customary to divide Portuguese into an archaic period (up to the fifteenth century) and a later period, which one may as well call modern. Well-defined phonological, grammatical, and lexical features serve to distinguish the two stages. For example, starting in the sixteenth century, many words and derivations borrowed (sometimes via Italian) from the literary Latin of antiquity entered the Portuguese lexicon, and it was also in this century that the linguistic norm was first organized in a disciplined way into grammars (Fernão de Oliveira, João de Barros, Duarte Nunes de Leão).

Sometimes the modern period is further subdivided into a classical period (sixteenth and seventeenth century) and a postclassical period in order to reflect changing styles in the literary language. The syntactic style of the classical period was tightly disciplined along the lines of literary Latin. Beginning in the eighteenth century, however, the influence of written French resulted in shorter sentences, syntactically independent of each other. Even considering only oral Portuguese, that is, the national language in a wider sense, there are still clear differences in the grammars of the sixteenth and seventeenth century on the one hand and later periods on the other. In fact, all evidence seems to indicate that the phonology of modern European Portuguese developed after the seventeenth century.

5. Being a somewhat conventional language of poetry with strong Galician and Provençal influences it was not really typical of the language spoken in Portugal. It is this poetic language, rather than normal Portuguese, that is called Gallaeco-Portuguese or Galician-Portuguese.

The Origin and Evolution of Latin

The Language of Rome

Establishment of Latin as the language of the region of Latium in Italy was one of the consequences of the Indo-European migrations from eastern Europe. Rome, which was the population center of the new Latin-speaking peoples, became its linguistic center as well when the urban dialect, at first quite different from that of the surrounding rural areas (from the lower Tiber to the Apennines and the Alban Hills), was adopted as the common language.

By the third century B.C. the city of Rome had assumed a leading role in the region. The key element in its social organization was an aristocratic class known as the 'patricians'. The members of this class originally controlled all political powers and remained politically, socially, and economically aloof from the great, somewhat anonymous, masses of the population. The latter, known as the 'plebeians', included freed slaves and immigrants both from the surrounding countryside and from foreign nations. The patricians seized upon the heterogeneous origin of the plebeians as an excuse for not considering them full Roman citizens.

The bipartite structure of Roman society led naturally to a corresponding dichotomy in linguistic usage. The patricians' usage, properly called 'elegant', contrasted markedly with the undisciplined, careless usage of the plebeians. Romanists, in an attempt to mirror this split in linguistic usage, have established the by-now-traditional theoretical division of Latin into *Classical* and *Vulgar* languages. The fact of the matter is, however, that a subtle dualistic concept of this type cannot be dismissed so easily. Classical Latin was the basis of the written language and the literary language *stricto sensu*. As such, it was a tightly disciplined language studied by intellectuals or, more exactly, grammarians, who followed the Greek school of grammar. As a studied and learned language it resisted the natural forces of linguistic change and was limited to a severe, supposedly immutable pattern that did not lend itself easily to daily social discourse. For this reason a dialect that was more vulgar than classical was used in ordinary dealings, even among patricians. Linguistic differentiation in social usage was further diminished by the numerous political, social, and economic gains won by the plebeians through extended class warfare. The patricians came to accept more of the usage of the plebeians, who in turn attempted to conform to the elegant usage of the patricians. At the same time, however, the grammatical discipline of the careful written and literary styles became more rigid and the ideal of Classical Latin as a fixed, static language became firmly established.

Vulgar Latin was really what we would now call a 'living' language. Classical Latin was a living language only to the extent to which it was influenced by Vulgar Latin and therefore became more malleable and dynamic. The degree to which this actually occurred in the literary language was variable and depended both on the nature of the work (e.g., the popular comedies of Plautus in the third century B.C.), and on the style of the author (e.g., in a later period and to a lesser extent, the lyric poetry of Catullus and the satires of Horace). An intensely vulgar character was added to the written language of Rome by the appearance of Christian religious literature for the masses, but at the same time the classical norm was at work in the vulgar language, tinging its usage to an extent that varied according to the social environment and the situations in which communication actually occurred.

Vulgar Latin can be defined only by contrast with the ideal norm of Classical Latin. Far from being a unique linguistic phenomenon, it is more correctly viewed as a collection of continuously changing social dialects. Insofar as Vulgar Latin was the dynamic, essentially oral, constantly evolving dialect, one may say that the Romance languages derive from it. Only those aspects of Classical Latin that entered the evolutionary process, that is, were 'vulgar', formed the origins of the Romance languages.

The Fragmentation of Latin

When Rome expanded into Italy and the other provinces of the empire, significant regional variation became possible. In the golden age (at least until the first century A.D.) dialect variation seems to have been minimal and was, in part, neutralized by the ideal of Classical Latin. The latter was used in all political and administrative activities, was taught in the provincial schools, and spread along with Roman literature. In later periods, however, two factors combined to increase regional variation. First the centrifugal forces that act upon any language spread over a large region began to take effect. Second, the administrative and educational network of the Romans fell into decay and the literary language became more and more distant from Classical Latin.

Given that such phenomena in themselves are not, however,

sufficient to account for the disintegration of the Vulgar Latin-speaking territory into linguistically distinct blocks, one must consider other causes. In the first place there was a time factor. Since the various regions were conquered and Latinized in different periods they assimilated dialects of Latin in different stages of evolution. Italy was the first to be Romanized, followed by Iberia, Gaul, and, much later, Dacia. Within Iberia itself Lusitania was Latinized after Baetica and most of Tarraconensis. In general the process of Romanization was based on the importation of large numbers of Latin-speaking people; however, the types of people who went to each region were quite different. In some regions one finds lower patricians and Roman plebeians, in others people from the rural areas of Italy, and in still other regions soldiers, or occasionally mercenaries, who did not speak Latin. Within the Iberian Peninsula there was significant variation from one region to the next. Thus, while most of the immigrants in Baetica came from the urban areas of the Italic Peninsula, elsewhere they were mainly from rural areas. Added to this social differentiation, there was also probably variation in the geographical origin of the colonists.

Variation in social and economic conditions of the various Romanized areas implies a corresponding variation in speech. Lusitania, unlike Baetica, was an essentially rural country, without the great urban centers typical of the latter. (For a general discussion see Wartburg 1941, 1952; Meier 1930, 1948; Baldinger 1963).

It is traditional to mention in this regard the fact that since Latin displaced languages of the most varied types, it acquired a correspondingly varied set of substrata. In the case of Lusitania, a Celtic, or at least Celtiberian, substratum has been suggested. In a later period, starting principally in the fourth century with the Germanic invasions, foreign governing elites were established in the provinces. Although they changed languages and adopted Latin, the abandoned languages became superstrata of the provincial dialects of Latin. In the Iberian Peninsula the small Swabian kingdom covered the part of Lusitania above the Tagus and for a while the whole peninsula was a large Visigothic empire. But, in fact, the effect of the linguistic substrata, which in any case involves only loans from the conquering language to the conquered language,[6] was in general of secondary im-

6. Many authors emphasize excessively the effect of substrata, even to the point of considering them almost mystical irrepressible latent forces.

portance in the Romance languages. The same is true for loans by the superstratum.[7]

A much more effective cause of fragmentation was the differing degree of contact with Roman Latin maintained by various regions. Rome, as the political, social, and cultural head of the empire, was the greatest center of radiation of linguistic innovations, and these innovations were becoming increasingly profound as time passed. The degree to which they affected particular regional dialects, however, depended both on the distance of the region in question from Rome and on its situation with respect to the main routes of communication. Some areas, like Italy and Gaul, participated intensely in the linguistic life of the capital; others, like Iberia, participated only marginally. There were even some 'isolated' areas, such as Sardinia or Dacia. Lusitania, the cradle of the Portuguese language, can be considered the most 'marginal' area of the three Iberian provinces.

The Structure of Latin and its Evolution

In the golden age of Latin both the verb and the noun were inflected. Although the norm of Classical Latin called for a fixed system of case endings, the truth of the matter is that this system had even then begun evolving toward a simpler one, particularly in regard to the noun. In fact, the dropping of nominal inflections in Vulgar usage began very early, affecting to a small extent even the written language. With the passage of the centuries this tendency became more and more pronounced, in defiance of the often purely conventional rules of classical grammar. Of course changes in nominal morphology require parallel changes in syntax. In particular, syntactic relations, which were formerly indicated by means of special desinences added to nouns, came to be expressed by means of word-order or connecting particles, the so-called prepositions.

The system of a nominative ending for the subject and an accusative ending for the object, which freely permitted stylistic variations of the type *puer vidit lupum, lupum puer vidit, lupum vidit puer, vidit lupum puer,* and so on, was replaced by a grammatical system based on the typical Romance order, i.e., *(o) menino viu (o) lôbo* 'the boy saw

7. Most Germanisms found in Iberian Latin entered the language long before the period of Swabian and Visigothic domination. They are common to the Latin of all regions in which Romance languages developed because they result from ancient contacts between Latin and Germanic languages (see Menéndez Pidal 1944, p. 19).

the wolf'.[8] There is some evidence that the new order came to be preferred quite early in the history of Vulgar Latin.

Prepositions, which were already used in conjunction with the accusative and ablative endings in order to indicate certain verbal complements, eventually took on a genuinely syntactic role in order to compensate for the phonetic weakening of the endings. The use of prepositions was also extended to other complement types that were formerly indicated by the dative or genitive endings. For example, instead of putting the indirect object in the dative case, the Romance languages use the construction *dar a(o) menino* 'to give to the boy'. This structure derives from the use of the preposition *ad* with an accusative object, a construction that could be used only with complements of direction in Classical Latin (ex: *ire ad templum, ir a(o) templo* 'to go to the temple'). In the same way the subordination of one noun to another by means of the genitive ending was slowly replaced by the "preposition followed by ablative" construction. By the second century A.D. one can find Christian epithets of the type *de Deo munus*, model for the Portuguese construction *dádiva de Deus* 'gift of God' in place of the classical construction *Dei munus*, with *Dei* in the genitive.

Likewise there was a strong tendency toward evolution in the phonological system. Vulgar Latin, heedless of classical orthoepy, offered no resistance to these tendencies, which often developed into radical changes. For example, the subtle interplay of vocalic quantities, which originally were distinctively long (as in *mālum* 'apple') or short (as in *mălum* 'bad'), was destroyed by the predominance of the stressed syllable and its contrast within the word to the unstressed syllables. Furthermore, both syllable types and the syllabification of individual words were altered, and extensive elisions reduced even the phonetic content of words.

As is in general true of social dialects, Vulgar and Classical Latin differed greatly with respect to the lexicon. In the case at hand such differences arose because the Vulgar dialect was subject to the indomitable dynamics typical of any spontaneous living language. As such, its lexicon was augmented and some of the original entries were replaced by words borrowed from other languages. Borrowing occurred not only in the 'cultural' sphere, but also as a result of intimate contact with other languages within a single region. New types of deriva-

8. The article, which is another grammatical innovation of the Romance languages, is put between parentheses.

guese and the Tupi considered all other Indians to be *tapuias,* a word meaning 'enemy' in Tupi. This is the historical origin of the opposition *Tupi-Tapuia,* which was long used as an ethnic and cultural division.

The Tupi of the coastal region between Bahia and Rio de Janeiro were a group of linguistically and culturally homogeneous tribes. When whites tried to learn the dialects they spoke, a generalized language for use in everyday contacts evolved. This language was basically the dialect of the Tupinambá, one of the most important groups and one of those that had most contact with the Portuguese. The language was studied and described in a normative way by Jesuit missionaries, who taught it with a view toward catechization. It was used not only in relations with Indians of the Tupi group, but also in contacts with all other Indians. In general, non-Tupi groups, unlike the Portuguese, learned the language quite easily.[9] In this way a Tupi-based *língua geral* (literally: general language) came into use alongside of Portuguese in the everyday life of the colony. Eventually *língua geral* acquired the status of a written and literary language through use in missionaries' translations of Christian prayers and in the religious hymns and plays (in the style of the old *autos* of Hispanic literature) that they themselves composed.

Portuguese acted as a superstratum for this indigenous language of communication, which was, in general, spoken quite well by the white sector of the population. As a superstratum the main effect of Portuguese was to modify the original phonology, causing Tupi sounds to conform to the Portuguese system. Thus, the Tupi guttural /i/ usually became Portuguese palatal /i/, although the Jesuits continued to use the graphy *y* in order to indicate its special status. Less frequently *y* became the group /ig/ (ex: *Iperoig* 'a place name'), which consists of palatal /i/ followed by guttural /g/. Similarly, the typically Tupi prenasalized consonants /ᵐb/ and /ⁿd/ were replaced by a Portuguese-style oral consonant with concurrent nasalization of the preceding syllabic vowel (ex: *imbu* 'a tree', *tamanduá* 'an animal'), and the single Tupi liquid became a Portuguese /r/, in distinctive opposition to /l/.

Occasionally semantic interpretations changed in the direction of Portuguese. This occurred both in the lexicon (ex: *tupã* 'thunder' became 'God') and in grammatical categories, especially in the semantic interpretation of verbal morphology.

9. Tupi and Jê are rather different lexically (exs: Tupi *i,* Jê *ko* 'water'; Tupi *tatá,* Jê *kuwi* 'fire'; Tupi *itá,* Jê *ken* 'stone'). They do, however, show significant phonological and grammatical similarities.

In contact with Portuguese, which also took root in the colony, the Tupi-based *língua geral* functioned more as an adstratum than as a true substratum—the two languages merely coexisted in the same territory.

The African Contribution

Beginning in the first years of the seventeenth century, importation of black African slaves to the farms and cities of Brazil at an ever-increasing pace added a new feature to the colony's linguistic panorama. Since the slaves, who came from such widely differing racial groups as the Bantu and the Yoruba, were forcibly thrown together in their new home they had to create a compromise language for use in daily life. It seems that since, as slaves, they were tightly integrated into all the principal activities of white society, they soon created a creolized Portuguese that served to unite together blacks of the most diverse origins. All available evidence indicates that they also learned the Tupi-based *língua geral* without much difficulty, stimulating and enriching it even further.

Brazilian Portuguese

Increased immigration from Portugal, combined with increased acceptance of European cultural values, caused the decline and, eventually, the almost complete disappearance of Portuguese-Tupi bilingualism, Portuguese winning out in the end. In fact, the decline of *língua geral* is documented as early as the middle of the seventeenth century.

Immigrants from both the north and south of Portugal, seemingly in approximately equal numbers, carried their respective dialects to Brazil. At the same time an appreciable number of administrators and nobles of the court brought the received language of Lisbon to the colony. Serafim da Silva Neto (1950, 10) has rightly observed that the coming together of such diverse dialects in a single overseas center must have set up conditions leading to a sort of linguistic compromise, a new kind of dialect. As an inevitable result of this process the received language also underwent certain modifications. Thus one can understand why conditions in Brazil since its founding have favored an independent linguistic existence and the development of a sub-norm, in the common language, quite different from that of European Portuguese.

Although the written language and the literary language *stricto sensu* (an epic poem in the style of Camões appeared in Pernambuco as early as the sixteenth century)[10] sometimes reflected these new conditions, other times they remained strictly confined to the patterns brought from Europe. The differences between the written and oral languages of Brazil were, however, reduced to a minimum as a result of a literary movement known as Romanticism that began a few decades after the country's independence in 1821. This same sort of process also occurred in Portugal, causing the differences between its written and spoken languages to be similarly minimized. In this way certain divergences between the written languages of the two Portuguese speaking nations were established. Although at times there have been attempts to force the written language of Brazil to conform to strictly, European patterns, most of the divergences remain. Indeed one can ascribe to them a certain vitalization of the Brazilian written language, which thus maintains a certain degree of contact with the common spoken language. This is not to say, however, that the written language and the spoken language (even in received usage) are identical. Orthographical conventions that do not truly represent Brazilian phonology, as well as forms and syntactic constructions that are either obsolete or entirely abandoned in the spoken language still can be found in the written language.

The Subnorms of Portuguese

The explanation for the discrepancies between the received languages of Brazil and Portugal cannot be ascribed to a supposed Tupi substratum or a supposedly profound African influence, as has sometimes been suggested. Rather, these differences are essentially a result of the circumstance that the language is spoken in two geographically and politically separate territories.

Since the implantation of Portuguese in Brazil during the classical period the language of each country has evolved in its own way, despite the fact that the two countries have maintained close social and cultural relations. For example, the typical *allegro* rhythm, the strong accent on the stressed syllable, and other important phonetic phenomena that developed in Portugal after the classical period are not to be found in Brazilian phonology. Nonetheless, the Brazilian phonological system is also the result of an evolutionary process, one that had as its starting point various overseas dialects as well as the

10. The *Prosopopéia* of Bento Teixeira (Pinto). The author was probably a Portuguese living in Brazil (see Coutinho 1955, I-1, 272).

received language. As far as the lexicon is concerned there are numerous instances of renovation, conservation, and dissimilar readings and borrowings. In the Brazilian subnorm there is a large stockpile of African and Tupi terms with which the common language was enriched during the period of Portuguese-Tupi bilingualism and the creolized Portuguese of the black slaves.

Of course, the popular dialects of Brazil are another matter. In this case it is quite possible that an indigenous, although not necessarily Tupi, substratum and various African dialects might have had phonological and grammatical effects. In another vein, in these same dialects there are also instances of the survival of certain features of archaic Portuguese, but only in areas that were either completely isolated or somewhat removed from the main lines of communication. In fact, the immense size of Brazil, combined with the intermittent and capricious way in which it was explored and settled, is by itself sufficient to create a complex array of dialects. Unfortunately, these dialects have not yet been satisfactorily studied.

Chapter 2

Phonology

PROSODY

Stress in Portuguese

Because of the fundamental importance of stress (or accent) to the entire phonological system, the study of Portuguese phonology must begin with the study of prosody, that is, the placement of stress. Stress in Portuguese is intensive but not violent. It is much weaker in Brazil than in Portugal, where there is a strong contrast between stressed and unstressed syllables. Since, in Portuguese at least, a syllable is stressed by increasing the relative strength with which the breath is released, it is necessarily accompanied by an increase in the frequency of the voice. This, in turn, creates a conditioned tonal accent that is not of relevance to the phonological system. Pitch functions independently only on the sentence level, where it establishes the melodic lines that constitute *intonation* and are character-istic of the various basic sentence types.[1]

Stress may be placed on the last, the penultimate, or the ante-penultimate syllable in Portuguese. Its placement is not determined by the phonological structure of the word. Although many expositive grammars attempt to establish rules for final and penultimate stress placement based on the structure of the last syllable of the word, these rules can do no more than reflect the relative frequency of the particular stress pattern that is considered 'regular'. Since the choice of the 'regular' pattern is always basically impressionistic, however, it would perhaps not agree with the results of rigorous statistical investigation.[2]

In Latin stress could be placed only on the penultimate or ante-penultimate syllable. Its placement was determined by the quantity of the penultimate syllable—if the latter was long it received stress, if it was short stress was placed on the antepenultimate syllable[3] (exs: *pérsĭcum, sólĭdum, apícŭla* vs *collīna, partīre*). With the disappearance of syllabic quantity in Vulgar Latin, rules for stress placement could no longer be given. Furthermore, words having final stress evolved when certain final unstressed syllables vanished or merged with the preceding stressed syllables. Thus *partīre*, with penultimate stress, gave Portuguese *partir*, with final stress, an example that is typical

1. These phenomena have not yet been sufficiently studied in a rigorous way either in Brazil or in Portugal.

2. Although one cannot deny that most words with a final syllable closed by /r/ have final stress, there are nonetheless certain words of this type that show penultimate stress (ex: *açúcar* 'sugar', and others). In the case of final /l/, on the other hand, the statistical distribution is balanced by the presence of adjectives ending in unstressed *-il* (exs: *fácil* 'easy'; *difícil* 'difficult'; *ágil* 'agile') and deriva-tives with the unstressed suffix *-vel* (*amável* 'kind'; *possível* 'possible'). In the case of final oral diphthongs, penultimate stress is rare (ex: *jóquei* 'jockey'), except for the plurals of nouns and adjectives with final unstressed *-il* or *-el* (ex: *fáceis* 'easy' (masc pl)). The written language obscures the balanced nature of the distribution of stress placement in words ending in the nasal diphthong *-ão* by adopting the purely conventional spelling *-am* in verbs (exs of penultimate stress: *órfão* 'or-phan'; *órgão* 'organ'; *sótão* 'attic'; *amam* 'they love'; *amavam* 'they used to love'; *amaram* they had loved'; ex of final stress: *amarão* 'they shall love'). The rules for the use of a diacritic to indicate stress in the written language are based on the impressionistic conclusions reached by certain scholars about the distribution of stress as a function of final syllable type.

3. A short syllable is an open one with a short vowel (ex: *so-lĭ-dum*). A long syllable is either an open one with a long vowel (ex: *par-tī-re*) or one containing a short vowel but closed by a consonant (ex: *be-ne-dĭc-tum*).

of all words having -*re* or -*le* as their final syllable. Latin *aviolum*, which had penultimate stress in Vulgar Latin, gave Portuguese *avô*, with final stress, because the final short *ŭ* (/o̧/ in Vulgar Latin) merged with the stressed *o*, as always happened when a consonant separating like vowels vanished. Thus, final stress is Romance in origin, although subsequent borrowings greatly increased its frequency of occurrence.[4]

On the other hand, most Portuguese words having antepenultimate stress did not evolve from Vulgar Latin. (One exception is *pêssego* from Latin *persĭcum*). Under most conditions the vowel immediately following the stress was dropped in the Iberian (and French) Romance, giving *soldo, abelha,* from *solĭdum, apicŭla,* and so on. In fact, most Portuguese words with antepenultimate stress are the result of a massive borrowing, beginning in the sixteenth century, of Latin and latinized Greek words from the classical language. Later there were direct borrowings from Classical Greek, but the tendency was to stress these words in accordance with the general principles of Latin prosody. The number of words with antepenultimate stress was also increased by a series of borrowings, beginning in the sixteenth century, from Italian, in which the dropping of the unstressed penultimate syllables did not occur.

In any case, penultimate stress is dominant, and one can consider antepenultimate stress to be somewhat marginal in Portuguese. Even in the received language there is an immanent tendency to modify such words in order to make them conform to the more usual penultimate stress pattern. Thus, in compounds or derivatives with a second unstressed element the stress has been shifted forward (ex: *quadrumano*, Lat. *quadrumănum*) and even in simple words stress has been shifted by analogy (ex: *oceano*, Lat. *oceănum*).[5] Antepenultimate stress

4. Final stress is frequent in Arabic loans (exs: *alvará* 'warrant'; *alecrim* 'rosemary'; *anexim* 'proverb'; *azar* 'bad luck'; *alguazil* 'bailiff'; *algodão* 'cotton'). In Brazil, certain loans from Tupi and various African languages also have final stress.

5. This stress shift is usually attributed to the influence of French by school grammarians, who fail to observe that in all clear cases influence of this type is strictly limited to helping along a tendency that is already immanent in any case. In fact, normative grammatical attempts to undo the stress shift often have resulted in a confused situation in which two stress patterns exist side by side. Such attempts have also caused the creation of certain hypercorrect forms such as *púdico* (antepenultimate stress) instead of *pudico* (penultimate stress) 'prudish' from Lt *pudicum*, on the analogy of a large set of words ending in unstressed -*ico*, from Lt *ĭcum*. (exs: *itálico* 'Italic'; *fatídico* 'fateful'; *típico* 'typical').

is eliminated from the popular language of Brazil by dropping a segment of the word between the stressed vowel and the final vowel (exs: *Petrópis* for the place-name *Petrópolis; exérço* instead of *exército* 'army'; *glóbo* instead of *glóbulo* 'globule'). Nevertheless, antepenultimate stress is well established in the received language.

As has already been said, stress may be placed on any one of the last three syllables. For this reason it cannot be denied that stress is distinctive; compare, for example, *dúvida* (noun) 'doubt', *duvida* (verb) 'he doubts'; *duvidara* (verb) 'he had doubted', *duvidará* (verb) 'he will doubt'. The example *dúvida : duvida* is typical of a frequent opposition between a noun and the corresponding verb in the present (*rótulo* 'label': *rotulo* 'I label'; *número* 'number': *numero* 'I number'), while a stress opposition of the type in *duvidara : duvidará* is valid for these two tenses in all 'regular' Portuguese verbs (*amara : amará* 'to love'; *temera : temerá* 'to fear'; *partira : partirá* 'to leave').

Stress as a Word-marker

In Portuguese, particularly in the received language of Brazil, stress serves not only to distinguish distinct words but also to mark the beginnings (or ends) of words, that is, to delimit them. Admittedly this may at first sight seem somewhat strange, given the fact that stress is, within certain limits, free.

In order to understand how words can be marked by stress it is necessary first to observe that there is a secondary prosodic difference between certain unstressed syllables: in words that have antepenultimate or penultimate stress, the syllables that precede the stress are slightly stronger than those that follow it. This phenomenon is particularly stable in Brazil where the posttonic syllables, or those that follow the main stress, are characteristically weak.[6]

The occurrence of a stress is in itself sufficient to signal the existence of a phonological word. In a breath group, that is, a continuous utterance without an intercurrent pause, the number of phonological words is equal to the number of stresses. The last stress, which is necessarily the strongest one and is therefore easily distinguished

6. The syllable that begins with the first consonant of the word is actually a bit stronger than the following pretonic syllables, but this difference can be ignored in the context of stress as a word marker. In Portugal the syllable beginning with the first consonant is the only one that is minimally unstressed. The rest of the syllables before the main stress are just as weak as those that come after it.

from the preceding weaker stresses, signals the end of the breath group and predicts a pause:

três grandes livros　'three great books'
　2　　　2　　　3

Secondary stress is distributed between the stress maxima in accordance with the principle that pretonic vowels receive stronger stress than posttonic vowels. Thus one has, for example,

oitenta volumosos livros　'eighty voluminous books'
1 2 0 11 2 0　3 0

As shown in the following examples, the stress pattern of isolated words, beginning with monosyllables, is therefore . . . (1)-(1)-3-(0)-(0) . . .:

só - *amor* - *casa* - *sólido* - *esplêndido* - *celebridade*
　3　　1 3　　3 0　　3 0 0　1 3 0 0　　1 1 1 3 0
'only'　'love'　'house'　'solid'　'splendid'　'celebrity'

Thus, in a breath group, 0-stress (minimum stress) followed by 1-, 2- or 3-stress (any stress except minimum) signals the end of a word, as does a 2-stress immediately followed by a 1-, 2-, or 3-stress:

três grossos livros　'three thick books'
　2　　2 0　3 0
três cadernos　'three notebooks'
　2　　1 3 0

It is this phenomenon that makes it possible, at least in the case of normal Brazilian pronunciation, to distinguish homophonemic sequences of the type *celebridade* 'celebrity' (one word) from sequences of the type *célebre idade* 'renowned age' (two words, a noun preceded by an adjective). In the second expression the initial vowel of *idade* merges with the final vowel of *célebre*, the minimum stress of the latter being maintained:

/selebridadi/
1 1　1 3 0　　(celebridade)
/selebridadi/
2 0　0 3 0　　(célebre idade)

Phonological Word versus Formal Word

A phonological word is a prosodic entity that is characterized by a stress maximum and two possible lesser stresses before and after the main stress. Although this concept corresponds on the level of form

to what Bloomfield calls a 'free form',[7] it is well known that phonological and formal units do not necessarily coincide. In Portuguese,
for example, there is a type of formal word that is not phonologically
set off by means of stress and is always pronounced in clitic position,
that is, as the initial or final unstressed syllable of a phonological
word.[8] The fact that such words can assume either initial or final
position within the phonological word shows that one is dealing with
individual units. Further evidence is given by the circumstance that
it is possible to insert one or more free forms between a clitic in initial
position and the rest of the word. In this case the clitic is phonologically attached to the first free form.

Pronominal objects may be placed either before or after their verb.
In the first case they are said to be in *proclitic* position and are
treated as a new initial syllable of the verb, while in the second case
they are treated as a new final syllable and are said to be in *enclitic*
position. Typical examples are:

o menino se feriu

            'the boy hurt himself'

o menino feriu-se

Free insertion occurs with a different series of clitics, but only in
proclitic position. Typical examples can be given with articles and
prepositions:

o livro de Camões   'the book of Camões'

o belo e imorredouro livro do grande poeta Camões

'the beautiful and everlasting book of the great poet Camões'

Most proclitics may receive 2-stress for emphasis, with or without
an accompanying pause, in certain styles. This tends to give them the
status of phonological words. As we shall see later, their vocalism,
which is not exactly the same as that of pretonic syllables, is in agreement with this tendency.

Juxtaposition of two phonological words to form a single formal
word is another process that results in a lack of coincidence between

7. An indivisible linguistic form or one that can be divided only into bound
forms and can serve as a communication in isolation (Bloomfield 1933, 160).

8. Although most clitics consist of only one syllable, there are a few two-syllable
clitics that may occur in initial position (ex: *para aqui* 'toward here' as opposed to
pára aqui 'stop here'). In final position, sequences of two monosyllabic clitics are
possible (ex: *ouve-se-lhe o ruído* 'people hear his noise') but are not used in normal
Brazilian speech.

these two categories, although it is of just the opposite sort as that exhibited by clitics. A typical example of juxtaposition, a process that occurs rather frequently in Portuguese nominal morphology, is _guarda-chuva_ 'umbrella'. This word has two successive stresses, a 2-stress and a 3-stress, just as in a breath group consisting of two free forms:

$$guarda\text{-}chuva \qquad \text{'umbrella'}$$
$$2 \quad 0 \quad 3\,0$$
$$forte\ chuva \qquad \text{'heavy rain'}$$
$$2 \quad 0 \quad 3\,0$$

It is only on the morpho-semantic level that a distinction can be made between the two sequences. On this level _guarda-chuva_ is distinct from _chuva_, whereas in the case of _forte chuva_ we are simply dealing with _chuva_ accompanied by a determiner. Thus the first element of the sequence can be deleted in a sentence like _caiu uma (forte) chuva_ 'a (heavy) rain fell', but if _guarda_ is deleted from _guarda-chuva_ the whole lexical entity is destroyed.

In Portuguese the process of formation of words by juxtaposition, in which two phonological words are maintained within a single formal unit, is distinct from agglutination, in which the formative element is incorporated into the simpler phonological word.[9] We return to the latter topic later.

VOCALISM

Evolution of the Latin System

The Latin vowels formed a _dreieck System_ (triangular system) in the sense of Trubetzkoy (cf. Camara 1953, 70). A single low vowel /a/, pronounced in a more or less central position in the mouth without lifting the tongue, was coordinated with two front vowels and two back vowels. The front series, constituting a two-step advance toward the front part of the mouth with a concomitant gradual raising of the tongue, consisted of a mid /e/ and a high /i/. The back series, characterized by a recoiling and simultaneous raising in two steps of the tongue, associated with a rounding of the lips, consisted of a mid /o/ and a high /u/. The vowels of a system of the type described above can be put in an abstract triangular array, the low vowel serving as

9. There are even minimal pairs of the type _extra-ordinário_ : _extraordinário_,
ex-posição : _exposição_.   2   0 1 1 3 0   1 11 1 3 0
2   1 1 3   1 1 1 3

the vertex and the two sides being composed of the front and back series:

$$/i/ \qquad\qquad /u/$$
$$/e/ \qquad /o/$$
$$/a/$$

The phonological system of Latin was complicated by the fact that each vowel of the triangle really represented two vowels—a long one, of somewhat greater duration, and a short one, pronounced rapidly. For this reason each vowel—low, mid front, high front, mid rounded back, and high rounded back—was really a distinctive pair, the members of which were distinguished by quantity, that is, temporal duration. Ordinarily quantity was not marked in writing, although for certain special grammatical studies (such as metrics) it was indicated by writing a diacritic above the vowel in question. A 'macron' was used for long vowels (ā, ē, ī, ō, ū), while short vowels were marked with a 'brachy' (ă, ĕ, ĭ, ŏ, ŭ). Since quantity was distinctive, each of the ten vowels was a phoneme. In fact the same vowel, except for quantity, was often used for distinct nominal case endings. In the first declension, for example, long ā was the ablative ending while short ă was the nominative ending (exs: *venit decimā horā* 'he arrived at the tenth hour'; *venit decimă horă* 'the tenth hour arrived'). There were also oppositions within single words—*mālum* 'apple' vs. *mălum* 'bad' (acc sing); *dĭco* 'I consecrate' vs. *dīco* 'I say'; *cĕras* 'a type of plant' vs. *cēras* 'wax' (acc pl); *mōlĭs* 'mass' (gen sing) vs. *mŏlĭs* 'mill' (dat-abl pl); *sŭdis* 'stake' vs. *sūdis* 'dry' (dat-abl pl). We have already seen how the intensification of stress in Vulgar Latin destroyed these subtle quantitative oppositions. At the same time vowels came to be conditioned by placement of the main stress or, in case they were unstressed, by their position with respect to the main stress. In this way the vowels lost the distinctive feature of quantity and developed three separate types: stressed, pretonic, and unstressed final.

A triangle of seven stressed vowels developed from the ten vowels of Latin, and the whole system of oppositions was modified because certain sets of distinct vowels converged into a single vowel and vice versa. The appearance of two degrees of tongue height between the low position (/a/) and the high position (/i/ and /u/) introduced an entirely new datum. The new 'close' mid vowels represent the convergence of the long mid vowels with the short high vowels. For this reason the only remaining high vowels were long /i/ and /u/, in which the quantity was, in fact, no longer distinctive. The correspondences between the two successive systems may be summarized as follows:[10]

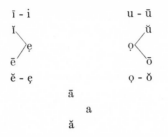

Although an opposition did not develop between open and close mid vowels in pretonic position, there was a change in the phonetic quality of the low vowel, /a/, which became more central and even somewhat back, resulting in what is usually called a 'close' [ɐ]. Thus, a system of five vowels evolved in position before the main stress:

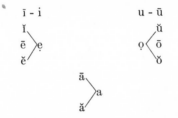

In final unstressed position a system of three vowels had evolved by the time one can correctly call the language 'Portuguese'. The back rounded series was reduced to the single vowel /u/ (traditionally written -*o*), and the front series, after an /i/ - /e/ stage, was reduced to /e/:

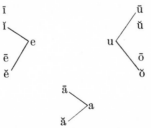

10. In certain phonetic environments these correspondences are not valid. For example, in Portuguese words with antepenultimate stress we sometimes find the close mid vowel in the place of a Latin short mid vowel or a high vowel in the place of a Latin long mid vowel or short high vowel. In such cases the determining phonetic factor is the presence of an unstressed final /i/ or /u/ to which the stressed vowel was assimilated (exs: *mĕtum* > *mêdo*, *fēcī* > *fiz* (intermediate *fezi* >

All available evidence indicates that it was this three-pronged vocalic system that was carried to Brazil during the earliest period of colonization. Further evolution, both in Brazil and in Portugal, introduced other developments.

The Vowels of Modern Portuguese

Although optional nasalization of stressed vowels in position before a syllable beginning with a nasal consonant constituted a new datum in the phonological system of European Portuguese, this process was always the general rule in Brazil, where it was associated with a concomitant change in timbre from /a/ to [ɐ] and from an open mid vowel to the corresponding close mid vowel. From the phonological point of view, it is the closing, rather than the slight nasalization that induces it, that is relevant. For this reason it is clear that at least in Brazil we are dealing with a positional variant of stressed /a/ and the elimination of the distinctive oppositions /ẹ/ - /ę/ and /ọ/ - /ǫ/. However, in Portugal, where closing is not obligatory, the oppositions /ẹ/ - /ę/ and /ọ/ - /ǫ/ are maintained and an /a/ - /ɐ/ opposition is made possible. The verbal inflections *-amos* (with close *a*) and *-ámos* (with open *a*) of the first person plural (exs: *falamos* 'we speak' : *falámos* 'we spoke') are, for example, distinguished in Portugal by means of this opposition. In summary, before a syllable beginning with a nasal consonant the Brazilian stressed vowel system is reduced to five members (with a positional variant for the low vowel), while the corresponding system in Portugal has eight vowels, with an added opposition between two low vowels.[11]

The unstressed vowel systems of the two subnorms reveal even greater differentiation than the stressed systems. Generally, in initial position before the main stress there were no changes in Brazil (exs: *morar* 'to reside' : *murar* 'to wall in'; *legar* 'to bequeath' : *ligar* 'to tie' : *lagar* 'wine press').[12] Under certain conditions, however, the opposition between high and mid vowels vanishes and only the high

---

fizi), *ovum* > *ôvo*). Since the final vowel is part of the ending, the same roots with other endings show the expected correspondences (exs: fem *ova* /ǫ/; pl *ovos* /ǫ/, final /o/ being at first maintained when followed by /s/; *fêz* from Lt *fēcǐt*).

11. Brazilian school grammarians sometimes insist upon distinguishing the two *-amos* endings, causing the phonological opposition to be used occasionally, if rather incoherently. In any case, one should note that the unnasalized version is possible in this position for Brazilian speakers.

12. In Brazil, *lagar* is, of course, a literary word imported from a European cultural milieu.

vowel is retained. The most important environment of this type is in position immediately before a stressed vowel, where contrasts of the type *suar* 'to sweat' : *soar* 'to sound'; *ciar* 'to hiss' (of animals) : *cear* 'to eat supper' are merely orthographic.[13] Similarly, before *s* in the first syllable of a word the only unstressed front vowel possible is /i/ (exs: *expor* /ispor/ 'to expose'; *estar* /istar/ 'to be'), although a diphthongized /e/ ([e:y]) is found under secondary stress (by juxtaposition, as in *ex-posição*).

A less permanent expansion in the use of high vowels in place of mid vowels resulted from a phenomenon known as 'vowel harmony' (Camara 1953, p. 79), in which a pretonic vowel is assimilated to a stressed high vowel. Vowel harmony, which is not indicated in writing, is somewhat colloquial and has entered formal elocution through indirect paths. For this reason certain words of a literary character (ex: *fremir* 'to tremble') are not affected, and the process may even be blocked under certain conditions in formal language. For example, *comprido* 'long' may be pronounced /ko(n)pridu/; in this case it would no longer be homonymous with *cumprido* 'executed'. Thus, in position before a stressed high vowel a system that includes the oppositions /e/ - /i/ and /o/ - /u/ is implicit, although the two phonemes do overlap.

Three facts of special importance cause the pretonic system to be much more complex in Portugal. The first of these is the existence of a central vowel tending somewhat toward a middle position, called neutral *e* [ə], an unstressed variant of /e/.[14] Another is the elimination of oppositions of the type *morar* : *murar*, caused by the merger of /o/ into /u/ except in absolute initial position, that is, at the beginning of a word. As mentioned earlier, such oppositions still exist in Brazil. Finally, a limited number of occurrences of /a/, /ę/ and /ǫ/ must be taken into account, giving a somewhat asymmetric system of seven vowels:

13. There are, however, some verbs that have radical /ei̯/, and these maintain the diphthong even in unstressed position, although it is then somewhat attenuated and written -*e*- (exs: *pear* 'to embarrass'; *piar* 'to chirp'; *enfear* 'to make ugly'; *enfiar* 'to thread').

14. In this position there is an opposition between /i/ and /ę/, the latter being realized as [ə] (ex: *ligar* : *legar*). At the beginning of a word, however, only /i/ is possible despite the fact that *e*- is sometimes written (ex: *erguer* /irger/ 'to lift').

Diachronically the vowels /a/, /ę/ and /ǫ/ have two sources. In the first place they are found in forms in which the geminate vowels of the classical period contracted. Typical examples are *vadio* 'idle' (/vadiu/, not [vɐdiu] as in Brazil) from *vaadio* (Lt *vagativum*); *pregar* 'to preach' (/pręgar/ as opposed to /prəgar/ 'to nail') from *preegar* (Lt *praedicare*); *corar* 'to color' (although *morar* and *murar* merged into /murar/, /kǫrar/ is distinct from *curar*) from *coorar* (Lt *colorare*). In the second place /a/, /ę/ and /ǫ/ appear in certain words borrowed from literary Latin in which the pretonic vowel was followed by a -*c* or a -*p* that later dropped (*ba(p)tismo* 'baptism'; *re(c)tidão* 'rectitude'; *ado(p)ção* 'adoption').[15]

Both in Brazil and in Portugal the vowels that may appear in the next to the last syllable of words having antepenultimate stress form an asymmetric system. In this position there are two front vowels /i/ and /e/ (in Portugal [ə]), and one back vowel /u/. Typical examples are *número* 'number'; *pálido* 'pale'; *pérola* 'pearl', rhyming with *cérula* 'sky-blue'.[16]

We turn now to final unstressed vowels. In Brazil /e/ underwent varying degrees of closure, but we can consider the standard articulation to be the true /i/ that evolved in Rio de Janeiro. In this pronunciation /i/ is symmetric to /u/, which, as we have seen, replaced final unstressed /o/ quite early in the history of the language. In southern dialects, however, -*e* has a more open timbre, sometimes even to the point of becoming an /ę/. Under these conditions there is an unstable distinctive opposition between /e/ and the final unstressed /i/ (written -*i*) of certain loan words, as in the pair *júri* 'jury' : *jure* 'may he swear' (from the verb *jurar*). However, in the received pronunciation there is a strong tendency to eliminate oppositions of this type, so that rhymes like *Bellini* 'a name' : *define* 'he defines', or *Vênus* 'Venus' : *serenos* 'serene' (masc pl) are accepted in Brazilian poetry. In Portugal final unstressed /e/ becomes [ə] and enters into a precarious *júri-jure* type distinctive opposition, giving a four-vowel system:

$$i \qquad\qquad u$$
$$ə$$
$$ɐ$$

15. Such forms are the cause of one of the discrepancies in the orthographical norms of the two Portuguese-speaking countries. In Portugal the silent consonant is phonologically significant since it serves indirectly to indicate the quality of the pretonic vowel.

16. In words of the type of *pérola* the spelling sometimes causes /o/ to be maintained in speech.

It must also be recalled that in Portugal vowels in all unstressed positions are significantly reduced. Since reduction occurs in various phonetic environments, the unstressed vowels of European Portuguese have a special character that clearly differentiates the European from the Brazilian language.

The Vowels of Clitics

The vowels of enclitic particles behave exactly like unstressed final vowels. For this reason, pairs of the type *falou-te* (verb with enclitic) 'he spoke to you' : *açoute* (noun) 'whip' and *sei-o* 'I know it' : *seio* 'breast' exhibit identical final vowels.

The vowels of proclitics act both as the unstressed initial vowel of a phonological word and as the unstressed final vowel of the particle itself. In effect, proclitics acquire a unique status because of their variable position. As we have already seen, in certain cases such particles may be attached not to the principal morphological word but rather to an interpolated word, forming a phonological word with the latter. In construction with a verb clitics may either be pre-posed or post-posed (exs: *te falou* or *falou-te* 'he spoke to you'). For this reason the particles themselves acquire a special status within the phonological system, and their vowels therefore behave like unstressed final vowels.

In Portugal no practical consequences result from the special status of proclitics because in both pretonic and final position /o/ and /e/ become /u/ and [ə], respectively. In Brazil, however, the pretonic vowel system is different from that of the unstressed final vowels with respect to the mid vowels /e/ and /o/. As we have seen, the vowels of proclitics behave like unstressed final vowels. Thus, despite the circumstance that they are in unstressed initial position, /e/ and /o/ are reduced to /i/ and /u/, respectively, in the pronunciation of Rio, and we can find minimal pairs like *Olavo* /olavu/ 'a proper name' and *o lavo* /ulavu/ 'I wash him', the latter consisting of the verb *lavar* and the pronoun *o*. Similarly we have the pair *sessenta* /sese(n)ta/ 'sixty' and . . . *se senta* /sise(n)ta/ 'he sits down' (the verb *sentar* with the reflexive pronoun *se*).[17]

As has already been mentioned, clitics can take 2-stress for emphasis, with or without a pause, in both Portugal and Brazil. Although

17. Although Sousa da Silveira (1937, p. 356) noted these distinctive oppositions along with several others, he limited his analysis to the phonetic level and did not draw any phonological conclusions.

the proclitic vowel then enters the stressed system, in Portugal it does not change in timbre. As a result we have a special instance of stressed /ə/, which therefore ceases to be a mere positional variant and becomes a true vocalic phoneme. A stressed pronunciation of this sort is particularly frequent with the particle *que* /kə/ 'that'. Under similar conditions the low vowel also maintains its unstressed back timbre—particles like *mas* 'but', *para* 'for', or *cada* 'each' can occur with a stressed /ɐ/.

In Brazil there is some hesitation in such words. In general the low vowel is open /a/ (/mas/, /para/, just like /cada/, which is, incidentally, more frequently stressed than unstressed). There is more hesitation in the specific case of *mas* 'but' due perhaps to a certain impulse to distinguish the adversative particle from the adverb *mais* 'more' with which it would be homonymous by virtue of a rule that diphthongizes a stressed vowel followed by /s/ in the same syllable. The most frequent pronunciation is /mɐs/, the back low vowel thus entering the stressed vowel system in an environment other than the nasal one. In general the mid vowels are reduced to high vowels even when stressed, and we therefore have, in contrast with Portugal, such forms as *que* /ki/. Very occasionally, however, the copula is pronounced /e/ instead of the much more frequent /i/.[18]

Thus, the stressing of proclitics for purpose of emphasis creates certain anomalies in the stressed vowel system. In Brazil /ɐ/ appears outside of the environment of a following nasal in the particle *mas* and in Portugal both /ɐ/ and /ə/ occur, the former much more frequently than in Brazil. These conditions create a supplementary stressed vowel system in both Portuguese-speaking countries.[19]

CONSONANTISM

The Latin Consonant System

Excluding such merely phonetic considerations as positional and free variants,[20] the Latin consonant system was particularly simple and

18. In any case the conjunctive particle is /i/ in Portugal. The very occasional instances of emphatic /e/ in Brazil are an interference from the written language in which the letter used is not in accord with the true phonological form of the particle. In school grammars particles with a front vowel are always given with /e/.

19. Diphthongs and the so-called nasal vowels will be discussed in the sections on syllabic structure.

20. This topic was first studied by Seelmann in the mid nineteenth century. See especially Sturtevant 1940.

is not in general the subject of extensive debates. It was characterized by the presence of a large number of stop consonants, that is, sounds produced when the speech organs block, at some point in the mouth, the stream of air coming from the lungs, producing a quick interruption in it. There were also two nasals, or sounds in which an oral closure is accompanied by a nasal resonance, and two fricatives, in which the stream of air is compressed rather than interrupted. Of the latter, one was a labial while the other had a 'sibilant' acoustic effect. Complementing the true consonants, we find two consonants of the type usually called 'liquid' and a consonant-like use of the vowels /i/ and /u/ in which these phonemes formed a syllable with a following vowel just as true consonants do.

There were three pairs of stops, each pair consisting of a voiced and an unvoiced consonant (that is, with or without glottal vibration): 1) labial (articulated without using the tongue): /p/ - /b/; 2) front (articulated with the tongue against the far front of the roof of the mouth—pre-palatal or on the dental ridge): /t/ - /d/; 3) back (the tongue coarticulated with the middle or back of the roof of the mouth—mid-palatal, post-palatal, or on the soft palate): /k/ - /g/. The consonants of the first pair were bilabial (coarticulation of the two lips), those of the second dental (coarticulation of the tongue with the upper ridge of the teeth), while those of the third pair had positional variants depending on the following vowel—they were post-palatal before /e/ and /i/ and velar before /a/, /o/, and /u/. The fricative /f/ belonged to the labial series (coarticulation of the lower lip with the upper ridge of teeth) while the other fricative, that is, 'the sibilant' /s/ was front. Both were voiceless. The /r/ was produced by vibrating the tip of the tongue against the back of the upper ridge of teeth, and the /l/ had two variants: 'thin' or *exilis* (apparently a dental articulation) and 'full' or *pinguis* (a back articulation, probably velar), depending on the phonetic environment.

As seen above, the Latin consonant system was perfectly symmetric with respect to the stops. As far as the rest of the consonants are concerned, however, the system was neither internally symmetric nor even symmetric in relation to the stops.

Aside from the oppositions already discussed, in environment between vowels in the same word, each consonant contrasted with an identical geminate articulation: /pp/, /bb/, /tt/, and so on. Gemination first became established in the prehistory of Latin through the agglutination of two morphemes into a single word (ex: *ad* + *tango* = *attingo*, *pel* + *do* = *pello*) or through certain processes of an expressive character, as seems to be the case in *bucca*. Thus we have such pairs as: *agger* 'mound' : *ager* 'field'; *annus* 'year' : *anus* 'ring'; *mollis* 'soft' : *molis* '(you) grind'.

The Portuguese Consonant System

A comparison of the Portuguese and Latin systems reveals that while the stop series remained essentially unchanged, the fricatives expanded to form a system phonologically analogous to that of the stops. The new fricative system consisted of three voiced-voiceless pairs that we may consider to be labial, front, and back, respectively, even though their points of articulation do not coincide with those of the stops. The labials (/f/ - /v/) were actually labio-dentals, the front pair (/s/ - /z/) were alveolars (articulation of the front part of the tongue, lowered toward the lower tooth ridge, against the alveolus of the upper tooth ridge),[21] and the back pair (/š/ - /ž/) were articulated by the mid-tongue against the mid-palate while the tip of the tongue advanced toward the upper teeth.

In the nasal series a new consonant that we can consider back developed alongside the original front nasal. The new nasal (ɲ) was articulated by the mid-tongue against the middle region of the palate, the tongue not being curved toward the bottom of the mouth as in /š/ and /ž/ to produce a 'hushing' effect, but rather unfolded against the soft musculature to give the consonant a simultaneous /i/ sound. Analogously an /ḷ/ developed.[22]

The geminate consonants were simplified and left no trace in the consonant system. Even though /rr/ remained distinct from simple /r/ in intervocalic position, it did lose the geminate articulation. Between vowels /r/ became the so-called bland /r/, while /rr/, as well as initial (or at least nonintervocalic) /r/, maintained the 'strong' vibrating articulation (/r̄/).

It is interesting to consider a table of the Latin consonant system

21. All evidence indicates that the Latin sibilant was also articulated in this way.

22. French grammarians of the seventeenth century called these consonants *mouille* or *mouillée* (softened). Later this term was erroneously translated into Portuguese as *molhado*, literally 'wet'.

in which the empty slots are filled in by the new consonants (in parentheses) that developed in Portuguese:

Stops:	/p/-/b/	/t/-/d/	/k/-/g/
Fricatives:	/f/-(/v/)	/s/-(/z/)	(/š/)-(/ž/)
Nasals:	/m/	/n/	(/ṇ/)
Liquids:		/l/	(/ḷ/)
		/ṛ/	
		(/r/)	

The Portuguese system, which is much fuller and more balanced, is the product of a general process of evolution in which the dominant tendencies are lenition and palatalization, that is, the utilization of the mid-palate, in conjunction with the middle of the tongue, as a complementary articulatory area. The only phenomenon contrary to the tendency toward lenition was the creation of a mid-palatal voiced fricative /ž/ and a labial voiced fricative /v/ from consonantal /i/ and /u/, respectively. The /v/, however, entered into symmetry with the voiceless /f/. Since both palatalization and lenition were in all cases contingent on particular phonetic environments, we proceed now to examine the conditions under which these two tendencies were manifested.

The Evolution of the Consonant System

In studying the changes that the Latin consonant system underwent while evolving toward Portuguese it is important to keep in mind that homorganic consonants do not necessarily occur in corresponding positions in a Latin word and its Portuguese reflex. The disappearance of a given consonant type in a given environment is, however, usually compensated by the evolution in some other environment of another type of consonant related to the one that disappeared. For this reason the net result is simply a change, or rather, an interchange in environments. This was accomplished without reducing the ability of each type of consonant to enter into oppositions.

In general, Latin consonant types did not change in word-initial position, although this is not true in word-internal position (exs: *pedem > pé, bonum > bom, tela > teia, dare > dar, carum > caro, gutta > gôta, faba > fava, salire > sair, manum > mão, nidum > ninho, legere > ler, rota > roda*). There were, nonetheless, three types of change in initial position:

1) /k/ - /g/ before /e, i/ (where the stops were post-palatal rather

than velar) were assimilated to the following front vowel, thus becoming front and also continuant. In the Lusitanian Romance /g/
eventually acquired a hushing sound that is still preserved today.
Thus, /g/ is one of the sources of Portuguese /ž/. The phoneme /k/,
on the other hand, became a dental fricative that for a long time was
not confused with /s/.[23] The merger of these two sounds is a relatively
recent development (exs: *gestum* /gestum/ > *gesto* /žestu/, *cera*
/kera/ > *cera* /sera/);

2) consonantal /i/, following the general Romance evolution toward
a full palatal consonant, became /ž/, merging with the reflex of
/g(e, i)/ (ex: *iustum* > *justo*)[24];

3) consonantal /u/ underwent an analogous consonantalization
just after the golden age of Latin, introducing a labio-dental voiced
/v/, in symmetry with /f/, into the consonant system of the language
(ex: *uacca* > *vaca*).

As a result of the last two developments the pair /i/ - /u/ lost its
consonantal value in initial position. However, the stops /k/ - /g/
did not cease to occur in position before /e, i/ because in this environment /k/ - /g/ followed by an asyllabic /u/ (which formed a diphthong with the following syllabic vowel)[25] took their place when the
/u/ disappeared (exs: *quem* /ku̯em/ > *quem* /ke(n)/, *guerra* /gu̯erra/
(from Gmc *werra*) > *guerra* /geṝa/).

As Martinet (1955) has correctly observed, the most crucial process
of word-internal evolution was simplification of geminate consonants
between vowels. In addition to destroying oppositions of the type
/pp/ : /p/, /gg/ : /g/, and so on, simplification resulted in the creation
of a much greater number of each type of single consonant. The general reaction seems to have been preservation of oppositions, although
under different conditions, through lenition.

In Portuguese, voiceless consonants became voiced (exs: *lŭpum* >
lôbo, *cĭto* > *cedo*, *lacum* > *lago*, *profectum* > *proveito*, *rosa* /rosa/ >
rosa /roza/), and as a consequence /k(e, i)/, which was already a
fricative, also became voiced, creating a voiced fricative that was

23. The letter *c* is still maintained in spelling despite the disappearance of the
phonological motivation for its use.

24. For a long time the letter *i* continued to be used with the new value. Finally,
beginning in the fifteenth century, a new letter *j* (called *jota* in Portuguese, from
the Greek *iota*) was introduced. The *g* - *j* distribution in modern Portuguese
spelling is a result of the phoneme's history. Gonçalves Viana (1904) instituted
an unsuccessful attempt to eliminate *g* in favor of *j*.

25. In Latin /k/ was written *q* instead of *c* in such cases, and the tradition has
been handed down to Portuguese.

represented in the written language by the letter *z* and eventually merged with the reflex of intervocalic /s/, just as the voiceless reflex merged with /s/ itself (ex: *acetum > azêdo*). Most of the voiced consonants disappeared between vowels (exs: *pedem > pee > pé, malam > maa > má*). However, /g/ remained at least when followed by /a/ or /u/ (exs: *digitum > dedo*, but *plaga > chaga, legumen > legume* and other examples that cannot be explained in this way (Williams 1938, p. 67)). The consonant /n/ was replaced by nasalization of neighboring vowels, and the nasal quality was either maintained, with diphthongization or contraction of the vowels (exs: *lana > lãa > lã, manum > mão*), or dropped, creating a hiatus (ex: *bona > bõa > boa*). The original labial /b/ underwent lenition to /v/, thus maintaining a certain distance from the /b/ that resulted from the simplification of the geminates. However, it did merge with the reflex of consonantal /u/ (ex: *faba > fava*).

The process of palatalization, an example of which we have already seen in the derivation of /ž/ from /g(e, i)/, poses a complex and many-faceted problem. In addition to the derivations already discussed, a palatal fricative, voiced or voiceless, was created when /s/ was assimilated to a following asyllabic /i/ that developed in Romance from Classical Latin syllabic /e/ or /i/ (exs: *passionem > paixão, caseum > queijo*). The voiceless phoneme, but not the voiced one, also resulted from the reduction of certain consonant clusters, a process in which /š/[26] was created directly from the sibilant immediately preceded by /k/ (written *x* in Latin orthography) or the inverse group /sk/ (exs: *buxum* /buksum/ > *buxo* /bušu/, *miscere* /miskere/ > *mexer* /mešer/).[27] Except between vowels, groups consisting of a labial fricative or a voiceless stop followed by /l/ became an affricative hushing sound with the beginnings of a dental stop articulation. This sound exists today only in certain dialects—in the common languages of both Portugal and Brazil it has become a pure fricative, merging with the reflex of /si/, /ks/ and /sk/ (exs: *planum > chão, clamare > chamar, afflare > achar*).[28] The phonemes /n/ and /l/ were palatalized

26. It is for this reason that the letter *x* has come to be used for the voiceless hushing sound in Portuguese.

27. In certain cases the preceding vowel is diphthongized (exs: *piscem > peixe*, **axum > eixo*, just as in *paixão* and *queijo*). In fact, it seems that free variation was the rule and that the spelling adopted was purely conventional.

28. The digraph *ch*, which came into Portuguese through Provençal, is still used. Gonçalves Viana (1904) justifies the maintenance of the digraph on the basis of the existence of the affricate in certain dialects.

only in intervocalic position. In the modern language instances of
/ḻ/ in initial position can be found only in a few borrowings from
Spanish (ex: *lhama* 'an Andean animal' : *lama* 'mud'). Similarly,
initial palatalized /ɲ/ occurs only in loans (ex: Tupi *nhandúti* 'a type
of lace work').[29] Liquid /ḻ/ is the reflex of: 1) a group consisting of a
labial fricative or a stop followed by /l/ between vowels (exs: *specŭlum*
> *speclum* > *espelho, scopŭlum* > *scoplum* > *escolho, tegŭla* > *telha*);
2) /l/ followed by a secondary asyllabic /i/ (ex: *palea* /palḭa/ >
palha). Nasal /ɲ/, on the other hand, comes from: 1) the group /gn/
(exs: *agnum* > *anho, ligna* > *lenha*); 2) /n/ followed by a secondary
asyllabic /i̯/ (*linea* > /linḭa/ > *linha*); 3) nasalization of stressed /i/
resulting from the reduction of /n/ between /i/ and /a/ or /o/ (ex:
pinum > *pĩo* > *pinho*).[30]

The Portuguese Consonant System

In principle the consonant system formed by the phonemes established and distributed as discussed above still functions in present-day
Portuguese. Generally, loan words have been modified in order to
conform to this system. However, /š/, /ɲ/, and /ḻ/ do not occur in
loans taken from literary Latin during or after the fifteenth century.
In such loans the letter *x* retains the original Latin value /ks/ (ex:
fixo /fiksu/ 'fixed') or, in certain very common words, simplifies to *s*
(ex: *próximo* /prǫsimu/, 'near'). Consonant clusters consisting of /l/
preceded by a labial fricative or a stop were reintroduced (exs: *flama*
'flame'; *planger* 'to lament'; *amplo* 'ample'; *clamar* 'to clamor'), as
were /gn/ and /l/ or /n/ followed by asyllabic /i/ (exs: *interregno*
'interregnum'; *óleos* 'oils', in opposition to *olhos* 'eyes'; *vênia* 'pardon',
in opposition to *venha* 'he may come'). However, even in loans
/g(e, i)/ and consonantal /i/ became /ž/ and /k(e, i)/ became /s/.[31]
In the case of /r/, the geminate was reduced to /r̄/, in opposition with
simple /r/. The latter, in turn, underwent lenition to bland /r/ in

29. Other examples are the vocative hypocoristics of black creole Portuguese:
nhonhô, from *sinhô* (senhor), and *nhanhã*, from *sinhá*, a feminine form derived
from *sinhô*.

30. The /i(n)/, that is, nasal *ĩ* stage seems to have lasted until at least the
twelfth or thirteenth century. The form *minha* 'my' (fem) is not the result of
lenition of intervocalic /n/ but rather of nasalization of /i/ by the preceding
/m/ (*mea* > *mĩa* > *mia* > *minha*).

31. In fact, even Classical Latin was read in a similar way since the accepted
practice was to read Latin in accord with the phonological system of one's own
language.

accord with the general tendency toward lenition in Lusitanian Romance.

Phonemes of non-Latin origin have never been admitted into the language of either Portugal or Brazil. Even in the most distant past, non-Latin phonemes in lexical borrowings were interpreted in terms of the system which evolved from Latin. For example, the Germanic labio-velar constrictive /w/ was assimilated to the Latin cluster /gu̯/, and was then simplified to /g/ in front of /e, i/ in the same way as original /gu̯/. Thus, we have words with Germanic roots like *guarnecer* 'to equip' and *guisar* 'to stew', alongside Latin terms like *igual* 'equal' and *águia* 'eagle'. Similarly, in loans from Arabic, Latin consonants were substituted for Arabic consonants which did not exist in Latin. We have, for example, Latin /f/ instead of the Arabic guttural in such words as *alfaiate* 'tailor', *alface* 'lettuce', and /š/, which evolved from /si̯/, /ks/ and /sk/ in the Lusitanian Romance, in such words as *xerife* 'sheriff', *xarope* 'syrup'. As we have already seen, no phonemes of Tupi or any other indigenous or African language have entered Brazilian Portuguese.[32]

Changes which occurred in the informal style as well as intrusions from certain sub-dialects[33] have, however, had repercussions in the modern consonant system, and even in the tense or careful style of the received language there are some unstable oppositions. After a labial fricative or a stop, for example, the /l/ - /r/ opposition is weakened by a preference for /r/, and there are even examples of free variation in the literary language (exs: *fluir* 'to flow (of a liquid)' : *fruir* 'to take pleasure in'; *frecha* or *flecha* 'arrow'). Similarly, the vibrated

32. One cannot deny, however, that superstrata, adstrata, and substrata can have otherwise unexpected consequences in certain lexical items. Thus, in *guedelha*, from Latin *uiticulam*, Latin consonantal /u̯/ became /g/ just as Germanic /w/ (but not /u/) did, and in *Tejo*, from Latin *Tagus*, /g/ was palatalized in front of /u/, a change that can only be explained by an Arabic adstratum. Similarly, it is possible that the reduction of intervocalic /l̯/ to /i/ in certain Brazilian dialects (exs: *foia*, instead of *fôlha* 'leaf', *oio*, instead of *ôlho* 'eye') can be explained with reference to the creolized Portuguese of the black slaves or perhaps the indigenous substratum since, in the latter, the /l/ - /l̯/ - /r/ opposition does not exist.

33. Subdialects of this type often have phonological systems that are quite different from those of the received dialect. A few examples, such as the affricate *ch* of Trás-os-Montes or the front rounded /ü/ (as in French) of the Algarve should suffice to establish this point. In the same vein, we have the elimination of /š/ in favor of /tš/ in certain Brazilian dialects as well as the substitution of /s/ by /š/ both in the north of Portugal and in the Brazilian states of Goiás and Mato Grosso.

/r̄/ has a velar (vibration of the root of the tongue in the back of the mouth) or even uvular (vibration of the uvula) variant that sometimes is reduced to mere guttural friction, as is very common in Rio de Janeiro. In post-vocalic position the phoneme /l/ has a velar variant that in Brazilian Portuguese, even in the careful pronunciation of the educated classes, can come dangerously close to an asyllabic /u̯/. When this occurs, certain types of oppositions are destroyed (exs: *mal* (noun) 'bad' : *mau* (adj) 'bad'; *vil* (adj) 'vile' : *viu* (from the verb *ver* 'to see') 'he saw'; *alto* 'tall' : *auto*, the usual abbreviation of *automóvel* 'car'). A particularly important development in the received language in a large part of Brazil was the creation of an affricative positional variant of /t/ and /d/ before /i/. In this environment the stop becomes a mid-palatal fricative with a slight hushing sound (exs: *tio* 'uncle'; *dia* 'day').

In fact, in both Brazil and Portugal, there is a tendency toward the creation of a slight differentiation between popular (or vulgar) speech and the normal, accepted pronunciation, although the latter can scarcely resist the impact of the former. As a result the consonant system has developed several new positional variants that modify the interrelations of the individual consonants. It is obvious, for example, that if velar [ɫ] becomes a vowel,[34] the distribution of /l/ is reduced. Similarly, the phonetic relationship of the two Portuguese /r/'s was upset by the creation of the uvular [rₒ] or, even more so, by its reduction to a mere glottal friction.

THE STRUCTURE OF SYLLABLES

Latin Syllable Structure

The syllable, a phonological entity created by the inner concatenation of phonemes in the stream of speech, is a functional unit of the second degree, starting from the phoneme. In effect, it is the syllable that determines the function of each phoneme within an utterance. In Latin, the central phoneme of this secondary unit was always a vowel, called the syllabic vowel. A syllable, then, could either be *simple*, that is, consist entirely of a syllabic vowel, or *complex*, that is, contain consonantal phonemes before or after the syllabic vowel. If there were no post-vocalic consonants, the syllable was said to be 'open' (exs: *a-* in Lt *amare* or *da-* in Lt *dare*); if such consonants were

34. In certain areas this occurs even in intervocalic position. In Lisbon, as well as in certain areas of southern Brazil, post-vocalic final /l/ remains dental but receives a vocalic support.

present, the syllable was called 'closed' (exs: Lt *est* or *dat*). Thus, as is generally true for all languages, syllable types were a function of the existence or nonexistence of asyllabic phonemes before or after the syllabic vowel[35] and, in case such phonemes were present, of their number, nature, and possible orders.

Aside from simple and open syllables, Latin had syllables closed by all types of consonants. Syllables containing an asyllabic vowel, forming what is traditionally called a 'diphthong' with the syllabic vowel, were rare. Although one finds *ae* and *oe* in the written language, these groups of letters, even within the classical language, were pronounced /e/, and in Vulgar Latin they underwent the normal evolution for /ĕ/ and /ē/, respectively. The diphthong /au/, written *au*, was in free variation with /o/ and, despite the fact that the latter was rejected by the grammarians, it soon became dominant in Rome and in most of the regions in which Romance languages eventually developed. Before a syllabic vowel, one finds only /u̯/ preceded by a back stop (written *gu-*, *qu-*); but the rising diphthong formed in this way was unstable, and even in the classical language there was hesitation between /k/ and /ku̯/ (exs: *cotidie* and *quotidie;* the pronunciation of *quis* as /kis/ reported by a Latin grammarian).[36]

As mentioned above, any consonant—stop, fricative, nasal, or liquid—was allowed after the syllabic vowel. Furthermore, the group formed in this way could be followed by the sibilant (exs: *nox* /noks/, *urbs, mens, ars*). A geminate consonant between vowels closed the first of the vowels since the syllable boundary fell in the middle of the geminate (cf. Brugmann 1905, p. 37). At the beginning of the syllable, before the syllabic vowel, Latin permitted the so-called *muta cum liquida* cluster (that is, a stop or a labial fricative followed by /l/ or /r/) and the sibilant followed by a stop.[37] In initial position the latter cluster created an 'impure' /s/, that is, an /s/ followed by a stop in the same syllable (exs: *speculum, stare, scopulus, smaragdus*).

35. Simple syllables and open syllables with only one pre-vocalic consonant occur quite generally in all languages and are among the earliest to be developed in child language (see Jakobson 1941). For some discussion of the theoretical aspects of syllable structure see Camara 1964.

36. Sturtevant (1941, p. 169) has suggested that *qu* is a digraph that represents a velar labialized stop distinct from /k/, written *c*.

37. Accordingly we should have syllable divisions of the type *fa-stus*. This is contradicted, however, by the circumstance that the first syllable (with a short vowel) was considered long in metrics. In any case, with three consonants the most probable division is, for example, *in-sta-re* or *per-spi-ci-o*.

In case the *muta cum liquida* cluster was in intervocalic position, the syllable boundary in Vulgar Latin could optionally be made between the *muta* and the liquid (ex: *in-teg-rum* instead of *in-te-grum*). The acceptance of this free variation by the literary language had various repercussions in the Romance languages.[38]

Evolution of Syllable Structure

In its evolution Vulgar Latin followed two main trends which had become apparent earlier in the history of the language: 1) the tendency to eliminate the 'impure' *s* cluster by introducing a supporting short /i/ (ex: *ĭstare*) in order to create a new initial syllable; 2) the tendency to reduce, or in certain cases completely eliminate, closed syllables.

In final position the latter process began with the dropping of syllable final nasals. Except in certain monosyllables such as the preposition *cum* (Ptg *com*) the labial nasal in final position was dropped quite early. As a consequence the *-m* desinence of the accusative singular was eliminated from nominal morphology, creating, for example, *lupu* instead of *lupum* and *rosa*, homonymous with the nominative *rosa*, instead of *rosam*. With the exception of monosyllables of the type of *in* (Ptg *em*) the dental nasal, which was less frequent, was dropped next, and in Lusitania and certain other regions final stops met the same fate. Typically, the preposition *sub* gave Old Portuguese *so'* although the latter in turn has been replaced by *sob* because of acceptance in the spoken language of an artificial *b* introduced in the sixteenth century in order to make the Portuguese and Latin forms look alike.[39] The dental stop /t/ was especially frequent in final position and was the desinence of the third person singular, which is therefore usually Ø (zero) in Portuguese (exs: *amat* > *ama*, *amabat* > *amava*). For the same reason the conjunction *et* became *e*, the preposition *ad* became *a*, and in general syllable final stops became phonologically unacceptable in Portuguese. *Sob* is pronounced /sobi/, with two syllables, and is therefore distinguished from *sobre* 'over' only by

38. The preceding syllable could be considered long for metrical purposes even though it had a short vowel (ex: /e/ in *integrum*) and the word thereby acquired penultimate stress. The stress shift was, however, merely a consequence of the change in syllable division and should not be considered primary.

39. Another example of the effect of learned spellings on pronunciation is words of the type *digno, benigno,* in which the /g/ is pronounced in modern Portuguese. Although such words are written with *g* in *Os Lusiadas,* they rhyme with *Alcino, divino,* etc. See Guimarães 1919, 2:82.

the absence of an /r/ after the /b/. In foreign names written with a final consonant and in certain onomatopoetic terms written with a final -*c* (exs: *tic-tac, toc-toc*) the final consonant creates a new final syllable and, as in the case discussed above, is supported by the front vowel of the final unstressed system ([ə] in Portugal, /i/ in Brazil). Even when the final unstressed vowel is unvoiced and becomes generally imperceptible in certain speech styles, it is still phonologically present and the putative 'final' consonant constitutes a second syllable. For metrical purpose *toc* counts as two syllables in both Brazil and Portugal, as is shown by the following lines from a Portuguese poem, each line consisting of eleven syllables.[40]

> Toc-toc-toc, como se espaneja
> 1 2 3 4 5 6 7 8 9   10 11
> Lindo, o jumentinho pela estrada chã!
> 1 2   3 4 5   6 7 8   9 10 11
> Clip-clip-clop, how he shakes himself clean
> Pretty, the little donkey on the flat road.

Loans with final consonants and modern abbreviations used in administrative and commercial language also acquire the sort of structure discussed above.[41]

In closed syllables within a word, final stops underwent lenition to an asyllabic high vowel. In this way, many falling diphthongs with /i/ or, much less frequently, /u/ were created in Portuguese. The latter occurs only in words that originated in the higher social levels and are more recent in the Lusitanian Romance (exs: *lectum* > *leito*, *conceptum* > *conceito*, *lactem* (vulgar masculine instead of the neuter *lac*) > *leite*, *Cepta* > *Ceuta*, *actum* > *auto*). Later, many loan words having an internal syllable closed by a stop entered the language. Most such words were sixteenth-century borrowings from literary Latin, which often did not retain their original structure. The incongruous stop was frequently elided and was probably never pronounced in many words. In fact, the process of elimination of syllable

40. Guerra Junqueiro, *Os Simples*, 9th ed. p. 25. Eleven syllables, not counting the final unstressed one.

41. Raul de Leoni, for example, rhymes *Liliput* with *lute* (see Camara 1953, p. 149). One of the most interesting instances of commercial abbreviations presently in use in Brazil is *Peg-Pag*, the name of a chain of stores in which the customer himself gets his own merchandise from the shelves (that is, 'o freguês *pega* a mercadoria') and pays (*pagar*) for it at the exit. Thus *Peg-Pag* is evidently simply an unusual way to write the imperatives *pegue* 'pick' and *pague* 'pay'.

final stops is still operative in both Portugal and Brazil although it is not reflected in the European spelling system. Thus, the words written *exceto* 'except', *Egito* 'Egypt', *reto* 'straight', in Brazil are written with a silent letter in Portugal: *excepto* /isętu/, *Egipto* /ižitu/, *recto* /rętu/.

Stops of the type discussed above are retained even today in certain other loans introduced via the written language, but in such cases Portuguese syllabification is different from that of Latin. Instead of a CVC syllable with a second consonant after the syllabic vowel, one has CV and CCV, in which the second consonant has joined the next syllable and become pre-vocalic. A word like *as-pec-tum* gave archaic Portuguese *aspecto*, syllabified *as-pe-cto*. Such groups are not of the same type as the *muta cum liquida* groups since the two consecutive stops are separated by a vocalic element that is articulatorily front. In the literary language of Brazil prescriptive grammar does not take into account this new vocalic element, but it is real nonetheless. In general, there is a tendency to reduce it as much as possible in formal styles, making it a very rapid phonetic syllable unlike most other pretonic syllables of Brazilian Portuguese. Because of this tendency, such vocalic elements are usually not counted in metrics. Nonetheless, in some cases they must be counted, as Sousa da Silveira has shown to be true of certain poems of Gonçalves Dias (Silveira 1935, p. 352).

In the popular language and even, in general, in the colloquial language, this rather ambivalent state of affairs was resolved by the complete acceptance of a new syllable containing either /i/ or, by vowel harmony, /e/. A verb like *ritmar* 'to make rhythmic' is really /ritimar/ and is therefore conjugated in the present indicative *ritimo*, *ritimas*, *ritima*, and so on, with stress on the new syllable *-ti-* in agreement with the prosodic pattern *número* 'number' : *numero* 'I number'; *fábrica* 'factory' : *fabrica* 'he manufactures'; that is, a verbal noun with antepenultimate stress corresponding to a verb with penultimate stress. Thus we have /adimitir/, /adevogado/, /abisulutu/, which are written *admitir, advogado, absoluto,* and so on.[42]

In Portugal, the phonetic situation is somewhat different because of the general tendency to reduce all syllables preceding the stress. In some instances pretonic vowels are even completely eliminated in

42. In certain scientific terms, borrowed in general from Greek, this same structure can be found in initial position (exs: *ptose, tmese, ctônio, pneumático, psicologia*). In such cases the initial group is treated in the expected way—for example, *pneumático* 'tire', popularized as *pneu*, is pronounced /penęu/.

both members of pairs of the type *ritmar-animar*, *admitir-adivinhar*, and *absoluto-aborrecido*. In this case one can talk about the phonological existence of a *muta cum muta* cluster at least in the quick, relaxed speech of Portugal. At any rate, the problem cannot be resolved in terms of the written language, and it would be preposterous to admit such clusters only when they correspond to groups of letters representing consonants.[43]

A new stress pattern was created by insertion of a vowel into posttonic consonant clusters found in certain Latin loans that originally had antepenultimate stress (ex: *rítmico* /ri'timiku/, with stress on the fourth vowel from the end). This pattern, however, is really not entirely new since verb forms with antepenultimate stress followed by a clitic pronoun were already of this type.

In summary, we have seen above that open syllables predominate in Portuguese and are of the following types: a) simple, b) with one consonant before the vowel, c) with a *muta cum liquida* consonant cluster before the vowel, d) with a disputable pre-vocalic *muta cum muta* consonant cluster that does not exist even in formal speech styles in Brazil (exs: *a(brir)* 'to open'; *pe(dir)* 'to ask'; *fra(co)* 'weak'; *blo(co)* 'block'; *tme(se)* 'tmesis'). Secondarily, we have closed syllables of the following types: a) closed by /r/ or /l/,[44] b) closed by a sibilant (a hushing sound almost everywhere Portuguese is spoken), c) closed by nasalization, d) closed by an asyllabic vowel (exs: *ar(te)* 'art'; *al(to)* 'tall'; *gas(to)* 'expense'; *cam(po)* 'field'; *pai(rar)* 'to hover'). If a syllable is closed by nasalization, by an asyllabic vowel, or by both, the sibilant may be added. In this way doubly and triply closed syllables are created (exs: *pais* 'parents'; *órfãs* 'orphans' (fem); *órfãos* 'orphans' (masc)). The sibilant cannot, however, be added directly to a syllable closed by /r/ or /l/ so that the plural of *mar* 'sea' is *mares*, the plural of *mal* 'evil' is *males* and the plural of *animal* 'animal' is *animais*,

43. Helmut Lüdtke (1952, p. 288) claims a two-syllable structure in all instances, as does Morais Barbosa (1965, p. 152). Barbosa went on to establish the phonological existence of the neutral vowel even in those styles in which it is phonetically elided by pointing out that the first consonant of the resultant groups constitutes its own syllable.

44. Syllable final /l/ is common in word-internal position. Although many of the words that have this property are loans from literary Latin, others (ex: *alto* 'tall') are part of a much older layer. Nonetheless, syllable final /l/ often underwent lenition to an asyllabic vowel. If the next syllable begins with a stop, this change is uniform and the /l/ becomes /u̯/ (ex: *salto* > *souto*). In *muito* < *multum*, the /l/ gave /i̯/ in order to increase the contrast with the syllabic vowel. Nasalization of the diphthong by initial /m/ occurred later.

in which the /l/ is dropped. The only exceptions to this rule are certain syllables created within words by the combination of a morpheme consisting of a syllable closed by /r/ or /l/ with a bound form beginning with impure *s* (exs: *perspectiva*, from *per* with the root *spec-*; *solstício* from *sol* with the root *sti*, that is *sta*, from the Latin *stare*). From this summary it is apparent that there are two types of syllables in Portuguese that do not occur in Latin—syllables closed by nasalization and an extensive system of diphthongs.

Nasalization in Portuguese

Any consonant, nasal or nonnasal, could close a syllable in Latin. But, quite early in the history of the language syllable final nasals were dropped in position immediately before /s/. As a result of this development, the first syllable was opened (exs: *consul* > /kosul/, *mensis* > /mesis/), and the /s/, which became intervocalic, subsequently underwent the normal lenition to /z/ (ex: *mesa* /męza/, from *mensa*). Later, syllable final nasals were reduced in the environment of any other following consonant and the phonological closing was completed by strongly nasalizing the vowel. This process, which is the origin of the so-called nasal vowels of Portuguese, occurred only in the Lusitanian Romance;[45] in Castilian the nasal consonant alone, as in Latin, persisted.

Phonologically, Portuguese nasal vowels consist of a vowel accompanied by a syllable-closing nasalization that cannot be distinguished from the vowel articulation itself. This sort of nasalization is quite different from the purely assimilative type that occurs with vowels in position before a syllable beginning with a nasal consonant.

As we have already seen, in final position post-vocalic nasal consonants dropped, just as did stops in the same environment.[46] As a result open syllables were created (exs: *lôbo* < *lupum*, *crime* < *cri-*

45. There was a somewhat similar evolution in French, but in this language the distinction between a nasal vowel and a vowel followed by a nasal consonant was retained (ex: *bon* /bõ/, masc; *bonne* /bon/, fem). The claim that Portuguese and French nasalization is due to a Celtic substratum is rash, if not totally gratuitous (see Jungemann 1955, p. 102 ss).

46. A trace of the post-vocalic nasal consonant remained at least in the environment of a following syllable initial stop. The syllable boundary, contrary to Hall's claim (1943), comes after the consonant. Recent investigations in experimental phonetics have quite unexpectedly shown the existence of a trace of the nasal consonant before other consonants (see Barbosa 1962; Lacerda-Head 1963).

men). Nasalization was not eliminated from this environment, because a new syllable-closing nasalization evolved when intervocalic /n/ was reduced and replaced by nasalization of the vowels that consequently merged or diphthongized. Whenever this change occurred in the last two syllables of a Latin word, Portuguese has a final vowel accompanied by syllable-closing nasalization that, in this case, is reduced to vocalic nasalization (exs: *bene* > *bẽe* > *bem, bonu* > *bõo* > *bom, fine* > **fĩe* > *fĩi* > *fim, unu* > *ũu* > *um, lana* > *lãa* > *lã, orphănu* > *órfão, *pones* > *pões*).[47]

There are two ways of indicating nasalization in modern Portuguese orthography—either a consonant letter (*m* or *n*) is used, or a diacritical mark called 'til' (-) is written above a vowel letter. In Latin *m* was written in front of a syllable beginning with a labial consonant (exs: *campus, ambo*) and *n* was written before all other consonants (exs: *legenda, sanguis*). The til was introduced by scribes in the Middle Ages as an abbreviation for *n*.[48] Eventually the modern language adopted the practice of writing *m* or *n* (according to the Latin usage) in syllable internal position and in syllable final position after *e,i,o,u* while reserving til for diphthongs or final *a*.

Final nasal vowels are phonetically diphthongized in Portuguese. Nobiling's observations about this phenomenon in the pronunciation of São Paulo (Nobiling 1904, pp. 139–52) are actually quite general, so that we find pronunciations of the type [ii̯(n)], [uu̯(n)], [ou̯(n)], and even [aɐ̯(n)] with closing of the final part of the low vowel. The phenomenon has received special attention in the case of nasal /e(n)/, which is a (phonetic) diphthong in both Brazil and Portugal, [ɐi̯(n)] being favored in the received pronunciation of Portugal. Phonologically, the diphthong /ei(n)/ does not exist in Brazil since there is no nondiphthongized nasal vowel with which it can contrast in order to create a distinctive opposition. What is true of /e(n)/ holds equally well for /i(n)/, /u(n)/, /o(n)/, and even /a(n)/ when the diphthong is conditioned by a nasal closing. In such cases we find a quick

47. When, as in the case at hand, there is no trace of the nasal consonant, considered phonologically to be syllable final, one can say that this consonant is reduced to zero (∅). The vocalic nasalization then becomes phonologically relevant. Granted the diphthongization of the final nasal vowel, however, one can consider the syllable-closing function to be transferred to the last part of the diphthong.

48. Til was also used as an abbreviation of *r* and *q*.

asyllabic vowel, which is necessarily homorganic to the syllabic vowel. The true diphthongs with nasal closing are the ones that have an asyllabic vowel that is heterorganic to the syllabic vowel. In this case there is a contrast and a distinctive opposition between the diphthong and a simple vowel (exs: *órfão* 'orphan' (masc) : *órfã* 'orphan' (fem); *irmão* 'brother' : *irmã* 'sister'; *mãe* 'mother' : *(ir)mã* 'sister'; *põe* 'he puts' : *(pom)pom* 'powder puff'; *muito* 'much' : *unto* 'grease'). In European Portuguese the situation is somewhat different since /e(n)/ and /ai̯(n)/ merged, and under these conditions what is missing phonologically is a mid front nasal /e(n)/.

The discussion above is valid only for final vowels. In nonfinal stressed syllables and in pretonic syllables diphthongs do not exist either phonologically[49] or phonetically. In these positions, both in Brazil and in Portugal, one has five vowels with a nasal closing: /a(n)/, /e(n)/, /i(n)/, /o(n)/, /u(n)/. At the beginning of a word, however, the opposition between unstressed /e(n)/ and /i(n)/ is unstable and in normal speech /e(n)/ becomes /i(n)/.

Portuguese Diphthongs

We have already seen that for all practical purposes there were no diphthongs in Latin with the exception of *au*, which varied with *o*, and *qu*, if the latter was not merely a labialized /k/ (see n. 36). In the Lusitanian Romance, *au* was in general preferred to *o*, and the occasional instances of the latter (ex: *paupere* > *pobre*) are probably forms taken from the Vulgar Latin of Rome. Although /au̯/ became /ou̯/ by assimilation, it was later (especially beginning in the sixteenth century) reintroduced into Portuguese as /au̯/, creating doublets of the type *causa* 'cause' : *cousa* 'thing' and *ouro* 'gold' : *áureo* 'golden'. Thus, the rather extensive system of falling diphthongs of modern Portuguese is necessarily a purely Romance innovation.

The Portuguese system of falling diphthongs is a consequence of several distinct processes of evolution. In the first place the strong stress characteristic of Vulgar Latin caused stressed syllables to become markedly differentiated from unstressed ones, and as a result diphthongs evolved when a stressed syllabic vowel was followed directly by another syllabic vowel. The latter was reduced and became tightly subordinated to the former, causing Classical Latin

---

49. The only exception is /ui(n)/ in *muito*. The origin of this example, which has already been discussed above, is explained in n. 44.

disyllables of the type *deus, fuit, fui* to evolve to Portuguese mono-syllables /deu̯s/, /foi̯/, /fui̯/.[50]

Other diphthongs, created by the dropping of certain intervocalic voiced consonants, are more fully characteristic of phonological and phonetic developments in Lusitanian Romance. If a high or mid unstressed vowel followed the dropped consonant, the former was subordinated to the preceding vowel, just as in the process discussed above, and a diphthong was created (exs: *malu > mau, caelu > céu, dedi > dei, magis > mais*). The reduction of syllable final stops, which (except at the end of words) became asyllabic /i/ or /u/, also resulted in diphthongs (exs: *lectu > leito, octo > oito, actu > auto, salto > sauto > souto*).

At some point between the archaic and modern periods, in a de-velopment internal to Portuguese, a diphthong was formed by di-vergence from the geminate /ee/ that resulted from the elimination of intervocalic /d/, the reflex of Latin /t/, in the second-person plural verbal desinence (ex: *sabees* (from *sabedes*) *> sabeis*). This process also occurred in forms with antepenultimate stress (ex: *amássedes > amássees > amásseis*) and, in fact, must have originated with such forms since they present a phonetic environment in which the /d/ would be particularly weak. In this way unstressed /ei̯/ appeared, just as had happened before in the case of certain plural adjectives (*faciles > facees > fáceis*).[51]

The developments discussed above led to the following system of falling diphthongs in Portuguese. Notice that /ou̯/ is missing:

/iu̯/	(*riu* 'he laughed')	. . . .	
/eu̯/	(*deu* 'he gave')	/ei̯/	(*dei* 'I gave')
/ɛu̯/	(*céu* 'sky')	/ɛi̯/	(*anéis* 'rings')
/au̯/	(*mau* 'bad')	/ai̯/	(*pai* 'father')
. . . .		/ɔi̯/	(*dói* 'it hurts')
/ou̯/	(*sou* 'I am')	/oi̯/	(*boi* 'steer')
. . . .		/ui̯/	(*fui* 'I went')

The existence of only one diphthong each for syllabic /i/ and /u/ is inherent in the structure of Portuguese since consonants of the type

50. In Classical Latin, a vowel in hiatus was necessarily short. In Vulgar Latin, however, *fūi*, in accord with the Indo-European root *bheu*, lived on, and as a result we have the Romance *fu-* alongside *fo*. It is in this way that one can explain the Portuguese morphological opposition *fui* 'I went': *foi* 'he went'. See Camara 1964, p. 286.

51. This is for all practical purposes the only case of an unstressed final diph-thong. The English loan *jóquei* 'jockey' fits into this pattern.

/y/ (as in the German *jemand*) and /w/ (as in the English *war*) do
not exist in that language, which, as we have seen, has only asyllabic
/i̯/ and /u̯/ as positional variants of /i/ and /u/, respectively. On
the other hand, the absence of /o̦u̯/ contributes a true asymmetry
which has perhaps favored the monophthongization of /ou̯/ to /o̦/ in
the received languages of both Portugal and Brazil. Although this
phenomenon tends to make the diphthong system more symmetric,
the written language persists in ignoring it. The replacement of /ou̯/
by /oi̯/ in a large number of words, especially in European Portuguese, may also be viewed as a tendency toward breaking the asymmetry (*ouro* > *oiro* 'gold').

In certain Brazilian dialects vowels are diphthongized before syl-
lable-final /s/. For example, in Rio de Janeiro, /as/ : /ai̯s/, /ɛs/ : /ɛi̯s/
and so on, are not in distinctive opposition since only the diphthong
is possible. Even the literary language has accepted the elimination of
such phonological oppositions, and rhymes like *Satanás - ais* or
luz - azuis are considered canonical. Phonologically, the most important consequence of this process is not the elimination of such
oppositions but rather the loss in status suffered by /ɛi/, which, in
the Portuguese lexicon, appears only before syllable final /s/ (but
see chap. 3, n. 18).

Before a hushing consonant in the following syllable there has been
at times a tendency to create diphthongs and at other times a tendency
to reduce them. The former process is exemplified by *peixe* 'fish' from
pexe and by certain popular forms in the written language (ex: *feicha*),
while the latter process, the reduction of diphthongs, is normal in
Brazilian pronunciation. Whichever way it may be, the diphthong is
phonologically eliminated since there can be no distinctive opposition
with a simple vowel.

Our analysis of certain strings consisting of a stressed vowel and a
high unstressed vowel as diphthongs is based on two circumstances—
first, such sequences contrast with simple stressed vowels and, second, they are perceived as single syllables, equivalent in the utterance
to a vowel and a syllable final consonant. In the metrics of the
literary language, for example, such groups are treated as a single
syllable. It is still worthwhile, however, to ask if they contrast with
disyllables containing the same vowels. In general, Portuguese
grammar books compare diphthongs with an unstressed high vowel to
groups in which the high vowel is stressed and the first vowel is unstressed (ex: *sai* 'he leaves' : *saí* 'I left'). It is clear that in such cases

the prosodic difference sets up distinct phonological environments. More meaningful are such contrasts as *rio* /riu/ 'river' or first-person singular present of *rir* 'to laugh' : *riu* /riu̯/ third-person singular preterite of *rir; a Rui* /aɾui̯/ 'to Rui' (in answer to the question 'Who did you give the book to?') : *arrue* /aɾui/, third-person singular present subjunctive of *arruar* 'to plan'. Another such contrast is provided by the indicative of the third conjugation and the subjunctive of the first—(*in*)*tui* /tui̯/ from *intuir* 'to intuit' : (*a*)*tue* /tui/ from *atuar* 'to actuate'. Although contrasts like the ones discussed above are quite stable in certain areas (for example, Rio de Janeiro), in other parts of both Brazil and Portugal the hiatus /iu/, written *-io*, has merged with the diphthong, and in Portugal the desinence of the subjunctive in the first conjugation is [ə] so that an /i/ : /i̯/ opposition is impossible. For this reason the only remaining criterion for talking about diphthongs rather than disyllabic sequences of vowels in Portuguese is an auditory or phonetic one. In unstressed position, conditions are analogous, and if a word is derived from another one in which the high vowel was stressed, a sequence of two vowels in hiatus may be used freely. Even in the metrics of the literary language both forms are used (ex: *tra-i-ção* 'treason' from the verb *trair* 'to betray' in free variation with *trai-ção*).

We turn now to the rather controversial matter of rising diphthongs. As we shall see, these diphthongs do not form a system analogous to that of falling diphthongs. After a velar stop (written with the letter *q* when voiceless) a diphthong with /u̯/ occurs (exs: *quadro* 'picture'; *freqüênte* 'frequent'). This Latin heirloom remains functional in Portuguese because of oppositions of the type *quais* /ku̯ais/ 'which' (masc pl) : *coais* /kuais/ 'you strain' (2d-pers pl). But, we have already seen that even in Latin this sequence has always tended to overlap with one in which the stop is followed immediately by the syllabic vowel (exs: *cota* - *quota* 'quota', *cociente* - *quociente* 'quotient', *questão* - *qüestão* 'question', *líquido* - *líqüido* 'liquid'). In all other environments we have free variation, whether the second vowel is stressed or unstressed. Thus *real* /rial/ 'real' can be either a monosyllable or a disyllable, *piedade* 'pity' either a trisyllable or a polysyllable, and *suave* 'soft' either a disyllable or a trisyllable. Although the *allegro* pronunciation in Portugal makes the diphthong more usual there, just the opposite is true for Brazil. Furthermore, the traditional debate over the syllabification of the unstressed final groups /iu/, /ia/, and /ua/ is not phonologically relevant (exs:

vário, vária 'various'; *níveo, nívea* 'snowy'; *tábua* 'board'; *mágoa* 'bruise').[52] The weakness of the final unstressed segment, however, does make a two-syllable pronunciation unlikely phonetically. Thus, from a purely phonological point of view, the state of affairs in Portuguese is the same as in Latin: there is only one rather special rising diphthong.

In Vulgar Latin, on the other hand, a whole series of rising diphthongs was temporarily set up in positions where Classical Latin had a mid or high vowel, stressed or unstressed, in hiatus with any other vowel (exs: *palea* [pa-lĕ-a], *ciconia* [ci-co-nĭ-a], *mulierem* [mu-li-ĕ-rem], *aviolum* [a-vi-ŏ-lum], *parietem* [pa-ri-ĕ-tem], *battuere* [bat-tu-ĕ-re]). In such cases the first vowel became asyllabic, the stress moving forward to the next vowel if the first one was originally stressed (/pali̯a/, /kikoni̯a/, /muli̯ére/, /avi̯ólu/, /pari̯éte/, /battu̯ére/). Although a series of rising diphthongs was created in this way, the new syllable structure was soon eliminated from Lusitanian Romance. When the first consonant in the syllable containing the diphthong was /l/, /n/, /t/, /d/, /s/, or /z/ (the latter from intervocalic /s/), asyllabic /i/ was absorbed by the consonant, which thereby changed in nature. The phonemes /l/ and /n/ became palatalized (*palha, cegonha, mulher*) while /t/ became a fricative. The latter is unvoiced in the less ancient or less popular parts of the lexicon and voiced in the older parts (cf. *ração* 'ration' and *razão* 'reason' from *ratione*). Eventually these fricatives merged with the sibilants /s/ and /z/, respectively. The phoneme /d/ became a voiced hushing phoneme (*hodie* > *hoje*) and /s/ gave a voiceless hushing phoneme or, when intervocalic, the voiced counterpart (*passione* > *paixão, caseu* > *queijo*). In all other cases, that is, if the first consonant in the syllable was not one of those in the list given above or if the asyllabic vowel was /u̯/, the latter was simply dropped (*avô, parede, bater*).

Sandhi

Within a breath group words are connected by *sandhi* in Portuguese and therefore behave as if they were bound forms within a single word. In speech of this type the structure of word-final syllables is altered if such syllables end in a consonant and the next word begins with a vowel since the consonant then joins the next syllable, which

52. In the case of *-uo* (ex: *assíduo* 'assiduous') there are two possibilities— /u/ alone as in the colloquial language or the more formal /uu/ (two syllables). In Brazil *-ie* is treated in the same way (/ii/ or /i/), but final *-e* is [ə] in Portugal.

thereby acquires a pre-vocalic consonant while the first syllable is simultaneously opened (exs: *mar alto* (*ma-ral-to*) 'high sea'; *sol ardente* (*so-lar-den-te*) 'burning sun'; *paz armada* (*pa-zar-ma-da*) 'armed peace'). In such cases we have bland intervocalic /r/, intervocalic /l/ instead of the post-vocalic velar variant,[53] and /z/ instead of /s/ (realized as a hushing sound almost everywhere Portuguese is spoken).

Furthermore, certain phonemic groups that do not occur in word-internal position are created through *sandhi*. For example, it is only in such cases that geminate[54] /ss/ and /rr/ can be found—*mar Roxo* 'Red Sea' is pronounced /mar-r̄ošu/, and there is a distinctive opposition in such pairs as *ar roxo* 'purple air' : *arrôcho*, 'tourniquet stick'. Similarly, *paz sólida* 'solid peace' is pronounced /passolida/ in contrast with *pá sólida* /pasolida/ 'solid shovel'. In the case of a stressed nasal -*i* or -*e* the final diphthong (/i(n)/) is extended to include a slight /ŋ/ that joins the syllable containing a following initial vowel (exs: *vim aqui* /viŋaki/ 'I came here' or *nem uma* /neŋuma/ 'nor one'). There is no *sandhi* with any other nasal vowel (exs: *manhã alta* /maŋa(n)alta/ 'high morning', *bom homem* /bo(n)ome(n)/ 'good man', *algum urso* /algu(n)ursu/ 'some bear'). Unstressed oral vowels, on the other hand, are connected by *sandhi* and either contract or form diphthongs accordingly as they are the same or different (exs: *campa ardente* /ka(n)parde(n)ti/ 'burning tombstone'; *campo ardente* /ka(n)pu̯arde(n)ti/ 'burning field'; *sêde ardente* /sẹdi̯arde(n)ti/ 'burning thirst'). If even one of the vowels is stressed, a hiatus, without *sandhi*, is established (exs: *campa alva* /ka(n)paalva/ 'white tombstone'; *campo alvo* /ka(n)pualvu/ 'white field'). Thus in the case of two identical vowels we find a vocalic gemination that would be inadmissible within a word. Note, however, that the above is valid only for Brazilian Portuguese. In Portugal, elision eliminates diphthongs (ex: *sêdardente*) and even replaces gemination with an intermediary syllable (ex: *campálva*), at least in some styles.

53. Evidently the situation is somewhat different in those dialects in which syllable final /l/ was replaced by /u̯/.

54. In writing the doubling of letters is used to indicate /s/ and /r̄/ between vowels (exs: *passo* /pasu/, *êrro* /ẹr̄u/).

Chapter 3

The Morphology of Nouns

NOMINAL CATEGORIES

Nouns and Adjectives in Latin

In Latin the two classes of words known as 'nouns' and 'adjectives' were joined into a single, more extensive noun-adjective class that was then partitioned according to syntactic criteria. When a given word of this class was used as the head of a syntactic construction internal to a given sentence it was a 'noun' (or, equivalently, a 'substantive'), while 'adjectives' were those words that referred back to nouns. The adjective's dependence on the noun was indicated by its 'agreeing' with the latter, that is, by showing a desinence of the same case, number, and gender as those (both implicit and explicit) of the noun. In subject position, where the noun functioned as the head, it was in the nominative and could be modified by an adjective in the same case. Each noun was, furthermore, either in the singular or plural 'number', accordingly as it referred to only one individual or to more than one individual,[1] and any accompanying adjective assumed the same number as its noun. Independent of its occurrence in any particular sentence, each noun was permanently assigned one of the three genders—masculine, feminine, or neuter—and an accompanying adjective in any given sentence was marked for the same gender as its noun. For example, in a sentence of the type of *puer vidit lupum* (or any other word order—*vidit puer lupum, lupum puer vidit, lupum vidit puer,* etc.) *puer* was the subject since it occurred in the nominative and *lupum,* which was in the accusative, was the (direct) object. If one were to expand the sentence by the addition of adjectives, they would have to be in the nominative if they referred to the subject or in the accusative if they referred to the object. Thus, in *abiectus lupum puer vidit famelicum* the adjective *abiectus* 'downhearted *or* haggard', in the nominative, tells us about the condition of the boy (*puer*), while the wolf (*lupum*) that he saw (*vidit*) is said to be famished (*famelicum,* acc). At the same time, since the nouns *puer* and *lupum* are both of the masculine gender and refer to only a single individual of each type, both adjectives are masculine in gender and singular in number.

In order to understand fully the typology of nouns in Latin it is important to note that although case and number were clearly expressed in this class of words, gender could, in general, be made fully explicit only by means of an associated adjective. For example, despite the fact that *lupus* 'wolf' was masculine and *quercus* 'oak tree' was feminine, both words had precisely the same desinences in all cases (accusative: *lupum, quercum,* etc.). An associated adjective of the type *abiectus* served to bring out the difference in an explicit way (*quercus abiecta : lupus abiectus*).

The circumstance that the six cases of Latin had desinences that varied from noun to noun led the grammarians to set up five formal groupings of nouns called the 'declensions'. In reality, however,

---

1. 'Number' as a nominal category corresponds to the concept of one individual as opposed to more than one individual. Notice, however, that the latter concept is a purely cultural and linguistic one. Although one human being or one animal is always considered a single individual in all cultures, the same cannot be said of any given concept to which a noun may happen to refer. For example, in Latin the concept 'city' could be conceived of as a plurality, and the corresponding noun was then obligatorily plural.

only three groups were justified by the fundamental patterns. The latter, called the first, second, and third declensions, were extended to include all nouns in Vulgar Latin.

We have already seen that the case system was gradually reduced, bit by bit, in a slow but steady process of syncretism. In Iberian Romance this process led to the eventual adoption of the accusative for all syntactic functions, including that of subject.[2] The basic accusative endings were *-m* in the singular and *-s* in the plural. The syllabic vowel that preceded these consonants determined which of the three basic 'declensions' a given noun belonged to: *rosam* : *rosas* (*-a-*, 1st decl), *lupum* : *lupos* ($\breve{u}/\bar{o}$, 2d decl, evolving to *-o-*), *artem* : *artes* (*-e-*, 3d decl). When final /m/ was dropped, the endings for all three groups of nouns became zero (∅) for the singular and *-s* for the plural. This general structure was carried over intact to Portuguese (exs: *rosa* : *rosas, lôbo* : *lôbos, arte* : *artes*).

Gender

In Classical Latin the neuter gender was not, even partially, associated with any particular concept. It was, in fact, merely a formal idiosyncrasy of certain nouns, and its distinctive material realization was, correspondingly, rather weak, consisting in essence of the desinence *-a* for both the nominative and accusative plural.[3] One way of eliminating this conceptually obsolete category consisted of reinter-

2. In certain other Romance languages the nominative-accusative distinction survived for quite a long time. Kurylowicz (1966, p. 169) views the loss of the nominative in Iberian Latin as a result of the comparative structure of the nominative and the accusative, singular and plural, of the third declension in Vulgar Latin. The nominative singular, nominative plural, and accusative plural all showed the same ending *-es* (ex: *panes*), while the accusative singular did not have an *-s* (ex: *pane*). Although this system clearly expressed the singular-plural opposition in the accusative, the opposition was not explicit in the nominative. Under these circumstances there were two possibilities: either the case distinction could be maintained at the expense of the number distinction, or the number distinction could be maintained at the expense of the case distinction. In Iberian Romance the second option was chosen because the category of number was still operational and that of case obsolete. The *pane - panes* pattern (singular *-∅*, plural *-s*) was then extended to the remaining two declensions, which therefore took on the accusative form (exs: *lupo* : *lupos, rosa* : *rosas*).

3. The identity of the nominative and accusative desinences was a fundamental feature of the neuter, being true even of the singular. In Indo-European the neuter was originally associated with entities that were thought of as inert and, therefore, incapable of being the active subject of a verb. It follows that even in subject position the neuter took the desinence of the accusative, a case incompatible with the subject function.

preting the nominative-accusative plural as a singular collective of the type *rosa*.[4] It was in this way that *Castella*, the plural of the neuter noun that designated the numerous fortifications raised by the Romans in the mid-north region of the Iberian Peninsula, came, as a singular, to designate the set of such fortifications (or the fortified front) and eventually became the name of a whole province.[5] Similarly, we have Portuguese *lenha* 'an armful of sticks and kindling for starting a fire' from the neuter plural *lĭgna* (*lĭgnum*, neuter, 'tree trunk') and *fôlha* 'leaf' from Latin *folia*, neuter plural, taken as a collective at first but later given a plural in *-s* (*folias* > Ptg *fôlhas*). Another morphological process tending toward the elimination of the neuter was the reassignment of the singular of certain neuter nouns to the masculine or feminine in order to provide them with a new plural agreeing with the new gender (ex: *castellum*, reassigned to the masculine with a new nominative *castellus* and the corresponding accusative plural *castellos*, whence Portuguese *castelos*). In any case, the neuter gender eventually disappeared from all of the Romance languages in one way or another.[6]

As we have already noted, the masculine-feminine opposition was explicitly marked only in adjectives, of which there were a large number that took the desinences either of the first declension or of the second declension, becoming thereby masculine or feminine, respectively. Such adjectives agreed with (explicitly or implicitly) masculine nouns by taking the first set of endings (*puer abiectus*) and with feminine nouns by taking the second set (*quercus abiecta*). As far as nouns were concerned, however, membership in one of the declensions was not sufficient to determine gender, although the second declension was primarily masculine and the first primarily feminine. Typical counter-examples to the above generalization are the feminine *quercus* and the masculines *nauta, poeta*, etc. In the third declension, the masculine-feminine opposition was not marked by any formal indication of gender. The adjectives of this declension, which constituted a sig-

4. A 'collective' is a noun that, though singular, designates a compound or secondary set composed of elementary or primary individual entities. The latter are, in turn, designated by a specific noun in the language (exs: *povo* 'people', a set of *homens* 'men'; *mata* 'forest', a set of *árvores* 'trees').

5. In Spanish *Castilla*, with a palatal /ḷ/ and the consequent change of /e/ to /i/.

6. The gender that is often called 'neuter' in Rumanian has no conceptual connection with the Latin neuter. In fact, the so-called neuter nouns of the grammars are actually masculine in the singular and feminine in the plural.

nificantly large set, did not vary according to the gender of the associated substantive (exs: *tristem : tristes, generalem : generales, parem : pares*), and we therefore have *tristem puerum, tristem quercum, tristem rosam, tristem poetam,* and so on.

It was exactly the structure described above that was carried over to Portuguese. For this reason Portuguese nouns do not necessarily have a morphological mark of gender; that is to say, they have the zero desinence (∅). A noun's implicit gender, however, is made explicit by agreement with any of a whole series of adjectives, derived from the Latin series mentioned above, having -*o* in the masculine and -*a* in the feminine (exs: *belo : bela* 'pretty'; *soberbo : soberba* 'superb or* haughty'). A structurally significant addition to this class of adjectives was the so-called article, a proclitic particle that in principle can precede any noun[7] and is used in the Romance languages as a 'determiner'. The article is *o* for masculine nouns and *a* for feminine nouns. If *poeta* is masculine in Portuguese, it is because one says *o poeta.* Similarly, *rosa* is feminine because one says *a rosa. Artista,* on the other hand, has no fixed gender since one can say both *o artista* (masc) and *a artista* (fem). Similarly we have *soberbo poeta : soberba rosa* and *soberbo artista : soberba artista.*

The Nature of Gender and Number

Number is both conceptually and morphologically simple in Portuguese. Conceptually, it corresponds to the opposition between one single individual and more than one individual, while morphologically it is merely the absence of a final -*s* in the singular and the presence of such an -*s* in the plural. The singular *lôbo,* for example, is theoretically *lôbo* + ∅ (no desinence), while *lôbos,* in the plural, is theoretically *lôbo* + *s.* This opposition ceases to exist only in nouns and adjectives that have antepenultimate stress and end in /s/ (exs: adj *simples* 'simple'; noun *ourives* 'goldsmith'), in which the plural desinence is missing. Under these conditions an adjective does not change in order to agree in number with its associated substantive (exs: *simples rosa* 'simple rose'; *simples rosas* 'simple roses'), and the number of a noun can be made explicit only by means of the agreement mechanism

7. There are, of course, nouns with which the article cannot occur, and it is precisely for this reason that such nouns do not have a fixed gender (ex: *Paris é belo* or *Paris é bela* 'Paris is beautiful'). Even proper nouns, which by definition are already definite, always take the definite article, or at least can take it optionally (ex: *o Brasil* 'Brazil', *o Amazonas* 'Amazonia'; *o Silva* 'Silva').

(exs: *grande ourives* 'great goldsmith'; *grandes ourives* 'great goldsmiths'; *o ourives* 'the goldsmith'; *os ourives* 'the goldsmiths').

Conceptually, the category of 'gender' turns out to be much more complex than that of 'number'. As far as nouns that designate members of the animal kingdom are concerned, the masculine-feminine dichotomy usually, but not always, coincides with the male-female distinction. Counter-examples can be found even in nouns that designate human beings (ex: *a testemunha* 'the witness', whether a man or a woman). The permanent assignment of nouns designating 'irrational' animals to a given gender is not at all unusual (exs: *o tigre* 'the tiger', whether male or female; *a cobra* 'the snake', whether female or male). Furthermore, in the case of many nouns of this type only one of the forms—masculine or feminine—is really used in the language, the other one being almost totally excluded. In such cases one grammatical gender usually refers to both sexes (exs: *a perdiz* 'the partridge'; *o elefante*[8] 'the elephant'). The category of gender is, furthermore, totally divorced from the concept of sex by the circumstance that all substantives must be assigned to one of the genders. Nonetheless, in the case of words referring to 'things' the masculine-feminine distinction sometimes corresponds to certain other, frequently rather obscure, concepts such as collectivity (exs: *o ramo* 'the branch'; *a rama* 'the foliage'; *o ôvo* 'the egg' : *a ova* 'roe'), mode of use (exs: *o sapato* 'the shoe' : *a sapata* 'low shoe, bed plate, brake shoe'), dimension (ex: *o barco* 'the boat' : *a barca* 'the ferryboat'), delicacy of manufacture and specialization (ex: *o jarro* 'the pitcher' : *a jarra* 'the vase'). Most nouns that designate things, however, have a single, conceptually arbitrary gender. In such cases we can view the content of the gender as being 'evaporated'.[9]

As is usual for the Romance languages, gender is morphologically quite complex in Portuguese. The fixation of nouns in the accusative, which caused the morphology of the number system to become so simple (Ø morpheme for the singular, /s/ morpheme for the plural), did not have the same effect for the morphology of gender. As we have already seen, gender was complex even in Latin, where only one series of adjectives exhibited a clear masculine : feminine distinction.

8. The hesitation on the part of normative grammars in the case of the feminine of *elefante* 'elephant' is a good proof of the fact that the feminine form is purely theoretical and almost never used.

9. Or, as Martinet (1962, p. 17) puts it, 'The contents of the feminine gender boil down to zero'.

This situation was, in principle, carried over intact to Portuguese, in which morphological patterns are determined by a single series of adjectives (including the 'article'). In this series the masculine has a theme in -*o*, the -*o* being dropped in the feminine upon the addition of the desinence -*a*.[10] This productive process is also found in a large number of substantives that have themes that do not end in -*o* (exs: *lôbo* : *lôba* 'wolf'; *mestre* : *mestra* 'teacher', in which the theme vowel -*e* is dropped; *autor* : *autora* 'author', in which the desinence -*a* is added directly to the last consonant in the absence of a thematic vowel).

In other nouns gender is not marked morphologically but is implicit in the word's lexical (rather than inflectional) structure. A final -*a* is the feminine desinence only if it is found in a nominal theme that would be masculine without such an -*a*. This is equivalent to saying that one is dealing not with the feminine desinence but merely with a theme-final *a* in such examples as *rosa* 'rose', *artista* 'artist', and *poeta* 'poet', the latter being a particularly clear case. The gender of such nouns is indicated by the presence or absence of the -*a* desinence in an associated adjective having a theme in -*o* (including the article). On the basis of this type of evidence one can say that *rosa* is always feminine, that *poeta* is always masculine, and that *artista* is feminine in some of its occurrences and masculine in others. It might be added that the same method can be applied to nouns that do not happen to end in unstressed -*a* and therefore do not look like forms with the feminine desinence (exs: *o papel* 'the paper'; *o sabiá* 'the thrush'; *o mar* 'the sea', always masculine; *a cal* 'lime'; *a juriti* 'the dove'; *a flor* 'the flower', always feminine). *O mártir* 'the martyr' is masculine because the associated article does not have the -*a* desinence and, by the same principle, *a mártir* is feminine because the article has this desinence.

In summary, gender is expressed in Portuguese by means of an -*a* desinence for the feminine as opposed to a Ø desinence for the masculine. This situation is quite similar to the one for number (-*s* in the plural). It is important to note, however, that although all members of the noun-adjective set (except those that have penultimate stress and already end in /s/) are inflected for number, gender is explicitly marked only in a proper subset of adjectives (those that have a theme

10. In Portuguese grammars the desinences are usually said to be -*o* for the masculine and -*a* for the feminine. The superiority of our treatment will become apparent in the discussion that follows.

ending in -*o*) and nouns (without regard to ending). Gender is not, in fact, explicitly indicated in most nouns or, to say the same thing in other words, has a variant desinence Ø that is incapable of distinguishing the feminine from the masculine since the latter always has the Ø desinence. Thus, gender is made explicit only by a speech act in which an adjective having a theme in -*o* is made to agree with a noun.

The Structure of Nominal Inflections
The Plural

Although the plural desinence is *s*, one cannot say merely that /s/ is added directly to the singular nominal theme because certain phonological changes that may accompany this addition must be taken into consideration. In fact, such changes can be totally independent of any phonological process currently at work in the grammar. An example is the change in quality of the stressed close mid /o̱/ of the singular to the open mid /ǫ/ of the plural, a phenomenon traceable to a very early process of metaphony that occurred in the singular of nouns and adjectives having a short stressed -ŏ- and theme final -*o*-, pronounced /u/. The following are typical examples: *ovo* /o̱vu/ 'egg' : *ovos* /ǫvus/ 'eggs', from Latin *ŏvum; grosso* /gro̱su/ 'thick' (masc sing) : *grossos* /grǫsus/ 'thick' (masc pl), from Latin *grŏssum.* Evidently the difference in quality between the singular and the plural quickly became morphological in nature and as such was redundant with the /s/ desinence. Upon acquiring the status of a morphological process, the quality difference was extended to a new class of words, those with stressed long -ō-[11] (ex: adjectives with the lexical suffix -*oso*, from Lt -*ōsum*), which thereby received plurals in stressed open /ǫ/. The same sort of opposition then began to appear in certain other types of nouns (exs: *forno* /fo̱rnu/ 'oven' : *fornos* /fǫrnus/ 'ovens', from Lt *fŭrnum : fŭrnos*).[12] From the synchronic point of view, therefore, one must recognize, in addition to the /s/ desinence, a complementary change in quality of /o̱/ to /ǫ/. The latter is not, however,

11. Unlike stressed short ŏ, stressed short ĕ became close in the plural as well as in the singular, so that a singular : plural /e̱/ - /ę/ opposition was not created (exs: *mĕtum* > *mêdo* /me̱du/, *mĕtos* > *mêdos* /me̱dus/).

12. The question of the exact role of metaphony in Portuguese historical grammar is still unresolved. The most complete treatment to date is that of Cavacas (1920). The common preoccupation with finding an explanation for the present situation exclusively in terms of phonetic evolution does not seem justified, however. One must always keep in mind that this originally phonetic phenomenon soon acquired morphological status.

perfectly general and often does not apply to words that are nouns exclusively (ex: *lôbo* /lǫbu/ 'wolf' : *lôbos* /lǫbus/ 'wolves').[13]

Phonologically conditioned changes in the latter part of the nominal theme may also occur when the /s/ desinence is added. As an example of such change, consider a set of nouns, derived from the third declension of Latin, in which theme-final -*e* was dropped when a preceding consonant (-*r*, -*s*, or -*l*) joined the (formerly) penultimate syllable. This change occurred only in the singular since the presence of the /s/ prevented the thematic vowel -*e* from dropping in the plural (exs: *mare* > *mar*, but *mares* (instead of the neuter *maria*) > *mares; mense* > *mês*, but *menses* > *meses; male* (substantivized adverbial) > *mal*, but *males* > *males*). This historical process reflects the fact that the final consonant clusters /rs/, /ls/, and especially the geminate /ss/ are incompatible with the structure of the language. As a consequence of this incompatibility we have such plurals as *revólveres* and *gases*[14] for loans like *revolver* and *gás*.

It is important to note, however, that when the final consonant is /l/, only *males* and the literary term *cônsules* are fully in accord with the process as described above. The dropping of intervocalic /l/, a phenomenon typical of the evolution of the Portuguese consonant system, caused the thematic vowel -*e* to come into contact with the preceding stressed vowel. This development, in turn, eventually resulted in several distinct types of evolution. If the preceding vowel was /a/, /o/, or /u/, a diphthong was obtained directly (exs: *sais*, pl of *sal* 'salt'; *sóis*, pl of *sol* 'sun'; *pauis*, pl of *paul* 'marsh'), and the dropping of /l/ with diphthongization came to be the general rule. In the case of /ę/ and unstressed /ẹ/[15] there was an intermediary geminate /ee/ stage (exs: *cruées*, from Lt *crudeles; amávees*, from Lt *amabĭles*), followed at the end of the archaic period, by diphthongization (exs: *cruéis, amáveis*). If the vowel in question was stressed

13. In Vulgar Latin these nouns had /ǫ/ (corresponding to Classical ō, ŭ) and were excluded from phonological alternation of the type discussed above. At the present time, however, such nouns are not treated uniformly in the common language. For example, in the normal pronunciation of Lisbon one hears *bolso* /bǫlsu/ : *bolsos* /bǫlsus/, 'pocket', while /bǫlsu, bǫlsus/ is normal in Brazil.

14. Similarly, we have examples of the type *açúcar* 'sugar' : *açúcares* 'sugars' in nouns with penultimate stress. If the word originally ended in /s/, the resulting antepenultimate stressed plurals disappeared from the language, or, putting it differently, the plural came to have the zero desinence Ø (ex: *ourives* 'goldsmiths' with the same form as the singular, instead of *ouríveses*).

15. The sequence */ęl/ does not exist because final /l/ causes the reflex of Latin ē to open (ex: crudēle > *cruel* /kruęl/).

/i/, the intermediate /ie/ stage was followed by /ii/ and eventually /i/, so that the descriptive rule involves nothing more than the dropping of the final /l/ of the singular (ex: *sutis*, from Lt *subtīles*). Unstressed final /il/, which was introduced into Portuguese through a series of loans from literary Latin (corresponding to *ĭle*, short *i*) remained distinct from /el/ because the /i/ : /e/ opposition was preserved in unstressed final position (exs: *flébil*, a literary loan corresponding to *flebĭlem; amável*, from Lt *amabĭlem*). In this case the disappearance of the /l/ in position before the *-es* of the plural [16] at first created /ies/, later /ees/, which then diphthongized in the same way as geminate /ee/. Thus we have the pattern sing *flébil* : pl *flébeis*.

In synchronic terms the developments sketched above reduce to three distinct morphophonological rules for the plural of nouns and adjectives ending in /l/. Rule 1: after /a, e, o, u/, the /l/ is dropped and a diphthong is introduced (exs: *animal* : *animais* 'animal'; *papel* : *papéis* 'paper'; *amável* : *amáveis* 'kind'; *anzol* : *anzóis* 'fishhook'; *azul* : *azuis* 'blue'). Rule 2: after stressed /i/, the /l/ is dropped (ex: *anil* : *anis* 'indigo'). Rule 3: after unstressed /i/, the /l/ is dropped, /i/ becomes /e/, and a diphthong is introduced (ex: *fácil* : *fáceis* 'easy').

Finally, we turn to the morphophonemic alternations that are found in some nouns and adjectives that end in stressed *-ão* /au(n)/. Formerly such words had themes ending in *-e* preceded by intervocalic /n/, but at a very early stage the final /e/ of the theme was lost in the singular (ex: Old Ptg *razom*, from Lt *ratiōne; pam*, from Lt *pane*). Just as in the case of /r, s, l/, the thematic vowel was retained in the plural where it was protected by the /s/ (exs: *razões, pães*). For quite a while it was exactly this situation—absence of final *-e* in the singular theme but presence thereof in the plural—that was found in Portuguese. However, stressed final *-om* and *-am* were eventually diphthongized to *-ão*,[17] causing the merger of these themes ending in *-e* with other themes ending in *-o* since the latter already had a final *-ão* (exs: *mão, são, irmão* from Lt *manu-, sanu-, (g)ermanu-*). For this reason Portuguese possesses three plural structures for nouns and adjectives

16. The dropping was a morphological process, following the pattern of the other nominals ending in /l/.

17. This process did not include forms that ended in *-õo* or *-ãa* at that time (exs: *bõo*, from Lt *bonu; lãa*, from Lt *lana*). Later these endings were reduced to *-om* and *-ã*, reintroducing final nasals (exs: *bom, lã*). See Vasconcelos (1911), p. 143.

ending in stressed -*ão:* 1) no morphological change (ex: *mão* : *mãos*);
2) the diphthong -*ão* changes to -*õ* in the plural and the thematic
vowel -*e* is added (ex: *razão* : *razões*); 3) the diphthong -*ão* changes to
-*ã* and the thematic vowel -*e* is added (ex: *pão* : *pães*). From a synchronic viewpoint, the distribution of the three plural types is arbitrary and in fact they are often confused, even to the point of free
variation, whether it be accepted by the grammarians (ex: *aldeãos* :
aldeões : *adeães* 'peasants') or not (ex: *cidadãos* is accepted while
cidadões is rejected as the plural of *cidadão* 'citizen'). Although there
is significant disagreement on this point among grammarians (as well
as in literary usage), a tendency toward fixation of the morphophonemic pattern -*ão* : -*ões* is apparent. This is a consequence of the
circumstance that words that formerly had -*om* are much more frequent in the modern language than those that had original -*ão* or
-*am*. The -*om* type includes, for example, all action nouns related to a
verbal radical (exs: *consolação* 'consolation'; *persuasão* 'persuasion';
omissão 'omission'). The leveling process, however, is a very slow one,
and common words that derive from an original -*ão* (exs: *irmão, mão*)
or -*am* (ex: *pão*) remain totally exempt from it. In the schools a
valiant attempt to save the three types of plural is under way. Such
efforts are based either on the Latin origin of the words in question,
their relation to the corresponding Spanish words, which really do
have distinct forms (exs: *razón* : *razones, hermano* : *hermanos, pan* :
panes), or the preferred usage of certain authors considered 'classic'
in the literary language.

The table on the following page summarizes the morphological processes that exist in the modern language.

The Structure of the Feminine

The feminine desinence, unstressed -*a*, contrasts with the zero (Ø)
desinence of the masculine, that is, the nominal theme itself in the
very same way as the -*s* desinence of the plural contrasts with the Ø
desinence of the singular. There are, however, certain morphophonemic alternations in the feminine of nouns and adjectives that must
be taken into account. Only a rather special set of nouns that end in a
consonant are exempt from such rules of morphophonemic altera-
tion in the feminine.

Some of the alternations mentioned above, namely those that are
phonologically conditioned, are a part of certain word restructuring
processes that, as we shall see in the discussion of verbal inflection

SINGULAR		MORPHOPHONE-MIC CHANGE	PLURAL	
form	examples		form	examples
. . . V V(n)	any vowel	—	. . . V +s	*lôbos* 'wolves' *sabiás*[18] 'thrushes' *jovens* 'young' (masc pl) *bons*[19] 'good' (masc pl)
. . . C	/r/, final stressed /s/ /l/ in *mal*, *cônsul*	+thematic *e*	. . . C +es	*mares* 'seas' *açúcares* 'sugars' *pazes* 'peace' (pl) *males* 'evils'[20]
. . . C	penultimate stressed /s/	—	. . . C +∅	*ourives* 'goldsmiths' *simples* 'simple' (pl)
. . . C	(a, e, o, u) /l/	−C+diphthong	. . . /i̯/ +s	*sais* 'salts' *amáveis* 'kind' (pl) *anzóis* 'fishhooks' *azuis* 'blue' (pl)
. . . C	(stressed *i*) /l/	−C	. . . +s	*sutis* 'subtle' (pl) *anis* 'indigo' (pl)
. . . C	(unstressed *i*) /l/	−C, *i*>*e*+ diphthong	. . . /ei̯/ +s	*verossímeis* 'verisimilar' (pl)
. . . ão	theoretical *-om*	−/u/, a>õ+ diphthong	. . . õe +s	*corações* 'hearts'
. . . ão	theoretical *-am*	−/u/ +diph- thong	. . . ãe +s	*pães* 'breads'
. . . ão	theme in *-o*	—	. . . +s	*irmãos* 'brothers'

18. In those regions where a final stressed vowel followed by /s/ is diphthongized (including Brazil, even in the language of poetry), the formula given is still valid and the oppositions *-ás* : *-áis* and *-és* : *-éis* (the latter in each pair being found in plurals of nouns and adjectives ending in V + /l/) are not removed from the structure of the language since the diphthongization persists in the second case, but not in the first, under conditions of *sandhi*. When the /s/ becomes /z/ and joins the initial syllable of the following word, we have, for example, *paz armada* /pazarmada/ 'armed peace' in opposition with *pais armados* /pai̯zarmados/ 'armed parents'. In effect, then, the morphological reality reappears when the phonological motivation for its masking disappears.

19. The change from *m* to *n* is, of course, merely the result of an orthographical convention to the effect that *m* is written only at the end of a word or before /p/ or /b/.

20. In the literary language, certain other words ending in /l/ show free variation. For example, Antônio Feliciano de Castilho uses both *méis* and *meles* as the plural of *mel* 'honey' in the very same book (the fourth) of his classic translation of Vergil's *Georgics*: '. . . *aliás do inverno o frio/congelaria os méis, e os derrereta o estio*' (vv. 52–54) and '*e espremia aos panais os meles abundantes*' (v. 199), (edition of Otoniel Motta, São Paulo, 1930).

and lexical derivation, are general and fixed. A clear example of an alternation of this type is the dropping of the unstressed vowel of a nominal theme upon addition of the vocalic desinence -*a* (ex: *bel(o)* + *a* = *bela* 'beautiful'). The loss of nasalization of a final nasal vowel when the addition of the -*a* desinence causes a hiatus to appear is another good example. The second rule explains why the feminine of *bom* /bo(n)/ 'good' is *boa* (*bo* + *a*). Notice that the same process also accounts for the feminines of nouns and adjectives that have a theoretical ending in -*om*, realized as *ão*, since in such words the feminine is formed from the theoretical radical, as is also true of the plural. For example, in the case of *bretão* 'Breton', the plural *bretões* suggests a theoretical *bretom*, yielding the correct feminine *bretoa*. Only in the subclass of augmentatives in -*ão* does nasalization become a consonant /n/ that is added to the next syllable (ex: *valentão* 'ruffian', theoretical *valentom*, pl *valentões*, fem *valentona*). If -*ão* corresponds to a true theme in -*o*, the -*o* is realized as the asyllabic vowel of the nasal diphthong in the masculine, while in the feminine this theme vowel is dropped without addition of any desinence at all (ex: *órfão* 'orphan' (masc) : *órfã* 'orphan' (fem); *são* 'healthy' (masc) : *sã* 'healthy' (fem)). In case -*ão* corresponds to a theoretical -*ã*, the feminine is realized as this theoretical form itself (ex: *alemão* 'German', theoretical *alemam*, pl *alemães*, fem *alemã*). Finally, in nouns and adjectives that end in -*eu* /eu̯/ we have a process of diphthongization that destroys the hiatuses -*eo* and -*ea* and is accompanied by a complementary change of /e̞/ into /ɛ/ and elision of the thematic vowel, asyllabic /u̯/ (ex: *europeu* 'European' (masc) : *européia* 'European' (fem)).

The /o̞/ : /ɔ/ alternation, which is not phonologically conditioned in the modern language, is found in the feminine just as it is in the plural. The historical development is the same in the two cases.[21] Thus, we have *ôvo* /ˈo̞vu/ 'egg', and *ova* /ˈɔva/ 'roe' parallel to the plural *ovos* /ˈɔvus/, as well as *formoso* /formˈo̞zu/ 'beautiful', fem *formosa* /formˈɔza/, parallel to the plural *formosos* /formˈɔzus/. In fact, this alternation becomes the sole mark of the feminine in *avô* 'grandfather' : *avó* 'grandmother' (and their compounds) since the -*a* desinence is missing.[22]

---

21. There are examples of an /ɛ/ in the feminine corresponding to an /e̞/ in the masculine even though there is no such alternation from singular to plural (ex: *capelo* /kapˈe̞lu/ 'hood' : *capela* /kapˈɛla/ 'chapel', both derived from *cappa* with the suffix -*ĕllu*).

22. The desinence -*a* of the intermediate form *avoa* /avˈɔa/ from Latin *aviŏla* was dropped.

The Feminine of Nouns

We have already seen that whereas adjectives with a theme in -*o* show fully explicit feminine inflections, nouns in general do not. In many instances the gender of nouns can be made explicit only by means of the mechanism of agreement with an -*o* theme adjective. For example, we classify *cobra* 'snake' and *testemunha* 'witness' as feminine nouns because they always take the feminine form of adjectives with thematic -*o* (exs: *tremenda cobra* 'tremendous snake'; *testemunha fidedigna* 'trustworthy witness'). By the same token, *tigre* 'tiger' and *cônjuge* 'spouse' are classified as masculine because they require masculine adjectives with theme in -*o* (exs: *pavoroso tigre* 'frightful tiger'; *cônjuge devotado* 'devoted spouse'). Both *artista* 'artist' and *mártir* 'martyr', on the other hand, may be either feminine or masculine, taking the corresponding gender of an -*o* theme adjective, accordingly as they refer to a woman or a man, respectively (exs: *magnífico artista* 'magnificent artist' (masc); *magnífica artista* 'magnificent artist' (fem); *heróico mártir* 'heroic martyr' (masc), *heróica mártir* 'heroic martyr' (fem)).

Nonetheless, under certain conditions nouns themselves may show explicit feminine inflections. Thus, despite the fact that -*e* theme adjectives are not inflected in the feminine, some nouns with theme in -*e*, as well as nouns with theme in -*o*, are so inflected (exs: *lôbo* 'wolf' (masc) : *lôba* 'wolf' (fem); *mestre* 'teacher' (masc) : *mestra* 'teacher' (fem)). There is a tendency to decline nouns ending in a consonant or thematic -*e* for gender if they refer to human beings. In the case of consonant-final nouns, the addition of the -*a* desinence is not accompanied by any morphophonemic alternations. The *mestre : mestra* example given above, as well as the more colloquial *parente* 'relative' (masc) : *parenta* 'relative' (fem), are typical of -*e* theme nouns, while pairs like the following exemplify consonant-final nouns: *autor* 'author' (masc) : *autora* 'author' (fem); *espanhol* 'Spaniard' (masc) : *espanhola* 'Spaniard' (fem); *freguês* 'customer' (masc) : *freguêsa* 'customer' (fem). This tendency was first manifested in the classical period for derived nouns and adjectives ending in the suffixes -(*d/t*)*or* and -*ês*.[23]

23. Certain forms derived by the addition of -*ês* do not take a feminine inflection. In general, forms of this type can function only as adjectives (exs: *cortês* 'courteous'; *montês* 'mountainous'; *pedrês* 'mottled'; as in *dama cortês* 'courteous lady'; *cabra montês* 'mountain she-goat'; *galinha pedrês* 'mottled hen').

In certain nouns, grammatical gender, i.e., the reflex of the division of the animal kingdom into the two sexes, is distinctively realized in a way that cannot properly be considered inflectional. Pairs of the type *duque* 'duke' : *duquesa* 'duchess'; *conde* 'count' : *condessa* 'countess'; *diácono* 'deacon' : *diaconisa* 'deaconess', for example, show in the feminine the addition of a variant of the lexical suffix *-ês*, in association with the feminine desinence, to the basic masculine form. The same is true of the pair *príncipe* 'prince' : *princesa* 'princess', except that the radical is reduced to *princi-* in the feminine, the unstressed final vowel being dropped by morphophonemic rules in position before the initial vowel of the suffix. In some cases, the feminine is derived from the masculine by the addition of the suffix *-inho*, in its feminine form *-inha*, to the basic masculine word. Typical examples are *galo* 'rooster' : *galinha* 'hen'; and *rei* 'king' : *rainha* 'queen', where in the last word the stressed *-i* of the suffix has caused the *-e-* of the radical to change to *-a-* and the asyllabic vowel has been dropped. In other cases the derived word turns out to be the masculine (exs: *ladrão* 'thief' (masc) : *ladra* 'thief' (fem); *lebrão* 'hare' (masc) : *lebre* 'hare' (fem); *perdigão* 'partridge' (masc) : *perdiz* 'partridge' (fem)).[24] Finally, there are a few instances of a masculine form having one lexical suffix while the corresponding feminine form has a different one. For example, in the pair *imperador* 'emperor' : *imperatriz* 'empress', the masculine shows the suffix *-dor* and the feminine the suffix *-triz*.[25] All the examples discussed above fall under the general heading of lexical distribution, a phenomenon that is quite different from the paradigmatic, regular, and precise inflectional process.

When the masculine : feminine opposition is realized by two words that have distinct radicals, it is even more evident that one is dealing with an essentially lexical phenomenon (exs: *homem* 'man' : *mulher* 'woman'; *cavalo* 'horse' : *égua* 'mare'; *bode* 'goat' : *cabra* 'she-goat'). Ever since the time of the ancient Indo-European languages, so-called

24. The consonant in the radical *perdic-* underwent different evolutionary processes in the environment of a following *-a* or *-i*.

25. The suffix *-triz*, which corresponds theoretically to the form 'suffix + ∅', includes the feminine gender implicitly. There are instances, however, in which the two suffixes appear in alternate forms of the same word. One can say, for example, *embaixadora* 'ambassadress' in the modern language, and *imperadora* was common in the classical language (ex: *Senhora, vós sois senhora/emperadora* 'My lady, you are the empress'; from Gil Vicente's *Obras*, edition of Marques Braga, Lisbon, 1951, 2: 11).

suppletion of radicals, as illustrated above, has been used alongside nominal and verbal inflection. Such suppletive processes are frequently employed in Portuguese nouns that refer to the animal kingdom, indicating sex through grammatical gender. Quite clearly this is a question of lexical distribution and is only marginally a part of nominal morphology.[26]

THE DISAPPEARANCE OF INFLECTION FOR DEGREE

Inflection for Degree

In Latin, special desinences were employed in order to express an increment in the quality expressed by an adjective with respect to two distinct situations, both of which were simultaneously referred to by a given occurrence of the adjective. It follows that inflection for degree is associated in an essential way with comparison and that it must occur with adjectives used in a specific type of syntactic construction. Comparison may be carried out in one of two ways. Either one or more entities may be viewed as exceeding another entity or other entities in some property, or one or more entities may be viewed as exceeding in some property a whole totality of which the former is a part. In the first case the comparison is said to be of the comparative degree (in the strict sense) and in the second case it is said to be of the superlative degree (in the strict sense).

In Latin, the comparative was expressed by the desinences *-ior* (masculine and feminine) and *-ius* (neuter). The adjective inflected in this way agreed in gender, number, and case with the noun compared, while the other noun was put in the ablative[27] (ex: Lt *vilius virtutibus aurum*, Ptg *o ouro vale menos que as virtudes* 'gold is worth less than the virtues'). The superlative was expressed by the desinence *-issim-* (*-im-* if the radical of the adjective ended in /l/ or /r/), followed by a second or first declension case desinence depending upon

26. Sometimes in the history of languages pairs of this type are replaced by a more regular inflectionally related pair, as for example in Latin *filius* : *filia* (whence Portuguese *filho* : *filha*) as compared to Greek *uiós* : *thugátēr*. In other instances, however, a pair consisting of two distinct members has been created in the evolutionary process. An example of the latter type is Portuguese *cavalo* : *égua* as compared to Latin *equus* : *equa*.

27. The ablative noun in this construction could alternatively be preceded by *quam* and put in the same case as the first noun. It was this syntactic pattern that was carried over to Portuguese, although the comparative inflection was dropped (ex: *o ouro é mais desvalioso que as virtudes*).

whether the noun was masculine or feminine.[28] Adjectives inflected in this way were followed by a noun in the genitive plural (ex: Lt *felicissima matrum*, Ptg *a mais feliz das mães*, 'the happiest of mothers'). The very same desinence *-issim-* (or *-im-*) was also used to indicate an increment in quality above the normal (ex: Lt *mater felicissima*, Ptg *mãe muito feliz* 'very happy mother') and the Latin grammarians, noting that the adjective in this construction had the same form as in the true superlative, improperly called it 'superlative' as well. To be more exact, they called the second construction the 'absolute superlative' and the first, that is, the true superlative construction, the 'relative superlative'.

Although the Latin system of inflections for degree did not survive in most Romance languages, Italian did retain the suffix *-issim-* (or *-im-*) to indicate an increment of a quality above the normal. Classical Portuguese, influenced by Italian, in turn borrowed from literary Latin forms like *felicissimu-*, *facillimu-*, and *pauperrimu-* in order to indicate an intensification in the quality referred to by the adjective. This occasional borrowing led to the creation of a secondary form of the adjective that often has a radical different from that of the corresponding primary form, a result of the circumstance that the former was borrowed from literary Latin during the Classical period, that is, after many phonological developments of Vulgar Latin had already occurred. For this reason the form corresponding to *pobre* 'poor' is *paupérrimo* 'poorest' (from Lt *pauperrimu-*, *pauper*), while the form corresponding to *feliz* 'happy' is *felicíssimo* 'happiest' (from Lt *felicissimu-*, *felic(is)*).[29]

In actual fact, intensification eventually came to be a synchronic process of adjective derivation, and new forms were therefore created directly from Portuguese (ex: *pobre* 'poor'; *pobríssimo* 'poorest').[30] This derivational process, however, is rather limited in extension, as well as in actual use, because many adjectives simply do not have the corresponding secondary form.

Since comparisons of degree are a matter of sentence types or

28. Of course, there was also a neuter, which had an identical nominative and accusative, both in the singular and in the plural. In the plural the neuter took the case desinence *-a*.

29. *Felicis* is the genitive; the nominative is *felix* /feliks/, with the *-s* desinence.

30. In Brazil adjectives of the type *paupérrimo* gave rise to a pejorative suffix used to intensify adjectives having a negative quality (ex: *infamérrimo* 'very infamous').

syntactic structures in Portuguese and have no connection with the modern inflectional system, we shall discuss them later along with other sentence patterns found in the language. Notice, however, that even intensification of an adjectival quality is more commonly expressed by a syntactic process, the placement of the adverbs *muito* 'very' or (in the case of a negative increment) *pouco* 'less' before the adjective (exs: *muito feliz* 'very happy'; *pouco feliz* 'less happy').

Fossilized Inflections for Degree

The adjectives *grande* 'big', *pequeno* 'small', *bom* 'good', *mau* 'bad', *muito* 'much', and *pouco* 'little' are associated with comparatives that have a different radical—*maior* 'bigger', *menor* 'smaller', *melhor* 'better', *pior* 'worse', *mais* 'more', *menos* 'less'. Historically, the first four have the Latin comparative desinence *-ior* while the last two are adverbs that, in construction with nouns, gained an adjectival use (exs: *mais livros* 'more books'; *menos livros* 'less books'). It is clear, however, that as far as the structure of the modern language is concerned it would be totally unjustified to claim that these forms contain vestiges of a process of inflection for degree. They are indivisible forms that in themselves signal the comparative degree. Their relation to the corresponding adjective is parallel to that of the feminine *mulher* 'woman' to the masculine *homem* 'man'.

A small series of adjectives—*superior, inferior, anterior, posterior, exterior, interior*—borrowed from literary Latin are also special lexical forms. Although all of these adjectives had the comparative inflection in Latin, some of them did not have a corresponding adjective. In fact, we find only *superus, inferus, posterus,* and *exterus.*[31] Furthermore, some of these adjectives are not usually used as comparatives in Portuguese and others cannot be so used under any conditions (exs: *espírito superior* 'very lofty mind'; *sentimento interior* 'inner feeling', that is, a feeling that cannot be sensed).

31. Superlative forms, either with *-ēmu-* or *-ĭmu-*, also appear in certain Portuguese words (exs: *supremo, ínfimo, extremo, íntimo*).

`                                                      `

Chapter 4

The Morphology of Pronouns

PRONOUNS AND MEANING

Relational Meanings in Language

In all languages the location of an element of the bio-social world relevant to linguistic expression can be determined within the context of a speech act by means of a system of forms that indicate the relative position of a given element at the moment a linguistic message is conveyed. Under a system of this type the bio-social elements of the world are not represented by linguistic forms that symbolize them or bring them into focus as a function of the particular concept that each such element entails for the speech community. The system differs from the nominal and verbal systems precisely in this respect, and the forms that comprise it must therefore be purely indicative or deictic

(in a broad sense). Such forms are classified as pronouns and function
within what Karl Bühler called the *Zeigfeld* (relational field) rather
than in the *Symbolfeld* (symbolic field) or *Zeichenfeld* (representative
field) (see Bühler 1934, p. 95).

The speaker-hearer axis, which is automatically set up by the act
of communication, was used in Latin, as in many other languages, to
indicate relative distance in the pronominal system. The existence of
a series of forms to indicate the speaker at any given moment, independently of the speaker considered as an individual, is a natural
consequence of this circumstance. Any person—*Marcus, Sextus,
Tullia,* or *Cornelia*—could call himself *ego,* that is, the person speaking right now, but the same person might equally well be called *tu*
when addressed by another speaker, say, *Publius, Septimus,* or
Iulia. Such pronominal forms showed morphological variation according to the category of case (nominative, accusative, genitive, etc.)
in the same way nouns did. Alternating with the nominatives *ego* and
tu, we find genitives *mei* and *tui,* datives *mihi* and *tibi,* and accusative-
ablatives *mē* and *tē,* respectively. In terms of the general morphological system of Latin the nonnominative forms were the ones that
were most frequently and constantly used since the desinence of the
verbal form was itself sufficient to indicate whether the speaker or
hearer was to be understood as the subject, a function that otherwise
would have been assigned to the pronouns *ego* and *tu.* Under these
conditions *ego* and *tu* were actually used only to emphasize the subject
redundantly, as 'vocatives' in an isolated communication, or in a
sentence without an explicit verb (ex: *ego bonus* 'I am good').

Parallel to the situations discussed above, which involve single
speakers and hearers, the morphological system of Latin included
forms that allowed the speaker to address more than one hearer or to
express himself not only in his own right but also on behalf of a larger
group associated with him in some way. These forms were *nōs* and
uōs. Their distribution according to case was somewhat different from
that of *ego* and *tu*—there were special genitive (*nostrum, uestrum*) and
dative-ablative forms (*nobis, uobis*), but the accusative was identical
to the nominative.

Corresponding to the system of the so-called personal pronouns
ego, tu, nōs, and *uōs,* we find a system of demonstratives in which
bio-social elements of the world other than the speaker or hearer were
indicated by means of their position relative to one of the poles of the
speaker-hearer axis. *Hic* was used to refer to that which was close to

the speaker, *íste* for that which was close to the hearer, while there was another independent system of forms for referring to elements that did not fall into either of these two relational areas. At first the latter consisted of three distinct pronouns: *ílle*, which had a precise indicative value; *is*, which was somewhat vague; and *ípse*, which repeated a previously given indication in a way similar to *o mesmo* in Portuguese or *the same* in English.[1] All of the demonstratives had specific forms for each of the three genders (masculine, feminine, neuter) and took the desinences of the five fundamental cases.

Possessives

The genitive of a personal pronoun was used in order to lay claim to an element of the bio-social world for either the speaker or the hearer. In such cases the element in question was referred to by means of a substantive (ex: *frequentia uestrum* 'your attendance (here)') and in Classical Latin an adjectival form of the personal pronoun, agreeing with the noun, was preferred to the genitive (ex: *frequentia uestra*). In Latin grammar the adjectival personal pronouns were called 'possessives', a name that derives from their use to indicate true possession (ex: *domus mea* 'my house'). Just like any other adjective with a theme in *ŭ/o*,[2] the possessives belonged to the second declension when masculine and the first when feminine. There were four series, one for each personal pronoun: *meus, mea* (*ego*, gen *mei*); *tuus, tua* (*tu*, gen *tui*); *noster, nostra* (*nos*, gen *nostrum*); *uester, uestra* (*uos*, gen *uestrum*).

Reflexives

The Latin system of personal pronouns did not include a form for a third person external to the speaker-hearer axis, as is evident from the discussion above. When the subject of a verb was neither the speaker nor the hearer a distinctive verbal inflection was used and the subject could be specified either by the appropriate noun or by means of a demonstrative pronoun operating within the *Zeigfeld*. The subject of *currit* 'runs', for example, could be specified either as 'Marcus' in *Marcus currit* or as 'that person you see over there' in *ille currit*. Analogous constructions were possible in other positions—as the

1. The correspondence is only approximate, if not actually wrong. In reality the best Latin translation for Ptg *o mesmo*, Eng *the same* would be *idem*, a compound of *is*. *Ipse* had a much more specific and particular value.

2. Of course there was also a neuter with plural in *-a* in the nominative-accusative and a second-declension singular, having identical forms in the nominative and accusative.

complement of nouns like *domus* 'house', we find the genitive (exs: *domus Marci, domus illius*); as the direct object of verbs like *uideo* 'I see', we find the corresponding accusative (exs: *uideo Marcum, uideo illum*), and so on.

There was a series of true third-person possessive and personal pronouns in Latin, but this series was used only when the third-person form was in complement position and identical to the subject. Putting the same thing in other words, one can say equivalently that Latin had a system of 'reflexive' pronouns in the third person. The accusative reflexive *se* appears, for example, in sentences like *se quisque diligit* 'each person loves himself', and the possessive reflexive, in its feminine ablative form, is found in *agit pro domo sua* '(he) acts for his own sake'.[3] The personal reflexive pronoun of the third person, which obviously had no nominative, took case desinences parallel to those of *tu* (*sui, sibi, se*), and the third-person reflexive possessive had the same structure as the other possessives, that is, the masculine *suus* was second declension while the feminine *sua* was first declension.

Personal Pronouns in Portuguese

A new series of third-person forms, generally based on one of the demonstrative pronouns stripped of its deictic content, developed in all the Romance languages. As early as the imperial period, this new role was turned over to *ille* in Vulgar Latin.[4] Since Portuguese followed the general Romance pattern, we find in the modern language a series consisting of *êle, ela, êles*, and *elas* (masc sing, fem sing, masc pl, fem pl, respectively) alongside the series *eu, tu, nós*, and *vós*.

It is important to recall that the third-person pronoun has a rather peculiar categorical character as compared to the first- and second-person pronouns. In essence it is a mere substitute for a noun that is either explicit or implicit in the linguistic context and to which it must refer. The third-person form can attain the extralinguistic context only indirectly, by means of the associated noun. *Êle*, for example, always takes the place of some noun, be it *livro* 'book', *jardim* 'garden', *professor* 'teacher', or *operário* 'worker', as determined by the linguistic context. *Eu, tu, nós*, and *vós*, on the other hand, unlike the third-person forms, are immediately and directly relevant to one of

3. *Domus* 'house' in a figurative sense.

4. In the Classical language the demonstratives were systematically and rigorously distributed according to the demonstrative nuance required by the sentence.

the poles of the speaker-hearer axis, that is, to the extralinguistic situation.

From a formal point of view, the third-person pronoun agrees in gender and number with the noun for which it is substituted. In place of *testemunha* 'witness', one must say *ela*, whether one is discussing a man or a woman, and similarly *cônjuge* 'spouse' can be replaced only by *êle*. The first- and second-person forms, however, retain the Latin structure, that is, they have independent forms for the singular and the plural and show a total absence of the category of gender.

The Portuguese system of personal pronouns is dichotomous in the conceptual, as well as in the morphological, sense. On one hand, there is the older Latin structure in *eu, tu, nós, vós*, and on the other hand there is the third-person series that has the nominal type structure of a feminine in -*a* and a plural in -*s*. The pronouns of the first group refer to the people who take an active part in a linguistic communication; those of the second group, given the linguistic context, replace a noun that refers to something that is inactive in the communication. The real difference between Portuguese *êle* and Latin *ille* is that *ille*, being a true demonstrative, was related directly to the bio-social world in which linguistic communication occurs. In *ille currit*, for example, we know that the subject is 'that person you see over there', not simply 'him'.

Terms of Address

Even in Latin the relational structure of the personal pronouns was altered by a social convention requiring the use of the plural for a single speaker or hearer under certain conditions. The reasons for this type of usage can be many and varied. In the first place the speaker may wish to imply that he is speaking not as an individual but rather as a spokesman for a more or less collective opinion. Examples include a general speaking to the enemy on behalf of the troops he commands or an author who wants to associate the reader with that which he is writing. Looking at the same situation inversely, the general, when addressing an enemy commander, would use the second-person plural as would a reader addressing an author taken to be the representative of a whole school of thought. In Classical Latin *nos* and *uos* even had special genitive forms with singular desinences (*nostri, uestri*) in case they referred to a single individual. Eventually the use of *uos* to refer to one individual came to be the general rule, and this pronoun, which was already the plural of *tu*, developed into a replacement for *tu* used in order to indicate a greater degree of deference toward the hearer.

The practice of analyzing a speaker in terms of his 'eminence' or social 'majesty' and then taking this qualitative status to be the goal of a communication was another type of usage that interfered with the structure of the personal pronouns. One did not address the Emperor of Rome as *Uos* but as *Uestra Maiestas* 'Your Majesty', and when the latter was the subject of a verb, the verb was put into the third-person singular. The intensity and scope of this new type of construction were especially marked. Although Portuguese, unlike Italian, did not go so far as to use the third-person pronoun for the hearer in subject position, in complement position this pronoun was employed with a subject of the *Uestra Maiestas* type (exs: *Vossa Majestade* 'Your Majesty' or *Vossa Alteza* 'Your Highness', used in addressing kings; *Vossa Mercê* 'Your Grace'; *Vossa Senhoria* 'Your Lordship'). Eventually the long, heavy expression *Vossa Mercê* contracted to a new, briefer, and lighter form, *você*.[5]

The possessives *suus, sua* eventually lost their strictly reflexive meaning in Vulgar Latin and came to be used for the new third person *ille*, just as *meus, mea* was the possessive for *ego*. The Portuguese reflex of *suus, sua* (*seu, sua*), having the new nonreflexive value, also became the possessive form for the hearer referred to as *Você* (or any equivalent complex expression).

Although the *tu* series survived in certain usages that vary from region to region, *vós* (the reflex of Latin *uos*) survived only in the written language. It is not used in the speech of either Portugal or Brazil.

Finally, we should mention that personal pronoun subjects are generally optional in Portuguese just as they were in Latin. The role of the verbal desinence in determining the person of the subject has not changed. Portuguese, unlike French or such non-Romance languages as English or German, shows a subject pronoun in front of the verb only for stylistic reasons (exs: Ptg *dou*, Lt *do*, Fr *je donne*, 'I give').[6]

5. There was also an intermediary stage—*Vosmecê*—that was finally abandoned in the common language. In Brazil a parallel usage of *o senhor, a senhora, os senhores, as senhoras* also developed. *Você* and the latter expressions are distributed accordingly as a lesser or greater degree of deference to the hearer is intended.

6. It should be noted, however, that since the various verbal desinences are less strongly differentiated in Portuguese, personal pronouns are more frequently used in subject position than they were in Classical Latin.

The Demonstrative in Portuguese

The tripartite structure of the Latin demonstratives was maintained in the corresponding Portuguese system. The modern language has *êste* for location near the speaker, *êsse* for location near the hearer, and *aquêle* for location distant from both speaker and hearer. The only change was the simplification of the third-person series of Latin, which was, as we have already seen, rather complex and elaborate. In other Romance languages, among them Italian and Rumanian, a two-member system of the English *this-that* type developed, and in French the deictic system consists for all practical purposes of only one element: *ce*.[7]

Like all the other Romance languages, Portuguese supplemented the system of position indicators with a type of pronominal adjective that adds the category 'definite' to a noun with which it agrees. This new pronominal form, unknown in Classical Latin, is usually called the 'article'. It developed slowly through an increase in the use of one of the demonstratives, usually *ille*,[8] in Vulgar Latin. By this mechanism the absence of the demonstrative became an ipso facto indication of indefinite reference. Such reference could be made more emphatic, however, by the addition of *unus, una,* and in fact we can find occurrences of this new function in Plautus (third century B.C.): *una lepida mulier* 'a pretty woman'.[9]

PRONOMINAL FORMS: SYSTEM AND EVOLUTION

The Personal Pronouns

Grammarians traditionally claim that the Latin case system was carried over unscathed to the personal pronouns of Portuguese, but this statement is inaccurate and reflects a confusion of two systems of entirely different formal types. In Portuguese there are three forms distributed according to the following uses—1) as a subject or in isolation, 2) as a clitic joined to a verbal form with which it constitutes a phonological word, and 3) as the head of a construction in which it is governed by a preposition and, as such, is subordinated to

7. The bipartite system, formed by adding the particles *-ci* and *-là* to *ce*, is used only when opposing one thing to another (ex: *ce livre-ci et ce livre-là*).

8. Ancient Greek also had an article that had evolved from a demonstrative. It is possible that the Greek model fostered the development of the article in Latin.

9. Since an isolated substantive could in principle be applied to a definite being, indefinite reference was normal in Classical Latin with other pronominal forms.

a verb.[10] A distribution of this type is totally different from the Latin one, in which case depended on the function of the noun or pronoun in a sentence.

The best terminology for the three forms of a given personal pronoun is: 1) isolated form, 2) dependent adverbal form, 3) form gov-

	Form 1	Form 2	Form 3
1st sing	eu	me	mim
2d sing	tu	te	ti
3d reflex	—	se	si

erned by a preposition. The first is a stressed free form, the second a clitic that is dependent on a preceding or following verbal form, and the third a stressed form that is also dependent since, in an autonomous utterance, it can appear only in association with a preposition. It is this system that we find in the two persons of the singular and in the third-person reflexive system. The latter, however, has identical singular and plural forms and lacks a stressed free form. The first form might occur in a miniature monologue like *Quem? Eu!?* 'Who? Me!?', the second in an example like *Ouve-me?* 'Do you hear me?', and the third in a sentence like *Que esperas de mim?* 'What do you expect of me?'

This system was entirely new. It was created at the expense of Latin forms that lost the true function of case. Although *eu* and *tu*, which come from *ego* and *tu*, respectively, did not really change in function, the two remaining Portuguese forms represent a total overhaul of the Latin forms of which they are reflexes. *Mim* can be traced back to *mī*, a contraction of the Latin dative *mĭhĭ*, while *ti* and *si* derive from Latin forms *tī* and *sī*, modeled after *mihi* and used in Vulgar Latin as replacements for the datives *tibi* and *sibi*. *Me, te,* and *se,* on the other hand, are reflexes of the accusative-ablative *mē, tē, sē*. In Portuguese, however, the adverbal clitics indicate a direct or indirect object, that is, they are equivalent to an accusative-dative. The form governed by a preposition, which evolved from the Latin

10. With a noun the adjectival (or possessive) pronoun is used, as we have already seen to be the case in Latin (ex: *frequentia uestra - vossa afluência, domus mea - minha casa*).

dative, corresponds roughly to an ablative (or accusative governed by a preposition).[11]

The first- and second-person plural have only one form each—*nós* and *vós*, respectively. In adverbal clitic position they lose the /ǫ/ of the stressed vowel system and acquire /u/ from the unstressed final system (written -*o*). The dative-ablative forms *nobis, uobis* were lost and were replaced by the nominative-accusative forms *nōs, uōs*.[12]

The third person subsystem, a creation of the Romance languages, has one stressed free form that varies in gender and number in the same way nouns do (*êle* 'he', *êles* 'they' (masc), *ela* 'she', *elas* 'they' (fem)), and two adverbal clitic forms that retain the distinction between the Latin dative and accusative. The accusative or direct object form is a monophonemic particle *o* that also has feminine and plural forms modeled after those of nouns (*o, a, os, as*). The dative or indirect object form does not vary with gender but does have a plural in -*s* (*lhe, lhes*). All of the third-person forms are connected in some way with the Latin demonstrative *ille*, as we have already seen. It was the nominative, masculine *ĭlle*, feminine *ĭlla*, that gave Portuguese *êle, ela*. The feminine form shows an open /ę/ that can be explained in terms of the morphological nature that was soon acquired

11. The preposition *com* governs a variant of Form 3. In this case a morphological word is formed in which the preposition agglutinates with radical *migo tigo sigo*, to give *comigo contigo consigo*. These radicals, however, already contain an agglutinated enclitic occurrence of *cum* with the Latin ablatives *mē tē sē*. The forms *migo tigo sigo* are the result of lenition of intervocalic /k/ and metaphony of -ē- (/ę/) caused by the final /u/ of *mecu(m) tecu(m) secu(m)*. One of the more striking differences between Old and Modern Portuguese is the occurrence in the old language of isolated *migo tigo sigo* with the full value of the preposition contained within the final syllable -*go*. Typical examples are:

> quando se foi posera *migo*
> que se veesse logo a seu grado,
> senon, que me enviasse mandado

(Nunes 1926, p. 249), where *posera migo* is equivalent to *combinara comigo*. The modern form, however, was even then in free variation with the older one:

> Madre, se meu amigo veesse,
> demandar lh'ia, se vos prouguesse,
> que se veesse veer *comigo:*
> se veer, madre, o meu amigo
> demandar lh'ei que se veja *migo*

(Nunes 1926, p. 226).

12. Whence *noscum uoscum* instead of *nobiscum uobiscum*, leading to modern *conosco convosco* from archaic *nosco vosco* (see n. 11). The open quality of *nós, vós* is a small enigma. Williams (1938, p. 142) accepts an explanation by 'analogy' to *nosso vosso* due to Isidore Dyen.

by the open vowel–close vowel alternation in the feminine.[13] The plural in -*s* was a Portuguese (more accurately: Romance) development, modeled on the plural of nouns. The particle *o, a, os, as* comes directly from the four forms of the Latin accusative of *ĭlle* : *ĭllum, ĭllam, ĭllos, ĭllas*. The latter underwent a gradual articulatory weakening which effected both the initial vowel and the consonant of the radical.[14] In archaic Portuguese there was a dative form *li* that evolved from the Latin masculine dative *illī*. The modern form with palatal /ļ/ evolved under the influence of the agglutinated form *lho*, from *li* and the old accusative *lo* used together with a single verb (*lilo* > *lio* > /lĭo/ > *lho*). It seems that *lho* was then analyzed as *lhe* + *o*, exactly as *mo* and *to* correspond to *me* + *o* and *te* + *o*, respectively. The plural *lhes* is of more recent origin and is not found up to the beginning of the classical period.

In the Brazilian colloquial language, even that of the educated classes, the third-person subsystem has undergone profound changes. Both *lhe* and its plural *lhes* have become adverbal forms indicating the hearer addressed in the third person and thus are now identical to *te* in function. In less-careful speech, *lhe* may even be replaced by *te* because *você* and *tu* are equivalent in this style. Since, furthermore, the forms *o, a, os,* and *as* have come to be quite simply obsolete, the third-person series is reduced to the forms *êle, ela, êles, elas* in any syntactic function.[15]

In the written language and in formalized speech the traditional system is fully operative. As I have stated elsewhere, 'In this case a split between the written and spoken languages is evident and there

13. The idea that final /a/ causes a reverse metaphony, opposite to that of final /u/, has also been suggested.

14. It is to the form *lo* (that is, *o* before the loss of the consonant of the radical) that one must look for the historical explanation of two morphophonemic changes that occur when the adverbal form *o* is in enclitic position. If the verbal form ends in /r/ or /s/, this consonant is dropped and the *lo* variant is added as the enclitic (exs: *amá-lo* 'to love him', *di-lo* 'he says it'). The historical evolution was: *amar* + *lo* > *amallo* > *amalo*, that is, assimilation of *r* to *l* in *rl* > *ll*, followed by simplification of the geminate. If the verbal form ends in nasal closure, on the other hand, the *no* variant of *o* is added (ex: *amam-no* 'they love him'). In this case the historical evolution was: *amam* + *lo* > *aṃam* + *no*, that is, assimilation of the /l/ to the nasal environment.

15. A similar reduction is found in the archaic literary language. In the archaic case, however, this occurred only under conditions of emphasis and was caused by the gross volume and stress inherent in the *êle* series. In Brazil, on the contrary, one is dealing with an autonomous structural fact that is to be explained by a process of remodeling (see Camara 1957).

seems to be no hope of compromise. Any Brazilian who has had some schooling spontaneously adopts a new attitude toward the morphology of *êle* when he sits down to write. The accusative forms *o*, *a*, *os*, and *as*, which are all but banned from the colloquial language, are used in the written language with perfect ease' (Camara 1963, p. 336).

Possessives

The Portuguese system of possessives, derived from the corresponding Latin accusatives, is a continuation of patterns established in the classical language. In late Vulgar Latin, however, the difference between the radical *meu-* of the first person and the radicals *tuu-*, *suu-* of the second and third reflexive persons set off a leveling process that tended to remodel the system in favor of *meu-* or *tuu-/suu-*, depending on the region. Although Spanish retained the two distinct radicals of Latin, Portuguese adopted the first-person model for the masculine of the second and third reflexive persons. In Portuguese, then, the masculine forms are *meu*, *teu*, *seu* (+/s/ in the plural) and the feminine forms are *minha*,[16] *tua*, *sua* (+/s/ in the plural). The first- and second-person plural forms *nostru-*, *vostru-* (a Vulgar form of *uestru-*) were not adopted in Lusitanian Vulgar Latin but were replaced by new forms based on the corresponding personal pronouns **nossu-* and **vossu-* (Bourciez 1930, p. 450). The latter may even have existed in the Roman version of Vulgar Latin at a very early date (Mohl 1900). At any rate the modern language has *nosso*, *vosso* (with the -*a* and -*s* desinences of the feminine and the plural, respectively).

Since a Portuguese possessive, like its Latin counterpart, does not in general add the category 'definite' to the noun with which it is associated, the article may be used for this purpose (ex: *o meu livro ali está* 'my book is over there'). In Brazil, however, the article is usually omitted if it is clear from context that the noun is to be taken as definite. Thus, corresponding to the indefinite phrase in *meus livros são numerosos*[17] 'my books are numerous', we may have the definite phrase either with the article, as in *os meus livros são os seguintes . . . ,* or without the article, as in *meus livros são os seguintes . . . ,* both meaning 'my books are the following ones . . .'. Only within the

16. Following the general rule for /ẹ/ in hiatus, the Latin form *mea* gave *mia* (cf *uĭa* > Ptg *via*), which in turn gave *mĩa* by nasalization. The word then entered the pattern of stressed nasal *ĩ* in hiatus (cf *pĩo* > *pinho*).

17. In Portugal *os meus livros são numerosos* is preferred despite the evident indefinite character of the phrase headed by *livros*.

predicate, when the possessive refers to a nominal subject, is the presence or absence of an article fully indicative of the definite-indefinite opposition (exs: indefinite *êsse livro é meu* 'this book is one of mine'; definite *êsse livro é o meu* 'this book is mine').

Just as in Latin, the Portuguese possessive is purely adjectival. Traditionally, the grammar books, noting the sentential pattern *êste livro é o meu* 'this book is mine', assign the possessive a substantive-like function. But, the fact is that the distinction between nouns and adjectives vanishes in predicative position, and even words that from a formal point of view are nouns exclusively take on an adjectival function in that position (cf. *êste homem é bom* 'this man is good' : *êste homem é Pedro* 'this man is Pedro'). Traditional grammar itself recognizes this implicitly by accepting the adjectival character of the possessive in the *êste livro é meu* pattern (possessive without article). It seems that the underlying reasoning was the idea that the article turned the possessive into a noun. In reality, however, the article serves to express the category 'definite' by its presence or the category 'indefinite' by its absence. It is once again the 'definite' category that requires the presence of the article in the second member of a nominal sequence of two possessives joined by *e* 'and' in which both possessives refer to distinct individuals of the same type, the latter being explicitly mentioned only in the first conjunct. Thus we have (*o*) *meu livro e o teu*[18] or in the inverse order *o meu e o teu livro*, both meaning 'my book and yours'.

Demonstratives

We have already seen that, as far as categories are concerned, the tripartite system of Latin survives unchanged in the Portuguese demonstratives, that is, both languages have forms denoting: 1) proximity to the speaker, 2) proximity to the hearer, and 3) distance from both speaker and hearer. This is not to say, however, that the actually occurring forms are the same in both languages. On the contrary, *iste*, formerly the second-person demonstrative, became first person in Portuguese and the empty second-person slot was filled by *ipse*, a form that had a rather different function in Latin. The basic cause of this shift in forms was the abandonment of the first-person form *hic*. The changed status of *iste* at first might have consisted of a simple extension in area. In this case, *iste* would have become a form de-

---

18. When the possessive has its own isolated form the situation is rather different. We have in French, for example, *ton livre* but *mon livre et le tien*.

noting the totality of the speaker-hearer axis in opposition to *ille,* which denoted all points exterior to this axis. We must note, however, that if such a process occurred, the older tripartite system was quickly reestablished by restricting *iste* to proximity to the speaker and adding *ipse* for proximity to the hearer. The use of emphatic *ipse* with the three personal pronouns, especially the second-person form, must have encouraged the latter change (ex: *Medice, cura te ipsum* 'Physician, heal thyself').

In the singular, the Portuguese forms correspond to the Latin nominative with a theme in *-e* and a feminine with the *-a* desinence. The plural, on the other hand, has the *-s* desinence in accordance with the nominal pattern. Unlike nominals, however, the Portuguese demonstratives have an explicit neuter form derived from the nominative-accusative of the neuters of Latin *iste, ipse, ille* (*istud, ipsum, illud,* respectively). In Portuguese, these forms have no plural and are used only as substantives denoting 'things', that is, entities considered inert or passive. As we have seen, the notion originally associated with the neuter gender was lost in the Latin nominal system and 'neuter' had come to be a mere morphological idiosyncrasy. In the substantive use of the demonstratives, however, even within Latin, the fundamental idea of the neuter remained intact and was passed on to Portuguese. The Portuguese reflexes of *istud, ipsum, illud* are used to refer to that which either does not belong to the animal kingdom or is not considered to belong to it. A 'thing' of this type is viewed as a single individual with a position in the *Zeigfeld.*

Reinforcement of demonstratives by a pre-posed occurrence of the particle *ecce* (modern *eis*) was a well-established usage of Vulgar Latin. Eventually the phrase *ecce eum* (*ecce* + the accusative masculine singular of *is*) agglutinated to *eccum,* which in turn replaced the original *ecce.* A variant of the former, *accum,* losing the final nasalization, then came to be used in Portuguese reinforced demonstratives of the type *aqueste, aquesse, aquêle.* All three reinforced demonstratives were in free variation with the corresponding simple variants in the archaic period. The form *aquêle* won immediate acceptance even in nonemphatic uses in order to make the demonstrative distinct in form from the third-person personal pronoun *êle,* which also derives from *ille.* The reinforced forms *aqueste* and *aquesse* did not survive.

The morphology of the modern Portuguese demonstratives shows the effect of the /ẹ/ - /ę/ alternation in the feminine and the /ę/ - /i/ alternation in the neuter. As in the case of /ęla/, one must keep in mind the fact that although the /ę/ - /ę/ alternation originated through metaphony, it quickly gained morphological status. As far as the /ę/ - /i/ alternation in the neuter is concerned, it should be noted that the archaic forms *esto* . . . became *isto* . . . without any similar change occurring in nouns with /ę/ and thematic *-o*. This fact confirms the hypothesis that the change was a morphological one rather than a phonetic one.

The following table will serve as a summary of the demonstrative forms of Portuguese discussed above:

	adjective use[19] substantive use (animal kingdom)	substantive use (neuter)
proximity to speaker	êste, -s; esta /ę/, -s	isto
proximity to hearer	êsse -s; essa /ę/, -s	isso
distance from both	aquêle, -s; aquela /ę/-s	aquilo

This system is used not only with reference to the spatial positions of the speaker and the hearer (deictic in the strict sense) but also within the more general sphere of the linguistic context. The latter function is called *anaphoric*, from Greek *ana-* 'back' plus *pherein* 'to carry', that is, 'to relate'. In their anaphoric usage, the *Zeigfeld* of the demonstratives is centered around the speaker. The tripartite system of Latin which is based on the speaker : hearer opposition, becomes quite inapplicable. What one is dealing with in this case is really an opposition between the general context of the moment at which communication occurs and any other time, either before or after that moment. In other words, the series *êste : êsse : aquêle* reduces to (*êste/êsse*) : *aquêle*, a two-membered series of the Italian, Rumanian, or English type.

Despite the nonequivalence of the demonstratives in their deictic and anaphoric functions, both in Brazil and in Portugal there has been a concerted effort within the written language to keep *êste* and *êsse* apart in the latter function. The rule created for this purpose, that of restricting *êsse* to that which is about to be said, does not correspond

19. 'Adjective' should here be understood somewhat loosely. As in the case of the possessives, the isolated use of a demonstrative that refers to a previously employed noun is included (exs: *aquêle livro e êste* 'that book and this one,' *o livro é êste* 'the book is this one').

to linguistic reality and is frequently ignored. In Brazil resistance to the would-be rule is greater than in Portugal. The norm inherent in the Brazilian written language requires the use of *êsse* for the moment of communication. The latter then enters into opposition with *aquêle*, and *êste* becomes an emphatic variant of *êsse*. Even in the deictic function the tripartite system is losing ground in Brazil since there is a tendency to eliminate the discrepancy between the tripartite deictic system and the bipartite anaphoric system.

The Article

The article, which derives from demonstratives in all Romance languages, is used to mark the opposition between a given determined instance of a species, viewed as definitively specified, and any other instance of the same species.[20] In Vulgar Latin the accusative of the demonstrative *ille*, stripped of its spatial connotations, eventually came to be used for this purpose in position before nouns (ex: *proferte mihi stolam illam primam* 'bring me the first stole'; see Grandgeant 1928, p. 72). The process of phonological weakening, which we have already seen at work in the case of *ille* in construction with a verbal form, operated in this case also. As a result, the article became a clitic and was eventually reduced to the modern form *o*, the bare root, by the fall of the initial /l/[21] of a transitional form *lo*. Like unstressed final *-o*, this *o*, which constitutes the theme, vanishes upon addition of the feminine *-a* desinence in accordance with the morphophonemic rules of the modern language. Thus, the Portuguese article has the forms *o, a, os, as* (masc sing, fem sing, masc pl, fem pl, respectively).

As far as category is concerned, the article is still a demonstrative pronominal particle, and its presence implies a definite position within the ideal *Zeigfeld* common to both speaker and hearer. In the Vulgar Latin example *proferte mihi stolam illam primam*, the two interlocutors are discussing a stole which is clearly situated in their memories. The absence of the article, on the other hand, is sufficient to establish that a substantive refers to an undetermined individual of the species.

20. *Species* should be understood as a linguistic division, that is, as a collection of individuals that are designated by the same noun in a given language.

21. It is this transitional form that provides the historical explanation for morphophonemic agglutination of *por* and *em* with the article. The first gives *pelo* (from *per + lo > pello > pelo*); the second *no* (from *em + lo > ēno > eno > no*). In modern descriptive terms one may say that the initial /n/ is equivalent to the preposition, or is a variant thereof, since it indicates the functional presence of *em*.

Evidently this is not true of Latin, although the same idea can be positively expressed in Latin, as well as in Portuguese, by using an indefinite pronoun as an adjective.[22]

One can conceive of a single instance of a species either as a definitely determined unique entity or as an archetype of the whole species. The latter, like the former, may be expressed by means of a singular noun with the article serving as a mark of 'typification' (ex: *o leão é animal feroz* 'the lion is a ferocious animal'), but one may also refer to a totality of this type by means of a plural (ex: *os leões são animais ferozes* 'lions are ferocious animals').[23]

The article, in any linguistic structure that contains it, serves also as a mark of the purely substantive status of a given member of the noun-adjective class. This fact has two immediate consequences, one of which is valid for all languages that have articles. The more general consequence involves the 'substantivization' of words that are morphologically adjectives by means of the addition of a pre-posed occurrence of the article (ex: *o belo* 'that which is beautiful'). This type of substantivization is in contrast with derivation by means of a process of a specific type (ex: *beleza* 'beauty'; from *belo* 'beautiful'). The former process can be extended to verbs, in the infinitive (ex: *o comer e o coçar* 'eating and scratching'), to adverbs (ex: *sei o que fazer, mas falta decidir o quando e o como* 'I know what to do, but I've got to decide the when and the how of the thing'), and even to personal pronouns, which lose their deictic pronominal value and function as substantives (ex: *o eu de cada um de nós* 'the "I" of each one of us' *or* 'the ego of each one of us'). The second, less general, consequence is the use of the article with proper nouns, that is, substantives that refer to a particular individual, distinguishing it from the set consisting of many other individuals of the same name.[24] In Portuguese, the presence of the article is obligatory with proper nouns denoting geographic entities of irregular formation (exs: *o Vesúvio* 'Mount Vesuvius', *os Alpes* 'the Alps', *o Amazonas* 'the Amazon'), and the classical practice of omitting the article with names of countries has been abandoned in

22. In the Romance languages, however, there is also an indefinite article derived from the numeral *one*.

23. In the latter construction (*leões são animais ferozes*) the disappearance of the article is the result of a latinism introduced in the archaic literary language.

24. This seems to capture adequately the concept of 'proper noun'. Note, however, that the exact definition of this concept has long been a subject of debate, reflected in an extensive literature.

the modern language (exs: *o Brasil* 'Brazil', *a França* 'France', *os Paises Baixos* 'the Netherlands'). The only exception is the proper noun *Portugal*, which does not take the article. Proper nouns denoting cities take the article unless they are specific words that do not correspond to any member of the common vocabulary (exs: *Lisboa, Paris*), originally denoted something other than the city (ex: *João Pessoa*), or are full noun phrases (exs: *Belo Horizonte, Caldas da Rainha*). The article is supposed to be used with names of people only when accompanied by a pre-posed adjective (exs: *o belo Brumel* 'Beau Brummell', *o grande Camões* 'the great Camões', *o doutor Silva* 'Doctor Silva'). In the colloquial language, however, the article is used quite freely with names of people,[25] as is also the case in Italian.

Despite the essentially adjectival nature of the article, its isolated, or substantive, function[26] still exists in certain constructions containing pronominal *o que*. A series parallel to that of the demonstratives, including a neuter form *o* corresponding to *isto isso aquilo*, is found in this usage. The article does not, however, cease to be a particle used to indicate the category of definiteness and enters into a stylistic alternation with *aquêle*, the latter losing its precise demonstrative function (exs: *os que trabalham merecem nosso aprêço* or *aqueles que trabalham merecem nosso aprêço* 'those who work deserve our esteem', *o que se estuda bem, não se esquece* or *aquilo que se estuda bem, não se esquece* 'that which is well studied is not forgotten').

THE INDEFINITES

The Latin System

Latin possessed a whole series of word forms that lacked both demonstrative and nominal character since they were devoid of positional and specific referential meaning, a circumstance that made them appropriate for use in questions as the designation of an unknown element about which the hearer was asked to supply information. The basic form of these so-called indefinite-interrogative words was the radical *$kw(i/o)$*—Classical *quis* (masc-fem), *quid* (neuter) were derived from the radical *kwi* in the nominative, but from the radical *kwo*[27] in all the other cases. These primary forms, in turn,

25. The use of the article adds a shade of intimacy.

26. The construction exemplified in *meu livro e o de Pedro* is, unlike the case discussed here, analogous to that of *o meu livro e o teu, aquêle livro e êste*.

27. The radical *kwo* gave a nominative feminine *qua* that sometimes appears, causing *quis* to become restricted to the masculine.

gave several derivative forms (exs: *quisquis,* by reduplication; *quidam, quispiam, aliquis, quiuis,* by composition). The derivatives expressed certain fine shades of meaning such as an attitude of indifference on the part of the speaker toward the 'indefinite' property, to give just one example. In actual fact the derivatives constituted an open-ended series, and Latin grammars did not even try to exhaust the possibilities.

As in other ancient Indo-European languages, the indefinite-interrogative was used in Latin for the purpose of subordinating one clause to another in the so-called relative clause construction. The pronoun then functioned either in both clauses simultaneously (ex: *cognosces quis sim* 'you'll find out who I am') or in the relative clause, as a link to a noun in the principal clause (ex: *libros quos scripsi* '(the) books that I wrote'). The fact that the **kwo* variant of the radical was preferred in the nominative of the second construction (*qui,* masc; *quae,* fem; *quod,* neuter) led the Latin grammarians to set up a 'relative pronoun' alongside the indefinite-interrogative *quis-quid.*

The striking unity of this set, based on a single primary radical, was broken in grammatical descriptions by the inclusion of a series of adjectives with theme in *-o/u* (exs: *unus,* originally the number 'one', and *ullus, alter, alius*). Semantically, such adjectives were either indefinites (ex: *ullus* 'anyone at all') or made anaphoric reference to an element of a previously mentioned group (exs: *alter* 'the other one of two', *alius* 'the other one of many'). Morphologically, they showed the special desinence characteristic of the demonstratives (genitive in *-ius,* dative in *-i* for all three genders). This morphological idiosyncrasy was also shared by the adjectives *totus* 'all' and *solus* 'only', which therefore were included among the pronominal indefinites.

The Portuguese System

The Latin system underwent an extensive process of remodeling in all the Romance languages. Portuguese in particular developed a marked separation between the indefinites on the one hand and the interrogatives on the other: the latter retained for the most part the **kw(i/o)* radical of Latin, while the former were completely revised.

Even if the Latin radical enters into the historical explanation of the indefinites, nonetheless it is entirely absent from any synchronic analysis of the present-day forms. The modern indefinites, like the demonstratives, are of two morpho-semantic types: 1) a general series, which varies with gender and number and is used in both substantive and adjectival functions, and 2) an invariable form, used only as a substantive. Unlike the corresponding demonstrative, however, the indefinite form, which is invariable with respect to gender and number, splits into two forms, accordingly as it refers to the animate or neuter gender. Putting the same thing in another way, we may say that there is one form for human beings (excluding all other members of the animal kingdom), and another, along the lines of *isto, isso, aquilo,* for 'things' or inert beings. Thus we have the following series:

general variable form (noun-adj)				invariable nominal form	
masc sing	pl	fem sing	pl	people	things
algum	+s	alguma	+s	alguém	algo[28]

In this particular series we find a base with theme *alge-* and oppositions established by the suffixes *-um* (for the general variable form), *-ém* (for the personal invariable form), and Ø (for the neuter).

Phonetic evolution as well as reinterpretation and redistribution of Latin forms with the **kw(i/o)* radical entered into the derivation of the Portuguese system. We have, for example, **aliqu'unu* (nonattested agglutination of *alĭquis* with *unus*) > *algum; alĭquem* (accusative of *aliquis*) > *alguém;*[29] *aliquod* (from the replacement of the *kwi* - theme of *alĭquid,* neuter of *alĭquis,* by **kwo*) > *algo.* The *algum* series manifests a pattern that is typical of the indefinites, and there is a corresponding negative series that differs only in the neuter form: *nenhum* (+*a,* +*s;* < Lt *ne(c)* + *unu-*); *ninguém* (<*ne(c)* + *quem*); *nada.*[30] *Outro* (+*a,* +*s*), derived from the accusative of *alter (alterum, alteram, alteros, alteras),* received an invariable form for people, *outrem,* in which the *-em* suffix is unstressed.[31] The indefinite *um,*

28. The form *algo* is used only in the literary language. In normal speech it is replaced by *alguma coisa.*

29. Final stress must have arisen in Lusitanian Romance by association with monosyllabic *quem.*

30. *Nada* (in Lt *natam,* the feminine perfect participle of *nasci* 'to be born') derives from *rem nata,* a textually attested expression that had roughly the meaning 'anything that exists' and was used for emphasis with a negative verb. French *rien* and archaic Portuguese *rem* (ex: *não dou eu por tal enfinta ren* (Nunes 1928, 2: 12), Mod Ptg *não dou nada por êsse fingimento* 'I don't give a hoot about such pretenses') derive from emphatic use of *rem* alone, as in the expression *não tenho coisa* 'I haven't a thing'.

31. Penultimate stress resulted from leveling with *outro.*

which we have already seen to be a reflex of the substantive for unity, *um* (+*a*, +*s*), retained (exclusively) the general variable form.

The invariable adjective *cada*[32] is a Romance innovation that resulted from a Greek loan to Vulgar Latin. It is applicable only in the singular with reference to the various elements, taken *de per si*, of a group that has already been brought into focus. The expression *qualquer*, pl *quaisquer*, was another innovation. Made up of *qual* (Lt *qualis*, acc *qualem*) and the verbal form *quer* (compare the expression *seja qual fôr o que se queira* 'whichever the one that is wanted may be'), it is used to denote indifference in choice among a series of elements.[33] This expression replaced *quilibet* (where *libet* is a verbal form derived from *libere* 'to think well of'), an analogously formed Latin compound that had the same use. *Cada* functions as an adjective while *cada um*, an expression containing the indefinite *um* (+*a*, +*s*), is used for the nominal function (exs: *cada livro* 'each book', *cada um dos livros* 'each one of the books', *cada um* or *cada pessoa cuida de si* 'everyone *or* each person looks out for himself'). *Qualquer*, which can function either as an adjective or a noun (exs: *qualquer livro* 'whichever book', *qualquer dos livros* 'whichever of the books'), also has a compound form *qualquer um* (+*a*, +*s*) in nominal functions.

We see then that in Portuguese the indefinite forms are clearly separated from the interrogative and relative ones. Only *qual*, which is basically interrogative-relative, is ever found in a pure indefinite usage, and this occurs exclusively in the classical literary language, where it is used to single out the various members of a list.[34] The Portuguese system of indefinites, on the other hand, is complex and even somewhat unbalanced, both with respect to distribution of meaning and with respect to distribution of forms into morphological series. In traditional grammars the situation is made even worse by inclusion of certain adjectives with theme in -*o* among the indefinites (exs: *muito* 'many', *pouco* 'few', *todo* 'all'). As far as *muito* and *pouco* are concerned, there is nothing that can be said in favor of this idea. The claim that they express 'indefinite' quantity is based upon a

32. Derived from Greek *katá* (with penultimate stress in Latin), used to enumerate articles in commercial documents.

33. *Qualquer* is an example of a phonological word (stress on *quer*) that consists of two morphological words. The morphological autonomy of the first element is shown by the fact that it varies with number.

34. As in the following verses of Camões: "*Qual do cavalo voa, que não desce;/qual, co'o cavalo em terra dando, geme;/qual vermelhas as armas faz de brancas; qual cos penachos do elmo açouta as ancas*" (Lusiadas, 6: 64, ed. Epifanio Dias).

concept unrelated to the indefinite character of the pronouns belonging to this class. Any adjective that does not imply an exact measure is as 'indefinite' as *muito* and *pouco*. Even within the field of quantity expressions we have such examples as *parco* 'scanty', *exíguo* 'exiguous', *raro* 'rare', and, in the opposite direction, *numeroso* 'numerous', *abundante* 'abundant', *imenso* 'immense'. Latin grammarians sensibly refrained from trying to classify *multus* and *paucus* in this way. In the case of *totus* (as well as *solus*, Ptg *só* 'only'), they did so because this adjective had the *-ius* ending of the genitive singular and the *-i* ending of the dative singular for all three genders, a morphological pattern typical of the demonstratives. In Portuguese one might give an analogous morphological argument: in addition to *todo* ($+a$, $+s$) there is a nominal form *tudo*, which is invariable and only applicable to things, just like *isto* and *algo*. One might even mention the /ǫ/ : /u/ vocalic alternation since it is parallel to the /ę/ : /i/ alternation in *isto, isso, aquilo*. For the sake of simplicity and clarity, however, it seems preferable to adopt a different criterion for classification. *Tudo* might be considered a substantive derived from the corresponding adjective by means of a process of vocalic alternation /ǫ/ : /u/,[35] rather than by means of a suffix (as in *beleza* from *belo*). The former is not normally found in the morphology of pronouns.

Portuguese Interrogatives

Portuguese interrogatives are much more closely related to Latin than are the indefinites. In fact, the Portuguese pronominal interrogatives derive directly from Latin *quis-quid* and *qualis*, a compound based on the **kwo-* radical. The masculine-feminine accusative *quem* was restricted in Portuguese to the 'personal' gender (only human beings), which we have already seen in the indefinites *alguém, ninguém*, and *outrem*. For descriptive purposes one may note the presence of the *-em* suffix in *quem* as well as in the other indefinites. The neuter *quĭd* gave the Portuguese *que*, which is of the neuter or 'thing' gender that we have also come across in the demonstratives and indefinites. *Qual*, from *qualem*, the accusative of *qualis*, has a rather peculiar function. It serves to indicate an undetermined element of a previously delimited group of beings, where the group as a whole is considered definite, and can refer either to a singular (*qual . . . ?*) or a plural

35. Since metaphony, being a purely phonetic process, would have also affected *todo* (Latin *tōtum, tōtam, tōtum*), it is apparent that the alternation under discussion is a morphological one.

(*quais . . . ?*, from the accusative plural Lt *quales*). Both *qual* and *que* may be used either as substantives or as adjectives (exs: *qual dos livros deseja?* 'which of the books do you want?' *qual livro deseja?* 'which book do you want?' *que livro deseja?* 'what book do you want?' *que deseja?* 'what do you want?'). In the modern languages of both Brazil and Portugal, however, *que* has a variant *o que* (in reality an indivisible word /ukẹ/) in its substantive use. Although *o que* is often considered 'not too correct' in the literary language, it is well established and very much alive in the common language.[36] *Quem* is used only as a substantive. In adjectival functions the *quem* : *que* opposition is neutralized and only the latter is possible (ex: *que homem é capaz disso?* 'what man is capable of this?').

The Relative Pronoun

The primary relative pronoun in Portuguese, *que*, resulted from the convergence of the Latin nominatives masc *qui*, fem *quae*, neuter *quod*, and the corresponding accusatives *quem, quam, quod*. The reduction of the vowel to /ə/ in Portugal or /i/ in most parts of Brazil can be explained by the articulatory weakness of the proclitic position that *que* assumed in the Vulgar Latin of the empire. As was true of *qui quae quod*, *que* functions only in relative clauses and is anaphorically related to a noun or pronoun of the other clause (ex: *leia os livros que escrevi* 'read the books that I wrote'). Because of its function within the relative clause, *que* may be governed by any preposition (exs: *os livros a que você se refere* 'the books to which you refer', *os livros com que você se entretém* 'the books with which you amuse yourself', *os livros em que se acha essa explicação* 'the books in which this explanation is found'). In nominal complement position the possessive construction governed by *de* (ex: *os livros de que Alencar é autor* 'the books of which Alencar is the author') may be replaced by the adjective *cujo* (+*a*, +*s*), which agrees in gender and number with the 'possessor'[37] (ex: *os livros cujo autor é Alencar* 'the books whose author is Alencar'). *Cujo*, which is usually preferred in the literary language, derives from a Latin adjective with theme in -*o* related to the relative

---

36. It seems that within the normative tradition Said Ali was the only grammarian to give preference to *o que*. He based his judgment on a type of phonic stylistics, saying that the particle would stand out more clearly if used in this way (Ali 1930, p. 26).

37. In the archaic language *cujo* was also used as an interrogative.

pronoun[38] in the same way that the possessive adjective is related to the personal pronoun. Parallel to *que*, an expression consisting of *qual* preceded by the definite article may be used as the relative. Since *qual* varies with number and the article varies with both number and gender, this relative agrees in gender and number with the noun to which it is anaphorically related (ex: *os livros com os quais você se entretém* 'the books with which you amuse yourself').[39] In its substantive use, functioning in both clauses, the particle *que* must be accompanied by the particle *o*, a neuter nominal form bearing the same relation to the series *o, a, os, as* as *aquilo* does to *aquêle*. The neuter relative formed in this way is used only for 'things', in the sense that word usually has for Portuguese pronouns. As a neuter relative it is in opposition with the personal relative, the pronoun *quem*. The latter is a readaptation within the Portuguese relative system of the Latin accusative *quem*. It retained the nasal closure since it occurred in utterances in which a certain amount of stress was placed on the pronoun[40] (exs: *não sei o que chegou* 'I don't know what arrived', *não sei quem chegou* 'I don't know who arrived').

38. *Cuius, cuia, cuium* should not be confused with *cuius* (invariable in gender), the genitive of *quis* and *qui*, from radical **kwo* + desinence *-ius*.

39. This form is favored in the literary language.

40. The restriction of *quem* to people is explained by the fact that emphasis was more usual in the case of a person.

Chapter 5

The Adverb

General Properties

Many Indo-European languages possess a series of nominal or pronominal forms used to contribute supplementary meaning to the essential import of a communication as expressed by the verb. The word
type called *epirrhema* by Greek grammarians ('added to the verb';
Gk *rhema* 'verb') was of precisely this sort. Latin grammarians provided the translation *adverbium*.

There are three basic types of adverbs, two of which are pronominal by virtue of their function in linguistic communication. The
latter are employed to locate a communicated event in space or in
time with respect to the spatial or temporal position of the speaker.
We may call these adverbs locative and temporal, respectively. Locative adverbs are associated with the demonstrative pronouns in both

the morphological and semantic senses. Examples are *hic* 'in this place where I am speaking', *istic* 'in that place where you are', *illic* 'in that place over there'. Temporal adverbs, on the other hand, serve to situate an event with respect to the moment at which communication occurs. Examples are *nunc* 'at this moment at which I am speaking', *tunc* 'then, at another moment'. Within the temporal group there was also a series based on the division of time into days—*hodie* 'today, on this day during which I am speaking', *heri* 'yesterday, the day before this one', *cras* 'tomorrow, on the day after this one'. Thus, temporal and locative adverbs operate within the *Zeigfeld* of the speaker.[1]

Adverbs of the third group are nominal, whatever their origin may have been. They denote 'manners of being' in an event and may therefore be generically called *modal* adverbs. The specific modal character of such adverbs, however, is of no relevance to grammatical structure. We have *semper* 'always, in a continuous manner', *iam* 'now, in an immediate manner', *tarde* 'tardily, in a tardy manner', *male* 'badly, in an imperfect manner', and so on.

Like other ancient Indo-European languages, Latin had two distinct processes for distinguishing adverbs from the nominal or pronominal forms upon which they were based—such adverbs were either obligatorily put in a given case, usually the ablative, or else they were given a distinctive structure containing a characteristic suffix. Adverbial expressions of more than one morphological word were also quite common. The elements of these expressions were sometimes agglutinated, sometimes juxtaposed, and occasionally even joined in a phrase in which each element was morphologically independent. In modern Portuguese, for example, we have agglutination in *talvez* (*tal* + *vez*) 'perhaps', juxtaposition in *anteontem* (/a(n)tio(n)te(n)/) 'day before yesterday', and a phrase in *muitas vêzes* 'often'.

The traditional definition of an adverb as 'a word that modifies a verb, an adjective, or another adverb' has reference to modal adverbs, in the general sense in which we have defined this term, since a 'mode of being' can equally well complement an activity, a quality attributed to a given substantive, or another 'mode of being'.

---

1. All locative and temporal adverbs may also be used as substantives to express the corresponding place or moment (exs: *os homens de hoje* 'men of today', *as idéias de então* 'former ideas', *os moradores daqui* 'residents of this place'). Except for adverbs that refer to 'days', they can all take on an anaphoric usage in addition to the deictic one.

46586

Adverbs in Latin

The Primitive Indo-European modal adverb system, which was complex and structurally heterologous, had undergone significant simplification by the time of Latin. Originally the modal system consisted of an extensive series of particles that could be arrayed as satellites around the verbal element, but many of these particles agglutinated to verbs (after a transitional stage as 'preverbs') while others came to be more closely associated with the nominal complement whose relation to the verb they were supposed to highlight. The category of 'prefixes', a new type of word-formation element that arose as a result of the first of these developments, was passed on intact to the Romance languages (ex: *sub*, originally an adverb indicating 'humble posture'[2] plus *placare* 'to calm someone's anger' gives *supplicare*[3]). In the new process a 'secondary'[4] word is obtained from a 'primary' one.

The second development sketched above, that is, association of an adverbial particle with a complement, created the category of prepositions, along with the now familiar processes that require a redundant accusative or ablative desinence in the expression of the verb-complement relation. This duplication through case ending and preposition was quite typical of the structure of Classical Latin.[5] Portuguese and other Romance languages eliminated the redundancy by dispensing with case endings.

Despite the processes of agglutination and association discussed above, Latin maintained a rather full set of adverbs within its phrasal structure. Some of these adverbs were inherited directly from Primitive Indo-European, but others were formed within Latin itself by various mechanisms, including agglutination, use of certain expressions as stereotypes, and fossilization of a noun or pronoun in a given case (perhaps with a slightly modified desinence or an added enclitic).

Locative adverbs in one-by-one association with the demonstrative pronouns formed a series in which spatial location (ex: *illic* 'over there') was, in principle, distinguished from direction (ex: *illac*

2. Here *sub* 'under' is taken in a figurative sense.

3. Latin morphophonemics included rules that assimilated the final consonant of a particle to the initial consonant of a verb, giving a geminate cluster. In addition, the root vowel /a/ changed to /i/ in an open syllable and to /e/ in a closed syllable.

4. This process was soon extended to nouns.

5. Prepositions made more specific the general relations that were covered by the accusative or ablative case (exs: *ire ad forum* 'to go to the forum'; *ire in silvam* 'to go into the forest'; *ire sub freta* 'to go under the waves').

'toward that place'). Corresponding to the indefinite for localization, there was another system based on the indefinite-interrogative radical, although the morphological derivation of these forms was already blurred in some cases. The system consisted of fundamentally interrogative particles that distinguished situation (*ubi*), provenience (*unde*), and direction (*quo*). Temporal position with respect to the moment of communication was indicated by the pair *nunc* : *tunc*, to which we have had occasion to refer earlier. For temporal location with respect to the concept 'day' there was the series *hodie*, an agglutination formed within Latin from *ho(c) die* (ablative); *heri*, inherited from Indo-European; *cras*, a word of uncertain origin but that is also found in Oscan-Umbrian.

Modal adverbs were of many different types, in both the morphological and semantic senses. They were formed by two processes of derivation: adjectives with a theme in *-ŭ/o* took the desinence *-e*, a variant of genitive *-i*, or *-o*, from the ablative, while those with a theme in *-e* took the suffix *-ter*, connected with the Indo-European suffix *-tero* (intensification). Since the process of derivation was quite productive, one could, in principle, derive an adverb from any adjective (exs: *male, bene, tarde, longe, raro, falso, certo, uero*,[6] from *malus, bonus, tardus, longus, rarus, falsus, certus, uerus*, respectively; *breuiter, audaciter, prudenter*, from *breuis, pruden(ti)s, audac(i)s* (written *audax*), respectively). The use of the nominative-accusative neuter singular as an adverb, even in the case of comparatives, was also common (exs: *multum*, theme in *-ŭ/o; facile*, theme in *-e; magis*, from *magnus*).

Adverbs in Portuguese

The locative and temporal systems of Portuguese are typologically parallel to those of Latin. Instead of phonetic evolution these systems have undergone morphological changes and substitutions.

In Portuguese there is a tripartite system of locatives, namely, *aqui* : *aí* : *ali*, corresponding to the demonstrative system *êste* : *êsse* : *aquêle*. *Aqui* derives from the agglutination in Vulgar Latin of *accu' hic*, which replaced the form *hic* of Classical Latin. *Aí*, which had a variant *i* (compare: Fr *y*) in the archaic language, is a derivative of the locative *ibi* (>It *ivi*), corresponding to the demonstrative *is*. The Portuguese form derives from Vulgar Latin *ad ibi*. *Ali*, on the same

---

6. In some of these examples there were alternative forms that, according to the normative grammars, were distinct in meaning (exs: *certo, certe; uero, uere*).

model as *aí*, is Vulgar Latin *ad illic*,[7] the replacement of *illic*, locative of *ille*.

In the tripartite system of locatives there is no sign of a tendency toward reduction to binary status despite the developments observed in the parallel system of demonstratives. This is not to say, however, that Portuguese possesses no binary locative system. On the contrary, in the series *cá* : *lá* nearness to the speaker is opposed to distance from the speaker without reference to the position of the hearer. These forms derive from Latin adverbs that expressed direction toward a place (*hac*, instead of *hic; illac*, instead of *illic*). Of the two Portuguese forms, *lá* comes directly from *illac* while *cá*, or *acá* in the archaic language, may be explained through Vulgar Latin *accu' hac*. The correlate form *acolá* from Vulgar *accu' illac* is used to express a second degree of distance from the speaker.

Both systems, the tripartite (*aqui* : *aí* : *ali*) and the bipartite (*cá* : *lá/acolá*), can be used indifferently for either location or direction (exs: *fica aí* 'stay there'; *venha aqui* 'come here'; *está lá* 'it is there' : *vai lá* 'go there'; *estamos cá* 'we are here' : *vem cá* 'come here'). In the common usage of both Brazil and Portugal the two systems overlap. In the received language of Lisbon, for example, *cá* often replaces *aqui*, although in Brazil the former is scarcely used at all. More generally, *lá* is added to the series *aqui* : *aí* : *ali* in order to indicate either a less definite location or one further removed than *ali*. In the colloquial language of Brazil *acolá* is almost as infrequent as *cá*.

The speaker may choose as his point of reference not only his own location, but also a point somewhere in front of himself. A location between the speaker and that point is then designated by *aquém* while any point beyond the chosen one is designated by *além*. Both of these locatives come from *ĭnde*, a derivative of *is* used to indicate provenience (*accu'inde, accu'ill'inde;* with intermediate forms *aquende, alende*).

The opposition between location (*ubi*), direction (*quo*), and provenience (*unde*) defines the basic structural type of the Latin interrogative system. Portuguese retained exactly this same basic typology, but nonetheless altered the system by replacing some of its members with other forms. In the case of location, archaic *u*, the reflex of *ubi*, was replaced by *onde* (<*unde*). For direction and provenience re-

---

7. This word has stress on the final vowel because the -*c* was a reduced form of -*ce*, which would have given penultimate stress.

course was had to the prepositions *a* and *de,* respectively, in association with *onde,* giving *aonde* and *donde.*[8]

In the temporal system *nunc* was replaced in the Vulgar Latin of certain regions by the ablative expression *hac hora,* or simply *hora,* whence Portuguese *agora* and *ora.* Along with *antes* 'at a moment before this one' and *depois* 'at a later moment', *agora* forms a tripartite series. In its own right, however, it is in opposition with *então* 'not at this moment'. All three of these forms are Latin adverbs that suffered no changes in value but were slightly altered in the Vulgar language by augmentation or agglutination. *Antes* derives from *ante + s,* the *s* being added in order to distinguish the adverb from the preposition *ante;*[9] *depois* comes from *de + post,*[10] and *então* can be traced to *in tunc.* Both *antes* and *depois* also function in the locational system to indicate position with respect to a point independent of that of the speaker. In this case the spatial continuum is divided into 'before' and 'after' the chosen point by reference to the speaker's location.

In the system based on the concept of 'day', the Latin agglutination *hodie* was conserved, giving the form *hoje* 'today' by normal phonetic evolution. Latin *heri,* which gave Spanish *ayer,* Italian *iere,* and French *hier,* became *eire* in the archaic language. In the modern language the Latin system was replaced by one based on a perspective that emphasizes the night of the day before and the morning of the day after (*ad noctem,*[11] by a complex phonetic evolution, *onte > ontem* 'yesterday'; *ad maneanam > amanhã* 'tomorrow'). The juxtaposed form *anteontem* 'day before yesterday' evolved on the basis of *ontem.*

Modal Adverbs in Portuguese

In the modern language a certain number of modal adverbs are specific words, either inherited from Latin (exs: *sempre, nunca, cedo, tarde, longe, mal, bem*) or formed within Portuguese, usually by agglutination (exs: *talvez; jamais; apenas* (cf. the expression *a duras penas*); *caro,* formed within Romance). Later the model of adverbs in

8. In actual use a certain amount of confusion sets in and even in the literary language *aonde* sometimes replaces *onde.* In Spanish *onde* lost out to *donde,* but new forms *adonde* and *de donde* were created for direction and provenience, respectively.

9. The ending *-s* must have been modeled after *depois.*

10. In the derivation from *post,* the diphthong is hard to explain. Various hypotheses have been suggested; see Nascentes 1932.

11. This way of looking at things is also responsible for the change in meaning of *uespera* from 'nightfall' to 'the day before another one'.

-*o* was extended to forms like *barato*. Side by side with such lexical units, Portuguese possesses another series of adverbs derived from adjectives by means of a productive mechanism of Vulgar Latin origin. This process, which replaced the Latin ones discussed above, consists of combining the form *mente*, originally the ablative of the feminine noun *mens* 'mind', with the adjective to be used as an adverb. The adjective is obligatorily pre-posed and agrees in gender with *mente*, which in this construction takes on the general meaning of 'manner' or 'way'. Even in literary Classical Latin one can find the beginnings of a construction of this type, but in the Classical period *mente* still preserves its original force (ex: *alta mente* 'with a loftier spirit').

The Portuguese construction has the status of an expression made up of two distinct phonological and morphological words fused together to form a secondary unit. In this larger unit, stress (one degree lower than in isolation) is retained by the adjective with *mente*.[12] Since the construction consists of two independent words only the last adjective in a conjoined series takes -*mente* (ex: *firme, serena, e corajosamente* 'firmly, serenely, and courageously').[13]

Supplementing the general process discussed above, there are several other less productive ones that generate expressions on the following patterns: a plural noun preceded by *a* or *de* (exs: *às vêzes* 'sometimes'; *de cócoras* 'squatting'), a feminine plural adjective preceded by *a* (ex: *às claras* 'publicly'), an adjective with invariable theme preceded by *de* (ex: *de repente* 'suddenly'), a compound consisting of an adjective and a noun in the plural (ex: *muitas vêzes* 'often'), a noun with a fixed preposition (exs: *sem dúvida* 'doubtlessly'; *por certo* 'surely').

Semantic and Functional Mobility of Adverbs

The description of Portuguese adverbs given above is in some respects merely theoretical since the extreme semantic and functional mobility characteristic of adverbs constitutes an interference with the system's general properties. Mobility is, in fact, inherent in adverbs. In ancient Indo-European it is precisely this factor that explains the

12. The practice of not putting adjectives ending in -*ês* into the feminine (exs: *burguêsmente, portuguêsmente*) is no more than a convention of the literary language based on archaic patterns. It can be maintained only because such adverbs are rather infrequent in normal language. In the case of -*or*, one has examples of the type *desesperadoramente*.

13. Fusion of the adjective and *mente* into a single word is merely a convention of the written language.

evolution of adverbial particles to preverbs and, eventually, prefixes. The creation of prepositions may be explained on the same basis.

In Portuguese, mobility takes on various forms. Semantically it is manifested by frequent deflection in meaning and use of temporal adjectives. The consistently clear meaning of adverbs based on the concept 'day' is exceptional. More typical examples are *antes* and *depois*, used with a point of reference outside the *Zeigfeld* of the speaker (ex: *Pedro e Antônio já se foram da mesma sorte que João; um já tinha ido antes, o outro partiu depois.* 'Peter and Anthony have gone just as John did; one had already gone *before*, the other left *after*'). In other usages *depois* indicates the order of ideas within a communication (ex: *a ordem é clara e não pode ser desobedecida; depois, não há qualquer motivo para fazê-lo.* 'the order is clear and may not be disobeyed; *after* (in the sense of 'after all') there is no reason to disobey it anyway'). Similarly, *antes* may be used to indicate preference.[14]

With the general exception of expressions in *mente*, in which the role of the adjective is decisive, modal adverbials have the same sort of mobility as particles (exs: *isso já é demais!* 'this is just too much (to bear) *already*'; *diga sempre . . .* '*always* say that . . .' or 'insist that . . .'; *êle mal tinha saído* 'he had *scarcely* left').

From the functional point of view, adverbs are frequently used in sequences of propositions as 'coordinating conjunctions'. In the modern language some adverbs have even become fixed in this usage, but in other cases the latter function is clearly distinguished from the adverbial one. In a few instances adverbs straddle both usages.

In order to express subordination in Portuguese, the preposition *de* or the conjunction *que* may be pre-posed to certain adverbs, which then become subordinating prepositions or conjunctions, respectively. The adverbial meaning persists in the head of such expressions, but a connective function is added (exs: *antes de* 'before'; *antes que* 'before'; *fora de* 'outside of'; *sempre que* 'provided that'; *longe de* 'far from').

It goes without saying that the mobility of adverbs must be in line with some general tendency or other. In order to present a full linguistic description it would be necessary to do further research and to set up a meticulous classification of the examples. If the conditions of context and distribution seem a bit arbitrary and unsure to us, it is because they have not yet been studied enough to permit exact deductions.

14. In *querer antes*, which is semantically equivalent to *preferir* 'to prefer', the adverb is lexically associated with the verb in a way functionally analogous to that of the Indo-European 'preverbs'.

Chapter 6

The Verb

FROM LATIN TO PORTUGUESE

Characteristics of Verbal Inflection

Latin verbs may be characterized typologically as a highly inflected word category. This fundamental property, which was passed on intact to Portuguese, has two important functions in language. First, inflections permit identification of the subject, or origin of communication. The subject may be either the speaker, the listener, or some other entity represented by a substantive. In any case, the content of the verb is subordinated to this element. Second, inflections designate certain characteristics that must accompany the intrinsic meaning of the verb as it is formulated in language.

Indication of subject by means of inflection constitutes 'desinence of person'. By means of this desinence the verb itself indicates the grammatical person (speaker, listener, or other being) of the element to which it is subordinated. 'Subordination' of this type is basically 'active' since the meaning of the verb is presented under the aegis of the subject, as if it were eternally dependent on the latter's activity. The view of the world imposed by Latin and Portuguese, as well as by the Indo-European languages in general, is that of a universal set of beings. Since all events must be referred back to this universe, the 'active voice'[1] is primary and the inversion of the subject-verb relation is possible only in a structure that has had secondary status ever since the days of Primitive Indo-European. Latin had a special inflectional process to indicate this 'passive voice', but it has vanished from the Romance languages.

The personal desinence is the last member of the inflection. It is preceded by another inflection that indicates inclusion of the communication in certain categories that language obligatorily takes into account. In Latin these verbal categories were three. The first was the concluded or nonconcluded 'aspect' of that which was communicated. An athlete's running, for example, could be viewed either with the runner already at the finish line or with him still on the track. The second category was 'tense', or time of an occurrence with respect to the moment of communication. The tense was *present* if the two were more or less coincident, *preterite* if the former preceded the latter (in other words, if the occurrence was in the speaker's past), or *future* if this occurrence was expected later. Finally, the third category consisted of a certain judgment by the speaker on that which was said, that is, this category reflected the *mode* (modern English '*mood*') in which he viewed his own communication. Latin opposed the subjunctive mood to a general form of the so-called indicative mood. The former explicitly indicated that an occurrence was doubtful, desirable, or hypothetical. Another verbal form, the 'imperative' mood, was used for the purpose of prohibiting or giving orders. Naturally the subject was always the listener in this case.

In addition to such forms of a true verbal nature, Latin verbs characteristically had other forms with nominal structure. The latter served as the head of a communication complete in itself but yet integrated into a larger unit. They included the infinitive, the gerund,

1. There are a certain number of 'impersonal' expressions in which the communication is centered directly about the verb rather than focused on the subject. Weather expressions are a good example. Formally, one has the third-person singular active in such cases (exs: Lt *pluit, tonat;* Ptg *chove, troveja;* 'it rains', 'it thunders').

and the participles. The first consisted of two invariable forms, one for concluded aspect and the other for nonconcluded aspect. The gerund, always of the nonconcluded aspect, took the genitive, accusative, and dative-ablative desinences of a substantive with theme in u/o. The participles were adjectival. There was a present with theme in -e, a preterite (concluded aspect) with theme in u/o, and finally a future, also with theme in u/o.

Aspect

Although Latin grammarians did not discuss the general concept of 'aspect' in their linguistic descriptions, beginning with Varro (first century B.C.) they did notice that Latin verbs formally distinguished concluded from nonconcluded events. Accordingly, they divided verbal forms into two large sets that they called *perfectum* 'perfect' (that is, completely finished, concluded) and *infectum* 'imperfect' (that is, not completely finished, nonconcluded). Although this opposition was treated rather inconsistently in Latin morphology, the perfect was generally the marked form. One indication of the marked aspect was presence of an element, usually -u- or less often -s-, added to a radical before inflections for tense-mood and person (exs: perfect *coluit vs.* imperfect *colit*, for the idea of 'cultivation'; perfect *scripsit vs.* imperfect *scribit*,[2] for the idea of 'writing'). Other verbs exhibited a mechanism, known as 'reduplication', in which the initial syllable of a root was said twice in a row, usually in a somewhat altered form the first time (ex: perfect *cucurrit vs.* imperfect *currit*,[3] for the idea of 'running'). In still other cases the root vowel changed (ex: perfect *fecit vs.* imperfect *facit*, for the idea of 'making'). Finally, in certain cases the roots of the two aspects were unrelated (ex: perfect *fuit vs.* imperfect *est*,[4] for the idea of 'being').

Latin grammarians considered the -u- suffix 'regular' in the perfect and, in fact, the addition of -u- was the most general and productive morphological process. See the table below:

	Preterite	*Present*	*Future*
Infectum	amabas	amas	amabis
Perfectum	amaueras	amauisti	amaueris

2. The final /b/ of the root becomes /p/ in position before the voiceless phoneme /s/. This is the very same morphophonemic rule that operates in prefixes.

3. The relevant feature of reduplication was presence of a new initial syllable having the same initial consonant as the root. Total identity of the reduplicated syllable was not required.

4. This distinction is preserved in Portuguese.

Even in Classical Latin the system sketched above had undergone significant changes.[5] In the first place, the aspectual notion 'concluded' came into conflict with the temporal notion 'present' and, as a result, forms of the type *amauisti* were reinterpreted as preterites.[6] This change left infectum *amas* without an oppositive form because *amauisti* entered into opposition with *amabas* as perfect and imperfect preterite, respectively. Preterite perfect *amaueras*, having to cede its place to *amauisti*, took refuge further back in the preterite, where it came to indicate a preterite concluded before another preterite, that is, a pluperfect. The net effect of these changes was to create a system in which the two aspects are asymmetrically related:

....	amabas	amas	amabis
amaueras	amauisti	....	amaueris

Vulgar Latin, unlike the classical language, did not favor the use of a future tense. The concept of a strictly temporal future is not, in fact, part of the colloquial usage of Indo-European languages. It is a sort of purely intellectual secondary formation. The use of a future tense, in the strictest sense, is always dependent upon special conditions within a given act of linguistic communication, and when it occurs it is more frequently required by objective reasoning than by a spontaneous communicative impulse. In such impulses the notion of future is always closely associated with that of doubt, desire, or imposition of will and therefore really functions as a *mood*. The future of Classical Latin itself arose from volitional (the -*b*- inflection of the first and second conjugations) or subjunctive forms (third and fourth conjugations). It was only later that grammatical discipline and the norm of written (or literary) language were able to deflect these forms toward a strictly temporal future.

On all levels of the social hierarchy of speakers of Vulgar Latin, the predominant tendency was replacement of the future tense by the present, unless there was some specific motivation to the contrary. For this reason the Latin indicative system, which is the starting point for that of Portuguese, was reduced to a set of four forms in which the

5. Here I follow Meillet (1931). These ideas have been attacked now and then, but never convincingly.

6. The basic reason for this was a change in the meaning of the perfect aspect. Originally it was 'permansive', that is, it indicated a concluded event that nonetheless still had certain present effects. In this original meaning it quite understandably had a present, of which one can find traces in a few verbs that have only a perfect form (exs: *odi* 'I got angry and still am angry'; *memini* 'I remembered and still retain the memory').

interplay of oppositions was profoundly modified. The present imperfect becomes isolated but retains its status as an imperfect because it is still associated with an imperfect in the preterite. The preterite pluperfect, in turn, retains its aspectual meaning since this meaning is inherent in the form's new role as a preterite preceding another preterite and therefore necessarily concluded. But in the new usage this form is asymmetrically isolated in the preterite zone which it occupied. In the first preterite zone, on the other hand, the opposition between the perfect and imperfect aspects survives intact. Here one still has morphologically and semantically distinctive forms like *amabas*, Ptg *amavas* : *ama(ui)sti*, Ptg *amaste*. Although it is true that the *-u-* of the perfect was eliminated, this in no way weakened the opposition since *-ba-* of the imperfect contrasts with zero (Ø) for the perfect. See the table below:

	Preterite		Present-Future
	II	I	
Imperfect		amabas	amas
Perfect	ama(ue)ras	ama(ui)sti	

The Future in Romance

The motivation for a mood-like future, which in Classical Latin favored promotion of certain volitional and subjunctive forms to a future, was also at work in Vulgar Latin. For this reason a volitional expression consisting of the imperfect infinitive and the present of *habere* (Ptg *haver*) was introduced in almost all Romance-speaking territories. The new construction emphasized, from the point of view of the present, a desire that a certain event occur. At the same time a parallel expression rooted in the past was also established. A speaker then had a choice: he could either declare that at the present moment he wants to sing, intends to sing, has singing as his goal, or he could refer back to some time in the past when he had the very same will, intention, or goal. For the first alternative expressions of the form *cantare habeo* were used, while the second alternative was represented by a parallel structure with the imperfect of *habere*, that is, *cantare habebam* (in Gaul and the Iberian Peninsula). In this way a future mood or, to put it another way, a mood-like future was established. Later, a slow, more refined categorial evolution led to a new temporal future or future tense in the Romance languages.

The new futures are not marked for aspect but are, nonetheless, of the imperfect aspect. They were added to the previous system without any internal displacement because they were superposed to it by creating two new zones, one starting out from the preterite and the other starting out from the present. The following table will serve as a graphic illustration:

	Preterite	*(Future)*	*Present*	*(Future)*
Volitional	amare habebam	→	amare habeo	→
Factual	amabam		amo	

From the purely formal point of view, the two individual words that constituted the future forms suffered agglutination, along with concomitant phonetic reduction of the forms of *habere*. The intervocalic /b/ vanished, and this loss was followed by assimilation, diphthongization, or contraction of the vowels that came into contact (exs: $a(b)eo > aio; a(b)e(b)a > ea > ia$[7]).

The Indicative in Portuguese

The developments outlined above led to an entirely new system in Portuguese. The first preterite maintains an opposition between concluded and nonconcluded aspect. Thus, within the concluded aspect, one has a second, more remote, preterite (pluperfect) that is already concluded by the time of the first preterite. In the temporal sense it is the preterite imperfect that is in opposition to the present. Starting out from each of these, there is a future that, following Said Ali (1930, p. 225),[8] we can call 'the future of the preterite' and 'the future of the present', respectively. These developments are summarized in the table below:

	Preterite	*Future*	*Present*	*Future*
Imperfect	amava	→ amaria	amo	→ amarei
Perfect	amei			
Pluperfect	amara			

Clearly the new structural correspondences do not lead to the same functional load for all forms. For one thing, the preterite future is necessarily very limited in usage because it depends upon rather special circumstances. As I have stated elsewhere, 'The speaker must, while remaining in the present, refer back to the past, and it is from this rather ubiquitous vantage point that he must consider an event that occurred after the moment of the past that he chose' (Camara 1956, p. 39). In other words, the speaker must summon forth a past moment at the present moment in which he is speaking.

7. The vocalic group /ea/ became /ia/ because of the hiatus; compare *uĭa* > Ptg *via; mea* > Arc Ptg *mia* > *minha*.

8. I have discussed this question at some length elsewhere (see Camara 1956).

On the purely temporal plane, the two futures are not unrestricted in usage. The same conditions that in Latin relegated the future to partial retirement operate also within the colloquial language. The future is, in fact, restricted to the written language and to certain formally oriented oral usages. For this reason a bipartite system consisting of the preterite on the one hand and the present, including future, on the other is fully functional alongside the tripartite system consisting of present, preterite, and future, as shown in the diagram below:

Preterite	Present	Future
amava	amo	→
amei		
amara		

There is still room for a preterite future in the simpler system but only in a way parallel to the usage of present tense for the future, that is, as an extension of the preterite imperfect (exs: *acho que êle vem* instead of the more elaborate *acho que êle virá* 'I think that he will come'; *achei que êle vinha* instead of *achei que êle viria* 'I thought that he would come').

The literary language takes advantage of the existence of these two systems for stylistic purposes. In the second system it can represent the present and its future or the preterite and its future as a unique cut in time (ex: *mandou lançar pregão por todos os arraiais que no dia seguinte se celebrava a festa do Senhor*[9] 'he ordered it to be proclaimed in all the encampments that the feast of the Lord would be celebrated on the following day').

Within the second system the future has a mood-like character and is equivalent to a subjunctive.

The Subjunctive

The subjunctive mood in Latin consisted of four tenses, two of the imperfect aspect and two of the perfect aspect. The structural symmetry between present and preterite, which we have already seen in the indicative of archaic Latin, was, at least in principle, maintained in the subjunctive despite the fact that Latin grammarians considered the present perfect a 'preterite perfect' and the preterite perfect a 'preterite pluperfect'. They were, apparently, motivated by a desire to model the nomenclature of the subjunctive after that of the indicative. The future, which was secondary even in the indicative

9. Example from Father António Vieira, the seventeenth-century sacred orator (Camara 1956, p. 78).

mood did not appear at all in the subjunctive mood. See the table below:

Imperfect	amares[10]	ames
Perfect	amauisses	amaueris

The basic functional difference between the Latin and Portuguese subjunctives is the circumstance that in the latter language subjunctive forms are used almost exclusively in subordinate clauses. They continue to express doubtful, desirable, or hypothetical events but only within a communication that is dependent on another communication. In isolated utterances the subjunctive is conditional upon a preceding occurrence of *talvez* 'perhaps'. Therefore, in two sentences of equivalent meaning, the subjunctive may indeed be opposed to the indicative to indicate doubt, but this is brought about by a formal process that depends crucially on the position of *talvez* with respect to the verb (exs: *talvez seja verdade* or *é talvez verdade* 'perhaps it is true'). In such communications the meaning of 'doubt' is expressed primarily by the modal adverb and does not depend in any significant sense on the presence of a subjunctive form. For this reason one can even dispense with the subjunctive entirely if *talvez* is postposed.

In subordinate clauses that obligatorily take the subjunctive, the modal element of 'doubt, desire, or hypothesis' is expressed, as in the case discussed above, primarily within the subordinate sentence, where it is represented by certain connectives. In other cases modal 'doubt' is present but nonetheless the verb is in the indicative mood (ex: *suponho que é verdade* 'I suppose that it is true').[11] Ultimately everything depends on the type of the subordinate clause.

We can say then that in Portuguese the use of subjunctive forms has become a formal idiosyncrasy of grammar, bereft of any semantic value. Classical Latin was already heading in that direction despite the fact that the subjunctive mood was still in opposition with the indicative mood on the semantic level. In Latin the subjunctive could appear freely in independent sentences, and in subordinate clauses a change in mood corresponded to a change in meaning. This was possible in several syntactic patterns. In Portuguese the two futures of Romance origin replace the Latin subjunctive[12] in isolated com-

10. Illustrative forms are always second-person singular.

11. In this structure (verb that expresses a hypothesis followed by a direct object subordinate clause) one finds free variation. Thus *suponho que seja verdade* is also possible.

12. In this modal usage the preterite future, just like the Latin preterite imperfect subjunctive, specifically expresses lack of reality, even with respect to the

munications (ex: *êle diz que está doente; será verdade?* 'he says that he is sick; can that be true?'; *êle disse que estava doente; seria verdade?* 'he said that he was sick; could that have been true?'). The difference between the two systems is made crystal clear by the natural Portuguese translation of the following Latin expressions:[13]

	Present	Preterite
Supposition	Lt: Dicat aliquis . . .	
	Ptg: Alguém dirá . . .	
Doubt		Lt: Quid facerem?
		Ptg: Que faria eu?
Inadmissible	Lt: Ego tibi irascar?	Lt: Ego tibi irascerer?
Hypothesis	Ptg: Eu lá me zangarei contigo?	Ptg: Eu lá me zangaria contigo?

Association of the perfect aspect with the preterite is especially clear in the subjunctive of Vulgar Latin. Here the so-called preterite pluperfect (ex: *amauisses*) came to be the *only* preterite because the preterite imperfect (*amarem*) was abandoned in almost all Romance-speaking areas. This change set up a unique opposition between the present (imperfect) and the preterite (perfect) in the subjunctive (ex: *ames : ama(ui)sses*, where *-u-* of the perfect is lost as in the indicative). It is precisely this opposition that one finds in Portuguese. In all syntactic structures that require the subjunctive, the present (ex: *ames*) alternates with the preterite (ex: *amasses*) on the temporal level (exs: *talvez venha hoje* 'perhaps he will come today'; *talvez viesse ontem* 'perhaps he came yesterday'; *nada aprende, embora estude* 'he learns nothing, even if he studies'; *nada aprendia, embora estudasse* 'he used to learn nothing, even if he studied'). In the bipartite system the present tense includes the future (exs: *talvez venha no próximo mês*[14] 'perhaps he will come next month'; *nada aprenderá, embora estude* 'he will learn nothing, even if he studies').

Portuguese retains a reflex of the Latin present perfect, the so-called preterite perfect (ex: *amaueris*). In the modern language this form appears in certain syntactic patterns where it has acquired a

---

present. The same is true of the preterite imperfect indicative in the same function and meaning. Murin (1959) brought out the modal function of the Portuguese preterite perfect indicative, but he incorrectly assigned this function a primary role, not noticing that it is the consequence of a subtle interplay of semantic relations.

13. Examples from Riemann (1927).

14. In the preterite, where the process of 'evocation' is involved, the situation is similar (ex: *resolvi esperar; talvez viesse no mês seguinte* 'I decided to wait; perhaps he would come the following month').

future connotation that is so strong that it is even called 'future' in the Portuguese grammatical tradition. Here the 'future' is in contrast with the preterite subjunctive, forming a future-preterite opposition on the temporal level. The present subjunctive is excluded from this second subjunctive system.

Syntactic structures in which the second system is obligatory are characterized by a correlation between a condition or, in terms of the Greek grammarians, a 'protasis', and its consequence, or 'apodosis'.[15] A present future indicative or simply the present itself in the apodosis is put into relation with a future subjunctive in the protasis (exs: *farei se quiseres* or *se quiseres, eu faço* 'if you want I will do it'). A preterite future or a preterite imperfect indicative in the apodosis requires a preterite subjunctive in the protasis (ex: *faria, se quisesses* or *se quisesses, eu fazia* 'I would do it, if you wanted'). Thus, the general structure of the Portuguese subjunctive is as represented below:

Present (*ames*)   . . . .   Preterite (*amasses*)

.

.

.

.

Future (*amares*)

The Imperative Mood

The morphological structure of orders and prohibitions in Classical Latin created a close association between the subjunctive and the imperative. In orders a subjunctive was used wherever the imperative lacked a particular form, namely, in the third person, when the hearer was so addressed, and in the first-person plural, when the speaker himself wished to participate in a task he was about to impose upon others. For prohibitions, characterized by a negative particle in position before the verb, subjunctive forms were obligatory in all persons.[16]

The situation in Portuguese is unchanged, although the imperative system was modified. Latin distinguished a present imperative, for orders to be carried out immediately, from a future imperative, for

15. Here *protasis* and *apodosis* must be understood in a broad sense, *not* restricted to the pattern of a protasis with the hypothetical conjunction *se* 'if' (ex: *farei quando quiser* 'I'll do it when I want to'; *faria quem quisesse* 'anyone who wanted to would do it').

16. In Classical Latin the preterite perfect form was preferred, but we know that this was in fact a 'present perfect'. Also used was the (imperfect) present, and it was only the latter that was adopted in Vulgar Latin. Thus we have ClLt *ne feceris*, VLt *non facias*, Ptg *não faças*, 'do not make'.

orders to be carried out later. The latter was eliminated from the
language, leaving only the present imperative, which lost its distinctive meaning.

Within Latin itself there was a certain amount of interchange between the true imperative and the subjunctive of desire. Use of the
subjunctive instead of the imperative was, in fact, a more polite way
to give an order in cultured colloquial speech and also in Vulgar
Latin. In Brazil there is a deep-seated tendency to replace the imperative by the present indicative, and the same is true of prohibitions,
where the subjunctive forms have similarly been replaced. The written
language, however, has not adopted this usage, which is occasionally
regarded as the result of confusing *tu* and *você* since the third person
singular of the indicative has the same form as the singular of the
imperative (for the second person).

Nominal Forms of the Verb

The rich and complex system of nominal forms[17] discussed above was
drastically reduced in the Romance languages. First, the accusative
of the gerund, which duplicated the uses of the imperfect infinitive,
was simply eliminated. Second, the genitive of this same form disappeared as a result of the general replacement of that case by the
accusative governed by *de*. In the structure under consideration *de*
then took the imperfect infinitive, so that a Latin expression like *ars
amandi* is represented in Portuguese by *arte de amar*. All that was left
of the gerund was the ablative, which in Portuguese and most other
Romance languages replaced the Classical present participle in the
so-called ablative absolute, a construction in which a verbal adjective
with its own subject was subordinated to an indicative with a different subject.[18] In this way a phrase of the type *regnante illo Tarquinio*
. . . came to be represented in Portuguese by *reinando então Tarquinio*. . . . At the same time, Portuguese accepted the Vulgar replacement of the present participle by the ablative of the gerund, a phenomenon of which one can find traces even in the Classical literary
language (ex: Lt *assurgens et populando* . . . Ptg *invadindo e deva-*

17. It should be noted that our treatment of nominal forms was intentionally
simplified. We did not even mention the supine (a noun, regularly accusative, of
the form of a perfect participle), which was already somewhat obsolete in Classical
Latin. The gerundive (an adjective with theme in *u/o* of the form of a gerund) was
similarly passed over.

18. The ablative absolute could also be nominal (ex: Lt *M. Messala et M.
Pisone consulibus*; Ptg *quando eram cônsules M. Messala e M. Pisão;* 'when Marcus Messala and Marcus Piso were consuls').

stando . . . , a present participle and an ablative gerund side by side in parallel usages; quoted from Tacitus, see Grandgent 1928, p. 89).

The survival of the ablative of the gerund is connected in this way with the disappearance of the present participle as a verbal form. The only Portuguese descendants of the participle in *-e* are nouns and adjectives that are entirely dissociated from the respective verbs (exs: *a amante* 'the lover'; *uma estante* 'a bookcase'; *um frequentador constante* 'a constant visitor'; *o agente* 'the agent'; *os pedintes* 'the beggars'). It is only in the literary language that, starting in the classical period, certain present participles with verbal characteristics were reintroduced in imitation of Latin usage. The form of such participles is noticeably influenced by Latin (ex: *superveniente* 'supervenient', from *sobrevir*). Even so, most of these loans have come to be more usual as pure nouns (exs: *o meu comitente* 'my constituent', from *cometer; uma medida conveniente* 'an advisable measure', from *convir*).

The future participle lost its verbal character; its descendants are nouns or adjectives in Portuguese (ex: *ventura* 'happiness', a nominalized neuter plural that became a feminine singular with theme in *-a*, from the future participle of *uenire*). In fact, the very word *futuro* is historically a future participle of the verb *esse* 'to be'.[19]

The developments outlined above created an entirely new system of deverbal nominal forms. In the first place, an infinitive (the imperfect) took on a substantive function (exs: *falar agora é desaconselhável* 'to speak now is not advisable'; *pare de falar sem pensar* 'stop talking without thinking'). Second, as verbal adjectives, we have one form of the perfect aspect and another of the imperfect aspect. The latter derives from the ablative of the gerund;[20] the former is an adjective with theme in *-o* and derives from the Latin perfect participle or preterite. Both of these adjectival forms may be used as adverbs in the manner of the Latin 'ablative absolute' (exs: *reinando*

19. In the classical literary language Camões, imitating Latin, used *futuros* as a participle in the following passage: *os duros/casos que Adamastor contou futuros;* 'from *all* that Adamastor did presage' (Lusíadas, V.60; Ptg. ed. Epifânio Dias, Eng. trans. Richard Fanshawe).

20. Traditional Portuguese grammar has oscillated back and forth between the names 'present participle' and 'gerund' for this verbal form. Recently the latter has gained favor on historical grounds, namely, the origin of the form in the Latin gerund (unlike the situation in French, where the gerund and the present participle coalesced). Certain grammarians have even asserted that the Portuguese form functions exclusively as a gerund, but this is noticeably at variance with linguistic reality.

Tarquínio, aconteceu que . . . 'while Tarquinius was reigning it happened that . . .'; *construída a cidade, deu-se um caso* . . . 'the city built, there occurred a case of . . .'). One of the most characteristic features of this system is the fact that an indeclinable adjective of the imperfect aspect is in opposition to an adjective of the perfect aspect that varies with gender and number in the manner of all other *-o* theme adjectives. The lack of morphological symmetry has an important consequence for the use of the two forms. The first is in essence verbal, and when it modifies a substantive it indicates a verbal process in that substantive (exs: *água fervendo* 'boiling water'; *crianças brincando* 'playing children'). On the contrary, the perfect participle, being a fully nominal form, is unrestricted in its use as an adjective.

The Personal Infinitive

One feature of Portuguese that sets it apart from the rest of the Romance languages is its possession of an infinitive that takes personal desinences in agreement with the subject. There has been much debate about both the origins and the linguistic function of this infinitive, traditionally called the 'personal infinitive' since its outstanding characteristic is the personal desinence.[21]

According to one theory, the origin of the personal infinitive is to be found in a deflection of the Latin preterite imperfect subjunctive to a new function. As we have seen above, this tense (exs: *amarem, timerem, partirem*) generally vanished as a subjunctive in the Romance languages and was replaced by forms in *-assem, -essem, -issem*. The argumentation in favor of this origin depends on two points: 1) similarity in form and 2) the hypothesis that the preterite imperfect subjunctive survived in certain regions when it appeared in a subordinate clause without a conjunction (ex: Lt *decrevit darent operam;* Ptg *decidiu dessem a obra*). According to the theory, a subordinate clause of this type would then have been equated with an infinitival clause of the traditional type (ex: *decrevit dare operam*), and *darent* would come to be equivalent to *dare* with personal desinences.

Other researchers prefer a simpler theory according to which personal desinences grew onto the infinitive in order to give it greater

---

21. Certain modern grammarians have objected to this name, claiming that 'personal' is the same as 'with its own subject'. They point out that either of the infinitives can have a subject. In the morphological sense, however, 'personal' means 'inflected for person'. The term 'inflected' alone is not satisfactory because both infinitives have the /r/ inflection as a suffix added to the theme.

syntactic autonomy with relation to the main verb. This innovation would be of the same type as a much later one that led in the popular language to the use of the nominative instead of the accusative for a pronominal subject of an infinitive (exs: *não vi êle sair* instead of *não o vi sair* 'I didn't see him leave'). According to this theory, the future subjunctive, which evolved from the preterite perfect subjunctive, would serve as a model for the personal desinences of the infinitive. This depends on the circumstance that in 'regular' verbs, that is, those that show no change of radical in the perfect, the loss of -*u*- caused the future subjunctive to take on precisely the form of an infinitive, except, of course, for the personal desinences (exs: *amar*, first and third person singular; *amares*, second person singular; *amarmos*, first person plural; *amardes*, second person plural, *amarem*, third person plural).[22]

The essential difference between the two theories is that the first supposes a syntactic model and the second a paradigmatic model for the source of the personal desinence. No matter which explanation is chosen, the Portuguese personal infinitive was the result of a creative impulse. What is important from the structural point of view is not the analogic motivation, whatever it may have been, but rather the appearance of the verb in a nominal form with personal desinences. For the synchronic structure of the present language, the most urgent problem is to determine up to what point the two infinitives are in complementary distribution, and when they are simply in free variation.

The semantic motivation for the creation and maintenance of the personal infinitive was a desire to give the infinitive the status of a clausal pattern, subordinated to a main verb like any other subordinate clause but without being associated with it in a compound secondary lexical unit. This clausal autonomy of the infinitive is obligatory in some structures; in others it is a matter of style.

Another problem for grammatical description is to determine whether the personal infinitive should be considered to be distinct from the future subjunctive despite the homonymy of the two forms. Differences in meaning and function alone are sufficient to provide a positive answer to this question without further consideration. There is also, however, a decisive formal argument. In those few verbs that have distinct forms for the perfect and imperfect, the infinitive takes

22. Good statements of these views can be found in Meier (1950) and Maurer (1951).

the latter and the future subjunctive the former. For this reason one has morphological oppositions of the type *querer* (infinitive) : *quiser* (future subjunctive).

Morphological Categories in Verbs

From the morphological point of view, the most fundamental partition of Portuguese verbs is into two groups accordingly as they possess or do not possess a special stem for the four tenses that derive from the Latin perfectum, namely, the preterite perfect indicative, the preterite pluperfect indicative, the preterite subjunctive, and the future subjunctive. We may call verbs that do have such forms perfectum verbs. The opposition between perfect and imperfect always involves some variation in the radical, as was already the case in Latin for two classes of verbs—those that had special radicals for the perfect (ex: Lt *est* : *fuit;* Ptg *é* : *foi*) and those that showed an alternation in the vowel of the radical (ex: Lt *facit* : *fecit;* Ptg *faz* : *fêz*). Both of these processes were carried over to Portuguese, as the examples above suggest. Furthermore, in some cases where Latin made the distinction by means of the suffixes *-u-* and *-s-*, this suffix has been incorporated into the radical of the corresponding Portuguese reflexes. Thus, here too the opposition is indicated by variation in the radical (exs: *habuit* > *haube* > *houve; dixit* > *dicsi* > *disse*). One must note, however, that the perfectum verbs in Portuguese are very limited in number and therefore have little structural importance in the statistical sense. Most Portuguese verbs have the same radical for the perfect and the imperfect because of the loss of the suffix *-u-*, the predominant mark of the perfect in Classical Latin and even more so in Vulgar Latin.

A second partition, encompassing all Portuguese verbs, is generated by the various theme vowels. Traditionally, classes determined in this way are called 'conjugations'. In principle, each verb belongs to only one conjugation because verbs generally maintain the same theme throughout the paradigm. It is important to note, however, that some perfectum verbs (exs: *dar, ver*) have one theme for the perfect and another for the imperfect.

Theme vowels have their origin in Latin, where the radical took one of the four vowels *-ā, -ē, -ĕ,* or *-ī* before infectum inflections or, when the vowels were *a* or *e*, before the *-u-* of the perfectum. Latin grammarians based their classifications on the imperfect infinitive, in which the inflection *-re* is preceded by the theme vowel, giving the endings *-āre, -ēre, -ĕre, -īre*. These were called the first, second, third, and fourth conjugations, respectively.

In Portuguese, as in Spanish, the third conjugation, with theme in -ĕ, vanished. The Portuguese reflexes of those third conjugation verbs that remained in the lexicon underwent a process of remodeling and received either the theme vowel of the Latin second conjugation -ē or that of the Latin fourth conjugation -ī (exs: *capēre*, instead of *capĕre*, >Ptg *caber*; *fugīre*, instead of *fugĕre* > Ptg *fugir*). In this way the number of conjugations was reduced to three in Portuguese: -*a* (1st conj.), -*e* (2d conj.), and -*i* (3d conj.).

Although the theme vowel is usually stressed, in certain forms it is in unstressed final position and the root vowel is stressed instead. This makes it possible to find out the true vocalism of the root, a fact indispensable in understanding its alternations. In certain other forms the theme vowel is pretonic and the suffix is stressed. If the inflection is a vowel, it sometimes vanishes, or becomes Ø, instead of remaining in final unstressed position.

The following table summarizes the 'regular' or most general pattern in the distribution of theme vowels:

Stressed	a : e : i	*Present Indicative*—1st and 2d-person plural: *amAmos, amAis; temEmos, temEis; partImos, partIs* *Preterite Perfect Indicative*—1st-person plural, 2d-person singular and plural, 3d-person plural: *amAmos, amAste, amAstes, amAram; temEmos, temEste, temEstes, temEram; partImos, partIste, partIstes, partIram* *Preterite Pluperfect Indicative: amAra; temEra; partIra.* *Imperative*—2d-person plural: *amAi; temEi; partI* *Preterite Subjunctive: amAsse; temEsse; partIsse* *Future Subjunctive and Infinitive: amAr; temEr; partIr* *Gerund: amAndo; temEndo; partIndo*
	o : e : i	*Preterite Perfect Indicative*—3d-person singular: *amOu; temEu; partIu*
	e : i	*Preterite Perfect Indicative*—1st-person singular: *amEi; temI; partI*
	a : i	*Perfect Participle: amAdo; temIdo; partIdo*
	a : Ø	*Preterite Imperfect Indicative: amAva; tem(Ø)ia; part(Ø)ia*
Pretonic	a : e : i	*Future Indicative: amArei, amAria; temErei, temEria; partIrei, partIria*
Final un-stressed	a : e[23]	*Present Indicative*—2d-person singular, 3d-person singular and plural: *amAs, amA, amAm; temEs, temE, temEm; partEs, partE, partEm.* *Imperative*—2d person singular: *amA; temE; partE*
	Ø	*Present Indicative*—1st-person singular: *am(Ø)o; tem(Ø)o; part(Ø)o* *Present Subjunctive: am(Ø)e; tem(Ø)a; part(Ø)a*

23. In Portugal, however, one finds [ə], indicating a theoretical /e/.

Several facts become apparent from the analysis presented above. First, verbs with theme in *a* are in general distinctly opposed to those of the other two themes. The only exception is the first-person singular of the present indicative. In the present subjunctive, where the theme vowel is always Ø, the first conjugation has a special suffix that distinguishes it from the other two conjugations. In the third-person singular and the first-person singular of the preterite perfect, the theme changes from -*a* to -*o* and -*e*, respectively. The reason for this is that the diphthongs /au/ and /ai/ of forms like *amaut* (< *amauit*[24]) and *amai* (<*amaui*, by the loss of the -*u*- of the perfect) became /ou/ and /ei/. However, verbs with theme in -*a* still remain distinct from those with theme in -*e* and -*i* (exs: *amou* : *temeu, partiu; amei* : *temi, parti*).[25]

The distinction between verbs with theme in -*e* and those with theme in -*i* is often lost. In the first place, the -*e* theme merges completely with -*i* in the perfect participle as well as in the first-person singular of the preterite perfect. In the preterite imperfect and in the present subjunctive, the theme vowel is reduced to Ø and an inflectional suffix common to both themes is added. In the second-person singular of the present indicative and of the imperative and in the third-person singular and plural of the present indicative, the two theme vowels merge since they are in final unstressed position. This is true regardless of whether the theme appears as a syllabic vowel after a consonant or as an auxiliary vowel /i̯/ after a root terminating in a vowel. In this connection it should be noted that in the third-person plural the theme vowel is nasalized by the personal desinence and therefore remains syllabic, in hiatus (exs: *temes,* from *temer* : *partes,* from *partir; móis, moem,* from *moer* : *atrais, atraem,* from *atrair*). A distinction between the two themes is to be found only when the vowel of a monosyllabic root is the same as the theme vowel (exs: *lês,* theoretically *lê(e)s; ris,* theoretically *ri(i)s*).

Structure of Suffixes

In principle, suffixes are not added directly to the radical *R* but rather to the theme *T*. Their composition is a function of two global categories that are expressed in Portuguese by means of the process of

24. In the third-person singular the /i/ of the sequence /uit/ was dropped instead of the /u/ of the perfect.

25. In *amei* 'I loved' the personal desinence is -*i* (/i̯/); it does not appear in *temi* 'I feared' or *parti* 'I left' because there is no phonological diphthong /ii̯/ in Portuguese.

inflection. First, there is a mark of *tense*, associated with a complementary indication of *mood*. We may call this part of the inflection the 'tense-mood suffix' *TMS*. Second, there is a *personal* desinence that indicates whether the subject is the person speaking (1st person), the listener (2d person), or some other being (3d person). Since this part of the inflection also gives a secondary indication of *number*—singular or plural—we may call it the 'person-number suffix' *PNS*. A complete inflection *S* results from the combination of these two totally distinct elements. The general formula for the morphological structure of verbs is therefore:

$$T (=R + V) + S (=TMS + PNS) .$$

As a specific example, consider the form *amávamos* 'we used to love':

$$amávamos = amá (=am + á) + vamos (=va + mos) .$$

This structure is exactly that of Latin verbs in the infectum, without a special mark for the perfect aspect. The corresponding Latin example is *amabamus* : *amabamus* = *ama* (=*am* + *a*) + *bamus* (=*ba* + *mus*). It goes without saying, of course, that any constituent of the general formula except the radical may be absent (or = $\emptyset$) in specific instances. For example, TMS is zero in the present indicative, just as it was in Latin:

$$amas = ama (=am + a) + s (=\emptyset + s) .$$

TMS is also zero in the singular and in the first- and second-persons plural of the preterite perfect indicative, again in correspondence with Latin, not counting the -*u*- or -*s*- of the perfect. PNS, on the other hand, is zero in Portuguese in those cases where Latin had final -*m* or -*t*, that is, in the first- and third-persons singular, respectively. In fact, since -*t* was the desinence of the third person, Portuguese has in general no mark for this person except in the preterite perfect indicative, where *amaut* (< *amauit*), *partiut* (< *partiuit*) became *amou*, *partiu*, and so on. The /u̯/ of the perfect then changed in function to become a personal desinence.

In Latin the first-person singular had the desinence -*o* in the present indicative (ex: *amO*), -*i* in the preterite perfect indicative (ex: *amauI*), and -*m* in other tenses.[26] The first and the second of these have the same roles in Portuguese. The latter, however, either became asyllabic /i̯/ (ex: *amaui* > *amai* > *amei*) or vanished after a theme in -*i* because Portuguese does not have /i̯i̯/ among its phonological

26. This is not true of the future indicatives, but these forms were quickly abandoned in Vulgar Latin and were therefore not adopted in Portuguese.

diphthongs (exs: *parti* and also *temi* since verbs with theme in -*e* take -*i* in the first-person singular of the preterite perfect indicative, as shown above). The -*i* desinence was even extended to the first-person singular of the Romance future present indicative, where it evolved from the -*i*- of *haio* (< *habeo*) as a result of a restructuring of the inflection caused by agglutination of expressions of the type *amare habeo* (*amare haio* > *amar hai* > *amarei*). Including Ø, we have the following pattern for tense-mood and number-person suffixes in Portuguese verbs:

TMS:

Ø	*Present Indicative*
	Preterite Perfect Indicative—singular and 1st- and 2d-person plural
VA (unstressed)	*Preterite Imperfect Indicative* (1st conjugation)
IA (stressed /I/)	*Preterite Imperfect Indicative* (2d and 3d conjugation)
RA (unstressed)	*Preterite Pluperfect Indicative*
	Preterite Perfect Indicative—3d-person plural
E (unstressed)	*Present Subjunctive*—singular and 3d-person plural (1st conjugation)
(stressed)	*Present Subjunctive*—1st- and 2d-person plural (1st conjugation)
A (unstressed)	*Present Subjunctive*—singular and 3d-person plural (2d and 3d conjugation)
(stressed)	*Present Subjunctive*—1st- and 2d-person plural (2d and 3d conjugation)
SSE /SE/ (unstressed)	*Preterite Subjunctive*
R	*Future Subjunctive*
	Infinitive
RE (stressed)	*Present Future Indicative*—2d-person plural, 1st-person singular and plural
RA (stressed)	*Present Future Indicative*—2d-person singular, 3d-person singular and plural
RIA (stressed /I/)	*Preterite Future Indicative*
NDO /(N)DU/	*Gerund*
DO	*Perfect Participle*

(Note: The unstressed /a/ of *-va-*, *-ia-*, *-ra-*, *-ria-* becomes /e/ before /i̯/; /r/ becomes /re/ before /s/ of the 2d-person singular and before the nasal of the 3d-person plural.)

In general the tense-mood suffixes given above derive from the corresponding Latin suffixes. The future indicative is, of course, an exception since this structure was created within Romance. The only element that evidences considerable phonological changes is *-ia* in the preterite imperfect indicative of the 2d and 3d conjugations. This suffix is the end product of a peculiar evolution of the Latin suffix *-ba-* in which the consonant vanished and the theme vowel was integrated into the tense-mood suffix.[27]

Consider now the person-number suffixes, that is, the personal desinences:

PNS:

1st sing.   *-o:* present indicative (exs: *amO, temO, partO*)[28]
             -i /i/: preterite perfect indicative, in the 1st conjugation (ex: *ameI*), present future indicative (*amareI, temereI, partireI*)
             Ø: all other tenses

2d sing.   Ø: imperative
             -ste: preterite perfect indicative (exs: *amaSTE, temeSTE, partiSTE*
             -s: all other tenses

3d sing.   *-u* /u/: preterite perfect indicative (exs: *amoU, temeU, partiU*)
             Ø: all other tenses

1st pl.   *-mos:* all tenses

2d pl.   *-stes:* preterite perfect indicative (exs: *amaSTES, temeSTES, partiSTES*)
             -des: future subjunctive and personal infinitive (exs: *amarDES, temerDES, partirDES*, present indicative, in 2d conjugation

27. TMS is *-ia*, in opposition with *-a* for the present subjunctive (exs: *temia, partia* : *tema, parta*). It would be incorrect to consider *-i-* the thematic vowel and *-a* the TMS because then the two tenses would be distinguished not by their respective TMS but rather by the presence or absence of the thematic vowel *-i*.

28. In the literary language this desinence undergoes a morphophonemic change to *-ou* when stressed but, as we have already seen, /ou/ is reduced to /o̜/ in the received dialects of both Brazil and Lisbon. In any case, monosyllabic verb forms such as *sou* 'I am', *dou* 'I give', and *vou* 'I go' are written with *-ou*. The form *estou* 'I am' shows this same morphophonemic change since the theoretical root is actually *-st-*. The initial /i/ is required because the raising consonant group /st/ is not allowed initially in Portuguese.

monosyllabic roots ending in *-e*, 3d conjugation monosyllabic roots ending in *-i* and any monosyllabic root ending in a nasal (exs: *leDES, iDES, ponDES*) imperative, under the same conditions as above, but the final *-s* is dropped (exs: *leDE, iDE, ponDE*).

-is /is/: in all other tenses; in the imperative the final *-s* is dropped[29]

3d pl.   /u(n)/: following stressed or unstressed /a/, in a diphthong; written *-ão, -am*, respectively (exs: *amarãO, temerãO, partirãO; dãO; amaM, temaM*)

/(n)/: following unstressed *-e* (exs: *ameM, temeM*)

In general this system of inflections succeeds very well in distinguishing the various verbal forms one from the other; homophonous forms are rare. Within a given tense, however, non-uniqueness in person occurs when the personal desinence is reduced to zero in the first- and third-persons singular (ex: *êle* or *eu amava*). With respect to two different tenses, non-uniqueness occurs when TMS has homonymous forms, as in the future subjunctive and the personal infinitive (TMS = *r*) and in the third-person plural of the preterite perfect and pluperfect (TMS = *ra*). Allowing both person and tense to vary, one finds the same forms for the third-person singular present indicative and the second-person singular imperative (exs: *ama, teme, parte*) and, in the case of verbs with theme in *-i*, for the first person of preterite perfect indicative and the second-person plural of the imperative (ex: *parti*).

The last mentioned identity of form is easily resolved by context, given the rather peculiar pattern of imperative sentences. In the case of the future subjunctive versus the personal infinitive, sentential patterns are sufficient to undo the ambiguity. The use of personal pronouns counteracts the homonymity of the first-person singular and the third-person singular.

The only non-uniqueness that tends to persist even in context is between the preterite perfect and the preterite pluperfect in the third-person plural (exs: *amaram, temeram, partiram*). It is precisely this non-uniqueness that must have caused, at least in part, the decline in use of the third-person plural of the pluperfect and, by extension,

29. In the third conjugation (imperative *parti* 'leave!', present indicative *partis* 'you leave') the asyllabic vowel of the personal desinences /i/ and /is/ vanishes (see n. 25).

of the whole tense in both Brazil and Portugal.[30] The functional load of the preterite pluperfect is, of course, much less than that of the preterite perfect.

VERBS WITH VARIABLE RADICAL

Vocalic Alternations

Up to this point we have discussed variation only in suffixes and have considered radicals to be constant. Although most Portuguese verbs are, in fact, of this type, nonetheless there are certain groups of verbs that show variation in the radical.

Still within the general compass of the term 'regular' are the following vocalic alternations: 1) between forms with stressed versus those with unstressed root vowels; 2) considering only forms in which the root vowel is stressed, between the second-person singular and the third-person singular and plural of the present indicative on one hand versus the first-person singular of the present indicative and the whole of the subjunctive on the other. Alternations of this type should be considered to be phonological alternations between vocalic phonemes or between a vocalic phoneme and a phonemic diphthong. The phonetic differences caused by the positional variation of 1) are an integral part of the phonological structure of Portuguese and therefore have no morphological significance. As far as grammatical structure is concerned, the following facts are irrelevant: a) a root vowel changes in quality in forms in which it is not stressed (ex: *la-* in *lavas* 'you wash' and *lavar* 'to wash'); b) an open mid root vowel closes when unstressed (exs: *re-* in *regas* 'you irrigate' and *regar* 'to irrigate'; *co-* in *cobras* 'you charge' and *cobrar* 'to charge'), c) a close mid vowel becomes a high vowel when in hiatus with stressed /a/ of the theme (cf. the usual pronunciation of *cear* 'to dine', *voar* 'to fly').

In fact there are only two types of vocalic alternation. The first, between forms with stress on the root vowel and those stressed elsewhere, has been shown above to be phonologically conditioned. The second, which occurs within forms stressed on the root vowel, is purely morphological.

Just as we consider the infinitive to show the true vocalism of the theme, we consider the second-person singular of the present indicative to contain the basic form of the root, revealing its true vocalism.

30. The preterite pluperfect was replaced by *tinham amado*, an expression having nearly the same value (see chap. 7). In the archaic language the two tenses under discussion had distinct desinences in the third-person plural. The preterite perfect was *amarom, temerom, partirom* (< Lt -*ŭnt*) while the preterite pluperfect was *amaram, temeram, partiram* (< Lt -*ant*).

The basic form, however, undergoes various changes. When the root ends in /ę/ (or, in some cases /ę̧/), this vowel diphthongizes to /eį/ (or /ę̧į/) in hiatus, a process that we have already seen in feminines of the type *européia* 'European'. More formally, we can say that phonological diphthongization occurs in the environment of /a/ or /o/ (reduced to /u/ in final unstressed position). In the second conjugation, verbs of the type of *ler* 'to read' (that is, *le* + *(e)r*) show such diphthongization with the desinence -*o* of the first-person singular present indicative and with the tense-mood suffix -*a* of the present subjunctive. In the subjunctive diphthongization occurs by morphological extension in the first- and second-persons plural even though the root vowel is unstressed (exs: *leio* 'I read', *leia* 'I read' (subj), *leias* 'you read' (subj), *leiamos* 'we read' (subj), *leiais* 'you read' (subj), *leiam* 'they read' (subj)). First conjugation verbs of the type *cear* 'to dine', *estrear* 'to inaugurate' (basic roots: /sę/, /istrę̧/) undergo phonological diphthongization in those forms of the present indicative that are stressed on the root vowel (exs: *ceio, ceias, ceia, ceiam*). It is only by morphological extension that the same process occurs in present subjunctive forms with final unstressed -*e* and stressed root vowel (exs: *ceie, ceies, ceie, ceiem*) .When the root vowel of such verbs is unstressed (that is, unstressed -*e* in hiatus with stressed or pretonic -*a*) it merges with -*i*.[31] The latter is the true vocalism of certain other roots in which diphthongization is not phonologically obligatory (ex: *variar* 'to vary' : *vario, varias*, etc.). Nonetheless, this process is often induced by the model of the opposition stressed /ei/ : unstressed /i/. In some cases the stressed /i/ vocalism is replaced by /ę/ (ex: /odę/ in *odeio* 'I hate', *odeias*, etc., but /odi/ in the noun *ódio* 'hate'), while in other radicals /ę/ and /i/ are in free variation (ex: *negoceio* 'I negotiate', *negoceias*, etc., alongside *negocio, negocias*, etc.).[32] The written language maintains the distinction between radicals with the letter -*e* and those with the letter -*i* even when this vowel is unstressed. The spelling used is *not* determined in accordance with the vowel found in root-stressed forms (exs: /sę/ in *ceio;* /odę/ in *odeio*) but rather by the original vocalism of the word, which can usually still be found in a cognate noun (exs: /odi/ in *ódio*, /negosi/ in *negócio*, just like /vari/ in *vário* and certain verbal forms).

31. The roots with -*i* are found in verbs borrowed from literary Latin. It is for this reason that -*ĭare* was adopted as -*iar*.

32. Brazilian normative grammars tend to condemn the free variation and prefer the radical with /i/.

The second type of vocalic alternation occurs in second conjugation roots that have an open mid vowel and in third conjugation roots that have either mid vowel, open or close. It is a purely morphological process that redundantly strengthens the indication of person present in the desinence. The true vocalism of the root, found in the second-person singular of the present indicative, is in opposition to that of the first-person singular and the associated present subjunctive forms.

In the second conjugation one finds oppositions of the type *open mid vowel* : *close mid vowel* (exs: *ced(es)* /ę/ 'you cede' : *ced(o)* 'I cede', *ced(a)* /ẹ/ 'I cede' (subj); *corr(es)* /ǫ/ 'you run' : *corr(o)* 'I run', *corr(a)* /ọ/ 'I run' (subj)). Historically, the origin of these alternations can be traced to Latin radicals in -ĕ- and -ŏ-. In stressed position these give Portuguese /ę/, /ǫ/ but in the first-person singular present indicative the desinence -*o* (phonological /u/) set off a process of metaphony, just as it did in nouns of the type *mĕtu-* > *mêdo, ŏvu-* > *ôvo*. As a result, present indicative forms stressed on the root vowel show the same sort of opposition as in masculine *ôvo* 'egg' versus feminine *ova* 'roe'. Despite this historical explanation, only an impulse toward creation of a secondary morphological process to complement inflection can explain two additional facts that turn out to be crucial: 1) the same alternation appears in verbs that historically have /ẹ/ and /ọ/, from Lt -ē- -ĭ- and -ō- -ŭ-, respectively (exs: *cēd-, cŭrr-*); 2) the present subjunctive, which has final -*a*, is included in the metaphonic alternation. The last-mentioned fact is a result of a structural association, inherited from Latin, between the present subjunctive and the first-person singular present indicative.

In the third conjugation one finds oppositions of the type *mid vowel* : *high vowel* (exs: *fer(es)* /ę/ 'you wound' : *fir(o)* 'I wound', *fir(a)* 'I wound' (subj); *cobr(es)* /ǫ/ 'you cover' : *cubr(o)* 'I cover', *cubr(a)* 'I cover' (subj); *sent(es)* /ẹ/ 'you feel' : *sint(o)* 'I feel', *sint(a)* 'I feel' (subj); in *sentes* the nasal closes /ę/ to /ẹ/). Alternations of this type are parallel to that found in the pairs *êste* : *esta* : *isto* and *todo* : *tudo*. The origin of the mid-high alternation once again can be traced to Latin verbs with radical -ĕ-, -ŏ-. In the case at hand it was the asyllabic /i̯/ of the first-person singular present indicative -*io* and of the present subjunctive -*iam* that caused metaphony in Vulgar Latin, giving the reflexes /ẹ/ /ọ/ for -ĕ-, -ŏ-. Thus, the verbs under discussion entered the same pattern as those with themes in -*e*, and the alternation was similarly extended to radicals in *ē/i* or *ō/u*.

Toward the end of the archaic period, a second bout of metaphony, conditioned by the *-o* /u/ of the first-person singular, set in and was extended morphologically to the present subjunctive. As a result /ę/, /ǫ/ became /i/, /u/.

A second morphological process is responsible for the existence of radicals with a mid vowel in the second-person singular and in the third-person singular and plural of verbs that originally had /i/ or /u/ from Lt *-ē-*, *-i-* or *-ō- -u-*. This resulted in an opposition with the high vowels of the first-person singular and the present subjunctive. As would be expected, the original vowel also survived in forms in which it was not stressed (exs: *freg(es)* 'you fry' : *frij(o)* 'I fry', *frij(a)* 'I fry' (subj), *frig(ir)* 'to fry' < Lt *frīgere; som(es)* 'you disappear' : *sum(o)* 'I disappear', *sum(a)* 'I disappear' (subj), *sumir* 'to disappear' < Lt *sūmere*).

As a consequence of this state of affairs, the vowels of non-root stressed forms underwent a bifurcation. In some cases such vowels are the same as that of the second-person singular, that is, a mid vowel (ex: *dormir*, like *dormes*), but in other cases they are the same as that of the first-person singular, a high vowel (ex: *frigir*, like *frijo*). In the modern language of Portugal, this bifurcation is actually limited to the vowels of the front series, where /e/ in pre-stressed position is realized as [ə] (ex: *ferir* [fərir], as opposed to *frigir*). In the back series one has only /u/ in unstressed radicals because of loss of the opposition /o/ : /u/. The orthography, however, carries on with the distinction, distributing letters according to the Latin (exs: *dormir*, *sumir*). In the case of Brazilian Portuguese, which still has the mid-high opposition in both series, the binary unstressed systems *e/i, o/u* remain operative but vowel harmony tends to eliminate the distinction through overlapping in certain geographic areas, including Rio de Janeiro.

Starting with the second-person singular of the present indicative, we find in modern Portuguese verbs of the second and third conjugations the following oppositional schemes of regular vocalic alternations:

second conjugation: /ę/ : /ę/—*ced(es)* : *ced(o)*, *ced(a)*, etc.
 /ǫ/ : /ǫ/—*corr(es)* : *corr(o)*, *corr(a)*, etc.

third conjugation: /ę/ or /ę/ : /i/—*fer(es)* : *fir(o)*, *fir(a)*, etc.; *freg(es)* : *frij(o)*, *frij(a)*, etc.; *sent(es)* : *sint(o)*, *sint(a)*, etc.
 /ǫ/ or /ǫ/ : /u/—*cobr(es)* : *cubr(o)*, *cubr(a)*, etc.; *som(es)* : *sum(o)*, *sum(a)*, etc.

The verb *prevenir* 'to prevent' and a small group of cognates based on the root *gred-* (Lt *grad-*, from *gradus*, Ptg *grau*) have /i/ in all root stressed forms of the present indicative and in all forms of the present subjunctive. They are, in effect, the vestige of a tendency to regularize /i/ as the vowel of all root stressed forms. Although this tendency was overcome in most third conjugation verbs, at one time it even reached the point of creating variants like *sigues* for *segues* on the model of *sigo* and *friges* for *freges* on the model of *frijo*.

From the discussion above we may conclude that the vocalic alternations that partition root stressed radicals into oppositive pairs in the second and third conjugations are regular and predictable from the radical of the second-person singular of the present indicative.

Further Variations in Root Stressed Forms

A limited number of verbs show irregular, unpredictable variation between the basic radical, found in the second-person singular of the present indicative, and the radical of the present subjunctive (*not* always the same as that of the 1st-person singular of the present indicative). One must, in such cases, resort to an enumeration or list in order to describe the oppositions.

Two subtypes of irregular variation are: a) a change in the final consonant of the radical; b) the addition of a final consonant to a radical that ends in an open syllable. Examples:

Type a

1. *perder*	'to lose'	*perd(es)*	: *perc(a)*, *perc(o)*
2. *valer*	'to be worth'	*val(es)*	: *valh(a)*, *valh(o)*
3. *ouvir*	'to hear'	*ouv(es)*	: *ouç(a)*, *ouç(o)*
4. *pedir*	'to ask'	*ped(es)*	: *peç(a)*, *peç(o)*
5. *medir*	'to measure'	*med(es)*	: *meç(a)*, *meç(o)*
6. *dizer*	'to say'	*diz(es)*	: *dig(a)*, *dig(o)*
7. *trazer*	'to carry'	*traz(es)*	: *trag(a)*, *trag(o)*
8. *fazer*	'to do'	*faz(es)*	: *faç(a)*, *faç(o)*
9. *poder*	'to be able'	*pod(es)*	: *poss(a)*, *poss(o)*

In examples 1–5 the radical of the second-person singular is maintained throughout the rest of the conjugation, but in examples 6–9 it survives only in the imperfect since these verbs have special radicals for the perfect. To this list should be added three radicals closed by a nasal that show a change to the palatal nasal consonant (/(n)/ : /ɲ/). Notice that the second radical is also found in the preterite imperfect indicative but with the additional change of a mid to a high vowel:

10. *ter*	'to have'	*ten(s)*	: *tenh(a)*, *tenh(o)*, *tinh(a)*
11. *por*	'to put'	*põe(s)*	: *ponh(a)*, *ponh(o)*, *punh(a)*
12. *vir*	'to come'	*ven(s)*	: *venh(a)*, *venh(o)*, *vinh(a)*

Type b

13. *ver*	'to see'	*vê(s)*	: *vej(a)*, *vej(o)*
14. *haver*	'to have'	*há(s)*	: *haj(a)*, *hei* (no inflection)
15. *estar*	'to be'	*está(s)*	: *estej(a)*, *estou* (general radical)

The alternations listed above have three distinct historical sources. First, the alternation in one of the examples, no. 9, *podes* : *posso*, is the direct reflex of the corresponding Latin opposition, *potes* : *possum*.[33] Second, certain of the examples, namely no. 6, *dizes* : *digo*, and no. 7, *trazes* : *trago*, show the consequences of the evolution of Latin *-c-* /k/ before *-e-* and *-o*, *-a*, respectively. Since these evolutions are, of course, distinct, one finds *dico* > *digo* but *dices* > *dizes* and similarly **traco* (VLt for *traho*) > *trago* but *tracis* > *trazes*. Finally, the remaining examples show a series of changes caused by asyllabic /i̯/ in the endings *-io -iam*, which in Classical Latin were bisyllabic. The /i̯/ of Vulgar Latin combined with preceding consonants and in so doing caused a change in their very nature. For this reason we find evolutions of the type *valeam*, *valeo* > *valha*, *valho* (like *muliere-* > *mulher*); *video*, *videas* > *vejo*, *vejas* (like *hodie* > *hoje*); *habeam* > *haja*; *facio*, *faciam* > *faço*, *faça* (like *ratione* > *ração*). Other forms that underwent similar changes are **petio* (instead of *peto*), *audio*, **perdio* (instead of *perdo*). In the last example, however, archaic *perço* was later replaced by *perco*.[34]

A second type of alternation is diphthongization of the radical vowel:

16. *caber*	'to fit'	*cab(es)*	: *caib(a)*, *caib(o)*
17. *saber*	'to know'	*sab(es)*	: *saib(a)*, *sei* (no inflection)
18. *querer*	'to want'	*quer(es)*	: *queir(a)*, *quero* (general radical)
19. *requerer*	'to require'	*requer(es)*	: *requeir(a)*, *requeir(o)*

In examples 16–19 it was once again the asyllabic /i̯/ of the desinence that caused a change. In these examples, however, /i̯/ metathesized instead of combining with the preceding consonant, a change in line with the general elimination of all raising diphthongs temporarily created in Vulgar Latin. For this reason we have the developments

33. The radical of *potes* served as a model for the VLt infinitive *potere*, which gave Ptg *poder*.

34. The historic cause of this replacement is somewhat of an enigma (see Williams 1938, p. 225).

capis > *cabes* but *capiam* > *caiba* (similarly *capio*); *sapes* > *sabes* but *sapeam* > *saiba;*[35] *quaeris* > *queres* but **quaeriam* (instead of *quaeram*) > *queira* and *quaero* > *quero.*

Variation of the Radical in Non-root-stressed Forms

The radical of the Portuguese reflex of *habere* shows a general *há-* : *hav-* opposition. The former is the basic radical found in the second-person singular of the present indicative (2d-person singular *há(s)*; 3d-person singular *há*, plural *hão*, that is, *há* + /u(n)/), while the latter is found in all nonroot stressed forms (*haver, havia,* etc.). This situation is the result of a reduction of the radical in the Latin present indicative (*habes, habet, habent*).

A different type of variation is found in the future indicative of second conjugation verbs with radical final /z/ (exs: *faz(es), fazer* 'to do'; *diz(es), dizer* 'to say'; *traz(es), trazer* 'to carry'). Here the theme vowel does not appear and /z/ is lost (exs: *direi, diria,* etc.; *farei, faria,* etc.; *trarei, traria,* etc.).

Radicals ending in a nasal (exs: *ten(s)* 'you have', *põ(es)* 'you put', *ven(s)* 'you come') lose the nasal and take no theme vowel in the infinitive and in the future indicative tenses. In the last example there is also a change in the root vowel, which becomes /i/. Certain of these forms show a theme vowel in addition to the root vowel (exs: *terei, teria; vir, virei, viria*), but others have only a root vowel (exs: *pôr, porei, poria;*[36] but *pões, põe,* with a theme vowel).

Verbs with a Special Radical for the Perfect

We have now reached a type of variation in the radical that is most important for a complete understanding of the structure of Portuguese verbs—the opposition between forms of the perfect aspect and those of the imperfect aspect. As noted above, this opposition vanished in the great majority of verbs as a consequence of the loss of Latin -*u*- of the perfect. The small number of verbs that still retain the distinction can be divided into three classes.

The first class, made up of only two members, actually shows an

35. The first-person singular *sei* is itself a radical without inflection and should be considered a variant of the radical *saib-* in the descriptive sense. Historically it is modeled after *hei*, which is also a radical alone (*haio* > *hai* > *hei*), in both the historical and the descriptive senses.

36. More of these futures without theme vowel existed in the archaic language (exs: *salrei, tenrei, adurei, verrei,* etc.).

opposition of themes rather than of radicals—*d(ás) d(ar)* 'to give' has a perfect with theme in *-e*[37] (except in the first-person singular of the preterite perfect indicative *dei*): *d(este)*, *d(era)*, *d(esse)*, *d(er)*, etc.; *vê(s) v(er)* 'to see' has a perfect with theme in *-i*: *v(i)*, *v(iste)*, *v(ira)*, *v(isse)*, etc.

The second class consists entirely of verbs with theme in *-e* and is characterized by so-called strong root stressed forms, with no inflectional suffix, in the first- and third-persons singular of the preterite perfect indicative. Here the theme vowel is reduced to final unstressed *-e*, which does not appear after /z/. Based on the vowel of the 'strong' third-person form, we can distinguish two situations: a) there is a mid-vowel–high-vowel alternation that distinguishes the third person from the strong first person; b) these two persons have the same vowel, that is, morphological identity occurs. In the first situation it is the high vowel in the first person, today extended to all nonroot stressed perfect forms, which shows the 'regular' inflection. Thus we have:

1. *-ou-* /ou̯/
   caber 'to fit' : *coube* (< VLt **capuĭ-*, instead of *cēpĭ-*); imperfect *cab(es)*
   saber 'to know' : *soube* (< Lt *sapuĭ-*); imperfect *sab(es)*
   trazer 'to carry' : *trouxe* (< VLt *traxuĭ-*, instead of *traxĭ-*, with the *-s-* of the perfect); imperfect *traz(es)*
   haver 'to have' : *houve* (< Lt *habuĭ-*); imperfect *há(s)*, *hav(er)*
   prazer 'to please' : *prouve* (instead of archaic *prougue* < Lt *placuĭ-*); imperfect *praz*
2. *-i-* /i/
   dizer 'to say' : *disse* (< Lt *dixĭ-*, with the *-s-* of the perfect integrated into the radical); imperfect *diz(es)*
   querer 'to want' : *quis* /kiz/ (replaced archaic *quige*, Lt *quaesii*); imperfect *quer(es)*
3. *-e-* /ẹ/
   fazer 'to make' : *fêz* (< Lt *fēcĭ-*, opposed to the imperfect *făcĭ-* by means of vocalic alternation); imperfect *faz(es)*
   ter 'to have' : *teve* (on the model of archaic *seve*, Lt *sedui-*, from *sedēre*, which gave Ptg *seer* > *ser*; later replaced by *foi*, *fui* from *esse*); imperfect *ten(s)*, *te(r)*
   estar 'to be' : *esteve* (same origin, replaced archaic *stede* < Lt *stetĭ-*, derived by reduplication from *stare*); imperfect *est(ás)*

37. In all verbs that have a special radical for the perfect the theme vowel *-e* is open /ẹ/. This can be explicated by reference to the perfect of *dare-*, namely, the reduplicated form *dĕd(i)*. In *dei* and *deu*, however, /ẹ/ closed to /ẹ/ because a diphthong was formed.

4. *-o-* /ǫ/

   pôr 'to put' : *pôs* /pǫz/ (< VLt **posĭ-* with /ǫ/, instead of *posuĭ-*); imperfect *põ(es)*, *pô(r)*

   poder 'to be able' : *pôde* (< VLt *potĭ-* with /ǫ/, instead of *potuĭ-*); imperfect *pod(es)* with /ǫ/

The most remarkable innovation in Portuguese was the creation of /ẹ/ : /i/ and /ǫ/ : /u/ alternations (exs: *fiz* 'I made', *tive* 'I had', *estive* 'I was', *pus* 'I put', *pude* 'I was able', all strong 1st-person forms). The source of these alternations is metaphony, caused by *-ī* desinence of the first person versus *-ĭt* of the third person.

Suppletive Radicals

Although the radical *fū-/fŭ-* was used in the perfect of only one Latin verb (namely, *esse* 'to be'), it has come to be associated with both *ser* 'to be' and *ir* 'to go' in Portuguese. Some Romance languages show both *fo-* and *fu-* as a result of free variation in quantity of the /u/. Portuguese eventually adopted *fo-*, but the /ǫ/ : /u/ alternation discussed above served as a model that caused *fu-* to be selected for the strong first person while *fo-* was established in the rest of the paradigm. The theme vowel survived only as a reduced asyllabic /i̯/ in the third person and in the strong first person (*fui, foi, foste; fôra, fôsse, fôr,* etc.).

The imperfect forms of *ir* and *ser* have heteronomous radicals. The first derives from Latin *ire*, which was regular in the fourth conjugation. Certain forms of another verb *vadere* 'to advance' were, however, incorporated into the paradigm, causing the adoption in modern Portuguese of *va-* for the present subjunctive and the root stressed forms of the indicative while *i-* remained in the rest of the paradigm of the imperfect.

In Latin *esse* 'to be' had three distinct forms in the infectum (*s-*, *es-* and *er-*, all derived from a single Indo-European root), but only one form (*fu-*) in the perfectum. Portuguese introduced into the paradigm certain forms of the verb *sedere*, which meant 'to sit' in Classical Latin. The archaic language even had a perfect form *seve*, derived from *sedere*. In the modern language the distribution of radicals is as follows:

1. *s-*, *so-*, *sa-* in the first-person singular, first- and second-persons plural, and third-person plural of the present indicative, respectively: *s(ou)*, *so(mos)*, *so(is)*, *sã(o)*.

2. *e-*, *er-* in the second- and third-persons singular of the present indicative

and in all forms of the preterite imperfect indicative, where the forms are root stressed and TMS is reduced to unstressed /a/ : *és, é, era*, and so on.

3. *se-, sej-* (< Lt *sed-*) in the infinitive, both future indicative tenses, the gerund, the perfect participle, and the present subjunctive (in the latter, /d/ combined with the asyllabic /i/ of the desinence of *sedeam*, giving /ž/) : *ser, serei, seria, sendo, sido, seja*, and so on.

THE PERFECT PARTICIPLE

History of the Perfect Participle

In principle, the Portuguese perfect participle has the same structure as its counterpart in Latin. Morphologically the latter was an adjective with theme in *-o/u*, inflected for gender, number, and case. Like other adjectives of this type, the form that survives in Portuguese is the accusative—masculine and feminine, singular and plural. The Latin participial suffix, *-tum* in the masculine accusative (fem *-tam*, pl *-tos, -tas*), was preceded in the first and fourth conjugations by a theme vowel (*-a, -i*, respectively), as was generally true of all perfects in *-u-*. Since the /t/ was therefore in intervocalic position in these forms, it underwent lenition to /d/ in Portuguese (exs: *amātu- > amado; partītu > partido*). In the second and third conjugation, on the other hand, the theme vowel usually did not appear. The participial suffix was either added directly to the radical (exs: *scripsi : scriptum, tenui : tentum*) or a connecting vowel *ĭ* was inserted, giving the participle antepenultimate stress (ex: *habui : habĭtum*).

The form involving a connecting vowel, not favored in Vulgar Latin, was replaced by a new structure in which the *-u-* of the perfect was incorporated into the suffix of the participle (exs: *tenutu-, habutu-*). Another tendency present in the Vulgar language was adoption of a theme in *-ī* for these participles. As a result, the archaic language had the following system of perfect participles: first conjugation *-ado*, third conjugation *-ido*, second conjugation *-udo* with a certain amount of free variation to *-ido*. Modern Portuguese rejected the forms in *-udo*, probably for two reasons: 1) lack of structural support in the rest of the paradigm for an *-u-* in the participle, and 2) homonymy with the nominal suffix *-udo*, used to derive adjectives from substantives (exs: *sanhudo* 'angry' from *sanha* 'anger'; *barbudo* 'bearded' from *barba* 'beard'; *membrudo* 'limbed' from *membro* 'limb'). For this reason the pattern *amado / temido, partido*, which we have already seen in verbal morphology, was established.

The structure without a thematic vowel was also adopted in Portuguese, both for participles that already had this structure in Classical Latin and for other similar participles that evolved in Vulgar Latin. Examples:

dizer	'to say'	: *dito*	Lt *dictu-*
escrever	'to write'	: *escrito*	Lt *scriptu-*
fazer	'to do'	: *feito*	Lt *factu-*
pôr	'to put'	: *pôsto*	Lt *posĭtu-* (with loss of the posttonic penult)
ver	'to see'	: *visto*	Lt *visĭtu-* (as above)
abrir	'to open'	: *aberto*	Lt *apertu-*
cobrir	'to cover'	: *coberto*	Lt *coopertu-*
vir	'to come'	: *vindo*	VLt *venĭtu-*

In the last example, fall of intervocalic /n/, with concurrent nasalization of the vowel, destroyed the suffix *-ido*, which survives in all other verbs with theme in *-ī*. The participle *vindo* derived in this way has the structure of a radical (*vin-*, a variant of *ven-*) followed directly by a suffix (*-do*). From a purely descriptive point of view, it does not make sense to posit a participial suffix in any of the other forms. In fact, it is more economical and more in line with functional reality to view these forms as themes in *-o* derived from a variant of the basic verbal radical (exs: *dit-* : *diz(es)*; *escrit-* : *escrev(es)*; *feit-* : *faz(es)*; *pôst-* : *põ(es)*; *vist-* : *vê(s)*; *abert-* : *abr(es)*; *cobert-* : *cobr(es)*).

We see then that there are two different types of perfect participles in Portuguese: 1) 'regular' participles, with the *-do* suffix and either *-a* or *-i* as thematic vowel (except in *vindo*); 2) irregular, unpredictable participles, with no suffix, made up of a verbal radical and the vowel of the nominal theme. The second type are root stressed or 'strong'.

New Root Stressed Participles

A very important aspect of Portuguese morphology is the tendency to introduce new root stressed participles into the conjugation. The new forms, which for many verbs are in free variation with participles in *-do*,[38] often appear through the reassociation with a verb of an adjective (without theme vowel) originally itself derived from the Latin participle of that verb (exs: *preso*, for *prender* 'to fasten'; *aceso*,

---

38. Many grammarians exaggerate the number of root stressed participles by including in their lists forms that, although derived from Latin participles, are pure adjectives in modern Portuguese.

for *acender*[39] 'to light'; *extinto* for *extinguir* 'to extinguish'). In some instances an adjective derived from a Latin participle has been put into association not with the reflex of that verb but rather with the reflex of a related verb (exs: *aceito*, from the verb *accipere*, for *aceitar* 'to accept'; *expresso*, from *exprimere* > Ptg *exprimir*, for *expressar* 'to express'; *expulso*, from *expellere* > Ptg *expelir*, for *expulsar* 'to expel'). In other instances a cognate adjective has been diverted to the participial function (exs: *livre* for *livrar* 'to free'; *limpo* for *limpar* 'to clean').

Many new participles are derived by addition of a nominal theme in *-o* or, in a few cases, *-e* to the verbal radical (exs: *pago* for *pagar* 'to pay', *ganho* for *ganhar* 'to win', *gasto* for *gastar* 'to spend', *entregue* for *entregar* 'to deliver'). One can cite further examples in both Brazil and Portugal, but these remain excluded from the literary language (exs: in Brazil, *pego* /ę/ for *pegar* 'to catch'; in Portugal, *fixe* for *fixar* 'to fix', *encarregue* for *encarregar* 'to put in charge of').

The incorporation of *morto* into the conjugation of *matar* 'to kill' in the role of a past participle is related to the third process of formation of root stressed perfect participles. The form in question was originally an adjective derived from the perfect participle of *mori* 'to die'. However, starting in the classical period, it was put into association with *matar* 'to kill' rather than with the Portuguese reflex of *mori*, namely, *morrer* (regular past participle *morrido*). In its new usage the participle was in free variation with the regular form *matado*. Although it is difficult to say what caused this complex chain of events, it is likely that the process was influenced by a euphemistic semantic impulse to express the result rather than the cruel deed itself.

Efforts made within normative grammar to limit the number of root stressed perfect participles and to rigorously define their proper use are mere conventions. What is important for the structure of Portuguese is the existence of a productive process for the formation of such participles. In fact, the process has a tendency to become even more productive as time passes.

39. In Latin there was a morphophonemic change of /t/ to /s/, depending on the phonological structure of the radical.

Chapter 7

Periphrastic Structures

Characteristics of Periphrastic Tenses

Side by side with inflected verbs, Indo-European languages have always had certain two-membered verbal compound expressions used to denote categories, or nuances thereof, not covered by inflections. The future tense of many Indo-European languages evolved from just such expressions. In Romance, for example, this tense was created when structures consisting of *habeo* and *habebam* plus an infinitive underwent agglutination.

The general tendency to change a periphrastic form to an inflected one appears to depend on three factors: 1) an increase in importance, within the general system of verbal categories, of the grammatical notion denoted by the periphrastic form; 2) obsolescence of the lexical meaning of the auxiliary verb, that is, the member of the compound that expresses grammatical functions; 3) propitious phonological conditions within the morphophonemics of the construction. All three of these conditions were satisfied in the case of *habeo* and *habebam* with an infinitive, and a new inflected future was therefore formed in Vulgar Latin.

In general, Indo-European languages form periphrastic tenses by associating a verbal noun or adjective with any of the inflected forms of some other verb that has been chosen as the 'auxiliary' of the periphrastic structure. The lexical meaning of such compounds is found in the verbal noun or adjective, just as that of ordinary inflected forms is found in the radical. The grammatical meaning of the compound is to be found in the inflected auxiliary form. It has two principal subparts: 1) number-person and time-mood categories; 2) the special categorial nuance of the construction, a consequence of association of the lexical meaning of the auxiliary with the particular nominal or adjectival form used in the construction. In Portuguese the latter include the perfect participle, the gerund, and the infinitive.

Despite the general semantic unity of periphrastic tenses, a fixed order of constituents is not necessarily required, nor is insertion of other expressions or words between constituents ruled out. The unity inherent in periphrastic tenses is a result of the existence of a direct and immediate relationship between constituents. For this reason the two elements of a periphrastic expression consisting of an auxiliary and a nominal form cannot be analyzed as separate parts, each associated with some other element. It would, for example, be incorrect to posit a periphrastic structure for the Portuguese construction consisting of *ter* 'to have' (with any inflection) followed by a perfect participle that agrees in number and gender with a noun. The latter is, in fact, one of the construction's immediate constituents (ex: *tenho guardados os papéis* 'I have the papers put away'; Ptg paraphrase *'guardados é a maneira que tenho os papéis comigo'*).[1] Similarly one cannot speak of a periphrastic construction in sentences like *vi-o sair* 'I saw him leave' because the correct analysis involves the two immediate constituents: *vi-o* 'I saw him', a verb with its object, and *sair* 'to leave'.

1. It is this construction that appears in the verses of Camões. The situation is somewhat obscured, however, because the object noun is in the masculine singular (ex: . . . *o nome que no peito escrito tinhas* 'that *Name* which printed in thy bosom was' (Fanshawe, ed. Ford, *Os Lusíadas*, III. 120).

Periphrastic constructions may be arrayed in a series in decreasing order of intensity of lexical meaning inherent in the auxiliary. Such series are open-ended, rigorously speaking. Their order corresponds to that of increasing grammaticalization. In the case of complete grammaticalization, the auxiliary loses all of its lexical meaning and becomes a mere index of the category to be expressed.

It is traditional in Portuguese grammar to treat completely grammaticalized constructions apart from all others. For this reason two specific compositional models are separated from the rest and are given the special label 'compound tense'. The first of these consists of an arbitrary inflected form of the verb *ser* 'to be' and a perfect participle. Under the name 'passive voice' this expression is viewed as a counterpart to the inflected active conjugation. The second 'compound tense' is an expression made up of certain tenses of the verb *ter* 'to have'[2] and an indeclinable participle. Traditional grammar considers these two constructions to be inflected forms; only the remaining constructions are considered true 'periphrastic tenses'.

As far as inclusion of the 'compound tense' *ter* construction in the 'simple' inflectional series is concerned, Said Ali (1931, p. 180) has rightly rejected this classification, which is based on a criterion that does violence to the morphological structure of the verbal expressions under discussion. The existence of two distinct, although correlate, systems must be recognized. At best, one is dealing with 'two branches of a single system of meaning' (Glinz 1953, p. 374), one branch being inflected radicals and the other periphrastic tenses.

With respect to the passive voice, here too it seems more correct, as Lenz has observed (1925), to speak of a sentence structure in which the verb *ser* 'to be' forms a connection between subject and predicate. In fact, the feature that characterizes uniquely the passive construction is the specific type of predicate involved, namely, a perfect participle of a transitive verb, rather than a true adjective. From the point of view of sentence structure, the following examples are of the same type: a) *os soldados foram punidos* 'the soldiers were punished'; b) *os soldados foram covardes* 'the soldiers were cowardly'. The difference is that *covardes* expresses an adjectival quality while the participle *punidos* has the force of a verb and denotes an activity that has been carried out.

We see then that the so-called passive voice has no special morpho-

---

2. The verb *haver* sometimes appears in this construction in the literary language, but this usage never occurs in normal speech (see Boléo 1936, p. 24).

logical characteristics in Portuguese. It is a sentence with a nominal subject based on an active sentence with a transitive verb, that is, a verb indicating an activity that has its origin in a certain being, the subject, and by the same token also has its goal in some other being, namely, the patient. The new structure consists of a sentence with nominal subject in which to the patient, as subject, is ascribed the condition resultant from an activity that impinges upon him. This is accomplished by using a perfect participle:

> *o general puniu os soldados*[3]
> 'the general punished the soldiers'
>
> ——*os soldados foram punidos*
> 'the soldiers were punished'

Parts of the structure discussed above existed in Classical Latin. The infectum, however, had a morphological passive voice that was distinguished from the active voice by a characteristic inflection, accompanied by certain morphophonemic changes (exs: Lt *amo* 'I love', but *amor* 'I am loved'; *amas* 'you love', but *amaris* 'you are loved'; *amat* 'he loves', but *amatur* 'he is loved'). In the perfectum, on the other hand, one finds a sentence structure analogous to that of Portuguese, with the single difference that the verb *esse* 'to be' was put in the infectum (exs: *amaui* 'I loved', but *amatus sum* 'I was loved', with the present form *sum* 'I am'; *amaueram* 'I had loved', but *amatus eram* 'I had been loved', with the preterite imperfect form *eram* 'I was').[4]

This combination of formally and intuitively heterogeneous passive expressions underwent two changes in Vulgar Latin. In the first place, the auxiliary *esse* switched to the tenses of the perfectum in the sentential passive of the perfectum system. Even the classical literary language was well disposed to this change, caused by a change in the semantic sector. Originally the infectum forms of *esse* had indicated only the state in which the subject found himself at a given moment. During this stage the construction was quite equivalent to the modern Portuguese (and Spanish) construction with *estar* instead of *ser*[5] (exs:

3. This pattern can be expanded by explicitly indicating the agent in the predicate (ex: *os soldados foram punidos pelo general* 'the soldiers were punished by the general').

4. Both forms, that of the infectum and that of the perfectum, appear under different circumstances in so-called deponent verbs.

5. The distinction between *ser* and *estar* is characteristic of both of these Romance languages of the Iberian Peninsula. It is the reflex of a new usage of Vulgar Latin in which *stare* became syntactically parallel to *esse* but at the same

Lt *templum clausum est*, Ptg *o templo está fechado*, 'the temple is closed'; Lt *clausum erat*, Ptg *estava fechado*, 'it was closed'; Lt *clausum erit*, Ptg *estará fechado*, 'it will be closed'). The general meaning of a concluded activity, ascribing a new attribute to the subject, required a structure with *esse* in the perfect (exs: Lt *clausum fuit*, Ptg *foi fechado*, 'it was closed'; Lt *clausum fuerat*, Ptg *fôra fechado*, 'it had been closed'). The second change was the elimination of the inflected forms of the infectum, with concurrent extension of the perfect participle structure to that aspect. The verb *esse* in the infectum then indicated a nonconcluded activity (exs: Lt *clausum est*, Ptg *é fechado*, 'it is (being) closed'; Lt *clausum erat*, Ptg *era fechado*, 'it was (being) closed'). In this way a sentence structure with the following properties was established in the Romance languages: 1) the predicate is a perfect participle; 2) to the subject is ascribed the result of an activity that impinges upon him.

A periphrastic construction, on the contrary, should be considered the result of a process of morphological composition that associates two phonological and morphological words into a higher lexical unit. Such constructions can be classified according to the verbal noun or adjective they contain: a perfect participle, a gerund, or an infinitive.

Periphrastic Structures with a Perfect Participle

The basic constructional model for the tenses to be discussed below may be considered to be an arbitrary tense[6] of the auxiliary *ter* 'to have' in association with an indeclinable perfect participle. Its origin can be traced to a sentence structure established in Latin to indicate the permansive aspect, which had vanished from the Latin perfect. The new permansive structure consisted of *habere* 'to have' in combination with an object modified by a perfect participle; the latter agreed in number, gender, and case with the former (exs: Lt *habeo litteras scriptas*, Ptg *tenho uma carta escrita (em meu poder)*, 'I have a letter written (in my possession)'). This particular structure still exists in the Romance languages, although the reflex of Latin *habere*

---

time entered into semantic opposition with it. Other Romance languages do not have the distinction. Thus French *la vitre est brisée* may be translated into Portuguese either as . . . *é quebrada* or . . . *está quebrada*, depending on the nuance of meaning intended (see Camara 1964, p. 186).

6. In modern Portuguese the preterite of the perfect may not occur in this periphrastic structure. It was quite common, however, in the archaic language (exs: *quando êle houve começado o sermom* 'when he had begun the sermon'; *depois que tive começada esta obra* 'after I had begun this work').

has been replaced by the reflexes of Latin *tenēre* in Portuguese and Spanish (*ter* and *tener*, respectively).

In Vulgar Latin, despite the continued vitality of the earlier structure, a periphrastic tense of the permansive aspect evolved when the perfect participle came into direct association with *habere*, and the object was subordinated to the expression as a whole, creating a perfectum. The new structure denoted presence of the effects of an action until the moment of time indicated by the tense of *habere*. From a morphological point of view there was no change; agreement of the participle with its nominal object continued for some time as a merely formal process. In the archaic language this is, in principle, the situation one finds (ex: *e perde os bẽes que d'ante auya fectos* /feitus/ 'and he loses the property which he had made before'; Vasconcelos 1922, p. 49). Frequently, however, the auxiliary *haver* is replaced by *ter* even in the archaic period, and the latter eventually came to be normal, thus distinguishing Portuguese from the rest of the Romance languages, including even Spanish, which maintain *habere*. The formal mechanism of agreement of the participle with its object vanished completely after a period of free variation in the classical literary language and at the same time the construction was extended to intransitive verbs, that is, verbs with no object (exs: *tenho ido* 'I have gone'; *tinha andado* 'I had walked'; *terei chegado* 'I shall have arrived').[7] To the modern reader, classical free variation in agreement of the participle seems especially strange.

Of all the Romance languages, Portuguese has best retained the meaning of the original permansive construction. It was for this reason that Said Ali called it a 'perfective', using a term familiar from Slavic linguistics (Ali 1931, p. 180). More rigorously, we can call it a perfect limited in time by the auxiliary. There is a periphrastic perfect in the present (ex: *tenho amado* 'I have loved'), the preterite (ex: *tinha amado*, 'I had loved'), the future (exs: *terei amado* 'I will have loved'; *teria amado* 'I would have loved'), and there is also a subjunctive (exs: *tenha amado*, present; *tivesse amado*, imperfect; *tiver amado*, future), an infinitive (ex: *ter amado*), and a gerund (ex: *tendo amado*).

The general semantic unity of the construction is not in conflict

---

7. In place of this construction Classical Portuguese had *ser* followed by a participle (exs: *somos chegados* 'we have arrived', *eram partidos* 'they had left'). The same pattern, originally an expression of the permansive aspect modeled after the perfectum of Latin deponent verbs, appears from time to time in archaicized modern literary language.

with certain special meanings that are associated with a few tenses. The present perfect, both in the indicative and in the subjunctive, is the only tense that indicates duration, continual or repetitive, until the present moment.[8] The preterite perfect coincides in the main with the preterite pluperfect, which also indicates the conclusion of an event in a given moment of the past. For this reason, the former often replaces the latter in Brazil. In the subjunctive, a true preterite pluperfect was created alongside the simple general preterite. In the present future, the future perfect is the same as one future before another. In its modal usage, to indicate a contrary-to-fact condition, the preterite future in the perfect projects this situation to a point before the present.

Periphrastic Structures with a Gerund

The periphrastic tenses involving a gerund serve to bring out and highlight a durative or continuative aspect in the tense indicated by the auxiliary. A model for this type of construction can be found in late Vulgar Latin (ex: VLt *stat spargendo medelas*, Ptg *está espalhando os unguentos*, 'he is scattering the ointment'; Bourciez 1930, p. 270). In the received language of Brazil this construction thrives to the present day, but in much of Portugal the gerund has been replaced by an infinitive (ex: *está a espalhar* 'he is scattering').

Normally the auxiliary used is *estar* 'to be' in any tense. Examples:

estou espalhando	'I am scattering'
estava espalhando	'I was scattering'
estive espalhando	'I kept on scattering'
estivera espalhando	'I had been scattering'
estarei espalhando	'I shall be scattering'
estaria espalhando	'I would be scattering'

8. Boléo (1936, p. 6) uses a popular quatrain to exemplify this continuative or iterative character, in opposition to the simple perfect preterite:

À sombra do lindo céu
eu jurei, tenho jurado
não ter outros amores
só a ti tenho amado

With shade of the pretty sky
I did swear and I have sworn
for to have no other love;
just you have I loved forlorn

Boléo considers this a type of durative aspect. But one may well ask why it should not rather be interpreted as a true perfect, that is, a permansive aspect, used in the quatrain in order to indicate an oath and a love that continue to have an external existence after their manifestation.

esteja espalhando	'may I be scattering'
estivesse espalhando	'may I have been scattering'
estiver espalhando	'(if) I shall be scattering'
estando espalhando	'being scattering'
estar espalhando	'to be scattering'
tenho estado espalhando	'I have been scattering'

In the last example even the auxiliary itself is in a periphrastic tense.

As in Vulgar Latin, the verb *ir* may also appear as an auxiliary (ex: VLt *errando vadit quasi caecus*, Ptg *vai errando como um cego*, 'he goes wandering about like a blind man'; Bourciez 1930, p. 270). The same is true of *vir* 'to come' and *andar* 'to walk'. The principal difference between *estar* and the other auxiliaries is an opposition between static duration in the former and dynamic duration in the latter. The dynamic element is added to the periphrastic construction by verbs of movement—the auxiliary *ir* highlights a movement in progress; *vir* a movement toward the speaker's location; *andar* directionless motion.[9]

The periphrastic construction with *acabar* 'to finish' is of a different type. It indicates the terminative aspect and presupposes a lengthy period of expectation (ex: *acabou saindo*, Ptg paraphrase *saiu afinal;* 'he wound up leaving', 'finally he left').

Periphrastic Structures with an Infinitive

Periphrastic structures involving infinitives are of the most variegated types, from both the morphological and semantic points of view.

First, there is a series of structures in which an infinitive is associated with a verb of mental state for the purpose of expressing any of a whole gamut of modal nuances (exs: *quero ir* 'I want to go'; *desejo falar* 'I wish to speak'; *pretendo estudar* 'I intend to study'; *conto viajar* 'I am counting on traveling'). This series is, in principle, open-ended and consists of the least grammaticalized of all the periphrastic structures. The general meaning of the construction is concentrated in the lexical meaning of the auxiliary, which retains all its vigor.

A similar, but distinct, construction may be used to express certain aspects. The similarity resides in two factors: 1) importance of lexical meaning of the auxiliary and 2) the open-ended property. One aspect

9. Thus, one finds examples like the following in the *Lusíadas: aqueles Reis que foram dilatando/a Fé, o Império, e as terras viciosas/de África e Ásia andaram devastando* 'Those Kings . . ./who sow'd and propagated where they passed *The Faith* with the *new Empire* (making dry/The *Breasts* of Asia, and laying waste/Black Affrick's vitious Glebe) . . .' (Fanshawe, ed. Ford; I.2).

of this type is the inceptive, which requires *começar* 'to begin' (or one of its equivalents) as auxiliary. Another is the terminative aspect, with *acabar* 'to finish' as auxiliary. Notice that a connecting preposition is placed between the auxiliary and the infinitive in this type of structure (exs: *começou a dizer*, Ptg paraphrases *principiou a dizer*, *pôs-se a dizer;* 'he began saying, put himself to saying'; *acabou de dizer* 'he finished saying').

A more grammaticalized construction is the auxiliary *ter* 'to have' joined to an infinitive by one of the connectives *de* 'of' or *que* 'that'.[10] Its meaning corresponds to that of the periphrastic structure that gave birth to the future in Romance, that is, it expresses obligation or compulsion. The construction includes all tenses (exs: *tenho de ir* 'I have to go'; *tinha de ir* 'I used to have to go'; *tive de ir* 'I had to go'; *terei de ir* 'I will have to go'). Grammars, however, tend to fix upon the present indicative of the auxiliary and call this special case the 'obligatory' or 'necessitative' future.[11]

Finally, we reach the periphrastic structure consisting of the auxiliary *ir* 'to go' and an infinitive. This structure is at once aspectual and modal because it both indicates intention to do something (a modal characteristic) and also expresses a *sui generis* aspect—the aspect of that which is still going to happen (exs: *vou sair* 'I am going to leave', *ia sair* or *fui sair*[12] 'I was going to leave', *irei sair*, 'I shall be going to leave'). It is the aspectual meaning that gives the construction characteristics of a future, based either on the present, the preterite, or another future. Furthermore, in colloquial usage, the modal nature of the construction favors its frequent use with *ir* in the present indicative as an alternative to the use of the simple present indicative with a future meaning (ex: *êle vai chegar às duas horas* 'he is going to arrive at two o'clock'). This usage commonly leads to a totally inadequate grammatical interpretation according to which the construction is a replacement for the simple future. On the contrary, the tense that replaces the future in colloquial speech is indeed the

10. Grammarians have tried to impose the use of the preposition *de* and no other, or at least to limit usage, restricting *que* to transitive verbs, as if it were a relative pronoun referring to an object.

11. With the auxiliary in the present indicative, there is a periphrastic construction consisting of an infinitive subordinated to *haver* by the preposition *de*. By using this construction the speaker injects his will into the situation (exs: *hei de sair* 'I am to leave'; *hão de se arrepender* 'they are to repent').

12. This is the least frequent usage. It is allowed only under certain conditions (ex: *para que você foi fazer isso!* 'why did you go and do *that!*').

simple present itself. Frequent use of expressions with the present of *ir* is motivated by their modal and aspectual meaning. Thus, what they actually replace is the simple present, not the future. Their use contributes an expression of psychological attitude of intention or expectation.

Verb-Pronoun Periphrastic Constructions

The Verb-Pronoun Construction

The Indo-European languages had a special process of inflection to indicate more intense participation of a subject in whatever the corresponding verb expressed. Greek grammarians called this construction the 'middle voice' in order to distinguish it from the 'active' and the 'passive' alike. In the infectum of Classical Latin there were still a certain number of verbs that were inflected in this way, but the inflections used were formally the same as those of the passive voice and were somewhat obsolete in the semantic sense. Just as occurred in the passive, in such cases the perfectum had an expression of the permansive aspect that consisted of a preterite perfect participle and the auxiliary verb *esse*. Latin grammarians called these verbs 'deponent', claiming that they had 'deposed' or abandoned their passive meaning and had thus become active verbs in the semantic sense while remaining passive in the morphological sense. In reality, however, it is the passive of the Latin infectum that is derived from the middle form—the notion of intense participation of a subject in a verbal expression evolved by extension to the idea of the subject as patient. In any case, the special notion associated with deponent verbs had been very nearly lost by the time of Classical Latin. One could no longer perceive how a subject would participate more intensely in the middle forms meaning 'death' (*morior*, rather than *morio*, for 'I die'), 'a gyratory movement of the body' (*uertor*), 'an exhortation' (*hortor*), and so on.

This does not imply, however, that the desire to express intense participation under certain circumstances had completely vanished. On the contrary, this desire was still quite alive, despite all that had happened, and accounts for the creation of a periphrastic construction consisting of an active verb and an oblique personal pronoun corresponding to the subject (exs: Ptg *volto-me* 'I turn', *levanto-me* 'I get up', *lembro-me* 'I remember'). At the same time the middle or 'deponent' inflection was abandoned in favor of the active forms (exs: *uerto*, even in literary Classical Latin, and *morio*, *nasco*, and *horto* in Vulgar Latin). The new verb-pronoun periphrastic construction is typical of the Romance languages, and Portuguese in particular makes much use of it. The periphrastic nature of the construction derives in essence from morphological considerations. Phonologically, the unstressed personal pronoun, the construction's most salient characteristic, is attached to the verbal form, although it can either be proclitic as a new initial syllable or enclitic as a new final syllable.

The Periphrastic Construction in the Third Person

Ever since the days of Classical Latin the verb-pronoun periphrastic construction has been used with any sort of third-person subject. This is in accord with the structure of active sentences, where the subject is treated as an 'agent' even when it is merely impinged upon by some activity. Thus, as far as sentence structure is concerned, there is no difference between *o menino anda* 'the boy walks' and *o menino dorme* 'the boy sleeps' or even *o menino sofre muito* 'the boy suffers a lot'.

The pattern 'verb with accusative reflexive pronoun' occurred first in literary Classical Latin and was very well received in Vulgar Latin. A good example can be given from Vergil: *clamor se tollit in auras* (Ptg *um clamor se ergue aos céus* 'a cry raises itself to the heavens'; Bourciez 1930, p. 116). Usually this construction is viewed as a sort of 'passive voice' (Bourciez, loc. cit.), but in fact this is not the most appropriate grammatical notion. The construction is actually an extension of the corresponding active, with the additional notion of the subject's intense participation. Thus, the example given earlier *um clamor se ergue aos céus* is parallel to *um clamor sobe aos céus* 'a cry goes up to the heavens'. Analogous examples are easy to cite: *a estrada avança* or *a estrada se estende* 'the highway stretches', *a casa desaba* or *a casa se esboroa* 'the house collapses'. Periphrastic verbal structures of this type are often used in Portuguese where other languages prefer passives on the model of *ser amado*.

An extension of the construction treated above led to sentences of the type *vive-se* 'one (indef) lives', *vai-se* 'one (indef) goes', *falou-se* 'one (indef) spoke', *combatia-se* 'one (indef) fought'. Such sentences indicate an ongoing activity that has no particular source. Thus, one is here dealing with a second submodel of the general verb-pronoun periphrastic pattern. Among the Romance languages, this model is found in Portuguese, Spanish, and Italian, but French, on the contrary, uses a simple active form with an indefinite or, more exactly, an indeterminate, subject that refers to a vague human collectivity (exs: *on vit, on va, on a dit, on a combattu*).

A third model is found with transitive verbs. Here the noun that would be the subject in the simple active form is dropped and we have, for example, *quebrou-se o vaso* 'the vase was broken' instead of *o menino quebrou o vaso* 'the boy broke the vase'. This particular verb-pronoun periphrastic structure has been treated in many ways in the Portuguese grammatical tradition and has always involved a certain amount of uncertainty. The two main ways of viewing it are: 1) as expressing an ongoing activity without any particular origin, as in the previous structure, but differing from that structure in that the activity finds its way back to an object; 2) as having its origin in the object, which thus becomes the subject. The second alternative has been especially favored by the literary language. In classical literature one even finds the construction used with a predicate complement that explicitly indicates the agent, just as in a sentence with the perfect passive participle (ex: *aqui se escreverão novas histórias/por gentes estrangeiras que virão* 'here shall be written modern histories/by a strange people that shall come' (modified Fanshawe), *Lusíadas* VII 55; cf. *os soldados foram punidos pelo general* 'the soldiers were punished by the general'). Even in the presence of an agent phrase, however, a different usage, in which agreement did not occur, was possible (ex: . . . *nas terras novamente descobertas primeiro se nota pelos mareantes que as descobrem os perigos do mar* 'in the newly discovered lands the dangers of the sea are first noticed by the sailors who discover them', a frequently cited example from João de Barros; see Carneiro n.d., 2d ed, p. 695).

In the modern literary language the agent phrase does not occur, not even as a special stylistic turn of phrase (see Dias 1918, p. 102). Despite this, according to the linguistic norm the patient noun is treated as subject and the verb is made to agree with it. In Brazil, and even in Portugal, however, the natural tendency in usual speech is quite different. Here the normal pattern always is to put the verb in the singular in order to express an activity with no particular origin or subject but nonetheless with a specific goal or object (exs: *já se escreveu muitas cartas* 'many letters have been written already'; *vê-se ao longe nuvens ameaçadoras* 'threatening clouds are seen in the distance').

Chapter 8

Connectives

Prepositions in Latin and Portuguese

One of the most important typological developments in the Romance languages was the creation of an elaborate system of prepositions used to subordinate constituents within a sentence. Although it is true that Latin had the beginnings of a system of this sort, it was limited to complements of verbs. Furthermore, such complements were always put in the accusative or the ablative cases, which were themselves sufficient to indicate subordination. The adverbial particle that preceded the complements served only to emphasize the subordinating bond and to more clearly demarcate exact conditions of dependence. These particles were called 'prepositions' in the terminology of grammar, as we have already seen in our discussion of the examples *ire ad forum, ire in silvam,* and *ire sub freta.* In the Romance languages, where inflection for case disappeared, prepositions became the sole indicator of subordination to verbs and at the same time the use of such particles with verbal complements increased significantly.

In Portuguese there are only two complement types that may appear without a connecting preposition: 1) the direct object, a constituent that completes the meaning of so-called transitive verbs, and 2) certain other complements of an adverbial[1] nature. In the second category specific conditions must obtain and the use of a preposition always remains a latent possibility (exs: *ir domingo* 'to go Sunday' or *ir no domingo* 'to go on Sunday'; *trabalhar três horas* 'to work three hours' or *trabalhar por três horas* 'to work for three hours'). Even in the first category, for objects that are 'people' rather than 'things', there is a special pattern with the preposition *a* 'to' in free variation with the general pattern (ex: *amar aos pais* or *amar os pais* 'to love one's parents').[2]

The feature most characteristic of Romance structure is the central role assigned to prepositions in subordination of nouns to each other. Latin employed a rather different process that required the dependent noun to be in the genitive case, in order to distinguish it from the head of the construction. Typologically, the most important development that occurred was the appearance of a new process for indication of the subordinating bond, namely, the use of the preposition *de* 'of'. Consider in this connection a Latin sentence like *historia est uita memoriae,* where *memoriae* is put in the genitive case (*-ae,* theme in *-a*) to indicate that it is subordinate to the noun *uita.* The corresponding

1. For example, complements of time, when spoken of in terms of days of the week, or divisions of time, when preceded by a demonstrative (exs: *chegou domingo* 'he arrived Sunday', *haverá esta noite* . . . 'there will be tonight . . . ', *choveu muito êste ano* 'it rained a lot this year'). Under these circumstances there is free variation with the preposition *em* (exs: *chegou no domingo* 'he arrived on Sunday', *haverá nesta noite* . . . 'there will be . . . on this night'). Similarly for duration (exs: *trabalhou seis horas* 'he worked six hours', *esteve ausente quatro meses* 'he was absent four months'). Here there is free variation with *por* or *durante* (exs: *trabalhou durante seis horas* 'he worked for six hours', *esteve ausente por quatro meses* 'he was absent for four months'). In the literary language Ø is in stylistic alternation with the preposition *de* for indication of 'instrument' (ex: *avançavam lança em riste* 'they went forward, lances poised for action'). In this case, however, it is much more usual to find a pre-posed *de* (ex: *avançavam de lança em riste* 'they went forward with lances poised for action').

2. This construction, very common with *amar*, is strictly stylistic. In Spanish, on the contrary, it is obligatory whenever the object is a 'person'.

sentence in Portuguese is (a) *história é* (a) *vida d(a) memória,* where the same relation of subordination is indicated by the preposition *de.* In fact, *de* became so widespread in this type of usage that it even eliminated a special Latin structure in which the preposition *ad* was used to indicate that the subordinate noun had a peculiar real-world functional relation to the head (ex: Lt *uas ad uinum,* Ptg *vaso de vinho,* but Fr *un vas à vin,* all meaning 'wine glass').[3]

Prepositions in Portuguese

The expansion in use of prepositions discussed above was accompanied by a conspicuous decrease in the actual number of distinct forms to be found in this class. Many Latin prepositions quite simply vanished as such, and therefore appear in the modern language only as 'prefixes' used in word formation. The essential cause of this phenomenon was an expansion in the use of certain favored prepositions that, for reasons of simplicity and economy, took on the duties of other prepositions.

In general, prepositional systems function on two levels of grammatical meaning. On the first, more concrete, level we have spatial location and, by extension, temporal location. The first level leads to a second one consisting of such modal usages as metaphorically derived concepts of state, origin, possession, goal, means, cause, objective, and so on.

If we group together all of the most basic Portuguese prepositions, we find that the members of this set operate on two levels in accord with the observation above. In fact, each particle possesses a complex and subtle set of abstract meanings derived from the locative meaning. Of course, a basic structural study of Portuguese prepositions must be limited for the most part to the more fundamental locative level.

To indicate 'general location' we have the preposition *em* 'in' or 'on' (< Lt *ĭn*). More specific information is given by *entre* 'between' (< Lt *ĭnter*), which specifies a location in terms of surrounding points, and by the pair *sôbre* 'over' : *sob* 'under' (< Lt *sŭper* : *sŭb*). Other prepositions add dynamic notions to the essentially static location of *em, entre,* and so on. Among these we have 'separation', expressed by *de* 'from' (< Lt *dē*); 'route', indicated by *por* 'through' or 'by' (< Lt *pro* which absorbed the uses of *per*); and 'direction', expressed mainly by the preposition *a* 'to' (< Lt *ad*). The preposition *para* (arc. *pera*) 'to'

3. Certain stereotyped expressions follow the French model (exs: *navio a vapor* 'steamboat', *fogão a gás* 'gas stove').

was created by agglutination of *per* and *ad* in the Vulgar Latin of the Empire. At first it denoted a directed route, but in Portuguese it has come to have a more complex directional meaning that includes such complementary notions as 'arrival' and 'length of stay'. For example, there is an opposition between *ir a Paris* 'to go to Paris' and *ir para Paris* 'to go to Paris (and stay there)'. The former indicates no more than a general directional notion.

The basic notional meaning of the preposition *contra* 'against' or 'facing' (< Lt *contra*) is derived by adding the idea of 'confrontation' to that of static location. The prepositions *com* 'with' (< Lt *cum*) and *sem* 'without' (< Lt *sine*) express, respectively, 'association' and 'isolation' in a given position.

Insofar as the meaning of individual prepositions is concerned, the principal differences between Portuguese and Latin are a natural consequence of the much greater abundance of such particles in the latter. For example, the original notion of 'separation' associated with *de* was strictly limited to 'movement from top to bottom'. The idea of 'provenience' was left to *ab* (morphophonemic variants: *a* and *abs*), while that of 'movement from inside to outside' was expressed by *ex* (or *e* before a stop). The Portuguese preposition *de*, the reflex of Latin *de*, took on all three meanings. Furthermore, the basis of the use of this preposition in subordinating nouns, the idea of 'possession', evolved by extension from that of 'provenience' (ex: *de tauro corium*, at first 'leather coming from a bull'; see Bourciez 1930, p. 100). The new and rather extensive distribution of *de* in Portuguese can be clearly seen by comparing the following Latin constructions with their true translations into Portuguese:

Latin	*Portuguese*	
se deiicere *de* muro	atirar-se *d(a)* muralha	'to throw oneself from the wall'
liber Petr*i*	(o) livro *de* Pedro	'Peter's book'
a fano tollere	retirar *d(o)* templo	'to carry off from the temple'
ex Epheso advenire	vir *de* Éfeso	'to come from Ephesus'

In the directional subsystem the uses of *a*, derived from Latin *ad*, were expanded at the expense of *in*, used in Latin with an accusative to express direction with the added notion of 'entrance'. Thus, instead of Latin *ire in silvam* we have modern Portuguese *ir à floresta* 'to go to the forest'. It is worth noting, however, that classical usage was much closer to the Latin model. Furthermore, this model is also preserved in Brazilian colloquial language, where one hears *ir na floresta* (*na* = *em* + *a*, as we shall soon see).[4] Of course, the entrance of *para*, a particle of Romance origin, into the prepositional system limited the extension of *a* in certain ways.

The notion of 'route' was expressed in Latin by *per*, while *pro* was used principally to indicate 'front position'. All evidence leads to the conclusion that Portuguese *por* evolved from the latter. For a long time the two particles were in complementary distribution, but *por* eventually took over all the usages—locative as well as metaphorical ('means')—of *per*.

Contractions

A characteristic morphological feature of Portuguese prepositions is their behavior in the environment of the definite article, where *de*, *a*, *em*, and *por* undergo processes of agglutination and consequent phonological variation.

In the case of *de*, one sees the effect of a general morphophonemic rule that elides final unstressed vowels before forms beginning with a vowel. The contracted forms are *do* (=*de* + *o*), *da* (=*de* + *a*), *dos* (=*de* + *os*), and *das* (=*de* + *as*). This indicates that the article and preposition have been integrated into a single form.[5]

For the combination of the preposition *a* and the article *o* we find a contracted form *o* (open /ǫ/) in the archaic language, but the form that was eventually adopted in modern Portuguese is *ao* /au/, where the article becomes an asyllabic vowel in a raising diphthong. In the case of *a* plus the feminine article *a*, contraction of the geminate vowels was definitive, and masculine *ao* /au/ is therefore opposed to feminine *à* /a/ when the preposition and a definite article are jointly expressed. Since European Portuguese typically has a vowel of open quality as the reflex of a contraction of this type, the agglutinated form [a] is there opposed to [ə] for either the preposition or the article alone.[6] In Brazil, on the other hand, neither the central

4. In the colloquial language of Brazil the differential distribution of *em* and *a* is quite distinct from that required by the Lusitanian norm. Brazilians have a noticeable tendency to prefer *em* (see Soares 1875, p. 16).

5. This is also true of demonstratives (exs: *dêste* 'of this', *daquilo* 'of that thing', *daí* 'thence').

6. In the written language the open quality of an unstressed vowel is indicated by the grave accent (ˋ) (see Camara 1963).

vowel nor the mid vowels are ever open when in unstressed position, but there is, in compensation, a secondary stress on the agglutinated preposition plus article form, which therefore is open just as above. There is a slight difference, however, since secondary stress is possible, and indeed frequent, even on the simple preposition. This results, of course, in the loss of the phonological distinction between the latter and the agglutinated form.

The morphophonemic explication that we have just given for the contractions of *de* and *a* with an article is strictly descriptive. A historical explanation would have to take into account as its starting point the fact that in the archaic language the article was *lo* (fem *la*). Historically it was the fall of intervocalic /l/ that created the conditions upon which we based the descriptive explication of these agglutinations (that is, *de + lo > de o; a + lo > a o*).

Phonological conditions were quite different in the case of the prepositions *per*, *por*, and *em* since these forms are closed syllables. In the first two, /r/ in contact with *lo*, *la* was assimilated to /l/, and the resulting geminates were simplified, giving *pelo*, *polo* (fem *pela*, *pola*). Although the distributions of *pelo* and *polo* were at first exactly the same as those of *per* and *por*, respectively, the dichotomy was slowly reduced. Strangely enough, this occurred in precisely the opposite way as with the simple prepositions—in this case it was *pelo* that invaded the field of *polo*, and the latter was eliminated entirely.

The evolution of the contractions of *em* was more complex. At first a contracted form *eno* (fem *ena*) evolved by assimilation of /l/ to /n/, but this form, in turn, soon lost its initial vowel and became *no* (fem *na*), which is in opposition with the simple article *o* (fem *a*) in the modern language. The opposition thus created gives /n/ prepositional force in the contraction, and /n/ itself therefore becomes a variant of /e(n)/ in the environment of a following vowel. For this reason we find a whole series of contractions, for example, with demonstratives (*neste* 'in this', *nesse* 'in this', *naquele* 'in that') as well as with indefinites (*nalgum* 'in some', *num* 'in a', *noutro* 'in another').[7]

Finally, we reach a morphophonemic process that ordinarily goes unnoticed in the written language since it is, in fact, only occasionally reflected in orthography and then only in poetry. This process is loss of final nasalization in the preposition *com* 'with' when a hiatus is formed with a definite article (exs: /ko u/, /ko a/ instead of /ko(n)u/,

7. Free variation is usual in this case (exs: *em algum, em um, em outro*).

/ko(n)a/). Only when the possibility for syneresis afforded by this phenomenon is actually used in poetry is it indicated by dropping the letter *m* and adding an apostrophe (exs: *co'o, co'a*).

The Complete Prepositional System

Up to this point we have restricted our attention to the most basic part of the Portuguese prepositional system. In reality this basic subsystem forms the nucleus of a much richer and more elaborate system that we shall now proceed to examine.

In the first place, we have not yet mentioned certain prepositions that, though inherited from Latin, have a very small frequency of occurrence even in the literary language. One such preposition is *ante* 'in front of' or 'before' (< Lt *ante*), used to denote 'forward position'. A derivative form *perante*, from the agglutination of *per* and *ante*, has more or less the same function, while the preposition of the opposite meaning *trás* 'behind' (< Lt *trans*)[8] is now obsolete. In the second place, certain particles formed in Romance through agglutination of Latin prepositions still occur with some frequency and retain a certain amount of vigor. Examples are *após* 'after' (< Lt *ad post*) for 'following'; *até* 'until' (<*ad tene*, instead of *tenus*)[9] for 'motion toward a final point'; *des* 'from' (<Lt *de ex*) or, more recently, *desde* for 'motion from an initial point'. Within the modern period, Portuguese has formed the combination *para com*, used only under certain rather special conditions to express a psychological attitude (ex: *proceder para com alguém* 'to behave (in a given way) toward someone').

The conversion of adjectival forms to prepositions within modern Portuguese has created a small and somewhat marginal system consisting of forms of the type *segundo, conforme*, and occasionally, in the literary language, *consoante*, all meaning 'according to'. The notion 'except' is similarly expressed by *salvo* or *exceto*. A peculiar morphological property of these prepositions makes their marginal character quite explicit—they govern the pronouns *eu* 'I' and *tu* 'you' rather than the forms that usually accompany prepositions in Portuguese

8. There was a change in meaning here since *trans* in Latin corresponds to modern Portuguese *através* 'across'. The prefix *trans-* preserves the original meaning.

9. Archaic Portuguese had *ataa* in addition to *atee*. Apparently these two particles are generically distinct: *atee* derives from Lt *ad tene* while *ataa* derives from Arabic *hattâ*. The exact etymology of these particles is, however, still a subject of debate (see Nascentes 1932, p. 80).

(ex: *exceto eu* 'except me', compare *para mim* 'for me', *de mim* 'from me', *a mim* 'to me').

The development that contributed most to the expansion of the Portuguese prepositional system was the evolution of an open-ended series of periphrastic prepositional expressions. Rigorously speaking, these expressions show three morphological patterns. First, we have the structure *de* (or occasionally *a*) preceded by an adverbial particle. The combination of these two elements becomes a preposition and governs a substantive (exs: *antes de* 'before' : *depois de* 'after', the latter more frequent than *após; diante de* 'in front of' *or* 'before'; *atrás de* 'in back of' *or* 'behind', the former more frequent than *ante* and the latter replacing the obsolete *trás; longe de* 'far from' : *perto de* 'near'; *além de* 'farther' : *aquém de* 'this side of'; *junto de* or *junto a* 'next to'). All of the forms of this first series give precise specification of location. The second series consists of periphrastic expressions in which all components are prepositions (exs: *embaixo de* 'under' : *em cima de* 'over', more common than *sob* : *sôbre; acima de* : *abaixo de*, *por cima de* : *por baixo de, de cima de* : *de baixo de*, all meaning 'on top of' : 'below'). Finally, one can create any number of prepositional expressions by surrounding a given noun with a preposition on either side (exs: *em conseqüência de, em virtude de, por causa de* 'because of').

CONJUNCTIONS

Class Membership

Two distinct types of connectives are joined in a single class under the name 'conjunction' in the Greco-Roman grammatical tradition. The first type, properly called 'coordinating conjunctions', estab-lishes a sequential connection between the words, lexical groups, or sentences of a given communication and indicates a summation of meanings, one added to the next, forming a total meaning in which all components are on the same level. A construction in which the elements are connected by means of a coordinating conjunction is what Greek grammarians called *syndeton*, whence it is the custom to call coordination with such a particle *syndetic*. On the other hand, when coordinated constituents are merely put one after another in a sequence the coordination thus established is called *asyndetic*. The second type of conjunction, unlike the first, removes from a sentence its autonomy, or status as a free communication, and makes it a constituent of a second sentence, where it functions as a determining or defining element. For example, in *digo e vejo* 'I say and I see', the activities of 'saying' and 'seeing' are coordinated and the resultant sentence communicates both activities. On the contrary, the sentence *digo que vejo* 'I say that I see' only communicates that which is said; the clause *vejo* 'I see' loses its own value and serves only to more clearly define the general meaning of the speaker's words.

From the formal point of view, subordinating conjunctions can be characterized by the fact that they are only applicable between propositional clauses, whereas coordinating conjunctions can establish connections between any of the elements of a communication, be they words (ex: *belo e grandioso* 'beautiful and imposing'), lexical groups (ex: *com grande entusiasmo e de coração aberto* 'with much enthusiasm and an open heart'), or propositional clauses (ex: *digo e vejo* 'I say and I see'). Thus, subordinating conjunctions are to clauses what prepositions are to words or lexical constructions.

Subordinating Conjunctions

An extensive and complex structural system of clauses subordinated by means of conjunctions had developed in Latin, principally in the written language.[10] At the same time there were two other processes of subordination: 1) a verb itself could express subordination by taking on a nominal or adjectival form, and 2) a so-called relative pronoun could be used. The latter both establishes a subordinating connection and also retains its pronominal meaning.

In Portuguese, as in other Romance languages, the whole system of subordinating conjunctions was profoundly remodeled. The most important fact to note in this connection is the appearance of the particle *que* 'that', homonymous with the relative pronoun *que*, as the subordinating conjunction *par excellence* (exs: *o homem que vejo* 'the man that I see'; *digo que vejo* 'I say that I see'). The principal cause of this was a loss of pronominal meaning suffered by the neuter indefinite-interrogative pronoun *quĭd* and its coalescence with neuter *quod*, a strictly relative form. Secondarily, there was the convergence in phonetic evolution of the comparative particle *quam* and the conjunction *quod*. Out of all this there arose a multifunctional particle *que*, used in the most varied sorts of phrasal structures. Its uses include the following: integration of one propositional clause into an-

10. In the written language subordination was often artificial, or more accurately, merely formal. The hierarchy of meanings put together in this way did not correspond to reality. It was this style, typical of Latin literary language, which was used in the Portuguese classical literary language.

other as subject or object (absolute subordination), subordination of
one term of a comparison to the other (comparative conjunction),
introduction of a propositional clause to indicate cause (causative
conjunction), and indication of a consequence (sequential conjunction). In certain styles *que* can even replace the coordinating particle
e 'and' in order to establish a formal bond of subordination where,
when all is said and done, there is no more than conjunction (ex:
maravilha feita de Deus, que não de humano braço 'a miracle made by
God, and not by a human hand').[11]

As the basic sign of clausal subordination, *que* is found in many
agglutinations and is also the last member of certain conjunctional
subordinating periphrastic constructions and expressions. The particle
porque /purke/ 'because' is a good example of an agglutinated form.
It occurs side by side with *que* as a causal conjunction. The expressions
referred to above are of two types. First, there is the combination of
an adverb with *que* (exs: *ainda que* 'although' a 'concessive' conjunction; *logo que* 'immediately' and *sempre que* 'whenever' for 'temporal
simultaneity'; *depois que* 'after' and *antes que* 'before' for 'temporal
relations'; *já que* 'since' for 'cause'). In the second pattern an adverbial expression consisting of a noun governed by either of the
prepositions *de* or *a* is made into a conjunction by the addition of *que*
(exs: *de sorte que* 'in such a way that'; *de modo que* 'so that'; *a fim de
que* 'in order that'; *ao passo que* 'whereas'; *à medida que* 'as').

Complementing the *que* series, we find other particles of the same
type. First, there is *se* 'if' ([sə] in European Portuguese; [si] in Brazil),
which evolved from the Latin conjunction *sī* and is used to express
'condition'. In Portuguese it acquired a new function, that of replacing
que in an embedded clause in order to indicate an attitude of doubt
with respect to the content of a communication. This usage occurs
only with a main verb that indicates lack of knowledge (ex: *não sei
se é exato* 'I do not know if it is accurate', but *sei que é exato* 'I know
that it is accurate'). Other particles that are of Latin origin are the
pronominal adverbs *quando* 'when' (< Lt *quando*) and *como* 'as' (Lt
quomodo > *comoo* > *como*). In Latin, as in Portuguese, these particles
function as subordinating conjunctions without losing their adverbial
force ('time' and 'manner', respectively).

The indefinite pronoun *quanto* is the basis for a small series of subordinating conjunctions formed within Portuguese. This series in-

11. This construction is literary *only*, of course.

cludes *conquanto* 'although' for 'concession', *porquanto* 'inasmuch as' for 'cause', and *enquanto* 'while' for 'simultaneity in time'. The expression *enquanto que* 'while', which developed from *enquanto* by addition of *que*, has a stronger conjunctional subordinating force.

Finally, one should mention here the adverb *embora*[12] 'although', which is now a concessive conjunction, and the forms *segundo* and *conforme* 'according to', which function both as prepositions and subordinating conjunctions.

Coordinating Conjunctions

The coordinating particle *par excellence* is *e* 'and', from Latin *et*. It is used to indicate explicitly that a word, lexical group, clause, or even an entire communication is the successor of some other such element. In Classical Latin the 'copulative' bond or grouping between elements established in this way could be indicated by any member of a whole series of synonymous particles, but in Vulgar Latin this series was reduced to the unique element *et*, which in any case was the most common and important conjunction even in the Classical language.[13]

Complementary notions like 'opposition', 'disjunction', and 'conclusion' may also be expressed in the coordinated elements. For the first the use of *magis* 'more' developed in Vulgar Latin. Implicit in this usage, of which one can find traces even in the literary language, was the idea of 'preference' (ex: Lt *non equidem invideo, miror magis*, Ptg *em verdade não invejo, admiro antes* or *mas admiro*, 'I do not envy, rather I admire'; quoted by Bourciez 1930, p. 121, from Vergil). Upon the adoption of *magis* the specifically adversative particles of Latin were dropped. For the notion of 'disjunction' Portuguese retained the reflex of Latin *aut* (> *ou* 'or') as well as that of the negative variant *nec* (> *ne* > *nem* /ne(n)/, with nasal closure caused by the initial nasal consonant, as in *mi* > *mim*). For 'conclusion' we find a conjunctional use of the adverb *post* 'after'. In Portuguese *pois* 'then'

---

12. This form evolved by agglutination from *em boa ora*, literally 'in good hour'. As Said Ali has noted, this expression was used 'to wish someone well or wish people a propitious *hora* for human endeavors. It was also introduced into optative and other clauses which indicate that one admits the possibility of something or that the individual speaking is not opposed to its occurrence. . . . This practice, in turn, led to the transformation of the adverb *embora* into a concessive conjunction in modern Portuguese. Naturally the context also changed' (Ali 1931, p. 217).

13. A copulative use of the adverb *sic* 'thus' also evolved and even survived for a while together with *et* in Old French. In Romanian the reflex of *sic* is the only copulative conjunction.

is used only as a conjunction; it is in opposition with the compound form *depois*, used only as an adverb.

The nucleus of coordinative conjunctions discussed so far does not exhaust the possibilities for syndetic coordination in Portuguese. For example, an adversative use of *porém* developed in Classical Portuguese, where this particle at first co-occurred with the adversative *mas* 'but'.[14] In the archaic language *porém*, being the natural descendant of the Latin expression *per ĭnde* or *pro ĭnde* (*ĭnde* 'thence'), was an explicative particle, equivalent to *por isso* 'because of that', 'therefore'. The nonsyncopated form *porende* also had a long existence and can even be found occasionally in literary Classical Portuguese.

A whole constellation of adverbs and adverbial periphrastic expressions may be used to emphasize certain notions in clauses or communications with respect to another previously uttered element of the same type. These expressions both serve as coordinating connectives and also carry specific notional properties. Some are pure modal adverbs that take on the duties of a conjunction. For example, the adverbs *demais* 'moreover' and *além disso* 'beside this' involve a copulative notion. Similarly we find *entretanto* 'in the meantime', *todavia* 'nonetheless', *contudo* 'notwithstanding', *não obstante* 'nevertheless', *apesar de tudo* 'despite everything' (or *apesar disso* 'despite this'), all of which express oppositional notions. Conclusions may be expressed by *assim* 'thus', *portanto* 'therefore', *por conseguinte* 'consequently', *daí* 'thence', *dêsse modo* 'in this way', and so on. This series is truly open-ended.

In order to express disjunction, adverbs and certain verbal forms were made into conjunctions through a process of specialization. Among the former we find *já*, which is repeated in each constituent of a disjunction to indicate temporal intermittence (ex: *já se deitava, já se levantava aos gritos* 'he would intermittently lie down and then jump up screaming'). Another adverb is *ora*, derived from the ablative of the Latin noun *hora*, just as *agora < hac hora* (ex: *ora se deitava, ora se levantava* 'sometimes he would lie down and sometimes he would jump up'). Certain verbal forms, all of the third-person singular present, indicate circumstances incapable of altering a given situation.

---

14. Cf. *O corpo nu e os membros genitais,/por não ter ao nadar impedimento,/mas porém de pequenos animais/do mar todos cobertos, cento e cento* 'His *Body* naked, and his *genitals*,/That he might swim with greater speed and ease:/But with *Maritime* little *Animals*/By Hundreds cover'd, and *all hid*, were *these . . .*' (Lusíadas, VI. 18; trans. Fanshawe).

These forms include the indicative *quer* and the subjunctive *seja*, both of which, like the adverbs discussed above, are repeated in each clause (exs: *quer faça sol, quer chova* 'whether it is sunny or rainy', *seja por displicência, seja por verdadeira tolerância* 'be it through indifference, or through true tolerance').[15]

In summary, syndetic coordination is a general process of linguistic expression. Its object is to lend unity to a series of bits of information by linking them together. In order to achieve this, Portuguese, like many other languages, uses two grammatical processes. First there is a set of particles, called 'coordinating conjunctions', used only for this specific function. Second, there is an open-ended series of adverbs and adverbial expressions that in addition to their modal function also serve to establish a coordinate bond.[16]

15. Since this expression still retains its original verbal character, *seja* is replaced by *fosse* in the past.

16. Genetically, coordinating conjunctions are always adverbs. In Classical Latin, for example, *et* still retained its original adverbial use with the meaning 'also'. (See our discussion of the evolution of *sic* as a copulative conjunction in Vulgar Latin).

Chapter 9

The Lexicon

Formal Typology of the Lexicon

The Portuguese lexicon, defined as the set of nouns, adjectives, and verbs used in that language, derives basically from Latin, and it is only against this fundamental background that the rather extensive effects of linguistic borrowing can be understood. The history of the Portuguese lexicon, starting from the earliest periods of Lusitanian Romance, corresponds closely to the language's external history, that is, to the history of contacts established between Portuguese-speaking populations and other peoples of the most varied linguistic stocks.

Within the principal part of the lexicon, words of Latin origin show a clear bifurcation into distinct strata. First, there is a lexical nucleus, the set of lexical items that entered Lusitanian Romance when Latin was adopted by the Iberians. Second, there is a rich and complex series of words borrowed from Classical Latin. Ever since the earliest periods of romanization, words have been entering the second stratum by way of various spiritual or intellectual paths and can still be said to possess a certain literary character, if this term is understood in a broad sense. In the Portuguese philological tradition, words of this type are called 'learned terms' in order to establish a contrast with words of Vulgar origin, the so-called popular terms of the lexical nucleus.

Popular terms are of predominant importance from a typological point of view because the lexical structure of the modern language is modeled after phonological and morphological patterns deduced from such terms. In particular, the basic phonemic system of modern Portuguese, as well as its rules of syllabification, are based on popular terms. Loans, including even learned Latin terms, were adapted to this system. Phonological innovations stemming from the second stratum are few in number.[1]

Terms of Vulgar origin were also of decisive importance in determining the morphological structure of Portuguese, that is, the totality of patterns found in nominal, adjectival, and verbal themes, in feminine, number-person, and tense-mood desinences, and so on. One clear indication of the correctness of this assertion is the fact that all nouns and adjectives have plurals in *s*, just as the Latin accusative did. This follows from the fact that it was precisely the accusative that came to be the only form used in Iberian Vulgar Latin. Learned words based on the nominative are very rare in Portuguese despite the fact that this was the central or, so to speak, primary case in Latin. Furthermore, the inflectional patterns of such nominative-based words were adapted to the structure imposed by popular terms. For example *ônus* 'onus', borrowed from the Latin nominative *onus* (3d declension neuter), is masculine in Portuguese and shows no formal change in the plural, conforming in this way with the structure of other Portuguese nouns and adjectives that end in -*s* and are stressed on the next to last syllable. Adoption of the nominative form *onus* did not imply similar treatment for the Latin nominative plural *onera* because the latter form would have no meaning within the general morphological system of Portuguese. To give another ex-

1. Among the most important of these phonological innovations are the *muta cum muta* clusters and final unstressed -*io*, -*ia*.

ample, the plural of the very old learned term *Deus* 'God', introduced in the nominative through the language of the Church, is *deuses* in Portuguese, following the pattern established for nouns ending in -*s* derived from the accusative of third declension forms by the fall of final /e/. In Latin, on the contrary, this word had a theme in -*o/u* of the second declension. Its feminine *deusa* was formed by addition of the popular -*a* desinence, and when the Latin feminine *dea* was borrowed in a much later period it took the form *déia*, conforming to Portuguese phonological structure by acquiring a diphthong. Similarly, the morphological structure of learned verbs is patterned after the popular morphological system. A good example is *preterir* 'to pass over' (< Lt *praeterire*, that is, *praeter* + *ire*), which follows the model of *ferir* 'to wound' in the root stressed forms just as if it were a simple verb.

Borrowings from other languages show the same general tendencies. In the case of languages typologically distant from Portuguese, the phonology and morphology of loans were altered to conform to Portuguese phonology and morphology, based, as we have seen, on the mass of popular words of Vulgar Latin origin. These remarks apply to Germanic, Arabic, African, and Asiatic languages, Tupi borrowings in Brazil, and so on.

Popular Terms

Popular terms, the basic linguistic stockpile of Vulgar Latin, are themselves of rather complex origins. First, there is a series of words that are both formally and semantically identical in Vulgar and Classical Latin (exs: Lt *terra-* 'earth', *mare-* 'sea'; *patre-* 'father', *matre-* 'mother', *filiu-* 'son'; *cane-* 'dog', *boue-* 'ox'; *oculu-* 'eye', *digitu-* 'finger'; *aratru-* 'plough', *uua-* 'grape', *uinu-* 'wine'; *annu-* 'year', *mense-* 'month'; *uiride-* 'green'; *rege-* 'king', *lege-* 'law' > Ptg *terra, mar; padre > pai, madre > mãe,*[2] *filho; cam > cão, boe > boi; ôlho, dedo; arado, uva, vinho; ano, mês; verde; rei, lei*). Second, we have certain terms that underwent a semantic shift (exs: Lt *causa* 'a juridical term' > Ptg *coisa* 'thing'; Lt *uenatu-*, the past participle of *uenare* 'to hunt' > Ptg *veado* 'male deer'; Lt *focu-* 'fireplace' > Ptg *fogo* 'fire'; Lt *nitidu-* 'bright' > Ptg *nédio* 'sleek'; Lt *mataxa-* 'strand' > Ptg *madeixa* 'skein'). Third, there are some cases in which Vulgar Latin preferred

2. *Pai* and *mãe*, which are innovations of modern Portuguese, probably should be ascribed to the forms *pade* and *made*, common in children's language (see Vasconcelos 1911, p. 88).

a derivative over the basic form of Classical Latin (exs: *aviolu-* instead of *auu-* > Ptg *avô* 'grandfather'; *apicula-* instead of *apis* > Ptg *abelha* 'bee'; *capitia-* instead of *caput* > Ptg *cabeça* 'head'; *cantare* instead of *canere* > Ptg *cantar* 'to sing'; *comedere* instead of *edere* > Ptg *comer* 'to eat'). Finally, there is a fourth series in which Vulgar morphological variants replaced a canonical form (exs: *dia* for *die-* > Ptg *dia* 'day'; *socra* for *socrus* > Ptg *sogra* 'mother-in-law'; *nura* for *nurus* > Ptg *nora* 'daughter-in-law'; *potere* for *posse* > Ptg *poder* 'to be able'; *padule-* for *palude-* > Ptg *paul* 'swamp').

In nominal phrases composed of a substantive and an adjective, ellipsis of one of the constituents, usually the former, was frequent. In such cases the remaining constituent took on the meaning of the whole phrase (exs: Lt *fructum persicum* 'Persian fruit' > Ptg *pêssego* 'peach'; Lt *mala Mattiana*[3] 'fruit of Mattius' > Ptg *maçã* 'apple'; Lt *nux Abellana* 'nut of Abella' > Ptg *avelã* 'filbert'; Lt *fratre germanu-*[4] > Ptg *irmão* 'brother'; *mantum* (or some other noun designating a piece of clothing) *uermiculu-* 'referring to a cochineal insect' > Ptg *vermelho* 'red'). Analogous examples can be given for phrases consisting of a verb and a noun (ex: Lt *plicare uela* 'to fold the sails' (in order to enter port) > *chegar* 'to arrive').

Since it was in essence a popular language, the Vulgar Latin used in normal speech abounded in metaphors, some of which, with the passage of time, were victorious over the basic meanings upon which they were based. A typical example is *serra* 'a notched implement for cutting wood', that is, 'a saw', which came to mean 'an uneven series of mountains', whence Portuguese *serra* in the latter sense. In the same way *rostrum* 'beak (of a bird)' came to be used for the central part of the human face, giving Portuguese *rosto* 'face'.

In other cases the popular language employed words that were studiously avoided in the Classical language (exs: *bŭcca* for *os* 'mouth'; *perna* for *crus* 'leg'; *casa* for *domus* 'house'; *caballu-* for *equus* 'horse'; *fabulare* for *loqui* 'to speak'; *afflare* for *inuenire* 'to find'; whence Ptg *bôca, perna, casa, cavalo, falar, achar*, respectively). The Vulgar terms were in general slang, ruralisms, or loans from languages of the most varied sorts. The latter were a result of the ethnic heterogeneity of the lower classes of Rome.

3. *Mattiana* is probably an adjective derived from the proper noun *Mattius*, for Caius Mattius, who wrote on agriculture in the first century B.C. (see Corominas 1961, p. 372).

4. The adjective *germanu-* is derived from *germen-inis* 'of the same ancestry'.

As time passed and Rome became a cosmopolitan city the number of popular loans increased. Greeks, spread out over Rome and other parts of the Roman territory, contributed vulgar Hellenisms (exs: *cara* for *caput* 'head'; *petra* for *lapis* 'stone'; *chorda* for *funis* 'cord'; whence Ptg *cara, pedra, corda*). Extensive contact with the Celts resulted in a certain number of Celtisms (exs: *camisia* 'a Celtic garment'; *caminu-* instead of *iter* 'road'; *basiare* instead of *osculare* 'to kiss'; whence Ptg *camisa, caminho, beijar*). Contact, warlike or peaceful, with the Germanic tribes resulted in Germanisms (exs: *guerra*, root *werr-*; *guardare*, from *wardan; raubare* from *rauban; riccu-*, root *rik-*; whence Ptg *guerra* 'war', *guardar* 'to guard', *roubar* 'to steal', *rico* 'rich', and so on).

The vulgar vocabulary of the various regions in which Romance languages eventually developed was not uniform. The tendency for each region to make its own formal and semantic selections is a natural one caused by the centrifugal nature of language itself, a factor that is always of special importance for the lexicon. From a study of lexical distribution one may draw many data important for a true understanding of the administrative, political, and cultural relations between various parts of the total Romance territory. In the Iberian Peninsula, Portuguese shows remarkable homogeneity in this respect with the central and southern dialects, including Castilian, which, in the guise of Spanish, was eventually superimposed on the other dialects. Catalan, on the other hand, shows a much greater affinity to Provençal and, *ipso facto*, to French, at least in part. The following table gives a sample of these relationships (see Rohlfs 1960, pp. 146ss):

	Portuguese	*Spanish*	*Catalan*	*Provençal*	*French*
'apple'	maçã	manzana	poma	pouma	pomme
'uncle'	tio	tio	oncle	ouncle	oncle
'leg'	perna	pierna	cama	camba	jambe
'to boil'	ferver	hervir	bullir	bouli	bouillir
'to eat'	comer	comer	menjar	manjà	manger
'to arrive'	chegar	llegar	arribar	arribà	arriver
'grape'	uva	uva	rahim	rasin	raisin
'to implore'	rogar	rogar	pregar	pregà	prier
'shoulder'	ombro	hombro	espatlla	espala	épaule
'to find'	achar	hallar	trobar	trobà	trouver
'lamb'	cordeiro	cordero	anyell	agnèu	agneau
'cheese'	queijo	queso	formatge	froumage	fromage
'head'	cabeça	cabeza	cap	cap	chef (arc.)[5]

5. In French *chef* was later replaced by a vulgar synonym *tête*, from Old French *teste*, Vulgar Latin *testa* 'pot, jug', used metaphorically for 'head'.

Phonetic Laws

By comparing popular terms of Portuguese with their Latin etymons one can deduce the main trends of Portuguese historical phonology, usually codified into so-called phonetic laws. The phonological structure of learned terms usually does not show the effects of the laws so deduced, although those terms that were introduced during historically early stages of Lusitanian Romance do show important phonetic modifications. These are, however, not always exactly the same changes that would be predicted by the basic phonetic laws. In any case, such words are generally considered to be of a different type and are therefore put in a special category labeled 'semi-learned'. For this reason the correspondences between the vowels of Portuguese and Latin discussed earlier are not valid for either learned or semi-learned terms. For example, in both of these categories Latin high vowels remain high even when short (exs: *mŭndu-* > *mundo* 'world'; *mĭssa* > *missa* 'mass'),[6] and mid vowels are usually open even if the Latin etymon had a long vowel (exs: *complētu-* > *completo* /ę/ 'complete'; *remōtu-* > *remoto* /ǫ/ 'remote'). Furthermore, the posttonic penult does not fall in either category, although an intervocalic voiced consonant following the penult was later elided in words of the second category, causing the penultimate stress pattern to appear upon contraction of the vowels brought into contact (exs: *populu-* > *poboo* > *povo* 'people'; *articulu-* > *artigoo* > *artigo* 'article').

The principal cause of so-called doublets in Portuguese is the difference in phonological treatment accorded popular terms on the one hand and learned or semi-learned terms on the other. It is important to note that the word used to designate this phenomenon is appropriate only in the morphological sense since the Latin etymon that serves as the source of both the popular and learned terms is usually associated with different linguistic contexts. There is sometimes a difference in meaning, often a significant one, involved. Consider, for example, the following instances:

Latin	*Popular Term*	*Learned Term*
articulu-	*artelho*[7] 'ankle'	*artigo* 'article'
atriu-	*adro* 'churchyard'	*átrio* 'atrium'
amplu-	*ancho* 'wide'	*amplo* 'ample'
actu-	*auto* 'ceremony'	*a(c)to* 'act'

6. These words are borrowed from the terminology of the Church. In French, on the other hand, we find the popular forms *monde, messe*.

7. Not in current use.

Latin	Popular Term	Learned Term
claue-	*chave* 'key'	*clave* 'clef'
communicare	*comungar* 'receive *or* administer Holy Communion'	*comunicar* 'communicate'
cogitare	*cuidar* 'to think'	*cogitar* 'to cogitate'
delicatu-	*delgado* 'slim'	*delicado* 'delicate'
factu-	*feito* 'act'	*fa(c)to* 'fact'
materia	*madeira* 'wood'	*matéria* 'material'
oculos	*olhos* 'eyes'	*óculos* 'glasses'
palpare	*poupar* 'to save'	*palpar* 'to palpitate'
plenu-	*cheio* 'full, filled up'	*pleno* 'full, total'
sigillu-	*sêlo* 'seal'	*sigilo* 'secrecy'
strictu-	*estreito* 'narrow'	*estri(c)to* 'strict'

The very first learned terms (or, more accurately, 'semi-learned' terms) found their way into Lusitanian Romance through the language of the Church, actual classroom teaching, or, in some cases, the exigencies of the Roman administrative system. Later, during the Middle Ages, certain specific terms were borrowed from Roman literature, most of which remained current. Mass importation of learned terms did not start until the Renaissance of the fifteenth and sixteenth century. The origin of this round of borrowing was literary, but the whole Portuguese lexicon soon underwent a process of renovation, causing many popular terms to vanish completely (exs: *considerar* 'to consider' for *consirar, martírio* 'martyrdom' for *marteiro; urso* 'bear' for *usso*, probably earlier *osso* (see Nascentes 1932, p. 803); *face* 'face' for *faz; flor* 'flower' for *frol* and *chor; calúnia* 'calumny' for *coima; insídia* 'ambush' for *enseija; ocasião* 'occasion' for *cajom*).

Simultaneously with the borrowings of the Renaissance, there developed a new process of word derivation based on Latin rather than popular Portuguese terms. It is this new process that is responsible for a series of adjectives that contain an allomorph of the radical of the corresponding noun (exs: *ocular* 'ocular' from Lt *oculu-*, but *ôlho* 'eye'; *digital* 'digital' from Lt *digitu-*, but *dedo* 'finger'; *capilar* 'capillary' from Lt *capillu-*, but *cabelo* 'hair'; *manual* 'manual' from Lt *manu-*, but *mão* 'hand'; *mensal* 'monthly' from Lt *mense-*, but *mês* 'month'; *áureo* 'golden' from Lt *auru-*, but *ouro* 'gold'; *plúmbeo* 'leaden' from Lt *plumbu-*, but *chumbo* 'lead'; *pluvial* 'pluvial' from Lt *pluvia-*, but *chuva* 'rain'; *celeste* 'celestial' from Lt *caelu-*, but *céu* 'sky'). Morphological unity was destroyed only when the Latin literary term chosen was not the etymon of the corresponding popular term (exs: *ígneo* 'igneous' from Lt *igne-*, but *fogo* 'fire'; *argênteo* 'argentive' from Lt *argentu-*, but *prata* 'silver'; *sáxeo* 'rocky' from Lt *saxu-*, but *pedra* 'rock').[8]

In a few instances we find a Latin present participle made into an adjective (exs: *cadente* 'falling' from Lt *cadente-cadere*, but *cair* 'to fall'; *conveniente* 'appropriate' from Lt *conveniente-convenire*, but *convir* 'to be suitable'; *comitente* 'constituent' from Lt *committente-committere*, but *cometer* 'to commit'). Derived superlative forms are another example.

External History of Loans

In discussing Portuguese words borrowed from other languages it is necessary to distinguish between what Bloomfield (1933, p. 461) calls 'intimate' loans and 'cultural' loans. The former are a result of intimate contact, within a given territory, of populations speaking different languages. They include loans by a substratum, by a superstratum, and by an adstratum. The first occurs when a defeated population accepts the language of the victors, the second when the victors accept the language of the defeated, and the third when the two languages exist side by side, creating a state of bilingualism.

In the case of Portuguese, native Iberian languages were the substratum, but the list of words that came from this source is small and very fragmentary (exs: *sarna* 'itch', *balsa* 'thicket', *manteiga* 'butter', *veiga* 'lowland', *arroio* 'brook'). Words borrowed later from Basque are historically separate (exs: *esquerdo* 'left' from Bsq *ezker; cachorro* 'dog'; cf. Bsq *txakur* 'to bark'; *zorro* 'fox', cp Bsq *zugur* 'astute'). Also to be included in this list is one word that seems to be a combination of two Basque elements (*bezerro* 'calf', cf. *bei* 'cow' and *zekor* 'bovine offspring', that is, 'calf').

An essentially Germanic superstratum would have resulted from the establishment of the Visigothic and other Barbarian empires, but the invaders found the Hispanic Peninsula in an advanced stage of romanization and their language was able to contribute little to either Portuguese or Spanish (see Baldinger 1963, pp. 78ss). As we have already seen elsewhere, germanisms found in Portuguese are of general Romance origin.

The Arabic adstratum is of singular importance in the history of Portuguese, but it must be clearly distinguished from a set of loans common to the whole of western Europe. These more widespread loans have several sources, including territories such as Sicily and

---

8. There is also a learned form *pétreo* 'petrous', derived from Latin *petra*.

Malta that were occupied by the Arabs at the beginning of the Middle Ages. Other words were borrowed during the Crusades and through communication with caravans that traveled the roads from the Volga to the Baltic (Baldinger 1963, p. 57, n. 35). Loans from the true Arabic adstratum occupy such semantic fields as agriculture and food (exs: *arroz* 'rice', *alface* 'lettuce', *cenoura* 'carrot', *alcaçuz* 'licorice', *albufeira* 'residual water of olives', *alfazêma* 'lavender', *algodão* 'cotton', *azeite* 'olive oil', *rês* 'cattle'),[9] names of territories (exs: *aldeia* 'hamlet', *azinhaga* 'narrow path', *bairro* 'neighborhood'), engineering terms (exs: *chafariz* 'fountain', *nora* 'scoop wheel', *azenha* 'water mill', *alcova* 'alcove', *alizar* 'lining'), professions (exs: *alfaiate* 'tailor', *açougue* 'butcher (shop)', *alfageme* 'armorer', *almocadém* 'captain', *almotacé* 'inspector', *alcaide* 'commander' or 'warden', *alferes* 'second lieutenant', *armazém* 'storeroom'), objects (exs: *alfinete* 'pin', *alforge* 'saddlebag'), weights and measures (exs: *quilate* 'carat'; *quintal* 'quintal', 100 kilograms, *arroba* 'arroba', about 15 kilograms), and so on.

The number of africanisms in common use in Brazil can be counted on one's fingers (exs: *cochilar* for European Ptg *dormitar* 'to doze', *quitanda* 'vegetable market', *batuque* 'any of several types of Afro-Brazilian music or dance', *moleque* for European Ptg *gaiato* 'young rogue', *quingombô* 'okra'). Terms of Tupi origin, which we may consider to be on the level of an adstratum, include several common words (exs: *xará*[10] 'namesake', *caipora* 'unlucky person', *pereba* 'sore'). Also of Tupi origin are several designations for plants, especially those native to Brazil (exs: *capim* 'a type of grass' used as fodder, *peroba* 'a type of timber tree', *acaju* 'various types of mahogany', *jacarandá* 'jacaranda'). Similarly we have several names of animals (exs: *perereca* 'tree frog', *tamanduá* 'tropical anteater', *tapir* 'tapir', *acará* 'a fish', *anum* 'a bird related to the cuckoo'). Typical of day-to-day Brazilian speech are the adjectives *açu* 'big' and *mirim* 'small', always post-posed to a noun as an augmentative or a diminu-

---

9. The Arabic article *al*, either with or without morphophonemic variation, is frequently found agglutinated in these loans brought to Spain by the Berbers, who formed the majority of the Muslim population. As Berber itself has no article, *al* was treated not as an article but rather as the initial syllable of a radical in Berberized Arabic. As Elcock has stated (1960, p. 280): 'The lesser proportion of Arabic words adopted into current Mozarabic without the article may be assumed to have reached the people more directly from the genuine Arab overlords'.

10. It is clear that this word was borrowed from Tupi, but documentation is lacking.

tive, respectively (ex: *uma planta mirim*, Ptg paraphrase *uma plantinha* 'a little plant').

Cultural loans, whatever the distance between the two peoples involved may be, are always a result of cultural interchange. In the archaic language the influence of Provençal and French was particularly strong (exs: *jaula* 'cage', *jardim* 'garden', *chapéu* 'hat', *charrua* 'plow', all from the other side of the Pyrenees). Contact with Spanish was, of course, always intense and brought into Portuguese several terms that show clear traces of uniquely Spanish historical morphology (exs: *vislumbre*[11] 'glimpse', *caudal* 'abundant', *hediondo* 'hideous', with the same root as genuine Ptg *feio* 'ugly', *colcha* 'bedspread', *lhano* 'frank', with typically Sp initial /ʎ/, *trecho* 'interval', *velar* 'to keep vigil', with intervocalic /l/).

Italian influence, both literary and artistic, is a hallmark of the Renaissance. From this source Portuguese took technical terms of poetics (ex: *sonêto* 'sonnet'), of painting (ex: *aquarela* 'watercolor'), of music (exs: *piano* 'piano', *violoncelo* 'cello', *arpejo* 'arpeggio'), and so on. In addition we find various terms of other sorts (exs: *pilôto* 'pilot', *bússola* 'compass', *fragata* 'frigate', *esdrúxulo* 'stressed on the antepenultimate'). The latter term is particularly relevant in Portuguese, since Italian influence often accounts for the stress pattern in question.

French loans once again became very important in the cultural sense beginning in the eighteenth century and even provoked, within the literary language, an unsuccessful puristic reaction against 'gallicisms'. This reaction later spread to loans from another modern language, English. Loans from English are much less numerous than gallicisms despite the rather early political relations established between Portugal and England. Certain anglicisms are, however, structurally significant because of the phonological patterns they contribute to Portuguese (exs: *revólver* 'a gun', distinguished by stress placement from the verb *revolver* 'to revolve'; *jóquei*, with the unstressed final diphthong /ei/; *túnel*, another instance of final unstressed *-el*, as in adjectives with *-vel* like *amável* 'kind'; *júri*, which creates an occasional contrast between unstressed /i/ and /ə/ in Portugal or /i/ and /e/ in southern Brazil).

Portuguese policies of colonial expansionism in the fifteenth and

---

11. From Lt *luminare*. Nascentes says, 'the treatment of the group *mn* of Lt *lum'ne* is typically Spanish.' (1932, p. 818).

sixteenth century led to a certain amount of direct Oriental influence on the Portuguese language (exs: *bengala* 'cane', *bonzo* 'bonzo', a Buddhist priest, *canja* 'chicken soup with rice', *catana* 'catan', a broad sword, *chá*[12] 'tea', *charão* 'lacquer', *jangada* 'raft', *mandarim*[13] 'mandarin', a public official in China, *manga* 'mango', *pagode* 'pagoda', *pires*[14] 'saucer'; see Dalgado, 1916).

Finally, we find a massive series of loans from ancient Greek used in cultural, technological, and scientific terminology. Since these words are usually compounds, we will postpone discussion of their structure until the appropriate section.

Composition of Some Semantic Fields

Semantic Fields in Portuguese

Since language, even on the lexical level, is always structured, it makes sense to array the lexical items of Portuguese in lists according to semantic field and historical origin. Naturally, semantic fields themselves may be arrayed in a hierarchy according to linguistic importance—some fields are clearly 'nuclear', and the words they contain are correspondingly fundamental from a linguistic point of view. By restricting our attention to nuclear semantic fields we can evaluate the importance of Portuguese borrowings from other languages.

The type of 'linguistic importance' that interests us here is a function of the fundamental cultural structure of society and of the designations used for basic things and human activities. Semantic fields referring to such things and activities contain words that are linguistically nuclear within a given cultural structure. They come from the most intimate and primitive levels of the total linguistic mass. Loans or lexical substitutions on these levels are therefore of the greatest significance.

Unfortunately, it is quite impossible to make a complete investigation of these matters in a section of a general discussion of the history and structure of Portuguese. All that is possible (and sufficient for our

12. From the Peking dialect, commonly called 'Mandarin'. The form *te*, of the Fu-Kiang dialect was adopted in Italian, Spanish, and French.

13. The Portuguese were the first to use this term, today commonly used in many Western languages. It seems to come from Malay *mantari* (Dalgado 1916, p. 746).

14. This form was unquestionably borrowed from an Oriental language, but the specific etymon is a subject of debate.

purposes) is a rapid and even somewhat superficial sampling of the relevant data. We proceed now to examine in this way five semantic fields:[15]

Distribution of Lexical Items in Five Semantic Fields

In the tables given below we consider: 1) the physical world, 2) body parts, 3) kinship, 4) time, and 5) climate. We restrict our attention to prime words in common use.

	Portuguese	Popular Latin	Learned Latin	Other
'world'	mundo		mŭndu-	
'earth'	terra	terra	. . . .	
'ground'	chão	planu-	. . . .	
'land'	solo		solu-	
'dust'	pó	pŭlu- (pŭluu-)	. . . .	
'mud, soil'	lama	lama		
'mud, slime'	lôdo	lŭtu-	. . . .	
'sand'	areia	arena	. . . .	
'mountain'	monte	monte-	. . . .	
'hill'	colina		collina (collis)	
'mountain range'	serra	serra		
'field'	campo	campu-		
'meadow'	prado	pratu-		
'plain'	vargem (arc *varga*)[16]			Celt (cf. Fr *berge*)
'valley'	vale	ualle-	. . . .	
'island'	ilha			Prov *iscla*
'continent'	continente		continente-	
'beach'	praia			Prov *playa*
'water'	água	aqua-	. . . .	
'sea'	mar	mare-	. . . .	
'ocean'	oceano		oceănu-	
'lake'	lago	lacu-	. . . .	
'gulf'	golfo			It *golfo*
'bay'	baía			Iber
'wave'	onda	ŭnda-	. . . .	
'river'	rio	rīuu-	. . . .	
'brook'	arroio			Iber
'stream'	córrego	corrŭgu-		
'fountain'	fonte	fonte-	. . . .	
'well'	poço	pŭteu-	. . . .	

15. When the Vulgar Latin etymon was also used in Classical Latin, dots are placed in the learned Latin column. It is clear, however, that in such cases the Portuguese is derived from the Vulgar usage.

16. From *varga* there developed *vargem* and also *várzea*, the latter showing depalatalization of /ž/.

	Portuguese	Popular Latin	Learned Latin	Other
'forest'	mata	matta[17]		
'forest'	floresta (arc foresta)[18]			Old Fr, Prov forest[19]
'jungle'	selva	silua	. . . .	
'woods'	bosque			Prov bosc
'tree'	árvore		arbore-	
'wood'	madeira	materia		
'stone'	pedra	petra		
'rock'	rocha			Fr roche
'cliff'	penha			Castil peña[20]
'sky'	céu	caelu-	. . . .	
'firmament'	firmamento		firmamentu-	
'sun'	sol	sole-	. . . .	
'moon'	lua	luna	. . . .	
'star'	estrêla	stēlla	. . . .	
'planet'	planeta		planeta	
'star'	astro		astru-[21]	
'light'	luz	lūce-	. . . .	
'shade'	sombra	ŭmbra[22]	. . . .	
'darkness'	trevas	tenebras	. . . .	
'fire'	fogo	fŏcu-		
'flame'	chama	flamma	. . . .	
'smoke'	fumo	fūmu-	. . . .	
'ash'	cinza	*cinītia		
'to burn'	queimar	*caimare[23]		
'to ignite'	acender	accendere		
'match'	fósforo		phosphŏru-	
'body'	corpo	*corpu-		
'skin'	pele	pelle-	. . . .	
'flesh'	carne	carne-	. . . .	
'hair'	cabelo	capillu-	. . . .	
'beard'	barba (arc barva)	barba	. . . .	

17. This appears to be a pre-Roman term of Sardinian origin that later spread to certain dialects through Vulgar Latin.

18. This word underwent a process of remodeling based on *flor* 'flower'. Both Portuguese and Spanish have the new form.

19. Probably a Frankish term derived from *forha* 'pine' (see Corominas 1961, p. 270).

20. Probably from Lt *pinna* 'turret' (Corominas 1961, p. 439). There is also a variant *pena* in Portuguese.

21. A Greek term, used in Classical Latin.

22. The initial /s/ in both Portuguese and Spanish probably comes from an association with *sol* 'sun'. There was also a compound form *solombra* 'penumbra, half-shade' (see Corominas 1961, p. 529).

23. This is the most probable etymon. It is derived from Gk *kaima* 'burning heat', used in the medical terminology of cautery (see Corominas 1961, p. 474).

	Portuguese	Popular Latin	Learned Latin	Other
'blood'	sangue	sangue-		
'bone'	ôsso	ossu-		
'skull'	caveira			Castil *calavera*
'head'	cabeça	capĭtia		
'cranium'	crânio		craniu-	
'cerebrum'	cérebro		cerebru-	
'face'	rosto	rostru-		
'face'	cara	cara		
'face'	face		face-	
'forehead'	testa	testa		
'chin'	queixo	*capseu-		
'nose'	nariz	narĭcae[24]		
'eye'	ôlho	ocŭlu-	. . . .	
'ear'	orelha	orĭcŭla		
'mouth'	bôca	bŭcca		
'lip'	lábio		labiu-	
'lip'	beiço			Celt (?)
'tongue'	língua	lingua	. . . .	
'tooth'	dente	dente-	. . . .	
'neck'	pescoço	*post + cocceu- (?)		
'throat'	garganta			onomatopoeic: *garg-*[25]
'shoulder'	ombro	ŭmĕru-	. . . .	
'arm'	braço	bracciu-		
'elbow'	cotovelo	cŭbĭtĕllu-		
'hand'	mão	manu-	. . . .	
'finger, toe'	dedo	dĭgĭtu-	. . . .	
'leg'	perna	perna		
'thigh'	coxa /koša/	coxa /koksa/		
'knee'	joelho (arc *geolho*)	genŭcŭlu-		
'foot'	pé	pĕde-	. . . .	
'heel'	calcanhar	*calcaneare-		
'nail'	unha	ŭngŭla[26]		
'chest'	peito	pectu-		
'heart'	coração (augmentative of *cor*)	cor		
'liver'	fígado	fīcătu-[27]		
'stomach'	estômago		stomachu-	

24. Nominative plural, used to designate the nostrils.

25. Whence also *gargarejar* 'to gargle', *gargalhada* 'peal of laughter', etc.

26. Latin *-ngl-* > *-nh-*; initial *u* due to the palatal nasal.

27. The corresponding term in Latin was *iecur*. *Ficatum*, a derivative of *fīcus* 'fig', was a culinary term used to designate the *foie gras* of a goose fed on figs. A fig sauce accompanied the liver. Variant forms *fīcātu-*, *fīcătu-*, and *fícătu-* occurred in various languages (cf. Fr *foie*, Ptg *fígado*, It *fegato*). There were interferences from the Greek terms for both 'liver' and 'fig' in the determination of the vocalism as well as the stress pattern.

	Portuguese	Popular Latin	Learned Latin	Other
'stomach'	barriga			Castil barriga[28]
'stomach'	ventre	uentre-	. . . .	
'intestine'	intestino[29]		intestīnu-	
'visceral organ'	víscera		uiscĕra	
'lungs'	rins (arc *rẽes*)	renes	. . . .	
'sweat'	suor[30]	sudore-	. . . .	
'family'	família		familia[31]	
'relative'	parente		parente-	
'husband'	marido	marītu-	. . . .	
'wife'	mulher	muliere-		
'spouse'	espôso, -a	sponsu-, -a		
'father'	pai (arc *padre*)	patre-	. . . .	
'mother'	mãe (arc *madre*)	matre-	. . . .	
'child'	filho, -a	filiu-, -a	. . . .	
'grandparent'	avô, avó	auiolu-, -a		
'grandchild'	neta, -o	nepta		
'uncle, aunt'	tio, -a	tiu-[32]		
'sibling'	irmão, -ã (arc *germão*)	germanu-, -a[33]		
'nephew, niece'	sobrinho, -a	sobrīnu-, -a		
'cousin'	primo, -a	prīmu-, -a[34]		
'father-in-law'	sogro	socru-		
'mother-in-law'	sogra	socra		
'son-in-law'	genro	generu-	. . . .	
'daughter-in-law'	nora	nora		

28. The same radical as in *barril* 'barrel', perhaps of Celtic origin. A bold metaphor is apparent.

29. The corresponding popular term is *tripas*, a word found in most Romance languages. Apparently it evolved from *extripare*, for *extirpare* 'to pull out, tear out', used in hunting terminology to designate the act of removing an animal's entrails (see Corominas 1961, p. 568).

30. Formerly pronounced with /ǫ/.

31. In the sense of a group of slaves or 'famuli', a meaning that is found in early periods.

32. Latin distinguished between *patruus* 'paternal uncle' and *auunculus* 'maternal uncle' (diminutive of *auus* 'grandfather'). Within the new social order this distinction vanished. Many Romance languages retained only *auunculu* (Fr *oncle*); Italian, Portuguese, and Spanish borrowed a popular Greek term *theios*.

33. The fall of *g*- in *germão* occurred within Portuguese.

34. This is the adjective *primus* 'first', that is, the 'first relative' after siblings.

	Portuguese	Popular Latin	Learned Latin	Other
'stepchild'	enteado, -a	antenatu-[35]		
'brother- *or* sister-in-law'	cunhado, -a	cognatu-		
'widower, widow'	viúvo, -a	uiduuu-, -a[36]		
'unmarried person'	solteiro, -a	solitariu-, -a		

'century'	século (arc *segre*)		saeculu-	
'year'	ano	annu-	. . . .	
'month'	mês	mense-	. . . .	
'week'	semana		septimana[37]	
'day'	dia	dia		
'hour'	hora	hora	. . . .	
'minute'	minuto (arc *ponto*)		minutu-	
'Sunday'	domingo	domĭnĭcu-		
'Saturday'	sábado	sabbătu-		
'winter'	inverno	hibernu-		
'summer'	verão	ueranu-		
'spring'	primavera	prima uera		
'autumn'	outono	autŭmnu-	. . . .	
'morning'	manhã	maneana		
'afternoon'	tarde	tarde		
'night'	noite	nocte-	. . . .	
'day before'	véspera		uespĕra	

'air'	ar (arc *aar, aiere*)	aere-	. . . .	
'atmosphere'	atmosfera			Gk *atmos*+ *sphaira*
'weather'	tempo	tempu-		
'climate'	clima		clima	
'wind'	vento	uentu-	. . . .	
'breeze'	brisa			uncertain, but general in Romance
'cloud'	nuvem (arc *nuve*)	nūbe-	. . . .	
'mist'	névoa		nebŭla	
'fog'	neblina			Castil *neblina*
'heavy fog'	ruço			Castil *rucio*
'dew'	orvalho	(?)[38]		

35. That is, born before a second marriage.

36. This form developed from *uiduu-* (cf. It *vedovo*). In Portuguese stress is shifted to the penultimate syllable.

37. This term was borrowed from ecclesiastic Latin.

38. This word occurs only in Portuguese. A dialectal form *rovalho* suggests the root *ros-roris* 'dew' (*roraliu- ?).

	Portuguese	*Popular Latin*	*Learned Latin*	*Other*
'rain'	chuva (arc chuiva)	pluuia	. . . .	
'snow'	neve	nĕue-		
'ice'	gêlo		gelu-	
'ray'	raio	radiu-		
'lightning'	relâmpago (arc relampo relampado)			Gk derived from *lampo*
'thunder'	trovão	tŭrbone- (?)		

Names of Persons

We turn now to a class of words that is lent singular importance by its social and cultural implications. This class, found in all linguistic communities, is used for the purpose of identifying each individual member of society. Its members are nouns that have no supplementary meaning beyond identification of an individual.[39] Together with place names, they make up the most important part of the category called 'proper nouns' in the Greco-Roman grammatical tradition (Gk *onoma kyrion;* Lt *nomen proprium*).

Latin had developed a system, peculiar to it alone among all the ancient Indo-European languages, for naming people. This system required the use of three names to identify an individual and was intimately connected with family structure in the context of the social organization of Roman aristocracy. One of the three elements used was the *nomen* or name of the individual's *gens*, a large kinship group to which he belonged and that was supposedly started by a common ancestor (exs: *Cornelius, Tullius, Iulius*). Also used were a *cognomen*, the name of a smaller kinship group, included in the rather extensive *gens* (exs: *Scipio, Gracchus, Cicero, Caesar*), and a *praenomen*, or personal name (exs: *Publius, Tiberius, Marcus, Caius*). These three terms were obligatorily put in the order *praenomen nomen cognomen* (exs: *Publius Cornelius Scipio, Tiberius Cornelius Gracchus, Marcus Tullius Cicero, Caius Iulius Caesar*).

Within the organizational structure of ancient Roman aristocracy the *nomen*, or name of an individual's *gens*, was the most important element and therefore had certain special functions. It was, for example, the only name used in public by women, a situation that led to the custom of using the feminine of a *nomen* as a sort of *praenomen*

39. As Coseriu puts it (1955, p. 6), 'no son multívocos como palabras (significante + significado) sino como 'meras palabras', como puros significantes'.

for women (exs: *Cornelia*, the mother of Tiberius Gracchus; *Tullia*, the daughter of Cicero; *Iulia*, the grandniece of Caesar). The *praenomen* was, of course, of little importance in general because Roman social structure revolved about the *gentes*. There were, in fact, very few names of the *praenomen* class, and these were used over and over again, one time after the next, in place after place. Many were merely ordinal numbers that originally indicated order of birth (exs: *Tertius*, *Quintus*, *Sextus*, *Septimus*, *Octavus* or *Octavius*, *Decimus*).

The whole Roman system of naming lost much of its vitality with the political and social ascension of the plebeians, but it was the advent of Christianity, combined with integration of the 'barbarians' into Roman society, that signaled its complete demise. Under Christianity the ceremony of baptism lent special significance to the first name, which therefore became the truly relevant element for purposes of social identification. Secondarily, the Germanic (or, most likely, general Indo-European) custom of indicating the father's first name was adopted, creating the so-called patronymic. In Iberian Latin patronymics were formed by the addition of an Iberian suffix consisting of -*k*- and a variable vowel followed by the Latin inflection for the genitive -*i*. The most common form of this suffix was -*ici*, from which we get Spanish -*ez* (unstressed) and Portuguese -*es* in a whole series of names that soon became associated with a particular family and lost their original patronymic value (exs: *Álvares* for *Álvaro*, *Gonçalves* for *Gonçalo*, *Henriques* for *Henrique*, *Mendes* for *Mendo*, *Nunes* for *Nuno*, *Rodrigues* for *Rodrigo*, *Vasques* for *Vasco*). In some cases the relation to a first name is no longer obvious (exs: *Alves*, an abbreviation of *Álvares*, *Dias* for *Dídaco*, *Pires* for *Pero*, a variant of *Pedro*).

Among several alternative processes for secondary identification was the use of the name of a place that an individual possessed, in which he was born, where he lived, and so on. This custom led to a series of last names of geographic origin. Other secondary processes can be traced to religious devotion (exs: *Ramos* for *Domingo de Ramos* 'Palm Sunday', *Assis* for Saint Francis of Assisi, *Pádua* for Saint Anthony of Padua), professions (ex: *Monteiro* 'a mountain hunter'), physical, social, or psychiatric peculiarities (exs: *Bravo* 'brave'; *Branco* 'white'; archaic *Cão* from Lt *canus* 'whitish-grey'; *Corpancho*, from *corpo* 'body' and *ancho* 'broad'; *Delgado* 'thin'; *Leal* 'loyal'; *Pimenta* 'pepper', and a derivative form *Pimentel*). Some, but not all, such names originally had a pejorative connotation. An associated series is comprised of names of animals (exs: *Lebre* 'hare', *Lebrão* 'big hare', *Coelho* 'rabbit', *Lobo* 'wolf', *Leitão* 'suckling pig').

The reestablishment of priority of family names over first names in the identification of an individual is a characteristic feature of Portuguese (or, more precisely, Iberian) culture. The practice of referring to two family names without mention of a first name is an old one. In the history of literature we can point to such examples as *Almeida Garrett, Gonçalves Dias, Castro Alves, Machado de Assis*, and so on.

The origin of traditional Portuguese first names is to be found in several sources, including Latin names, frequently involving the change of a *nomen* or *cognomen* to a first name (exs: *Cornélio, Júlio, César*). Other sources are Greek names (exs: *Felipe, Eusébio, Alexandre*); biblical names, sometimes completely Latinized (exs: *João, Maria, Ana, Joaquim, Manuel*);[40] Germanic names, also Latinized (exs: *Afonso, Adolfo, Alfredo, Geraldo, Rodrigo, Carlos*, the latter with the Latin nominative -*s*- desinence). Finally we find a series of names of characteristically Christian origin (exs: *Renato* from Lt *renatus* 'born again through baptism', *Deodato* 'dedicated to God').

The use of many first names and family names derived from foreign sources is an indication of the constant integration of foreigners into Portuguese social life during the Middle Ages and the Renaissance. Foreign first names include *Dinis* (French, from Lt *Dionysius*), *Luís* (Germanic, *Ludwig*), and also the examples of n. 40, *Jaques* (French) and *Jaime* (Catalan). Foreign family names include *Noronha* and *Camacho* (Spanish), *Belfort* and *Bettencourt* (French), *Lencastre* and, by popular etymology, *Alencastro*[41] (English).

Ever since the earliest periods, when names were borrowed from medieval tales of chivalry, the stockpile of first names has been constantly expanding through loans taken from literature, from political history, and from the history of Western culture in general. In more

40. The Hebrew name *Iakob* (with no Latin inflection) gave *Iago*, which was soon agglutinated to *Santiago* in the Iberian Peninsula because of the special devotion of warriors to this saint (*Santiago!* was the usual battle cry). A reanalysis of the agglutinated form gave *San Tiago* and thus the modern form *Tiago*. The variant form *Jaime*, of Catalan origin, is related to the Latin form *Jacomus*, which also gave Italian *Giacomo*. Another variant *Jaques*, borrowed from French *Jacques*, comes from the nominative of *Jacobus* by assimilation of -*cb*- to -*cq*-. The names *Jaime* and *Jaques* are very old in Portuguese and attest close political and cultural relations between Portugal and the countries where these names originated.

41. *Alencastro* is the form that Camões uses for the Duke of Lancaster himself (Lusíadas, VI. 46).

recent times Brazil has shown great fluidity in this field, and a penchant for originality or innovation is quite apparent. In Portugal, on the contrary, there is a tendency to stick to traditional first names. Particular choices are usually determined by religious considerations, continuity within the family, and so on. In Brazil, first names have even been invented by combining syllables taken from various traditional names (see Camara 1964B, p. 45), and names of Tupi origin are common. Some Tupi-based names were taken from colonial history, others from the Indianist school of literature. Among the latter is the very popular *Iracema*, a name invented by José de Alencar in his famous novel of the same title.[42]

Place Names

Place names acquire special significance to the extent that they reflect the political and social history of a region. Among the varied sources of such lexical items one may cite the following: a designation of some feature peculiar to a region, the name of an important person, words associated with religious cults, and so on. Of the first type, Portuguese possesses an extensive series with transparent etymologies (exs: *Barbosa*, a place where there are *barbas* 'creepers, moss-like plants'; *Campos* 'fields'; *Varginha* 'small plain'). Also found are certain descriptive phrases (exs: *Águas Belas* 'beautiful waters', *Belo Horizonte* 'beautiful horizon', *Campo Grande* 'big field'). Many place names of this type later became family names (exs: *Barbosa, Barroso, Cardoso, Dantas*, derived from the plural of *anta* 'dolmen', *Rocha, Pena*, a variant of *penha*).

The political and social history of Portuguese is abundantly reflected in another series of place names. First, we find vestiges of pre-Romance Iberian names, although in Latinized form (exs: *Braga*, Lt *Bracara; Coimbra*, Lt *Conimbriga; Lima; Mondego*, Lt *Mondaecus*). The period of Roman domination contributed such forms as *Castro* 'fortress', parallel to the neuter diminutive plural *Castela* 'fortified front', and *Sagres*, derived from the ablative plural *Sacris* of *sacer* 'sacred'. The latter is in accordance with the custom, traditional in Latin, of designating places by means of an ablative plural with

---

42. The structure of this name is not genuine Tupi. A deliberate association of the ideas of 'flowing' and 'honey', as in the corresponding literary Latin compound form *mellifluus*, is evident. Alencar himself gives the translation *lábios de mel* 'lips of honey'. Note that as a Tupi word the compound is also false in the semantic sense since it involves a connotation of 'honey' peculiar to Western culture.

locative meaning. Another form that was originally an ablative plural in *Chaves*, derived by loss of the first member, from *Aquis Flaviis*, a thermal bath dedicated to the Emperor T. Flavius Vespasianus. From the Christian period one may cite *Santarém* (from Lt *Sancta Irene*), a form obviously motivated by religious devotion. The Visigoths, in turn, left behind a large number of place names based on names of Germanic landowners (exs: *Resende*, *Guimarães*, with the Latin genitive ending). These are more numerous in the north of the country and in Beira since they disappeared from the south during the Arab occupation (Vasconcelos 1931, p. 142). Arabic itself contributed many place names, mostly in the south. In origin these names are usually descriptive and many of them eventually became family names (exs: *Almeida* 'the table', that is, 'the clearing'; *Almada* 'the mine'; *Algarve* 'the west'; *Faro* 'a man's name'). In certain other cases names that were originally Latin underwent a process of remodeling in the mouths of the Arabs. One example is *Beja*, derived from *Pace Iulia* 'Augustan Peace, Pax Romana' by loss of the second element. In the Latin word *pace*, ablative of *pax*, both /k/ and /a/ show developments normal for Arabic words.

In Brazil, a large number of Tupi-based names reveals the vitality this language had in the colony's early history as a general vehicle of communication (exs: *Pará*, *Paraná*, *Pernambuco*, all names of Brazilian states). In addition we find *Piauí* and *Paraíba*, both with the element *y* from /ï/ (high back vowel) 'water'.[43] Other place names, copied either from Portugal (exs: *Bragança*, *Santarém*, *Viseu*) or other European countries (ex: *Friburgo*), show the origin of the first colonizers.

LEXICAL EXPANSION AND RENOVATION

Grammatical Processes

Portuguese, like all living languages, has certain grammatical processes that provide for lexical expansion and renovation on the basis of already existing words. These processes, inherited from Latin, have come to be known as 'compounding' and 'derivation'. The first involves formation of a bond, both semantic and formal, between two

43. The adoption of the Quechua name *Copacabana* for a famous beach in Rio de Janeiro can be traced to religious motivations: there was once a small church dedicated to Our Lady of Copacabana located on the beach. This special cult of Our Lady reached Brazil from Peru at a very early date and was based on the renown for miracles of the Peruvian city of that name.

words, which thus joined constitute a new word with a meaning based on the meanings of the components. Derivation, on the other hand, occurs when the final section of one word is added to another word, creating a new lexical structure with the same basic meaning as the word from which it is derived.

From the phonological point of view, the two combining elements can either be agglutinated, forming a single phonological word, or juxtaposed. In the latter case each constituent remains a separate phonological word with its own stress and its own final vowel.

Compounding

The stereotyped use of two nouns, each with its own inflectional pattern (and therefore morphologically independent), constitutes the weakest type of compounding from the point of view of formal structure. In such cases one can more properly speak of a 'phrase' than of a true 'word'. A good example of a structure of this type is Latin *respublica*, where the noun *res* 'thing' and the adjective *publica* 'public' jointly designate the government of Rome. The noun continues to be declined for case and number and the adjective agrees as expected. Portuguese has stereotyped noun-adjective compounds of exactly the same type (exs: *obra-prima* 'masterpiece', *parede-mestra* 'main wall').[44] In such phrases the noun can be inflected for number, and the adjective will agree, just as it would in any normal phrase consisting of an arbitrary noun and an arbitrary adjective.

The Portuguese names for the days of the week between the Christian and Jewish days of rest have exactly the structure discussed above. The days of rest themselves are, however, designated by the nouns *domingo* 'Sunday' (from Lt *domenicus*, a derivative of *dominus* 'Lord') and *sábado* 'Saturday' (from *sabbatus*, a borrowing from Hebrew *sabbath* 'rest'). The intervening days have the compound forms *segunda-feira* (second-fair) 'Monday', *terça-feira* (third-fair) 'Tuesday', *quarta-feira* (fourth-fair) 'Wednesday', *quinta-feira* (fifth-fair) 'Thursday', and *sexta-feira* (sixth-fair) 'Friday'. Other Romance languages show a completely different type of structure for these five

---

44. When the adjectives *grande* 'great, big' and *recente* 'recent' are used in compounds of this type, the last syllable is omitted and the form thus obtained does not vary with number (exs: *grão-duques* 'grand dukes'; *recém-formados* 'recent graduates'). The phonological form *grão*, which is a reflex of *grã* or *gran* (cf. *pão* 'bread' < *pan*), was eventually felt to be a masculine. It thus came into opposition with a feminine *grã* created on the model *cristão : cristã* 'male Christian' : 'female Christian' (ex: *grão-duque* 'grand duke'; *grã-duquesa* 'grand duchess').

days, preferring the use of a name of a celestial body, sometimes combined with Latin *dies* 'day'. Compare in this respect Portuguese *segunda-feira* with Spanish *lunes*, Italian *lunedì*, French *lundi*, and Romanian *luni*, all of which are derived from Latin *luna* 'moon'.

The basis of this differentiation within the Romance group is the rejection by Portuguese of the designations established in the Roman Empire for weekdays when the division of months into 'weeks' was first introduced. This concept, foreign to Greco-Roman cultural traditions, is of oriental origin. It was the influence of Egypto-Chaldaic astrology that suggested a system of nomenclature based on stars. As might be expected, the Christian Church tried from the very start to eradicate the new system and insisted on the Judaic tradition of numbering the days. Accordingly, the Church, following a traditional Latin pattern, invented a phrase consisting of an ordinal number and the word *feria* 'consecrated day', where the understood meaning is 'consecrated to God'. For sociopolitical reasons this effort was successful only in Portugal, where the Church wielded exceptional influence, primarily through the agency of local priests in an essentially agricultural country.[45]

A variant of the adjective-noun compound structure just discussed is the structure consisting of two juxtaposed nouns (exs: *mestre-escola* 'schoolmaster', *couve-flor* 'cauliflower', *manga-espada* 'a type of mango with a shape that gives the impression of a sword-edge'). In this structure the second element modifies the first but is not subordinated to it by means of the preposition *de* 'of', as is usual in Portuguese for a phrase consisting of two nouns (exs: *estrada de ferro* 'railroad', *mestre de cerimônias* 'master of ceremonies', *oficial de justiça* 'officer of the peace'). This process has become in modern Portuguese the normal way to designate numerous subvarieties of vegetable products (exs: *manga-espada*, 'a type of mango' for the fruit *manga* 'mango'; *couve-flor* 'cauliflower' for the vegetable *couve* 'kale'; *rosa-chá* 'tea-rose' for the flower *rosa* 'rose'). The same structure is also used in the literary language to translate compounds of other languages that make greater use of such expressions (ex: *guerra-relâmpago*, a recent innovation based on German *Blitzkrieg*).[46] There is, however, a tendency to equate the structure under consideration to the noun followed by

45. This explanation is not universally accepted. Direct Judaic influence, in combination with Christian influence, has also been suggested. Mozarabic usage or even the Greco-Christian religious language would be other possibilities. See the summary given by Kuhn (1951, p. 439).

46. But note *jardim de infância* for *Kindergarten*.

adjective pattern, and as a result the second noun agrees with the first in number (exs: *couves-flores, rosas-chás*).

A variant structure of late Vulgar Latin origin, probably inspired by Greek lexical typology, consists of a phrase in which the first element is a verbal form and the second is a noun used as a complement of the first (exs: *guarda-chuva* 'umbrella', *beija-flor* 'humming-bird', *ganha-pão* 'livelihood'). The verb in this structure is stressed on the root and shows a theme vowel in addition to the radical.[47]

The three processes discussed above are productive in modern Portuguese, although there is a natural tendency toward greater unity of form and thus toward the creation of single phonological words through agglutination. When this occurs, the first element of the compound is structurally integrated into the second if the former is a noun, and inflection for number is found only at the end of the word (exs: *planalto - planaltos* 'plateau', *aguardente - aguardentes* 'firewater', *burgomestre - burgomestres* 'burgomaster', *vanglória - vanglórias* 'vanity').

Portuguese, like all other Romance languages, did not maintain the Latin process of compounding that consisted of combining a special thematic variant of a noun with another noun, the latter being the nucleus of the compound (exs: *armiger* 'an armor bearer', *agricola* 'a tiller of fields'). Some of these compounds, however, did manage to enter literary Portuguese as learned loans and, after becoming established in the language, even served as models for compounds based on certain nominal forms. Some of these are parallel to the corresponding Portuguese words, but others are based on purely Latin elements (exs: *-forme*, as in *cordiforme* 'cordiform, in the shape of a heart'; *-gero*, as in *belígero* 'bellicose'; *-fero*, as in *frutífero* 'fructiferous, productive of fruit'). As in Latin this process of compounding requires addition of the vowel *-i-* to the radical of the first element (exs: *cordi-, beli-, fruti-*).

Also of literary origin is a type of compound consisting of two adjectives juxtaposed, the first of which always has a theme in *-o* and is often a variant of the corresponding normal adjectival form. This process is productive for adjectives of nationality and serves to indicate the association of two nations in a given activity (exs: *guerra franco-prussiana* 'Franco-Prussian war'; *tratado anglo-americano*

47. This type of compounding is usually considered to have originated with the use as a true noun of a second-person singular imperative form followed by its complement. If this was actually the origin of such expressions they acquired a new semantic interpretation.

'Anglo-American treaty'; *amizade luso-brasileira* 'Luso-Brazilian friend-ship').

The only truly productive process of compounding in Portuguese is that of 'prefixation'. This process, which encompasses nouns, adjectives, and verbs, was fully developed in Latin, where it originated with 'pre-verbs'. For a full discussion of prefixion in Portuguese see the appropriate section of this chapter.

Derivation

Although derivation was a somewhat limited process in Classical Latin, it was quite highly developed in the Vulgar language. In the latter, the use of suffixes that were already part of the Classical language increased, and new suffixes were introduced by combining old ones or borrowing from other languages, principally Greek. A tendency to favor stressed segments over unstressed ones is quite clear in these developments.

From the structural point of view, suffixes have two properties of special importance. First, there is always a certain amount of variability in the boundary between a suffix and the corresponding radical. In the history of languages, suffixes are often observed to expand by acquiring a phoneme from the radical or to contract by giving up a segment that used to be an initial phoneme. As Bourciez puts it, 'at various times there have been changes in intuitions regarding just which portion of a word was felt to be the suffix' (1930, p. 60). Even within a synchronic description of language, variability of this type can occur in a given suffix, causing it to differ in the way it combines with other elements. The second property of structural significance is integration of a theme vowel into a suffix. As a result of this process, the derived word acquires a fixed theme independent of the word from which it is derived (exs: *artista* 'artist', *pianista* 'pianist', *harpista* 'harpist', all with theme in -*a;* derived from *arte* 'art' with theme in -*e*, *piano* 'piano' with theme in -*o*, and *harpa* 'harp' with theme in -*a*, respectively). This circumstance leads us to posit the existence of a nucleus within the segment that constitutes the suffix, and we view this as the central part of the suffix. The nucleus is then considered to show thematic variation (exs: -*ez* in *palidez* 'paleness', -*eza* in *tristeza* 'sadness'). In derived words it is the suffix together with its theme vowel that is inflected.

When a suffix is joined to a simple word the theme vowel of the latter may be elided by the general morphophonemic rule that drops an unstressed vowel before another vowel (ex: *lobinho* 'little wolf' from *lôbo* 'wolf'). In other cases this vowel is reduced and becomes a mere 'connecting vowel' between the radical and the initial vowel of the suffix (ex: *amenidade* 'amenity', from *ameno* + *dade* with reduction of *-o* to *-i-*). Of course, the above remarks apply only to agglutination; in juxtaposition, as for example with the suffix *-zinho*, a phrase is created, and both the suffix and the phonological word that corresponds to a simple word are inflected (ex: *lôbazinha* 'little she-wolf', with the feminine desinence on both *lôba* and *-zinha*).[48]

Finally, we reach certain suffixes that show divergence in form caused by the differences between popular, learned, and semi-learned developments. The basis for this phenomenon is the survival *as a derivative* in Portuguese of a Latin derivative both in the popular form, altered by phonetic laws, and the learned form, without such alterations. In either case the suffix—altered and popular or unaltered and learned—can be used in Portuguese. Both occur indifferently with popular and learned radicals.

The productivity of a given suffix within the grammar of Portuguese is a function of its prominence in derived words of Latin origin or in borrowed words of other origins. Putting the same thing in another way, we may say that certain derived words serve as a model for the creation of new words, giving the language new processes of suffixation by generalization in use of their final element. When this does not occur, any suffixes that may be deduced by analysis of existing derived words are not productive and do not function in grammar as a means of creating lexical items.

SUFFIXES

Derivation in Nouns and Adjectives

Modern Portuguese possesses a series of very productive suffixes that may be used, within certain functional and semantic areas, to derive both adjectives and nouns. The following suffixes derive adjectives from previously existing nouns:

-OS (*o*, *a*) < Lt *-ōs(u-)* (ex: *ardiloso* 'crafty' from *ardil* 'cunning'). This suffix is often used to create an adjective based on a noun that is itself derived by the suffix *-dad(e)* from a simple adjective (ex:

48. In the plural the first part of such structures obeys the normal morphophonemic rules of plural formation, but the desinence *-s* is somewhat attenuated in the oral language and is never written (exs: *florezinhas* 'little flowers'; *animaizinhos* 'little animals').

bondoso 'good-natured'[49] from *bondade* 'goodness', based on *bom* 'good').

-UD(o, a) < VLt *-ūt(u-)*, by extension of the perfect particle suffix (ex: *pontudo* 'pointed' from *ponta* 'point'. This suffix often contains the category 'excessive', giving it a pejorative connotation (exs: *ossudo* 'big-boned' from *ôsso* 'bone', *bochechudo* 'blub-cheeked' from *bochecha* 'cheek', *cabeçudo* 'big-headed' from *cabeça* 'head').

-IC(o, a) < Lt *-ĭc(u-)*, borrowed from Greek and carried to Portuguese through learned loans from literary Latin (exs: *melancólico* 'melancholic', *simbólico* 'symbolic'). As an unstressed suffix it is productive only in scientific language (ex: *pérmico*, and also *permiano*, 'Permian, a geological period' from *Perm* 'Perm, a former province of Russia').

-ÁTIC(o, a) < Lt *-atic(u-)*. Also of learned origin, by way of literary Latin (exs: *asiático* 'Asian', *lunático* 'lunatic').[50] In a few new formations this suffix has become popular (ex: *asnático* 'asinine' from *asno* 'ass').

Derivation of adjectives from verbs is also possible, and in this case the vowel of the verbal theme is maintained. The following suffixes are typical:

-VEL < Lt *-bĭl(e-)* (exs: *cobrável* 'collectible' from *cobrar* 'to collect', *vendível* 'saleable' from *vender* 'to sell', *suprível* 'suppliable' from *suprir* 'to supply'). The latter two examples show the theme vowel *-i* of the second and third conjugations. The second form *vendível* is semantically distinct from *vendável*.[51] In classical Portuguese the learned variant *-bil* was introduced and is still used as the basic form for new derivatives of adjective in *-vel* (ex: *exequibilidade* 'feasibility' from *exequível* 'feasible').

Popular *-DIÇ(o, a)* and learned *-TICI(o, a)*, from Lt *-ici(u-)* by integration of a consonant from the suffix *-t(u-)*[52] (exs: *abafadiço* 'stuffy' from *abafar* 'to stifle', *acomodadiço* 'accommodating' from *acomodar* 'to accommodate').

49. Here the syllable *-da-* is omitted from the suffix in accordance with a general morphophonemic rule of Portuguese known as 'haplology'. This rule, often confused with a 'phonetic law', requires the omission of the initial syllable of the second member of a compound if the first ends in the same consonant.

50. In the archaic language the popular form *-ádego* is sometimes found. See n. 14.

51. The latter can be explained as a derivative of the nominal form *venda* 'sale' and means 'that which sells easily'.

52. This suffix occurred both in the supine, which was a type of infinitive, and in the perfect participle.

Popular -*DI*(*o, a*) and learned -*TIV*(*o, a*), from Lt -*īu*(*u*-) by integration of a consonant from the suffix -*t*(*u*-) (exs: *escorregadio* 'slippery' from *escorregar* 'to slip'; *pensativo* 'pensive' from *pensar* 'to think').

Alongside suffixes like the ones discussed above, which create words that are essentially adjectival in nature, still other suffixes form essentially nominal words. The latter, however, may be used as adjectives in certain contexts. Derivatives of this type are principally nouns denoting people of a given nationality or other regional origin and nouns denoting people characterized by a given social activity. Examples of the first kind are:

Popular -*ÊS*(. . . , -*a*) and learned -*ENS*(*e*), from Lt -*ens*(*e*-) (exs: *burguês* 'villager' from *burgo* 'village', *francês* 'French' from *França* 'France', *vienense* 'Viennese' from *Viena* 'Vienna'). Feminine inflections did not become established in the popular form until the modern period. In accordance with the general morphology of -*e* theme adjectives, such inflections were never extended to three forms that may be used *only* as adjectives (*cortês* 'courteous', as in *uma dama cortês* 'a courteous lady'; *montês* 'of the mountains', as in *uma cabra montês* 'a mountain goat'; *pedrês* 'spotted with black and white', as in *uma galinha pedrês* 'a mottled hen'). The most productive form in Brazilian Portuguese is the learned one, used for all sorts of adjectives of origin (exs: *piauiense* from *Piauí*, a Tupi form used as the name of a state; *niteroiense* from *Nitreói*, a Tupi form used as the name of a city; *catarinense* from *Santa Catarina*, the name of a state).

Popular -*ÃO*[53] and learned -*AN*(*o, a*). The popular form is of very limited productivity in modern Portuguese, while the learned one, on the contrary, is very productive in the formation of adjectives of origin (exs: *petropolitano* from *Petrópolis*, the name of a Brazilian city; *goiano* from *Goiás*, a Tupi form used as the name of a state). Variant forms with alternate stressed vowels were first associated with this suffix in Latin and continue to be so associated in Portuguese. Thus we find -*EN*(*o, a*), from a Latin form with long -*ē*-, and -*IN*(*o, a*), with long -*ī*- in Latin (ex: *agareno* 'descendant of Agar' from *Agar*, a term used for 'Arabic'). Another variant -*IAN*(*o, a*) evolved from derivative forms in which a vowel of the radical, in this case -*i*-, was integrated into the suffix (exs: *italiano* 'Italian' from *Itália* 'Italy', *permiano* 'Permian' from *Perm* 'Perm'). Derivatives based on the

---

53. The feminine is either -*ã* or -*oa* (exs: *coimbrão* : *coimbrã* 'native to Coimbra'; *beirão* : *beiroa* 'native to Beira').

name of a famous person, used to designate a quality associated with that person, are often of this class (ex: *wagneriano* 'Wagnerian' from *Wagner*).[54]

Examples of the second type are:

-IST(a) from Lt *-ist(a-)*, itself borrowed from Greek. Usually used to derive nouns connected with artistic or scientific activities (exs: *violinista* 'violinist', *cientista* 'scientist', *psicologista*, alongside *psicólogo*, 'psychologist'). Also used in nouns and adjectives of origin (ex: *campista*, from the Brazilian city *Campos*). A nonproductive variant is *IT(a)* (exs: *jesuíta* 'Jesuit', *cenobita* 'cenobite' from *cenóbio* 'cenoby, convent').

Popular *-EIR(o, a)* and learned *-ARI(o, a)*, from Lt *-ari(u-)*, which was greatly extended in Vulgar Latin on the model of certain nouns like *operarius* and *tabernarius* (found in Cicero). It is used to form adjectives (exs: *verdadeiro* 'true' from *verdade* 'truth', *diário* 'daily' from *dia* 'day') and, either as an adjective or as a noun, characterizes people on the basis of a given social activity (exs: *obreiro* and *operário*, both for 'worker', the first of popular origin and the second of learned origin). In Brazilian Portuguese the learned form is systematically used for salaried professionals (exs: *comerciário* 'tradesman' for someone employed in *comércio* 'trade'; *securitário* 'insurance salesman', a learned form derived from Lt *securitas*, for someone employed by a *companhia de seguros sociais* 'an insurance company'; *bancário* 'teller' for someone employed by a *banco* 'bank'). The last example contrasts with *banqueiro* 'banker, someone who owns or directs a bank'.

As we have already seen, many suffixes, including the one just discussed, may be used to derive nouns from other nouns. In this process the most varied types of relations come into play. In particular, we note:

-EIR(o) or *-EIR(A)* (obligatorily fixed in one of the genders). Among its uses are: indication of a tree by reference to its fruit (exs: *pitangueira* 'Surinam cherry tree' from *pitanga* 'Surinam cherry', *cajueiro* 'cashew tree' from *caju* 'cashew'); indication of a container by reference to its contents (*mantegueira* 'butter dish' from *manteiga* 'butter', *açucareiro* 'sugar bowl' from *açúcar* 'sugar'); indication of a set by reference to its members (*pedreira* 'quarry', from *pedra* 'stone'), and so on. The learned form *-ÁRI(o)* or *-ÁRI(A)* also appears

54. This structure is also found in Latin (ex: *ciceronianus*, derived from *Cicero, Ciceronis*).

occasionally (exs: *fichário* 'card file'[55] from *ficha* 'file card'; *mobiliária* 'furniture' from *mobília*[56]).

-AD(A) from Lt *-at(a)*, the suffix of the perfect participle in the first conjugation, used in Vulgar Latin to derive nouns. Its modern uses include: indication of an action by reference to a means or instrument (exs: *facada* 'stab' from *faca* 'knife'; *punhalada* 'stab' from *punhal* 'dagger'); indication of a collective set (*boiada* 'herd of cattle' from *boi* 'ox'), occasionally with a pejorative connotation (ex: *papelada* 'pile of papers' from *papel* 'paper'); and, finally, indication of a product obtained from a fruit (exs: *marmelada* 'quince marmalade' from *marmelo* 'quince'; *cajuada* 'soft drink made of cashew juice' from *caju* 'cashew').

-AL from Lt *-al(e)*, which acquired a greatly expanded range of uses in Vulgar Latin. This suffix is used for derivation of adjectives from nouns (ex: *formal* 'formal' from *forma* 'form') or adjectives from adjectives (ex: *celestial* from *celeste*, both meaning 'celestial'). In addition it also indicates a set as a function of its members, particularly in connection with areas of land (exs: *areal* 'beach, sandy area' from *areia* 'sand'; *bananal* 'banana grove or plantation' from *banana* 'banana'). A variant form *-ZAL*, which evolved from forms with radical in *-z* (exs: *arrozal* 'ricefield' from *arroz* 'rice'), is used particularly for radicals ending in a stressed vowel (ex: *cafèzal* 'coffee plantation' from *café* 'coffee').

-AGEM from French and Provençal *-age*.[57] The original Latin suffix *-ātic(u)* gives learned Portuguese *-ÁTIC(U)* (ex: *viático* 'viaticum', a doublet of *viagem* 'trip' used in religious terminology for Holy Communion given to a sick person who cannot leave his house). This suffix is also used, as we have seen, to derive adjectives.

-ARI(A) from VLt *-ari(a)*, with stressed /i/. The stress shift was

55. In Portugal *ficheiro* is used in the sense of Brazilian *fichário*, a situation that is quite common for variants of a given suffix.

56. This form is itself a derivative of the latinism *mobil*, Ptg *móvel* 'mobile', applied to a certain type of *bens móveis* 'mobile goods' that are found in the interior of a house. An older and more popular synonym is *traste*, from the Catalan *trast* (< Lt *trastru-* 'a type of bench').

57. The true popular Portuguese form is *-ádego* (see n. 7, above). The French form and its analogue in Provençal spread at an early date to Spanish (*-aje*) and to Portuguese (*-agem*). In the latter, contamination by the ending *-agem* of semi-learned words like *imagem* 'image' (< Lt *imagine-*) explains the appearance of a nasal and the feminine gender. The *-agem* ending also appears occasionally in adjectives (ex: *selvagem* 'savage'). For a good study of this matter see Levy (1965, 1967).

caused by combination of -*ari*(*u*) with the Greek suffix -*ĭa*, in place of Latin -*ĭa*. An equally ancient variant form is -*ERI*(*A*). Apparently this suffix was first used in Gaul, where the form *glanderia* is documented in the sixth century. It denotes relations of various semantic types. The most common of these in modern Portuguese are the relation between a product and the place where it is made or sold (ex: *papelaria* 'stationery store' from *papel* 'paper') and the relation between a professional man and the place where he carries out his profession (ex: *alfaiataria* 'tailor's shop' from *alfaiate* 'tailor').

Nouns indicating the agent of a verbal process may be derived from verbs by means of the suffix -*DOR* (. . . , -*a*), which evolved from Lt -*tor*(*e*), a Vulgar combination of the suffixes -*t*(*u*) and -*or*(*e*). In Portuguese the verbal theme vowel is maintained under derivation (exs: *pescador* 'fisher' from *pescar* 'to fish', *varredor* 'sweeper' from *varrer* 'to sweep', *abridor* 'opener' from *abrir* 'to open'). The variant -*OR* (. . . , -*a*), from unchanged Lt -*or*(*e*-), is not productive (ex: *professor* 'professor', from Lt *professore*-, relatable in the descriptive sense to *professar*).

The place of an action is indicated by the suffixes -*DOUR*(*o*) (popular) or -*TORI*(*o*) (learned), derived historically from Lt -*tori*(*u*) by integration of a consonant from the suffix *t*(*u*-) into the suffix -*ori*(*u*-) (exs: *matadouro* 'slaughterhouse' from *matar* 'to kill', *lavatório* 'washroom' from *lavar* 'to wash', *bebedouro* 'drinking place' from *beber* 'to drink', *dormitório* 'bedroom' from *dormir* 'to sleep').

Abstract Nouns

Latin and the Romance languages both have a particular category consisting of nouns that correspond structurally to nouns of 'verbal processes' or 'qualities', the latter logically expressed in adjectives. Such nouns are traditionally called 'abstract' to indicate that they designate a mental abstraction that does not correspond to any concrete thing in the extralinguistic universe. In general, abstract nouns and adjectives are related to the corresponding verb as a derivative is to a simple form. Classical Latin itself had productive suffixes for the derivation of abstracts. The following are of particular importance in Portuguese for the derivation of nouns of quality from adjectives:

-*DAD*(*e*) from Lt -*tat*(*e*-), which was quite common in Vulgar Latin. For adjectives with theme in -*o* the thematic vowel, reduced to -*i*-, acts as a connecting vowel between the radical and the suffix (ex:

amenidade 'amenity' from *ameno* 'pleasant'). Since a morphophonemic rule of this type was also part of Latin grammar, the connecting vowel *-i-* sometimes appears in nouns that correspond in Portuguese to adjectives ending with *-l*. The reason for this is that such adjectives had a phonetic *-e* in Latin and this vowel was, of course, reduced (exs: *facilidade* 'facility' from *fácil* 'easy', but *crueldade* 'cruelty' from *cruel* 'cruel' and *lealdade* 'loyalty' from *leal* 'loyal'). For adjectives ending in *-io*, the connecting vowel is *-e-*, contrasting with *-i-* for the cases discussed above (exs: *seriedade* 'seriousness' from *sério* 'serious', *sobriedade* 'soberness' from *sóbrio* 'serious').

-UR(a) from Lt *-ūr(a-)* (ex: *brancura* 'whiteness' from *branco* 'white').

-EZ, *-EZ(a)* from Lt *-ĭti(e-)* *-ĭti(a-)*, much used in Vulgar Latin (exs: *palidez* 'paleness' from *pálido* 'pale', *magreza* 'thinness' from *magro* 'thin'). Variant forms include semi-learned *-IC(e)*[58] and fully learned *-ICI(e)*, both of which are very productive (exs: *tolice* 'foolishness' from *tolo* 'foolish', *calvície* 'baldness' from *calvo* 'bald').

Popular *-DÃO*, semilearned *-TUD(e)* from Lt *-tudĭn(e)* (exs: *escuridão* 'darkness' from *escuro* 'dark', *amplitude* 'vastness' from *amplo* 'vast').

-I(a) from VLt *-ī(a-)*, borrowed from Greek as a replacement for the Classical Latin unstressed suffix *-ĭa* (ex: *valentia* 'valor' from *valente* 'valiant'). The unstressed version survives only in *-ÂNCI(a)*, *-ÊNCI(a)*, a combination of *-ia* with the present participle suffix *-ante*, *-ente* (exs: *arrogância* 'arrogance' from *arrogante* 'arrogant', *clemência* 'clemency' from *clemente* 'clement'.

-ISM(o) from Vulgar Latin *-ism(u-)*, borrowed from Greek and much used in Christian Latin. The main application of this suffix was, and continues to be, for the purpose of expressing 'professions of faith'. In such cases it is attached to adjectives (ex: *cristianismo* 'Christianity' from *cristianu-*, the latter today represented by *cristão*, a new form derived from *Cristo* by addition of the popular suffix *-ão*). If the adjective is of Greek origin and ends in *-ic(o)* from *-ĭcu-*, this element is lost upon addition of *-ismo* (ex: *simbolismo* 'symbolism' from *simbólico* 'symbolic'). One indication of the productivity of this suffix in Brazilian Portuguese is its use in the derivation of nouns from initials of political parties. Nouns of this type denote the political ideology of the party in question (ex: *pessedismo* from *PSD*, the initials

58. Semi-learned *-iça* from *-itia* appears in *justiça* 'justice', which came straight from Latin.

of *Partido Social Democrático*). Similarly, the suffix is often used in derivations from the name of a philosopher, politician, or artist. In this case the derivative denotes the ideas associated with that person (exs: *comtismo* from Auguste *Comte; malarismo* from Stéphane *Mallarmé; miguelismo* from D. *Miguel,* a king of Portugal).

For derivation of abstract nouns of action from verbs the following three suffixes are of prime importance:

-MENT(o) from Lt *-ment(u-)* (exs: *julgamento* 'judgment' from *julgar* 'to judge', *cozimento* 'cooking' from *cozer* 'to cook').

-ÇÃO from Lt *-tiōn(e-)*, evolved from the suffix *-iōn(e-)* by integration of a consonant from the suffix *-t(u-)* (exs: *consolação* 'consolation' from *consolar* 'to console', *perdição* 'perdition' from *perder* 'to lose', *fundição* 'fusion' from *fundir* 'to fuse'). The variant *-ão*, from Lt *-ōn(e-)* is not productive (ex: *expressão* 'expression' from *expressar* 'to express').

-DUR(a) from Lt *-tūr(a-)* by combination of a consonant from the suffix *-t(u-)* with *-ūr(a-)*, which by itself is not productive in the derivation of abstract nouns of action (exs: *armadura*[59] from *armar* 'to arm', *benzedura* 'benediction' from *benzer* 'to bless', *urdidura* 'intrigue' from *urdir* 'to intrigue').

Notice that nouns of action are not always derived by suffixation. A different structure, widely used in Vulgar Latin, developed on the model of certain forms that already existed in Classical Latin. This structure consists of a verbal radical followed by a thematic vowel *-a*, *-o*, or *-e* (exs: *consolar* 'to console' : *consôlo* 'consolation', *comprar* 'to purchase' : *compra* 'a purchase', *atacar* 'to attack' : *ataque* 'an attack'). Some Portuguese derivatives of this type are of Latin origin (exs: *fugir* 'to flee' : *fuga* 'flight' from Lt *fūgĕre* : *fūga; provar* 'to prove' : *prova* 'proof' from Lt *probare* : *proba*). Another process used is nominalization, in the feminine, of a perfect participle (exs: *chegada* 'arrival' from *chegar* 'to arrive', *vinda* 'coming' from *vir* 'to come'). The second process is also of Latin origin, but it happens that often phonetic evolution caused Latin forms of this type to enter the first pattern (ex: *perder* 'to lose' : *perda* 'loss', the latter form evolved from Lt *perdĭta, perdĕre*). Finally, we also find the infinitive used as a noun. In this usage infinitives can take the nominal plural ending *-es* and may be preceded by an article (ex: *o falar* 'speaking', *os falares de uma língua* 'the dialects of a language').

59. This word became a concrete noun and took on the meaning 'armament of a medieval knight'.

In the case of nouns of quality, there is a parallel process that consists of the use as a noun of an adjective in the masculine singular thematic form. Historically, this pattern is related to the use in Latin of a neuter adjective as an abstract noun (ex: *o belo* instead of *a beleza* 'beauty').

Degrees

Suffixal derivation is employed in order to indicate a greater or lesser degree, dimension, or intensity of a derivative noun or adjective with respect to the corresponding simple form. In the case of nouns, this process generates the categories 'augmentative' and 'diminutive', which are put into opposition with a degree considered normal by means of specific suffixes.

Formation of diminutives through suffixation was common in Latin, but the principal diminutive suffix *-ŭlu-* (variant *-cŭlu-*) was slowly abandoned in the Vulgar language because it was unstressed. When it survives in Portuguese it no longer has diminutive force and is integrated into the radical, creating a new single word that replaces the original one. Furthermore, such words acquired penultimate stress through fall of the post-tonic penult (ex: *apicŭla* > *apecla* > *abelha* 'bee', instead of *apis*). The most important replacement for *-ŭlu-* was *-IN(u-)*, a suffix that acquired diminutive value by generalization from certain specific instances (ex: *collina*, from *collis* 'hill'). Another suffix of the same type was *-ELL(u-)* (ex: *vitellu-*, instead of *vitŭlu-* 'calf', > It *vitello*, from which Portuguese *vitelo* is probably borrowed). In Vulgar Latin we also find the diminutive suffix *-ITT(u-, a-)*, which seems to have been borrowed from Greek (ex: *melitta*, instead of *melissa* 'bee'), and is first attested with people's names (exs: *Julitta, Salvittus*). Although the suffix originally had short *-ĭ-*, a variant with *-ī-* was adopted in the Iberian Peninsula. All three suffixes were sometimes used merely to indicate affection or care, as was also the case with *-ŭlu-* and *-cŭlu-* in Latin (see Alonso 1951, pp. 195ss).

The two principal diminutive suffixes in Portuguese are:

-INH(o, a) from VLt *-in(u-, a-)*. Nearly unrestricted in use (exs: *livrinho* 'little book', *casinha* 'little house').

-IT(o, a) from VLt *-itt(u-, a-)*. Infrequent in Brazilian Portuguese (ex: *boquita* 'little mouth' from *bôca* 'mouth'). Both diminutive suffixes have variants with initial *-z-*. Originally the *-z-* occurred as the final consonant of certain radicals (ex: *rapazinho, rapazito* 'little boy' from

rapaz 'boy'), but in modern Portuguese the variant form is usually preferred. In this case the suffix is juxtaposed to a simple word to form a phrase in which both the latter and the former are inflected (exs: *lobozinho* 'little wolf', *lobazinha* 'little she-wolf').

The forms -*ET*(*o, a*) and -*ET*(*e*) are loans from Italian or French (Fr -*et* > Ptg -*ete*), both of which adopted the Latin variant with short -*ĭ*-. Another loan from French is -*OT*(*e*), from the Latin variant -*ott*(*u*-, *a*-) (exs: *lembrete* 'memorandum', *saleta* 'sitting-room', *rapazote* 'little boy'). Finally we mention in passing the two suffixes -*OL*(*a*) (ex: *rapazola* 'childish person') and -*UCH*(*o*) (ex: *papelucho* 'scrap of paper'), both of which have predominantly pejorative connotations.[60]

The augmentative developed in Vulgar Latin through use of certain word endings such as -*ōn*(*e*-), -*ace*(*u*-, *a*-), and *astr*(*u*-, *a*-) for this purpose. Augmentatives differ from diminutives in both frequency and functional value. They are, in fact, of only occasional use and always emphasize a strongly pejorative meaning. One can state quite simply that the augmentative occurs only in affective, or more specifically, abusive, language. The three augmentative suffixes of Vulgar Latin correspond in Portuguese to:

-*ÃO*, fem. -*ON*(*a*) (ex: *valentão, valentona* 'ruffian'). This is, so to speak, the basic augmentative suffix and can even be used to derive nouns from verbs (ex: *brigão* 'brawler' from *brigar* 'to fight'). There is also a whole series of variants that result from integration into the suffix of certain parts of radicals or other suffixes (exs: -*ALHÃO* in *grandalhão* 'enormous person', -*ARRÃO* in *santarrão* 'falsely sancti-monious person, bigot', *pedinchão* 'constant beggar', *homenzarrão* 'huge man, big shot').

-*AÇ*(*o, a*) (ex: *barbaças* 'man with a huge beard' from *barba* 'beard').

-*ASTR*(*o, a*) (ex: *poetastro* 'charlatan poet').

The suffix -*ARR*(*a*) (ex: *bocarra* 'big mouth' from *bôca* 'mouth') is of Basque origin. Also found is -*ACH*(*o, a*), which in the descriptive sense is a variant of *AÇ*(*o, a*) but is historically a reflex of endings in -*ascŭlu*-, with the diminutive -*ŭl*(*u*-) (ex: *vulgacho* 'rabble' from *vulgo* 'the common people').

A vestige of inflection for degree in adjectives can be found in the 'superlative absolute' suffix -*ISSIM*(*o, a*) and its variant -*IM*(*o, a*) (before /l/ or /r/), which was carried along to the modern language through loans from literary Latin by classical Portuguese. These

---

60. The suffix -*ola* is a French loan and -*ucho* comes from -*cŭlu*- integrated into a radical in -*us*-, whence -*uscŭlu*-.

inflections functioned quite regularly in Latin but vanished in Portuguese. It is true, nonetheless, that to a certain extent one can find innovations like *pobríssimo* 'very poor' from *pobre* 'poor' (or even *coisíssima* in an intense negation like *coisíssima nenhuma* 'nothing at all'). From *-IM(o, a)* combined with radicals in /r/ there evolved in popular modern Portuguese a pejorative suffix *-érrimo* (exs: *grandérrimo* 'too large', *infamérrimo* 'very infamous').

Derivation of Verbs

The most general process for derivation of verbs from nouns is simply addition of verbal inflections to a noun (ex: *muro* 'wall'; *murar* 'to wall'). The use of the suffix *-izar* is another process of the same type:

-IZ(ar), a borrowing from Greek found especially in Christian Latin. Because of its rarity in both the archaic and the classical languages, this suffix does not seem to have reached Portuguese directly, and its productivity in the modern language is, in any case, closely connected with an influx of French items. Not infrequently it is associated with adjectives in *-ic(o)*, the verb being derived by omission of the adjectival suffix (exs: *civilizar* 'to civilize' from *civil* 'civil', *harmonizar* 'harmonize' from *harmônico* 'harmonic').

A few verbs derived from nouns show both a verbal inflection and one of the prefixes *en-* (prep *em* 'in') or *a-* (prep *a* 'to') (exs: *acalmar* 'to calm' from *calmo* 'calm', *embandeirar* 'to adorn with a flag'[61] from *bandeira* 'flag').

Certain aspectual categories not normally associated with Portuguese verbal inflections are found in verbs derived by suffixation. The most important of these aspects are listed below:

1. *Frequentative* or *iterative*, that is, indication of an indefinitely repeating process:

-E(ar) from VLt *-ĭdi(are)*, which evolved from the popular pronunciation of the Greek suffix *-izz(are)*. In cultured speech the same suffix gave *-iz(ar)* (ex: *ondear* 'to undulate' from *onda* 'wave').

-EJ(ar) from VLt *-ĭdi(are)*, with /dia/ diphthongized to /dịa/, as in *hodie* > *hoje* 'today' (ex: *gotejar* 'to drip' from *gota* 'drop').

2. *Inchoative* aspect, that is, indication of the beginning of a process.

-EC(er), sometimes spelled *-ESC(er)*,[62] from Lt *-sc(ere)*, where *-sc-* itself was an inchoative suffix. Usually accompanied by *en-* or *a-*

61. Traditionally called a 'parasynthetic derivative'.

62. The official orthography frivolously adopts *-escer* when the word comes directly from Latin.

(exs: *entardecer* 'to grow late' from *tarde* 'late', *amanhecer* 'to dawn' from *manhã* 'morning').

Finally, we note in passing that the suffix *-IT*(*ar*) (ex: *saltitar* 'to hop') has a diminutive connotation through its relation to the diminutive suffix *-IT*(*o, a*).

Prefixion

We have already seen that in Latin a system of 'prefixes' evolved from the 'pre-verbs', or adverbial particles. This development led to the establishment within the structure of Latin of an important process for the creation of compound words from 'simple' words. Since prefixes are in essence adverbial particles, they modify the basic meaning of such compounds by contributing an adverbial component (ex: *exire* 'to go out' from *ire* 'to go').

Latin prefixes formed a system symmetric to that of the prepositions—a given particle, in principle, could either appear autonomously or integrated into a verb. In the first case it functioned as a preposition, relating a noun to a verb, and in the second as a prefix, creating a new word (ex: *ire ex Epheso* 'to go out of Ephesus', *exire* 'to go out'). We have already seen, however, that the actual number of distinct prepositions diminished significantly in Vulgar Latin and therefore also in Portuguese. This development broke the parallelism between prepositions and prefixes that had been so perfect in Latin. In Portuguese many particles quite simply vanish as prepositions while continuing to function as prefixes, usually in a learned shape since, for the most part, they were gleaned from words borrowed by classical Portuguese from literary Latin. In certain other learned words, however, a divergent form based on a Portuguese preposition of popular origin is found in the role of a prefix. In still other instances, a corresponding preposition was lacking even in Latin. This occurred because several prefixes had evolved from Indo-European adverbial particles that are found in Latin only as pre-verbs.

In summary, we see that Portuguese prefixion is based on three groups of particles: a) those that also function as prepositions; b) those that are learned variants of prepositions; and c) those that are prefixes exclusively. From the phonological point of view, a compound word formed by prefixion can be either agglutinated or juxtaposed. In the latter type prefixes have a secondary stress and their vowels undergo the normal treatment for unstressed final position if the prefix contains more than one syllable. In the written language juxta-position is sometimes indicated by separating the prefix from the simple word by a hyphen, but this usage is rather inconsistent. Examples:

Group a

A-. Prep *a* 'to' (exs: *apor* 'to attach'; *acalmar* 'to calm', para-synthetic).

ANTE-. Prep *ante* 'before' (exs: *antebraço* 'forearm', juxtaposition; *antepor* 'to put before, prefer').

EN-. Prep *em* 'in' (exs: *enraizar* 'to take root'; *embandeirar* 'to adorn with a flag', parasynthetic).

CON-. Prep *com* 'with' (ex: *conviver* 'to live together'). Variant *co-* before a liquid or a vowel (exs: *colaborar* 'to collaborate'; *corroer* 'to corrode', *coagir* 'to coerce').

CONTRA-. Prep *contra* 'against' (ex: *contradizer* 'to contradict').

DE-. Prep *de* 'down from', that is, the Latin meaning of the preposi-tion (ex: *depor* 'to put down').

ENTRE-. Prep *entre* 'between' (ex: *entrever* 'to catch sight of').

SO-. Prep *sob*, arc *so* 'under' (ex: *sobraçar* 'to put under one's arm').

SOBRE-. Prep *sôbre* 'over' (ex: *sobrescrito* 'envelope').

MENOS-. Adv *menos* 'less' (ex: *menosprezar* 'to underrate, scorn').

Group b

AD-. Lt prep *ad*, Ptg *a* 'to' (ex: *adjungir* 'to adjoin').

IN-. Lt prep *in*, Ptg *em* 'in' (ex: *incorrer* 'to incur'). Variant: *i-* before a nasal or a liquid (exs: *ilustrar* 'to illustrate', *irromper* 'to rush in').

INTER-. Lt prep *inter*, Ptg *entre* 'between' (ex: *intervir* 'to inter-vene').

PRO-. Lt prep *pro*, 'before, in front of', Ptg *por* 'at, through' (ex: *propor* 'to propose').

SUB-. Lt prep *sub*, Ptg *sob* 'under' (ex: *submeter* 'to submit'). Variant: *su-* before /p/ or /b/ (ex: *supor* 'to suppose').

SUPER-. Lt prep *super*, Ptg *sôbre* 'over' (ex: *superpor* 'to super-impose').

Group c

AB-. Lt prep *ab* 'from' (ex: *absorver* 'absorb'). Variant: *abs-*, before /t/ (ex: *abster-se* 'to abstain').

BIS-. Lt adv *bis* 'twice' (ex: *bisavô* 'great-grandfather'). Variant: *bi-* before a consonant (ex: *bidestro* 'bidexterous').

CIRCUN-. Lt prep *circum* 'around, near' (ex: *circunvalar* 'to enclose with a rampart').

DES-. This form is a combination of the prepositions *de* and *ex* that developed in Lusitanian Romance. It has a negative value and is of great productivity in the modern language (exs: *desfazer* 'to undo, demolish', *desigual* 'unequal', *desunião* 'disunion, separation').[63]

EX- /es/. Lt prep *ex* 'from'. This prefix is very productive in the modern language to indicate 'that which has ceased existing'. It is juxtaposed to the simple word (ex: *ex-posição* 'former position', *ex-presidente* 'former president'). With the meaning 'outside of' it forms compounds by agglutination, but these are less frequent (ex: *exposição* 'exposition'). In verbs derived from nouns it emphasizes intensity of movement and is spelled *es-* (exs: *esforçar* 'to strengthen', *espernear* 'to kick one's legs', *esburacar* 'to pierce with holes'. The variant *e-*, which is the same as that of the Latin preposition before a consonant, appears in words that existed in Latin (exs: *emigrar* 'to emigrate', *elaborar* 'to elaborate').

EXTRA-. Lt prep *extra*, related to *ex* 'from' (ex: *extravasar* 'to extravasate, flow out of a vessel').

IN-. A Lt prefix for 'negation' homonymous with the prefix and preposition *in* and exhibiting the same morphophonemic patterns (exs: *inapto* 'inapt', *irreal* 'unreal', *ilegal* 'illegal', *imaturo* 'immature').

INTRA-. Lt prep, related to the preposition *in* 'within' (ex: *intravenoso* 'intravenous').

INTRO-. Lt prefix denoting the notion 'inward', related to the preposition *in* (ex: *intrometer-se* 'to interfere').

INFRA-. Lt prep *infra* 'below', equivalent to *sub*. In scientific terminology this prefix is now productive, creating many juxtaposed compounds (ex: *infravermelho* 'infrared').

JUSTA-. Lt prep *iuxta* 'near by' (ex: *justalinear* 'line by line').

PER-. Lt prep *per* 'through' (ex: *perpassar* 'to pass through or by').

PRE-. Lt prep *prae* 'before' (ex: *prever* 'to foresee'). This prefix is especially productive in the contemporary literary language, where it is used in juxtaposition and therefore maintains an open /ę/. It indicates a phase previous to another phase that is taken as a point

---

63. There is a certain amount of confusion with *dis-*, a common Latin prefix for 'separation'.

of reference (exs: *pré-romântico* 'pre-romantic', *pré-histórico* 'prehistoric', *pré-história* 'prehistory').

RE-. Lt prefix indicating 'repetition'. It is extremely productive in the formation of verbs (exs: *retomar* 'to retake, recover', *reconsiderar* 'to reconsider'). In certain instances *re*- indicates a movement opposite to that of the simple word (ex: *reação* 'reaction').

RETRO-. Lt prefix related to *re*- meaning 'backward movement' (ex: *retroagir* 'to retroact').

SUPRA-. Lt prep *supra* 'above', related to *super* (ex: *supracitar* 'to mention earlier'). Also used in the modern literary language as an adverb (ex: *a frase supra* 'the above sentence').

TRANS-. Lt prep *trans* 'through' (ex: *trans-atlântico* 'transatlantic'). The old variants *tras-* and *tres-* are no longer productive (exs: *trasmudar* 'to transmute', *trespassar* 'to trespass').

ULTRA-. Lt adverb meaning 'beyond', of the same pattern as *intra, infra, supra* (ex: *ultramar* 'overseas').

VICE-. Adverbialized ablative of the noun *uice*, from which evolved Portuguese *vez* 'time'. This prefix, juxtaposed to a simple noun, is very productive to indicate a person who is the contingent replacement for another person exercising certain powers (ex: *vice-presidente* 'vice-president') or a person who can, up to a certain point, exercise such powers (ex: *vice-rei* 'viceroy').[64]

Hellenisms

The lexical structure of Ancient Greek included processes of compound formation that were quite frequently used to improve and enrich philosophical or literary terminology. Classical Latin soon borrowed a large number of compound lexical terms formed in this way (exs: *philosophia* from *philo* + *sophia; paradigma* from *para* + *deigma; prototypus* from *proto* + *typus*). The literary dialects of the Romance languages, as well as of most other European languages, adopted these latinized Greek loans. A later round of borrowing occurred when the modern languages took more structures of the same type directly from Greek itself, mainly for the purpose of enriching scientific terminology. The model set up in this way then led to further expansion in the use of Greek elements, even to the point of creating new items like *telefone* 'telephone' from *tele* 'far' plus *phone* 'voice'

---

64. In classical Portuguese there was a variant *vizo-*. A reduced form appears in *visconde* 'viscount'.

(exs: *metatarso* 'metatarsus, instep'; *acorese*, medical term for 'decrease in the capacity of certain organs to contain liquids').

The presence of a large number of learned Hellenisms, which eventually became well-integrated into the structure of Portuguese, caused certain prefixes to stand out clearly as such, and these prefixes then became eligible to function in the formation of further literary or learned words. Notice, incidentally, that this occurred also in other Romance, and even non-Romance, languages. In some cases certain Greek terms having a definite meaning came to function as suffixes in given semantic areas. A good example is *-polis*, which is used to indicate a 'city' in many compound terms of Brazilian toponomy (exs: *Petrópolis*, named after the Emperor D. Pedro II; *Florianópolis*, named after Floriano Peixoto, a leader in the Republican movement). Another suffix of the same type is *-logia* used to indicate 'study' or 'science' (ex: *sociologia* 'sociology', first used in French but later exported to other languages, including English).

Among the prefixes of Greek origin that are now found in Portuguese, the following are especially significant. Note that they are often synonyms of Latin-based prefixes.

a-, used for 'negation' (exs: *amoral* 'amoral', *anormal* 'anomalous').

anti-, used for 'opposition' (ex: *anticoncepcional* 'contraceptive').

arqui-, used for 'preeminence' (ex: *arquimilionário* 'multimillionaire').

hiper-, used for 'excess' (ex: *hipercorreto* 'overcorrect').

meta-, used for 'change' (exs: *metanálise* 'meta-analysis'; *metalíngua* 'metalanguage', where the prefix has acquired the sense 'beyond' on the model of *metafísica* 'metaphysics').

para-, used for 'alongside' (ex: *paraestatal* 'partially controlled by the state').

proto-, used for 'first, earliest known' (ex: *proto-língua* 'proto-language').

tele-, used for 'far' (exs: *televisão* 'television'; *tele-comunicação* 'telecommunication').

Chapter 10

The Sentence

Nominal and Verbal Sentences

Latin sentences are characterized structurally by a basic pattern in which a nexus is established between the 'subject' and the 'predicate', to use a pair of technical terms borrowed by Latin grammarians from the Greek grammatical tradition. The first of these terms designates a substantive (noun or pronoun) that may be considered the 'theme' or origin of a communication cast in sentence form. The essence of the communication is expressed by the 'predicate', a noun, verb, or adjective, which is put into direct confrontation with the subject, setting up a relationship like that of two opposite magnetic poles. It is this confrontation that creates the nexus that links the subject to the predicate. Since the latter is the most important element, Latin sentences and their Portuguese descendants may be classified as verbal or nominal accordingly as the predicate is a verb on the one hand or a noun or an adjective on the other.

In Latin the nexus of a nominal sentence was often expressed by means of 'intonation', that is, a sequence of rising and falling melodic lines. A rising intonation on the subject and a falling intonation on the predicate, for example, were sufficient to distinguish a sentence like *homo bonus* from the same sequence of words acting as a noun qualified by an adjective (see Camara 1964, p. 163). Complementing this structure in which the nexus was expressed by purely phonological means, Latin also had a parallel structure in which the normal intonational pattern was accompanied by a form of the verb *esse* 'to be' (ex: *homo bonus est*). This second structure was adopted by Portuguese, in line with a general Romance trend, but *ser*, the Portuguese verb that corresponds to *esse*, is normally placed between the subject and the predicate (ex: *o homem é bom*). The impulse that led to use of *esse* must have been the opportunity it affords for explicit indication of 'tense' through verbal inflection (exs: Lt *homo bonus erat*, Ptg *o homem era bom* (*antes da sua queda no Paraíso*), 'man was good (before he fell in Paradise)'; Lt *homo bonus erit*, Ptg *o homem será bom* (*quando se redimir do pecado*), 'man will be good (when he redeems his sins)').

The distinction between *ser* and *estar*[1] that was created in Portuguese, as well as in Spanish, caused the structure of nominal sentences in these languages to bifurcate according to the verb chosen. For this reason, a sentence of Latin or of a Romance language that has a unique verb for the general idea of 'being' sometimes corresponds to a Portuguese structure containing *estar* (exs: Lt *Gallia est omnia diuisa in partes tres*, Ptg *a Galia tôda está dividida em três partes*, 'all of Gaul is divided into three parts'; Fr *la vitre est brisée*, Ptg *a vidraça está quebrada*, 'the pane of glass is broken').

For verbal sentences Portuguese maintains the Latin model, in which pronominal subjects are not obligatorily expressed. Thus, it sometimes happens that the subject-predicate relation, in a strictly

---

1. Before this distinction was firmly established we find a period of free variation between *esse* and *stare* in Iberian Vulgar Latin. In the modern language *estar* is used for concrete situations that come about as the result of an actual change, or a supposed change in the future. From the semantic point of view, the general unmarked form is *ser*.

formal sense, is concentrated entirely within the verb itself. This pattern is normal in Portuguese, as in Latin, for first- or second-person subjects, which are obligatorily pronominal if actually expressed (exs: Ptg and Lt *amo* 'I love'; *amas* 'you love'). In the third person, where the subject is normally a noun, development of a third-person pronoun (a Romance innovation) led to the option of replacing virtual subject nouns with the new pronoun (ex: *todos o escutam com entusiasmo, quando êle fala* 'everyone listens to him enthusiastically when he speaks'). In a parallel Latin sentence one would say merely *loquitur* (Ptg *fala*) since a demonstrative pronoun of the type of *hic* or *is* could appear only under special conditions.

Use of either Portuguese *ser* or Latin *esse* to indicate nexus in nominal sentences has as its automatic consequence the expression of a first- or second-person subject by the verb itself (ex: Ptg *sou bom;* Lt *sum bonus*). For the third person, on the other hand, Portuguese usually has an explicit pronoun, and this structure is typical of the Romance languages in general (ex: *todos o escutam com entusiasmo, porque êle é um grande orador* 'everyone listens to him enthusiastically because he is a great orator').

In general the structural patterns found in verbal sentences depend on the nature of the predicate. For such sentences Latin in particular had three formal schemata that were a function of the meaning of that element. The first schema includes a series of verbs that are semantically complete in themselves. These verbs may be called 'intransitive' or, more accurately, 'intransitive absolute' since there is no meaning beyond the verb (ex: Lt *ambulo*, Ptg *ando*, 'I walk'). The second schema is generated by a series of verbs that co-occur with an accusative noun, and are called 'transitive' because their meaning would otherwise be incomplete (ex: Lt *video puerum*, Ptg *vejo o menino*, 'I see the boy'). The third and last schema contains verbs that occur with nouns in the dative. These, like the first group, are 'intransitive' but are more properly termed 'intransitive relative' since their meaning is expressed relative to the state of the being designated by the dative element (ex: Lt *loquor puero*, Ptg *falo ao menino*, 'I speak to the boy').

The predicate of a transitive or intransitive relative verb was, of course, a pronoun rather than a noun in the first and second persons (exs: *video te* 'I see you', with an accusative; *loquor tibi* 'I speak to you', with a dative). In the third person, nouns could be replaced by demonstrative pronouns under exactly the same conditions as in subject position (exs: *video illum, video eum, video hunc; loquor illi, loquor ei, loquor huic*).

The general Romance tendency toward elimination of case distinctions, which led in Portuguese to the systematic adoption of the accusative as the unique case, caused a new type of pattern to appear in the two schemata involving a verb and a noun. For transitive verbs there was no longer any formal distinction between subject nouns and predicate nouns, the latter traditionally called 'objects' or 'direct objects'. New processes to indicate this distinction were therefore in order for transitive verbs, and the elimination of the dative created an exactly parallel situation for intransitive relative verbs.

The dative was replaced by a structure in which the indirect object is governed by the preposition *a* 'to' (ex: *falo ao menino* 'I speak to the boy'). In this way indirect objects came to be characterized by the circumstance that they are governed by a particular preposition. Notice, however, that the distinction between 'direct objects' of 'transitive' verbs and 'indirect objects' of 'intransitive' verbs is unstable, at least in part, because the preposition *a* may also be used for the former in the case of a 'person' (ex: *o homem deve amar a Deus* 'men should love God').[2] Furthermore, *a* is also used with nouns to indicate a position that is the goal of a movement (exs: *vou a Paris* 'I am going to Paris' or even *vou ao menino* 'I am going to the boy', that is, to the place where he is located).[3]

Transitive verbs and intransitive relative verbs with pronominal objects underwent two fundamental changes. First, in the first and second persons the accusative and the dative converged to the unique forms *me* (1st sing), *nos* (1st pl), *te* (2d sing), *vos* (2d pl). This convergence caused the distinction between direct and indirect objects to vanish. Second, the new forms lost their stress and were attached to the verbal word in either enclitic or proclitic position. In the third person, however, the appearance of new forms derived historically from the demonstrative *ille* caused a very clear formal distinction to be established between the dative and the accusative. This dis-

2. In Spanish this is the general pattern for direct objects that refer to people.

3. This was the initial function of phrases with the preposition *a* and corresponds to a Latin accusative governed by *ad*. The replacement of the dative by this construction for indication of indirect objects originated in a tendency to associate the latter with complements of direction, which could analogously appear in the dative during periods in which the case system was fully operative (ex: Lt *educere caelo*, Ptg *atirar para o céu*).

tinction is based on the opposition between *o* (with plural and feminine variants) and *lhe* (with a plural variant). In the modern language these forms constitute the only formal criterion that may be invoked in order to distinguish direct from indirect objects and indirect objects from complements of direction. For example, the phrase *a Deus* in *amo a Deus* 'I love God' may be considered direct because it becomes *amo-O* under pronominalization. Similarly, by switching persons the structurally ambiguous *amo-te* is resolved to unambiguous *amo-o*. For indirect objects the situation is the same. Corresponding to *falo a Deus* 'I speak to God' we have *falo-Lhe*, and by switching persons ambiguous *falo-te* gives unambiguous *falo-lhe*. For complements of direction we have only *êle* governed by the preposition *a*. Thus, *vou ao menino* 'I go to the boy' pronominalizes as *vou a êle* while *falo ao menino* 'I speak to the boy' gives *falo-lhe*.

Since the third-person accusative and dative forms have been almost entirely eliminated from the colloquial language of Brazil, the transformations demonstrated above are no longer operative. The distinction between indirect object and complement of direction therefore vanishes completely (ex: *falo a êle, vou a êle*),[4] while the distinction between direct and indirect object comes to rest solely on the use of *a* as a governing preposition for indirect objects. As a result of the latter circumstance, the use of *a* with direct objects is systematically avoided. The direct-indirect distinction also receives independent support from the fact that a sentence with a direct object, but not one with an indirect object, can be transformed to a nominal sentence of the 'passive' type (exs: *Deus deve ser amado* 'God should be loved'; *esperamos os viajantes hoje* 'we expect the travelers today' : *os viajantes são esperados hoje* 'the travelers are expected today').[5]

Finally, we mention in closing a particular type of verbal sentence in which the verb is in the verb-pronoun periphrastic form. This structure replaced the so-called deponent verbs of the Latin grammatical tradition and led to the third-person verb-pronoun periphrastic construction, which we have already discussed in chapter 7.

4. Here we see the final phase of a process of convergence between indirect objects and complements of direction that started in Classical Latin.

5. This was not true in Latin because the passive voice could be used with intransitive verbs as well as transitive ones (ex: *diu atque acriter pugnatum est*, from Caesar). In such cases Portuguese would use the verb-pronoun periphrastic construction (ex: *combateu-se muito tempo e encarniçadamente* 'people fought fiercely for a long time'; see Camara 1964A, p. 267).

Negative Sentences

Corresponding to variations in the purpose of particular speech acts, we find a matched series of modifications of the basic sentential schemata of nominal and verbal sentences.

First consider negative sentences, where the underlying motivation is a desire to indicate rejection of that which is enunciated. The key element in this type of sentence is the negative particle *não*, derived historically from Latin *non*. The functions of these two particles are identical, and both are pre-posed to the verb (ex: Lt *non amo*, Ptg *não amo*, 'I do not love'). Portuguese, in general, does not permit a second reinforcing negative particle after the verb (ex: Fr *je n'aime pas*), but negative indefinite pronouns are allowed in this position (ex: *não quero nada* 'I don't want anything'). Strictly speaking, the pronoun *nada* 'nothing' is a negative direct object, as is shown by the fact that it alternates with the synonymous expression *coisa nenhuma*. Nonetheless, negative reinforcement undeniably predominates over syntactic function[6] in this pattern as well as in the similar schema involving *ninguém* 'nobody' (ex: *não vi ninguém* 'I did not see anybody'). Under certain circumstances both *nada* and *ninguém* may precede the verb either as subjects or, by virtue of free word order, as objects. In this case the literary language omits the particle *não* in accordance with Latin usage of negative pronouns (exs: *nada sei* 'I know nothing', *ninguém chegou* 'nobody arrived').[7] Furthermore, *não* is also omitted when either the subject or the object is pre-posed to the verb and is modified by the adjectival negative indefinite *nenhum* 'no' or its feminine and plural variants (exs: *nenhum livro li* 'I read no book', *nenhum viajante chegou* 'no traveler arrived').

Question and Answer

Nominal and verbal sentences become 'interrogative' when they are presented to the hearer not as an assertion, but rather a question, that is, a request for information. In this case too it is intonation, a phonological phenomenon, that characterizes the sentential schema,

6. It was for this reason that the Brazilian writer Machado de Assis anomalously omitted the pre-verbal particle *não* when he wished to emphasize the nominal character of *nada* as a direct object (ex: *êle pegou em nada, levantou nada e cingiu nada* 'he grasped nothing, lifted up nothing and fastened nothing'; see Camara 1962, p. 61).

7. Archaic Portuguese and the modern popular dialects of both Brazil and Portugal have double negation even here.

indicating the theme of the question by means of a rising melodic line in the voice.[8] In the yes-no questions, where the theme is the predicate as a whole, the sentence ends with a rising pitch (ex: *Pedro saiu hoje?* 'did Peter leave today?'). Notice that this intonation pattern is the *only* mark of yes-no questions in Portuguese. The interrogative particle *ne*, which was the formal mark of a question in Latin, was abandoned by Portuguese and the other Romance languages. (ex: Lt *estne frater tuus?* Ptg *é teu irmão?* 'is he your brother?'). Unlike French, which replaced *ne* by systematic inversion of the obligatory subject pronoun (ex: *est-il ton frère?*), Portuguese adopted no new formal mark to replace Latin *ne*.

In certain other structures sentence elements, which may be said to 'absorb' the interrogation, are expressed as indefinite interrogative pronouns. Such elements are obligatorily placed in sentence initial position. For questions that refer to a constituent functioning as an adverb, the corresponding indefinite interrogatives are *quando* 'when' for time, *como* 'how' for manner, and *onde* 'where' for place. The latter are all pronominal interrogative adverbs accompanied by a rising pitch on the beginning of the sentence and an abruptly falling pitch at the end of the utterance.

In the colloquial language of Brazil an additional formal mark of interrogation has evolved—the phrase *é que* 'is it that' is inserted after the interrogative particle (exs: *quem é que disse?* 'who said that?', *que é que êle faz?* 'what does he do?', *qual dos livros é que êle quer?* 'which book does he want?', *quando é que você parte?* 'when are you leaving?', *como é que você se feriu?* 'how did you hurt yourself?', *onde é que êle está?* 'where is he?'). In the literary language there are two patterns. If the questioned element is the subject, it is expressed by the corresponding indefinite pronoun (ex: *quem disse?* 'who said that?'). In all other instances of *qu-* questions, the subject is postposed (exs: *que faz êle?* 'what does he do?', *como se feriu o menino?* 'how did the boy hurt himself?', *quando partem os viajantes?* 'when do the travelers leave?', *onde estão os livros?* 'where are the books?').

All questions, whether of the yes-no or *qu-* type, are naturally associated with an answer by the hearer, who takes on the role of the speaker for the purpose of responding. The structural schema of the answer is a function of that of the question and is, in fact, joined to it.

---

8. In questions, ascending pitch indicates a phrase that will become complete only upon presentation of the answer.

For this reason the answer may be 'elliptic', that is, limited in theme to the information requested by the first speaker.

For answers to yes-no questions, an affirmative particle, in polar opposition to the Latin negative particle, evolved in the Romance languages. This development brought with it the possibility of restricting answers to one of these two particles, according to whether one wished to affirm or deny a questioned predicate. The affirmative particle of Portuguese, like that of Spanish and Italian, evolved from the Latin adverb *sic* 'so, thus' by loss of the final consonant. In modern Portuguese this monosyllable also acquired a final nasal and became *sim*. It is important to note, however, that the usual affirmative reply in Portuguese is not *sim* but rather a repetition of the main verb of the question (exs: *Pedro saiu hoje?* 'Did Peter go out today?' *Saiu.* 'Yes'; *É teu irmão?* 'Is he your brother?' *É.* 'Yes').[9] Negative answers, on the other hand, usually consist simply of the particle *não* (exs: *Pedro saiu hoje?* 'Did Peter go out today?' *Não.* 'No'; *É teu irmão?* 'Is he your brother?' *Não.* 'No').

The answer to a *qu-* question is quite naturally limited to a statement of the element (noun, adjective, pronoun, verb, or adverb) that fills the semantic vacuum left by the indefinite (exs: *Quem é que disse?* 'Who said that?' *O professor.* 'The teacher'; *Qual dos livros quer?* 'Which of the books do you want?' *Aquele.* 'That one'; *Que é que êle faz?* 'What does he do?' *Trabalha.* 'He works'; *Quando é que você parte?* 'When are you leaving?' *Amanhã* 'Tomorrow').

Comparatives

The Latin comparative consisted of a special type of nominal sentence that indicated that the subject noun had more of the quality expressed by the corresponding predicate adjective than some other single being or than all beings of a given type considered as a set. Two different constructions, called the 'comparative' and the 'superlative' by the Latin grammarians, existed for these two types of comparison.

In the comparative the adjective that was the basis of comparison took a special inflection (*-ior* for masculine and feminine; *-ius* for neuter), and the second noun was subordinated in the ablative case to this adjective (ex: *Publius fortior Tertio* 'Publius is stronger than Tertius'). The superlative, which involved comparison to a whole

9. In case the adverb *já* occurs in the question, it is this particle that is repeated (ex: *Êle já saiu?* 'Has he gone out yet?' *Já* 'Yes').

class, also had a special inflection (masculine *-issimu-*, feminine *-issima-*), and the second noun, that is, the one that designated a class, was put in the genitive plural (ex: Lt *Niobe felicissima matrum*, Ptg *Níobe era a mais feliz das mães,* 'Niobe was the happiest mother').[10] Portuguese, like all the Romance languages, lost the comparative inflections in both schemata but, unlike Italian, it did not replace the ablative and genitive cases by the governing preposition *de* despite the general Romance correspondences between cases and prepositions. Portuguese chose instead a later Latin model in which *quam* is used to connect the second part of a comparison to the first (ex: *Publius fortior quam Tertius*). From *quam* evolved archaic *ca* and modern *que* (ex: *Públio é mais forte* que *Tércio*).

It should be noted, however, that the *de* construction, which is normal in the superlative (ex: *Níobe era a mais feliz das mães*), also survived in another particular comparative context, namely, that in which the second member is the pronoun *o* (< Lt *ille, hoc*) followed by a relative clause (ex: Lt *peor hoc quod erat*, Ptg *foi pior do que antes era,* 'it was worse than it was before'). As Maurer has recently shown (1967), on the basis of this pattern an equivalence was established between the comparative particle *que* and *do que*, and the two therefore alternate in modern Portuguese (ex: *Públio é mais forte do que Tércio*). Putting the same thing in other words, we may say that *pior do que antes era* came to be viewed as equivalent to *pior que antes era*, and then *do que* was extended to all contexts. For this reason the second noun of a comparative sentence may be governed by either *que* or *do que*.

When the second position is occupied by a first- or second-person pronoun, the stressed isolated form is used rather than the prepositional form[11] (exs: *mais forte do que* or *que eu* 'stronger than me'; *mais forte do que* or *que tu* 'stronger than you').

The use of the new patterns discussed above resulted in a convergence between nominal and verbal comparisons because the latter had the particle *magis* (> Ptg *mais*) even in Latin (ex: Lt *miror magis*

10. We have already seen that in modern Portuguese *-issim* (*o, a*) is used only in the so-called superlative absolute. It is a borrowing taken from Latin by the classical literary language.

11. In archaic Portuguese the oblique forms *mi, ti* governed by the preposition *ca* could be used as the second member of a comparison.

quam invideo, Ptg *admiro mais que invejo*, 'I marvel more than I envy'). Comparisons of 'inferiority' (or 'downward' comparisons), on the other hand, were a completely new phenomenon since the Latin inflectional system provided only for comparisons of 'superiority' (or 'upward' comparisons) of the type *tristior, felicissima* (exs: *Públio é menos forte que Tércio* 'Publius is less strong than Tertius'; *É a menos feliz das mães* 'she is the least happy mother').

In comparisons of 'equality', the pair *mais* (or *menos*) . . . *que* is replaced by *tão* . . . *como* (or *quanto*). Aside from this difference, the syntactic schema is the same as in comparisons of superiority or inferiority.

In summary, then, we see that Portuguese acquired distinctive structures to express all types of comparisons through the use of the particles *mais* (< Lt *magis*), *menos* (< Lt *minus*), *tão* (< Lt *tantum*), *que* (< Lt *quam*), *como* (< Lt *quomodo*), and *quanto* (< Lt *quantum*). The latter two replaced *ut* in analogous functions.[12]

Subordination

Subordination is a process that creates structural unity between two or more nominal or verbal sentences. In general, this process requires the particle *que*, acting either as a relative pronoun or as a subordinating conjunction, but in some cases subordination is implicit in the use of nominal forms of the subordinated verb.

Among the subordinating particles that we have already mentioned *se* 'if' is particularly important because it forms the pivot of the 'conditional' construction and establishes a pairing of clauses in which a condition formulated in the protasis is related to its consequence in the apodosis. This is the same pattern found in Latin with the conjunction *si*. Notice, however, that the protasis can also be a relative clause or a temporal expression.

A subordinating connective is not always the only formal mark of subordination since such connectives are in some instances accompanied by subjunctive inflections on the verb of the subordinate clause. For example, in the conditional schema a protasis is marked not only by *se* but also by a subjunctive. The tense of this subjunctive is a function of the type of future used in the apodosis. The patterns

---

12. Other Romance languages adopted *plus* instead of *magis*. Both of these were used in Classical Latin (ex: Lt *hoc plus ne facite*, Ptg *não se faça mais de que isto*, 'let more than this not be done'; from the Law of the Twelve Tables).

found are: 1) future subjunctive : present future indicative; 2) preterite subjunctive : preterite future indicative. Examples:

1) *se puder . . . farei* 'if I can . . . I will do'
   quando puder . . . farei 'when I can . . . I will do'
   quem puder . . . fará 'he who can . . . will do'
2) *se pudesse . . . faria* 'if I could . . . I would do'
   quando pudesse . . . faria 'when I could . . . I would do'
   quem pudesse . . . faria 'he who could . . . would do'[13]

The subjunctive also appears in concessive clauses introduced by the conjunction *embora* 'although' or its synonyms and in purpose clauses introduced by the conjunctional expression *para que* 'so that' or its synonyms. In these clause types, however, the choice of subjunctive tense is between present or preterite indicative, respectively (exs: *embora queira . . . não consegue* 'although he may want to, he cannot' or *embora queira . . . não conseguirá* 'although he may want to, he will not be able to'; *embora quisesse . . . não conseguiu* 'although he may have wanted to, he could not' or *embora quisesse . . . não conseguia* 'although he may have wanted to, he used not to be able to' or *embora quisesse . . . não conseguira* 'although he may have wanted to, he had not been able to').

The same distribution of subjunctive tenses is also found in relative or complement clauses introduced by the particle *que*. Here the appearance of a subjunctive is conditioned first by the form and second by the meaning of the verb of the main clause, which is itself a nominal sentence with a predicate adjective. The subject of the main clause is, in turn, either the whole of a complement clause or the antecedent of a relative clause (exs: *é preciso um livro que explique . . .* 'a book that explains . . . is necessary', *foi preciso um livro que explicasse* 'a book that explained . . . was necessary'). The meaning of the verb of a main clause must involve a subjective expression of emotion, volition, or supposition of the part of the subject in order for the verb of a subordinate relative or complement clause to be obligatorily subjunctive (exs: *desejo um livro que me ensine . . .* 'I want a book that will teach me . . .'; *quero que compreendas* 'I want you to understand').

There is a strong tendency to diminish the use of subjunctive forms,

---

13. In the binary past-present system (instead of ternary past-present-future) we have *se puder . . . faço* 'if I can, I'll do it'; *se pudesse . . . fazia* 'if I could, I'd do it'.

and certain schemata even exhibit free variation. For example, when the verb of the main clause expresses an expectation and therefore explicitly projects into the future, the future indicative (present or preterite accordingly as the verb of the main clause is present or preterite) may be used in place of the subjunctive (exs: *espero que virás* 'I hope that you will come', *esperava que virias* 'I hoped that you would come', instead of *espero que venha, esperava que viesses*). Similarly the present indicative or the preterite present periphrastic may replace the future subjunctive or even the present subjunctive in the protasis of conditionals. In fact, one can cite examples like the following from literary texts: *se dais a Deus o que Deus vos dá, dareis muito, mas se dais a Deus o que o mundo vos promete dais muito mais* 'if you give to God that which God gives you, you will give much, but if you give to God that which the world promises you, you give much more' (Father A. Vieira; apud Ali, n.d. p. 235); *se mana Piedade tem casado com Quincas Borba, apenas me daria uma esperança colateral* 'if my sister Piedade had married Quincas Borba, that would only give me a secondary hope' (Machado de Assis; apud Camara 1956, p. 88).[14]

Syntactic Processes

Governance

Prepositions acquired a central role in syntax upon the elimination of the Latin system of cases. In Portuguese, but not in Latin, so-called nominal governance, that is, subordination of one noun to another, is accomplished by means of a preposition, and this is also true of subordination of a complement to a verb, so-called verbal governance.

Nominal governance is assigned almost exclusively to the preposition *de* 'of', which, as we have seen, replaced a syntactic construction involving the genitive case. In verbal governance, on the other hand, one of the prepositions—*a* 'to', *para* 'for, to', *em* 'in', *de* 'of', *por* 'through, for', or *com* 'with'—is associated with a given verb in order to subordinate to it the basic obligatory complements. For this reason all complements, with the exception of direct objects and certain temporal or 'instrumental' phrases, are characterized by prepositions that agree in grammatical meaning with the complement.

14. In this construction the contrary-to-fact condition is presented to the hearer as a *fait accompli* in order to make the imaginary conclusion more realistic (see Camara 1956, p. 88).

It is customary to say that a given verb 'takes' (Portuguese: *exigir* 'to require') a certain preposition, but the truth of the matter is that given complement types systematically appear with given verbs and that it is the complement type that determines the choice of preposition. It is, for example, the grammatical meaning of 'direction' that explains the occurrence of *a* 'to' as a governing preposition of the complement of the verb *aspirar* 'to aspire'. Similarly, the verb *incorporar* 'to incorporate' is found with *em* 'in' for place, *a* 'to' for direction, and *com* 'with' for association. Sometimes, of course, the choice of preposition is a mere convention in the present state of the language. For example, complements of *gostar* 'to like' occur with the preposition *de* 'of' because under the first meaning of this verb, which was 'to taste', *de* was used as a 'partitive', that is, an indication that only a small portion of the substance in question was to be tasted (cf. Lt *gustare de potione*).[15]

The range of grammatical meanings associated with prepositions covers the basic locative level and also the level of abstract relations derived from locatives. The notion of 'reference' associated with the preposition *a* is a typical example of the latter and is clearly connected in some way with the use of this preposition for 'indirect objects'. Other examples are the meaning of 'purpose' found with *para* and that of 'means' found with *por*. The interdependence between the abstract and locative levels of grammatical meaning is very clearly illustrated by the choice of preposition used to indicate the 'agent' of 'passives'. As we have seen above, this type of nominal sentence is obtained by transposing a verbal sentence and turning the direct object into a 'patient'. In the new structure the 'agent', that is the subject of the original verbal sentence, may be indicated within the predicate. This type of 'complement of agent' was an ablative governed by the preposition *ab* in Latin and originated when the locative meaning of provenience was transposed to the abstract meaning of cause (ex: *Tullia a Marco amata est* 'Tullia was loved by Marcus'). Later *de* replaced *ab* in Portuguese, and it is this preposition that governed the agent phrase during the archaic period, a usage that is still found occasionally in the literary language (ex: *quem de muitos é temido, a muitos teme* 'he who is feared by many people,

15. The partitive with *de* developed in Vulgar Latin and found its way into the Romance languages. It was quite normal in Portuguese until the classical period and is still a typical syntactic feature of French.

fears many people'; apud Carneiro, 2d ed., p. 747). Beginning in the classical period, however, a marked preference for *por* is apparent. The basis of this change was a merger between the ideas of cause and means, the latter indicated by *por* (see Ali 1931, p. 236). In this way a Portuguese structure analogous to that of the Latin passive with agent phrase was established (ex: *Túlia é amada por Marco*).

Agreement

In Latin prepositional governance was a mere handmaiden to the ablative and accusative cases, but agreement was a sort of syntactic primate, serving to interconnect the various parts of a sentence. With the obvious exception of agreement in case between a noun and an adjective, this process has retained its original importance in Portuguese, where the relevant categories are number and gender.

In the phonological sense, agreement in number provides a more consistently clear association between linguistic elements because the distinction between singular and plural vanishes in only one special case—that of penultimate stressed words ending in /s/. For the feminine on the other hand, distinctive inflections are lacking in the whole class consisting of adjectives with theme in -*e* and also in many nouns, namely, those with a radical in which gender is implicitly present but cannot be made explicit except through agreement itself (exs: *artista prodigioso* 'prodigious artist' (masc), *artista prodigiosa* 'prodigious artist' (fem)). These deficiencies in the nominal inflectional system are not, however, sufficient to seriously disturb the syntactic process that guarantees agreement because nouns are, in principle, always accompanied by an article. Since this element clearly indicates number and gender, nouns automatically receive these categories and can therefore be clearly associated with adjectives (exs: *os pires brancos* 'the white saucers', *a artista maravilhosa* 'the marvelous artist' (fem)). The process of nominal agreement becomes truly inoperative only in case it is the adjective that shows no inflection for number (ex: *os homens simples* 'the simple men') or no inflection for gender (*as crianças tristes* 'the sad children').

Coordination of two or more nouns presents a certain amount of difficulty from the point of view of associating a given adjective to each of the conjuncts. Normally adjectives agree with a contiguous noun and in this case the association of an adjective with all the other nouns of a series would have to be deduced without any formal cues (ex: *o amor e a amizade verdadeira* 'true love and friendship'). To resolve this problem an alternative was created in the literary language—the adjective is put in the masculine plural when agreeing globally with two or more nouns of different genders (ex: *sangue .e água verdadeiros* 'true blood and water'). However, even this somewhat artificial practice does not provide a formally unique analysis in all cases (ex: *praças e ruas cheias de sangue* 'squares and streets full of blood').

In Portuguese the most basic process for association of a third-person verb to the corresponding subject noun is agreement in number. Latin, of course, also possessed verbal agreement of the same type, but in that language the formal mark that directly identified the subject was a nominative desinence.

Since verbal agreement is the fundamental syntactic mechanism for indication of subject nouns,[16] invariability in number of a third-person verb is the mark of the so-called impersonal construction, that is, a sentential pattern in which the subject-predicate dichotomy vanishes upon elimination of the former. Verbs that indicate atmospheric phenomena had a structure of this type in Latin and still do in Portuguese. For this reason they have no subject noun and are obligatorily third-person singular (exs: Lt *pluit, tonat,* Ptg *chove, troveja,* 'it rains, it thunders').

A different type of impersonal developed in Portuguese, as in other Romance languages, with the verb *haver.* This construction consists of *haver* in the third person of any tense and two complements, one a place name governed by a preposition (or an adverb) and the other a noun. The latter acts as a direct object, and the verb therefore does not agree with it (exs: *na África há leões* 'in Africa there are lions', *no Brasil já houve numerosas populações indígenas* 'in Brazil there were once many indigenous populations'). The 'error' of allowing the verb to agree with the second noun, which is in fact the tendency in popular speech, is sufficient to make this noun the subject. The whole con-

---

16. When the subject consists of two or more singular nouns the verb is plural (ex: *Pedro e Maria sairam* 'Peter and Mary went out'). If the subject is post-posed to the verb, however, free variation between the plural and the singular, in agreement with the immediately following singular noun, is more usual (ex: *sairam* or *saíu Pedro e Paulo* 'Peter and Paul went out', Ali, n.d. p. 205; *desapareceu o explorador e todos os seus companheiros* 'the explorer and all his companions disappeared', idem, p. 206). In such cases the subject as a whole must be deduced from context.

struction then enters a sentence schema that is typical of such verbs as *existir* 'to exist' (ex: *no Brasil haviam*—or *existiam*—*numerosas populações indígenas*).[17]

The origin of the impersonal *haver* construction can be traced to a Latin personal construction in which a place name was the subject of *habere* in the sense 'to have'. The change that led to the impersonal construction consisted of a transposition that made the place name a locative complement by subordinating it to the preposition *in*, Portuguese *em* (ex: *in arca Noe habuit homines* instead of *arca Noe habuit homines;* see Bourciez 1930, p. 252). The same transformation later re-occurred in Brazil in the case of the verb *ter* (ex: from *a África tem leões* 'Africa has lions' evolves *na África tem leões* 'in Africa there are lions').

Another case in which lack of agreement in third-person verbs creates an impersonal (or subjectless) pattern is the verb-pronoun periphrastic construction. The impersonal character of this construction is, in fact, the feature that permits its extension to intransitive verbs for the purpose of indicating 'an ongoing activity that has no particular source' exs: *combateu-se* 'people fought', *vive-se* 'people live', *falava-se* 'people used to speak'). Notice, however, that in this case it is not really the verb's invariability in number but rather the nonexistence of a noun that could act as a subject that establishes the pattern as an impersonal. It is clear, of course, that no such noun could be present when the verb is 'intransitive absolute'. Furthermore, although 'intransitive relative' verbs do have an 'indirect' object, this object is governed by a preposition and therefore cannot serve as subject. The situation is exactly the same when the object of a 'transitive' verb is governed by the preposition *a*, a usage that can be found in the literary language (ex: *a Bernardes admira-se e ama-se* 'Bernardes is admired and loved'; an oft-cited example from Antonio de Castilho; see Camara 1964b, p. 47). The same result may also be obtained by allowing a transitive verb to remain invariable in number, but this construction is not accepted in traditional literary language. Agreement of the verb with its complement noun in the verb-

17. This 'error' never occurs in the present indicative, where the singular *há* is well established. The use of the new pattern is dependent on the similarity in form between singular and plural exhibited by each tense and is therefore much more frequent in the preterite imperfect indicative, where these forms are *havia* and *haviam*, respectively.

pronoun periphrastic construction, a usage advocated by grammarians, makes this noun the subject, and the whole periphrastic schema becomes equivalent to a 'passive' (ex: *aqui se vendem relógios* = *aqui relógios são vendidos* 'watches are sold here'). Lack of agreement in the popular language is an indication of lack of a subject (ex: *aqui se vende relógios* 'watches for sale here').

Word Order

The third syntactic mechanism that serves to interrelate sentence constituents is relative placement within a sentence. This mechanism did not exist in Latin because in that language word order was absolutely 'free' from the grammatical point of view. Some orders were, of course, more usual than others, but the fact of the matter is that word order was of no use whatsoever in deducing the meaning of a sentence. For this reason the literary language was perfectly free to use highly arbitrary word orders for stylistic purposes.

In Portuguese, word order is not as rigid as in French but qualifies nonetheless as a syntactic process, albeit an unstable one. The basic principle is this: the last member of an utterance has the greatest information content. Notice, for example, the differences in information content inherent in the following versions of the same sentence: 1) *eu saio às três horas* 'the time when I leave is three o'clock'; 2) *às três horas eu saio* 'what I do at three o'clock is leave'; 3) *às três horas saio eu* 'the person who leaves at three o'clock is me' (see Camara 1967, p. 103).

The same basic principle is applicable to the relative placement of adjectives and nouns within noun phrases. An adjective may either be pre-posed or post-posed to the noun it modifies, but the latter is the more fundamental pattern because the adjective usually contains a new bit of information with respect to the noun. In essence, an adjective is a supplementary descriptive element that adds something to the noun's meaning. As a consequence, when two successive nouns are in a determiner-determined relationship and neither is formally marked as adjectival, it is the syntactic process of placement that identifies which element is functioning as the adjective—this element is always put in second place. Thus *um amigo urso* is an *amigo* 'friend' who is classified as an *urso* 'bear' because he is false and an ingrate. No one would ever think that this phrase could refer to a friendly bear; such an entity would be designated by the expression *um urso amigo*, with *urso* pre-posed.[18]

In general, placement of an adjective before the noun it modifies is allowed, but this order is associated with a loss in the adjective's information content and typically occurs only for stylistic reasons. As I have stated elsewhere, 'Post-position of an adjective brings out its denotative meaning, as contrasted with the predominant connotative meaning which the adjective may have to a greater or lesser extent when pre-posed. For this reason adjectives which indicate predicates that easily conjure up connotations sometimes seem at first sight to be insensitive to placement. This impression is, however, deceptive and does not reach the true core of the phrase's expressive possibilities' (Camara 1967, p. 104). In the case of pronominal adjectives (demonstratives, possessives, indefinites), and elements referring to number or indefinite quantity, the situation is precisely inverse, that is, adjectives of this type are generally pre-posed (exs: *estes livros* 'these books'; *meus livros* 'my books'; *alguns livros* 'some books'; *cinco livros* 'five books'; *muitos livros* 'many books'; *todos os livros* 'all the books', the latter with an inserted article). Only in special contexts that require an increase in information content is it possible to post-pose such adjectives, and this placement is therefore often purely stylistic.

The position of a subject with respect to the corresponding verb is analogous to the case discussed above. Here the theme of the information contained in the predicate is the subject, and it is therefore this element that begins the sentence if there are no special reasons for adopting another order. An example of the latter type is the insertion or addition of a verb of saying to an utterance quoted in direct discourse (exs: *é muito tarde—disse êle—para partirmos* 'it is very late, he said, for us to be leaving'; *não desanimemos por tão pouco—aconselhou meu pai* 'let us not despair over so little, advised my father'). The presence of an initial emphatic adverb to indicate an important circumstance is another cause of inversion (exs: *lá vêm*

18. Machado de Assis used this syntactic process when, in *Memórias Póstumas de Brás Cubas* (Garnier, 4th ed., p. 1), he put the following words in the mouth of his main character: *eu não sou pròpriamente um autor defunto, mas um defunto autor para quem a campa foi outro berço* 'I am not really an author who is dead but rather a dead man who is an author. For me the gravestone was a second cradle'. In the second part *autor*, which is usually used as a noun, becomes adjectival because it is placed after *defunto*.

êles 'there they come', *só então chegaram os viajantes* 'only then did the travelers arrive').

Since the basic pattern requires subjects to be pre-posed, subject and object are normally found distributed on either side of the verb (exs: *o menino viu o lôbo* 'the boy saw the wolf' or *o lôbo viu o menino* 'the wolf saw the boy'). In relative clauses, of course, the pronoun *que* is obligatorily put in initial position even when it is the direct object, but this is compensated by the fact that the subject remains in pre-verbal position (ex: *o lôbo que o menino viu* 'the wolf that the boy saw'). Under other circumstances *que* is normally felt to be the subject (ex: *o lôbo que viu o menino* 'the wolf that saw the boy').[19]

Putting a verb before its subject lends a clearly stylistic turn to a sentence and helps to focus on the verbal action as the theme of communication. For this reason the literary language, and to some extent even the colloquial language, often prefers so-called inversion of subject if there are no blocking elements such as a direct object. Furthermore, even when there is such an object, inversion is still allowed if the mechanism of agreement is available. For this reason we frequently find the inverted pattern in two cases: 1) with intransitive verbs (ex: *chegaram os viajantes* 'the travelers arrived') and 2) with transitive verbs when the subject and object are of different numbers (ex: *viram os meninos um lôbo* 'the boys saw a wolf'). But the option of inverting the normal order goes even further. Often the subject is post-posed despite the fact that word order is the *only* relevant syntactic mark. This occurs, however, only in those cases in which the general context implicitly makes clear which noun is the subject (ex: *comeu o lobo o menino* 'the wolf ate the boy'). If this is not immediately clear or the sentence causes a certain amount of perplexity, then we have a case of what the Greek grammarians used to call 'synchysis', a device sometimes used in certain hermetic schools of literature such as seventeenth-century Gongorism in Spain and Portugal. For example, one seventeenth-century Portuguese poet refers to *Bato que em dura pedra converteu/Mercúrio pelos fatos que revela* 'Battus who(m) into hard stone converted/Mercury for the facts revealed' (see Camara 1964B, p. 76). Here the poet had in mind the legend according

19. In French this is one of the few cases in which the subject is post-posed. Notice, however, that the form of the relative pronoun distinguishes subject (*qui*) from object (*que*). Thus, *le loup qu'a vu l'enfant* contrasts with *le loup qui a vu l'enfant*. Through the influence of the French model, the Portuguese literary language occasionally post-poses the subject despite the consequent formal ambiguity.

to which Mercury turned the gossip Battus into a stone, but the message is confused linguistically since the position of *Mercúrio* after the verb marks it syntactically as an object.

The syntactic role played by word order in the association of constituents within a sentence creates a certain amount of obligatory ordering, but quite independently of this Portuguese also follows certain preferential arrangements inherited from Latin. The two languages diverge, however, with respect to the position of the verb—in Latin this constituent was normally in clause-final position while in Portuguese it is usually between the subject and its complements (ex: Lt *Labienus litteras Caesari remisit*, Ptg *Labieno enviou uma carta a César*, 'Labienus sent a letter to Caesar').

The preferential order is what grammars call 'direct order', often falsely associating it with a supposed logical order of ideas. Portuguese has much less freedom than Latin in permissible variation from this order, a fact that the literary language has used to a greater or lesser extent to create an 'inverse order' that is at times so foreign to normal usage that it reaches the level of the rhetorical figure called 'hyperbaton'. Placement of a noun governed by *de* before the noun it modifies is an instance of hyperbaton found in the literary language (ex: *de um vasto edifício nas frias escadas/eu vi-a sentada* 'on the cold steps of a large building I saw her seated'; verses of Gonçalves Dias, see Camara 1964b, p. 76).

The manner in which adverbial pronominal complements are attached to verbs is also a matter of preferential word order. In general, a pronoun may become either a new initial syllable or a new final syllable of the phonological word it forms with a verb, entering proclitic or enclitic position respectively (exs: *eu a vi, eu vi-a* 'I saw her'). The placement of these particles is, in fact, one of the features that separates archaic from modern Portuguese and also modern European Portuguese from Brazilian Portuguese. In the archaic language the pronominal particle was not necessarily joined to the verb and could even be placed before the subject (ex: archaic *tanto que lh'eu este cantar oi*, modernized *assim que este cantar lhe ouvi*, 'as soon as I heard this song'; Nunes 1926, p. 174). For the modern language one can say that enclisis is favored in Portugal while proclisis is favored in Brazil. This divergence is especially great for sentence-initial position, where clitic personal pronouns may not occur in the European language. Normative grammarians have arbitrarily declared this to be the 'correct' usage for the Brazilian written language, but their rule is unknown in the colloquial language (ex: *me dê o livro* 'give me the book').

The only particle for which enclitic position is favored in Brazil is *se* in the verb-pronoun periphrastic construction, which indicates an activity without a definite subject. In this case pre-verbal position, associated with the fronting of the 'patient' noun, imparts to the latter the functions of an active subject. Thus, *o livro se vende* 'the book sells' could be paraphrased as *o livro tem boa aceitação do público* 'the book is well received by the public', but the sentence *vende-se o livro* 'the book is sold' means *o livro está à venda* 'the book is for sale'. In the first case one may also say, in active form, *o livro sai* 'the book sells (well)', which is of the same formal pattern as *o homem sai* 'the man leaves'.[20]

When an unstressed pronoun is found between two members of a periphrastic verbal form it is proclitic to the second rather than enclitic to the first, although the latter is normal in Portugal. In other words, for the sentence *tinha me dito* 'he had told me' we have the phonological word *medito* in Brazil but *tinhame* in Portugal. The position of the hyphen in the written language follows European usage (ex: *tinha-me*).

In both countries the insertion of an adverbial complement between the members of such phrases is conditioned by their phonological structure. Thus, in Portugal *tinha-me repetidamente dito* 'he told me repeatedly' is normal, whereas in the Brazilian colloquial language *tinha repetidamente me dito* is more usual. The Brazilian written language, of course, tries to follow the first pattern.

Phonological Division as a Syntactic Device

The instability of Portuguese word order is often compensated to a certain extent by the distribution of breath groups within a sentence. For example, in a sequence of two adjectives pre-posed to a noun, it is by means of phonological grouping that one can indicate that the second adjective modifies the complex unit made up of the noun and the first adjective. In writing this is reflected by omission of a comma or presence of the copula *e* 'and' between the two adjectives (ex: *um céu azul/magnífico;* cf. *um ceu/azul/magnífico, um ceu/azul/e magnífico*). Placement of *magnífico* before the noun, an order permitted

---

20. Said Ali (1930, p. 158) noticed the difference between these two constructions, but he attributed it exclusively to the position of the subject without considering the position of *se* (exs: *vende-se êste livro: o livro vende-se*).

by the meaning of this adjective, would give the same result: *um magnífico céu azul.*

When a phrase consisting of noun governed by *de* follows the direct object of a verb, it is once again the distribution of breath groups that determines whether this phrase refers to the preceding noun as a Latin genitive or whether it refers to the verb as a Latin ablative with *de, ab,* and so on (exs: *tenho um livro/de Pedro* 'I have (or got) a book from Peter', say, as a present; *tenho/um livro de Pedro* 'I have a book of Peter's', say, one that he owns). Variant word orders are possible (exs: *tenho de Pedro um livro; tenho um livro de Pedro,* respectively). In short, the phenomena of word order, which did not exist in Latin, and phonological division, which was irrelevant in Latin, correct in a very subtle way for the ambiguity that would otherwise result from the disappearance of the following two syntactically distinct patterns: *librum a Petro habeo, librum Petri habeo.*

References

References are here listed alphabetically by last name of author. In the text works are referred to by author's name and date of publication. Only items specifically referred to in the text, or consulted during its preparation, are listed. In cases in which a translation was used, the original is also listed even if it was unavailable to me.

Abbreviations:

BCEFL - *Boletim do Centro de Estudos Filológicos de Lisboa.*
BSCAC - *Boletim da Segunda Classe da Academia de Ciências de Lisboa.*
ELH - *Enciclopedia Lingüística Hispánica*, edited by M. Alvar, A. Badía, R. de Balbín, and L. F. Lindley Cintra.
HSSN - *Estudos Filológicos, Homenagem a Serafim da Silva Neto*, edited by Leodegário de Azevedo Filho.

MEB - *Manual de Estudos Brasileiros*, edited by W. Berrien and R. Borba de Morais.
RBF - *Revista Brasileira de Filologia*.
RFH - *Revista de Filología Hispánica*.
RLFEC - *Revista do Laboratório de Fonética Experimental de Coimbra*.
RPF - *Revista Portuguesa de Filologia*.
RPH - *Romance Philology*.
RIL - *Readings in Linguistics*, 2, edited by E. Hamp, F. Householder, and R. Austerlitz.
SBAW - *Sitzungsberichte der Bayerischen Akademie der Wissenschaften, Philosophisch-historische Klasse*.
SIL - *Studies in Linguistics*.
SRL - *Société Roumaine de Linguistique*.

Ali, M. Said. n.d. *Gramática secundária da língua portuguesa*. S. Paulo.
———. 1930. *Dificuldades da língua portuguesa*. Rio de Janeiro.
———. 1931. *Gramática histórica da língua portuguesa*. S. Paulo.
Allen, J. H. D. 1941. Portuguese word-formation with suffixes. Supplement to *Language*, vol. 17, no. 2.
Alonso, A. 1951. *Estudios lingüísticos: temas españoles*. Madrid.
Alonso, D. 1962. Temas y problemas de la fragmentación fonética peninsular. ELH 1, Suplemento. Madrid.
Baldinger, K. 1963. *La formación de los dominios lingüísticos de la peninsula ibérica*. Spanish translation by E. Lledo and M. Macau. Madrid (*Die Herausbildung der Sprachräume auf der Pyrenäenhalbinsel*. Berlin, 1958).
Barbosa, J. Morais. 1962. Les voyelles nasales portugaises: interpretation phonologique. *Proceedings of the Fourth International Congress of Phonetic Sciences*, Helsinki 1961. The Hague.
———. 1965. *Études de phonologie portugaise*. Lisbon.
Battisti, C. 1949. *Avviamento allo studio del latino volgare*. Bari.
Bloch, O., and W. von Wartburg. 1950. *Dictionnaire étymologique de la langue française*. Paris.
Bloomfield, L. 1933. *Language*. New York.
Boléo, M. de Paiva. 1936. *O perfeito e o pretérito em português em confronte com as outras línguas românicas*. Coimbra.
———. 1942. *O estudo dos dialectos e falares portugueses: um inquérito linguístico*. Coimbra.
———. 1946. *Introdução ao estudo da filologia portuguesa*. Lisbon.
Bosch y Gimpera, P. 1932. *Etnología de la peninsula ibérica*. Barcelona.
Bourciez, E. 1930. *Éléments de linguistique romane*. Paris.
Brøndal, V. 1948. *Substrat et emprunt en roman et en germanique*. French translation, SRL, Copenhagen-Bucharest (*Substrater og Laan*, Copenhagen, 1917).
Brugmann, K. 1905. *Abrégé de grammaire comparée des langues indo-européennes*. French translation by A. Meillet et A. Ernout, Paris (*Kurze vergleichende Grammatik der indogermanischen Sprachen*. Strasbourg, 1902–4).
Bühler, K. 1934. *Sprachtheorie, die Darstellungfunktion der Sprache*. Jena.
Camara, J. Mattoso, Jr. 1938. *Uma alternância portuguêsa* 'fui : foi'. RFH, 1–3.

————. 1949. Filologia. MEB, Rio de Janeiro.

————. 1953. *Para o estudo da fonêmica portuguêsa.* Rio de Janeiro.

————. 1956. *Uma forma verbal portuguêsa.* Rio de Janeiro (reprint: *A forma verbal portuguêsa em* -ria. Washington D.C., 1967).

————. 1957. Êle comme un accusatif dans le portugais du Brésil. *Miscelánea-Homenaje a André Martinet* 1. La Laguna.

————. 1962. *Ensaios machadianos.* Rio de Janeiro.

————. 1963. Europäische Sprachen in Übersee: das brasillianische Portugiesisch. *Archiv für das Studium der neueren Sprachen und Literaturen,* 115 Jahrgang, 5 Heft.

————. 1964a. *Princípios de linguística geral.* Rio de Janeiro.

————. 1964b. *Dicionário de filologia e gramática.* Rio de Janeiro.

————. 1967. Um caso de colocação. HSSN, Rio de Janeiro.

Carnoy, A. 1906. *Le latin d'Espagne d'après les inscriptions,* Brussels.

Cavacas, A. d'Almida. 1920. *A língua portuguesa e a sua metafonia.* Coimbra.

Cintra, L. F. Lindley. 1954. Enquêtes au Portugal pour l'Atlas Linguistique de la peninsule ibérique. *Orbis.*

Cornu, J. 1906. *Die portugiesische Sprache.* Strasbourg.

Corominas, J. 1961. *Breve dicionario etimológico de la lengua castellana.* Madrid.

Coseriu, E. 1955. El plural de los nombres propios. RBF 1 : 1.

Coutinho, A. (ed.). 1955. *A literatura no Brasil* 1. Rio de Janeiro.

Cuesta, P. Vasquez, and M. A. Mendes da Luz. 1961. *Gramática portuguesa.* Madrid.

Dalgado, S. Rodolfo. 1916. Gonçalves Viana e a lexicologia portuguesa de origem asiático-africana. BSCAC 10 : 3.

Devoto, G. 1944. *Storia della lingua di Roma.* Bologna.

Dias, A. Epifânio. 1918. *Sintaxe histórica portuguesa.* Lisbon.

Elcock, W. D. 1960. *The Romance Languages.* London.

Entwistle, W. J. 1936. *The Spanish language together with Portuguese, Catalan and Basque.* London.

Ernout, A. 1909. *Les éléments dialectaux du vocabulaire latin.* Paris.

Ettmayer, K. R. von. 1919. *Vademekum für Studierende der romanischen Philologie.* Heidelberg.

Glinz, H. 1952. *Die innere Form des Deutschen.* Bern.

Gonçalves Viana, A. 1883. Essai de phonétique et de phonologie de la langue, portugaise d'après le dialecte actuel de Lisbonne. *Romania* 12.

————. 1892. *Exposição da pronúncia normal portuguesa para uso de nacionais e estrangeiros.* Lisbon.

Grandgent, C. 1928. *Introducción al latin vulgar.* Spanish translation by F. Mohl. Madrid (*Introduction to Vulgar Latin,* Boston, 1907).

Guarner, M. Sanchis. 1960. El mozarabe peninsular. ELH 1. Madrid.

Hall, Jr., R. 1943. The unit phonemes of Brazilian Portuguese. SIL 1 : 4.

Head, B. 1964. *A comparison of the segmental phonology of Lisbon and Rio de Janeiro.* Austin (unpublished doctoral dissertation).

Hoffman, J. B. 1936. *Lateinische Umgangssprache.* Heidelberg.

Huber, J. 1933. *Altportugiesisches Elementarbuch.* Heidelberg.

Iordan, I. 1967. *Lingüística románica,* Spanish translation by M. Alvar, Madrid (*Introducere în studiul limbilor romanice,* Bucharest, 1963).

Jakobson, R. 1941. *Kindersprache, Aphasie und allgemeine Lautgesetze.* Uppsala.

Jungemann, F. H. 1955. *La teoría del sustrato y los dialectos hispano-romances y gascones.* Spanish translation by E. A. Llorach, Madrid.

Kuhn, A. 1951. *Romanische Philologie. Erster Teil: die romanischen Sprachen.* Bern.

Kurylowicz, J. 1966. La nature des procès dits 'analogiques'. RIL, Chicago.

Lacerda, A. de, and B. Head. 1963. Análise de sons nasais e sons nasalizados do português normal. RLFEC, Coimbra.

Lafon, R. 1960. La lengua vasca. ELH 1, Madrid.

Lapesa, R. 1950. *Historia de la lengua española.* Madrid.

Leite de Vasconcelos, J. 1900. *Estudos de filologia mirandesa,* 1. Lisbon.

———. 1911. *Lições de filologia portuguesa.* Lisbon.

———. 1922. *Textos arcaicos.* Lisbon.

———. 1928. *Antroponimia portuguesa.* Lisbon.

———. 1931. *Opúsculos III: onomatologia.* Coimbra.

Lenz, R. *La oración y sus partes.* Madrid, 1925.

Levy, A. Katz. 1965. Contrastive development in Hispano-Romance of borrowed Gallo-Romance suffixes, 1. RPH, 18.

———. 1967. Contrastive development in Hispano-Romance of borrowed Gallo-Romance suffixes, 2. RPH, 20.

Lüdtke, H. 1952. Fonemática portuguesa: I, Consonantismo. BCEFL 13.

———. 1953. Fonemática portuguesa: II, Vocalismo. BCEFL 14.

Malkiel, Y. 1954. *Studies in the reconstruction of Hispano-Latin word families.* Berkeley-Los Angeles.

Martinet, A. 1955. *Economie des changements phonétiques.* Bern.

———. 1962. *A functional view of language.* Oxford.

Maurer, Jr., T. Henrique. 1951. *Dois problemas da língua portuguesa. O infinitivo pessoal e o pronome 'se'.* S. Paulo.

———. 1959. *Gramática do latim vulgar.* Rio de Janeiro.

———. 1962. *O problema do latim vulgar.* Rio de Janeiro.

———. 1967. A origem da locução conjuntiva 'do que'. HSSN, Rio de Janeiro.

Meier, H. 1948. *Ensaios de filologia românica.* Lisbon.

———. 1950. A génese do infinito flexionado português. BCEFL 11.

Meillet, A. 1931. *Esquisse d'une histoire de la langue latine.* Paris.

Melo, G. Chaves de. 1946. *A língua do Brasil.* Rio de Janeiro.

Menéndez y Pidal, R. 1944. *Manual de gramática histórica española.* Madrid.

———. 1950. *Orígenes del español.* Madrid.

———. 1960. Dos problemas iniciales relativos a los romances hispanicos. ELH 1.

Meyer-Lübke, W. 1920. *Einführung in das Studium der romanischen Sprachwissenschaft,* Heidelberg.

———. 1935. *Romanisches etymologisches Wörterbuch,* 3d ed. Heidelberg.

Mohl, G. 1899. *Introduction à la chronologie du latin vulgaire.* Prague.

————. 1900. *Les origines romanes: Études sur le léxique du latin vulgaire.* Prague.

Monteverdi, A. 1952. *Manuale di avviamento agli studi romanzi. Le lingue romanze.* Milan.

Murin, L. 1950. *L'imparfait portugais.* Brussels.

Nascentes, A. 1932. *Dicionário etimológico da língua portuguesa,* 1. Rio de Janeiro.

————. 1939. *Estudos filológicos.* Rio de Janeiro.

————. 1952. *Dicionário etimológico da língua portuguesa,* 2. Rio de Janeiro.

————. 1953. *O linguajar carioca.* Rio de Janeiro.

————. 1966. *Dicionário etimológico resumido.* Rio de Janeiro.

Navas Ruiz, R. 1963. *'Ser' y 'estar': estudio sobre el sistema atributivo del espãnol.* Salamanca.

Nobiling, O. 1904. Die Nasalvokale im Portugiesischen, *Die Neuren Sprachen* 11.

Nogueira, R. de Sá. 1938. *Elementos para um tratado de fonética portuguesa.* Lisbon.

Nunes, J. J. 1926. *Cantigas d'amigo dos trovadores galego-portugueses,* 2. Lisbon.

————. 1945. *Compêndio de gramática histórica portuguêsa.* Lisbon.

Pallotino, M. 1954. *Etruscologia.* Milan.

Pisani, V. 1953. *Le lingue dell'Italia antica oltre il latino.* Turin.

Porzig, W. 1954. *Die Gliederung des indogermanischen Sprachgebiets.* Heidelberg.

Ribeiro, E. Carneiro. 1915. *Serões gramaticais ou nova gramática da língua portuguesa.* Bahia.

Ribeiro, J. 1917. *História do Brasil, curso superior.* Rio de Janeiro.

Riemann, O. 1927. Syntaxe latine. *7° edition révue par E. Ernout,* Paris.

Rodrigues, A. Dall'Igna. 1958. Contribuição para a etimologia dos brasileirismos. *RPF* 9.

Rohlfs, G. 1956. *Sermo vulgaris latinus.* Tübingen.

————. 1960. *Diferenciación léxica de las lenguas románicas.* Spanish translation by M. Alvar, Madrid (*Die lexikalische Differenzierung der romanischen Sprachen,* SBAW, 1954).

Rossi, N. 1964. *Atlas prévio dos falares baianos.* Rio de Janeiro.

Silva Neto, S. 1950. *Introdução ao estudo da língua portuguêsa no Brasil.* Rio de Janeiro.

————. 1952. *História da língua portuguêsa.* Rio de Janeiro.

————. 1957. *Manual de filologia portuguêsa.* Rio de Janeiro.

Silveira, A. F. Sousa da. 1937. *Lições de português.* Rio de Janeiro.

Soares, A. de Macedo. Dicionário brasileiro da língua portuguêsa. *Anais da Biblioteca Nacional* 13, Rio de Janeiro, 1875–88.

Steiger, A. 1932. *Contribución a la fonética del hispano-árabe y de los arabismos en el ibero-románico y el siciliano.* Madrid.

Sten, H. 1944. *Les particularités de la langue portugaise.* Copenhagen.

Sturtevant, E. 1940. *The pronunciation of Greek and Latin.* Philadelphia.

Tagliavini, C. 1952. *Le origine delle lingue neolatine.* Bologna.

Tovar, A. 1960. Lenguas preromanas no indoeuropeas. *ELH* 1, Madrid.

Tovar, A. 1960. Lenguas preromanas indoeuropeas. ELH 1, Madrid.

Vidos, B. E. 1963. *Manual de linguística románica.* Spanish translation by F. Mohl, Madrid (*Handboek tot de romaanse taalkunde*, s'-Hertogenbosch, 1956).

Wartburg, W. von. 1941. *Les origines des peuples romans.* French translation by Guenot de Maupassant, Paris (*Die Entstehung der romanischen Völker*, Halle, 1936).

———. 1946. *Problèmes et méthodes de la linguistique.* French translation by P. Maillard, Paris (*Einführung in die Problematik und Methodik der Sprachwissenschaft*, Halle, 1943).

———. 1952. *La fragmentación lingüística de la Romania.* Spanish translation by M. Muñoz Cortés, Madrid (*Die Ausgliederung der romanischen Sprachräume*, Bern, 1950).

Williams, E. B. 1938. *From Latin to Portuguese.* Philadelphia.

Analytical Bibliography of
Joaquim Mattoso Camara, Jr.

With Index by Date of Publication
and
Index of Reviewers

Note: In the bibliography that follows we have listed only books, articles, and commentary that seemed to us to be relevant to university-level studies. We have omitted nearly all works intended for the secondary level, brief commentaries and letters, shorter non-critical notices of publications, and reviews that did not seem to us to attain a certain minimum of substantive content. Some items of this sort are, however, mentioned in the translator's preface.

Works are arranged by topic in a scheme invented ad hoc for the purpose. Reviews of Mattoso's publications are placed after each topic listing, while reviews by Mattoso are listed separately as a group. We have made every effort to keep our own comments as short as possible. They are not intended to be critical; indeed, since we do not share the author's theoretical orientation, a true critical commentary on the items listed in this bibliography would probably turn out to be longer than the whole book as now constituted.

Although the bibliography is intended to be complete within the limitations mentioned above, it has been compiled rather speedily under far from ideal conditions. Considering the fact that the book has been in process since 1963 we felt that any further delay could not be justified at this time.

We have worked exclusively from bibliographies, indexes of learned journals, and footnotes. We have not had access to the author's personal files. Insofar as materials were available to us on the shelves of the Library of the University of Chicago, the Newberry Library of Chicago, the Library of the University of Illinois at Urbana, and the Library of Congress in Washington, D.C., we have examined the complete runs of all journals to which Mattoso was known or likely to have contributed or in which reviews of his works were known or likely to have appeared. These sources were not exhaustive, however, and given the delays involved in publication, shipping, cataloguing, and binding, they did not go beyond 1968 in most cases. Many items not available at the libraries named above were graciously and promptly supplied to us by Miss Helen M. Smith of the University of Chicago Library. In a few cases, however, we were unable to examine items to which we found references. These are marked with an asterisk and the source of the reference is given.

Despite its deficiencies we hope that this bibliography can serve as a small indication of our esteem for Professor Mattoso Camara and his work.

Anthony J. Naro
John Reighard

I. Grammatical Studies in Portuguese

Phonemics

[1] *Para o estudo da fonêmica portuguêsa.* Coleção Rex. Rio de Janeiro: Organização Simões, 1953 [revised version of items 2, 3, and 4].
[2] Para o estudo da fonêmica portuguêsa: fonética e fonêmica. *Boletim de*

Filologia (Rio) 3 (1949): 71–100 [chapter 1 of M's doctoral dissertation, Universidade do Brasil, 1949].

[3] Para o estudo da fonêmica portuguêsa: os fonêmas em português. *Boletim de Filologia* (Rio) 3 (1949): 1–30 [chapter 3 of M's doctoral dissertation, Universidade do Brasil, 1949].

[4] A rima na poesia brasileira. *Anais do Congresso Brasileiro de Língua Vernácula*, 1: 298–333. Rio de Janeiro: Casa de Rui Barbosa, 1949 [M refers to this work as 'unpublished' in the preface to item 1; revised and expanded version of item 5].

[5] Imperfect rimes in Brazilian poetry. *Word* 2 (1946): 131–35.

Reviews: [1]: Antenor Nascentes in *Jornal de Filologia* 2 (1954): 300–302; Francis M. Rogers in *Language* 30 (1954): 503–9; Marilina dos Santos Luz in *Revista Portuguesa de Filologia* 7 (1956): 459–560. [3]: Helmut Lüdtke in *Boletim de Filologia* (Lisbon) 12 (1951): 353–55; Paul Garvin in *Studies in Linguistics* 8 (1950): 93–96. [4]: Amália Beatriz Cruz da Costa in *Anais do Congresso Brasileiro de Língua Vernácula*, 3: 435–36. Rio de Janeiro: Casa de Rui Barbosa, 1959.

M's treatise on Portuguese phonology consists of three quite separate subparts. First, there is an introductory exposition of general phonological theory as it had developed up to approximately 1948, with special emphasis on the Prague Circle and its North American extension. The second chapter is a treatment of Brazilian Portuguese phonology based on the theoretical orientation of the introduction. Concluding the treatise, the final section is presented as an example of the application of phonemics to a practical philological problem—imperfect rhyme in Brazilian poetry.

A detailed summary of M's main conclusions on Portuguese phonemics is given in Rogers's thorough review, to which we refer the reader.

The synchronic sections of the second chapter of the present work are based largely, though not entirely, on M's earlier studies. The main divergences are: (1) recognition of /ř/ in *carro* 'car' as a phoneme, and (2) denial of phonemic status of /w y/. The second of these is based on phonetic considerations, perhaps following a hint from Rogers (p. 505).

M's original analysis of [ř] was /rr/, that is, geminate /r/. Phonetically /rr/ was to become [Øř], the second *r* being realized as ř as it normally would in nonintervocalic position. One bit of evidence presented by M in favor of this representation that would still be of interest today is consideration of the relationship between certain standard vs. popular forms. His example is *cirurgião* 'surgeon', which has a popular form *cirrugião* (with [ř]). If /r/ and /ř/ are separate units the relationship between the two forms is accidental, but if [ř] is the realization of /rr/ the two forms can be related through the mechanism of metathesis.

Both Garvin and Lüdtke objected to M's analysis and he himself formally retracted it in item no. 56, p. 233. Garvin felt that the analysis represented, at least in part, a confusion of morphophonemics with phonemics; Lüdtke pointed out that /rr/ would be the only phonemic geminate. Of course today, in 1971, few linguists would take Garvin's objection seriously since the distinction has turned out not to be well founded, and on the systematic phonemic level there are certainly geminates (ex: /ll/ versus /l/; only the first vanishes between vowels), not to mention geminates created in derivations (exs: *irregular, fazê-lo* 'to do it' from /fazer + lo/; both geminates arise through assimilation). Thus, there seems to be no reason for abandoning M's original insightful analysis.

[6] Sôbre as consoantes palatalizadas. *Boletim de Filologia* (Rio) 1 (1946): 225–29.

[7] O consonantismo histórico português. *Revista de Cultura* (Rio) (1956): 244–46 [* reference in *Bibliographie linguistique de l'année 1957*, p. 143. Utrecht-Anvers: Spectrum, 1959].

[8] 'Muta cum muta' in Portuguese? *Word* 24 (1968): 286–89.

Synchronic Morphophonemics

[9] Para o estudo descritivo dos verbos irregulares. *Estudos Lingüísticos* 1, no. 1 (1966): 16–27.

[10] Considerações sôbre o gênero em português. *Estudos Lingüísticos* 1, no. 2 (1966): 1–9.

[11] A note on Portuguese noun morphology. In *To Honor Roman Jakobson* 2: 1311–1314. The Hague: Mouton, 1967.

Much of this material is reflected in the present book, especially in chap. 3 and chap. 4.

The theoretical position implied by M's work on morphophonemics is, to us at least, very unclear. In dealing with plural formation of nouns and adjectives ending in *-ão*, for example, three main classes must be considered:

'lion'	leão	leões
'bread'	pão	pães
'brother'	irmão	irmãos

In item no. 11, M sets up two morphological classes— *-e* class and *-o* class— and the 'patterns' *leõe pãe* (*-e* class), *irmão* (*-o* class). Since the patterns are explicitly based on the plurals, plural formation is simply a matter of addition of *-s*. The singular results by shift of *-e* class items to the *-o* class and change of *-õ* stems to *-ã* stems.

The intended theoretical status of the 'patterns' is difficult to determine. Since nasal vowels do not exist for M even on the phonemic level the italicized representations with nasal vowels, which certainly are not phonetic, must be merely expository.

In the present work the table at the end of chap. 3 takes a different view. Here all three types of items are listed under the singular *-ão*, and plural formation, rather than singular formation, is described in a complicated way. Nonetheless, at least for items of the types of *leão* and *pão* the 'theoretical' endings *-om* and *-am* are given in parentheses, and in the next section it is said that the feminines of such items are formed on the 'theoretical' radical. Furthermore, it appears that the 'theoretical' radical is to be deduced from the plural, as in item no. 11. Even the status of the word 'theoretical' is, however, not clear. In note 8, chap. 3, M uses this very term to describe a nonexistent feminine of *elefante* 'elephant' invented in the imaginations of certain school grammarians. Thus, 'theoretical' is perhaps intended to convey the meaning 'unreal' or 'fake'.

Conditional or 'Preterite Future' Verb Forms

[12] *Uma forma verbal portuguêsa: estudo estilístico-gramatical.* Rio de Janeiro: Livraria Acadêmica, 1956 [definitive version].

[13] *A forma verbal portuguêsa em* -ria. Washington D.C.: Georgetown University Press, 1967 [reprint of 12].

[14] Une catégorie verbale: le future du passé. *Proceedings of the Ninth International Congress of Linguists,* edited by Horace G. Lunt, pp. 547–51. Janua Linguarum, Series Maior 12. The Hague: Mouton & Co., 1965 [summary of 12 in French].

[15] Sôbre o futuro romance. *Revista Brasileira de Filologia* 3 (1957): 221–25 [reply to Eugenio Coseriu, Sobre el futuro romance. *Revista Brasileira de Filologia* 3 (1957): 1–18].

Reviews [12]: J. H. D. Allen Jr. in *Word* 13 (1957): 520–25; Kund Togeby in *Romance Philology* 16 (1962–63): 258–59.

Viewing matters from a diachronic as well as a synchronic viewpoint, M discusses the italicized verb forms found in such sentences as:

> a. se eu tivesse dinheiro, *compraria* uma casa
> 'if I had money, I would buy a house'
> b. disse que *viria* sem falta
> 'I (*or* he) said that I (*or* he) would definitely
> come'

Such forms are usually called 'conditional' because of their use in sentences like *a*, which have the shape of a logical statement, but M's central thesis, following the lead of Said Ali in traditional Portuguese grammar, is that these forms are really a 'preterite future', that is, a future when viewed from a vantage point in the past. This is particularly clear in *b* and corresponds to the historical origin of the form through agglutination of the infinitive with the preterite of *habere*, parallel to the formation of the future itself from the infinitive plus the present of this same verb. Reasoning on the basis of consistency of form, versus variability of intuition, M sees it as a mistake to separate *a* and *b* into different categories and therefore insists on a single classification—the future preterite—for the verbs of both sentence types.

In general, according to M, verbal forms may be categorized with respect to aspect, tense, mood, and voice, but these categories seldom appear in an unmixed form. In particular, the future is so thoroughly impregnated with potential, optative, or imperative coloration that in temporal terms the most basic linguistic division is present/past, the former being an essentially 'cursive' tense that includes events still to occur. Future forms morphologically distinct from the present evolve because speakers feel the need to express a future event not simply in temporal terms (for this the 'cursive' present forms would do), but also in terms of their own psychological attitude. Thus, in Indo-European at least, the future is often a secondary morphological formation involving a word meaning 'to want', 'to will', or 'must'.

But, human language is caught in an eternal swing between unhindered externalization of the inner psyche and controlled expression of a developed system of logic. When the latter prevails, the originally spontaneous modal forms are 'intellectualized', and their weak logical value as a strict future is strengthened to the point of obliterating the modal coloration. On the other hand, in thoroughly spontaneous colloquial styles there can be no place for logic and pure information. It is for this reason that the Classical Latin future vanished from Vulgar Latin and the Romance languages.

It is clear, then, that the future is not on the same functional or semantic level as the present and the past; rather it represents a new category which is superposed to the latter.

From the point of view of the present, an event viewed as future to a point in the past can have three outcomes: the event may already have occurred or, if not, it may still occur or else it may never actually occur (falsifying, in the latter case, the original prediction). This last circumstance carries the future preterite to the domain of the unreal.

In conditional sentences the conditioning clause may mention an event that serves to establish a past vantage point from which to view the event in the result clause. But these sentences, like *a*, may also be essentially intemporal, that is, realization of the event in the conditioning clause may be viewed independently of time. In this case we have a metaphoric use of the past in the *if*-clause (the imperfect subjunctive in *a*) to indicate lack of reality. Psychologically, the metaphor rests on two grounds: the unclearness intimately associated with the past and the fact that a past event can no longer be realized in the present, making it unreal. Naturally, once the condition is formulated in the past its result, although unreal, must be put in the preterite future. This explains in a uniform way the two seemingly disparate uses of *a* and *b* in terms of the intuitive semantic system within which speakers operate.

Of the reviewers, Allen considers M's work to be essentially 'unscientific' since it depends so heavily on the use of psychological semantically oriented data in the explanation of linguistic change. To him it seems as if the intuitive semantic system which M refers to must necessarily be 'unsystematic' and thus that M's usage involves a contradiction in terms that would lead to unverifiable results. Togeby's review, on the other hand, states that M's work avoids 'vain semantic explanations', and praises its historical orientation. Thus the two reviews appear to be flatly contradictory since one praises M for avoiding semantic speculation while the other criticizes him for excessive reliance on semantic arguments. The germ of this confusion rests in M's rejection of intuition as a basis for synchronic description while accepting it enthusiastically as the primary cause of linguistic change. Witness his insistence on classifying the verbal forms of *a* and *b* as identical because of their identity in *form*, in spite of the great intuitive difference that separates them. At the same time, however, he insists that the disappearance of the future in

Vulgar Latin cannot be explained on the basis of the fact that it came to be nearly homophonous with several other tenses. For M, the real cause lies in the stylistic-semantic factors outlined above.

Êle *as an Accusative*

[16] *Êle* comme un accusatif dans le portugais du Brésil. In *Miscelánea Homenaje a André Martinet*, edited by Diego Catalán, 1: 39–46. Canarias: Universidad de La Laguna, 1957.
Reviews [16]: Helmut Lüdtke in *Zeitschrift für Romanische Philologie* 75 (1959): 394; Hans-Jürgen Rein in *Revista Portuguesa de Filologia* 10 (1960): 316–17.

In popular Brazilian Portuguese *êle* 'he', a reflex of the Latin nominative *ille*, is used as an accusative:

> a. vejo-o
>   'I see him'   (standard)
> b. vejo êle
>   'I see him'   (popular)

Although the usage in *b* is fought in the schools, it is typical of the normal speech of all social levels in Brazil.

Sentences of the type of *b* are found in the archaic language, but M argues that the Brazilian usage must be an independent phenomenon since it is found only with the third person, whereas the archaic language had similar constructions also in the first and second persons. The same argument serves to rule out several other possible explanations.

According to M, the true diachronic genesis of *b* is not extension of the nominative to the accusative, but rather a morphological realignment—*êle* is detached from the case-sensitive pronominal system and becomes associated with the nominal and demonstrative systems:

Pedro anda	falo a Pedro	vejo Pedro
'Peter walks'	'I speak to Peter'	'I see Peter'
êle anda	falo a êle	vejo êle
'he walks'	'I speak to him'	'I see him'

This process produces a morphologically uniform system since *êle*, unlike *eu* and *tu*, has the usual nominal desinences (*êle, ela, êles, elas*). Semantically *êle*, again unlike *eu* and *tu*, is associated with nouns because it functions linguistically as a replacement for the latter.

The causes of the realignment of *êle* must be sought in developments of other aspects of the system 'où tout se tient', and these causes must, furthermore, be specific to Brazil since *êle* does not function as an accusative in Portugal. The causes proposed are: (1) in normal Brazilian speech, unstressed pronouns tend to be put in proclitic position, which is particularly weak since word initial vowels tend to be dropped. This affects only the third-person forms *o, a, os, as* since the other forms *me, te, nos, vos* begin with consonants. The process is, on the other hand, inoperative in Portugal, where unstressed pronouns tend to be enclitic. (2) In Brazil the most usual semantically second-person forms are syntactically third person (*você, o senhor* 'you') and therefore take third-person oblique forms. But this leads to an excessively ambiguous status for *o* (direct object) and *lhe* (indirect and also direct object in some styles), which accordingly become specialized in the semantically second-person use. Thus, *estou lhe falando* becomes exclusively 'I am speaking to *you*', while 'I am speaking to *him*' is expressed by *estou falando a êle*. This process is inoperative in Portugal because *tu* and *vos* may be used there.

Lüdtke's brief review calls into question the causes suggested by M. He points out that initial position is weak in Portugal, as well as in Brazil, but he forgets M's assertion that enclisis, not proclisis, is favored in Europe. Similarly, he points out that *vós* is not used in large areas of Portugal, but he forgets to mention that *tu* may be used. Thus, he seems to have missed M's point. Rein states that *êle* appears as an accusative in European Portuguese child language, but he makes no mention of the state of affairs with the other two grammatical persons.

In his article M emphasizes the point that the development under discussion is strictly Brazilian, and he therefore seeks to explain it in Brazilian terms. It is interesting to note that the explanation he offers is basically of the same type as the one he rejects in the case of the future verb forms: homophony occasioned in part by morphological factors and in part by phonetic factors.

Miscellaneous Topics in Morphology

[17] Una alternancia portuguesa: *fui* : *foi*. *Revista de Filología Hispánica* 1 (1939): 257–61.

[18] A alternância portuguêsa *fui* - *foi*. *Revista de Cultura* (Rio) 34 (1943): 98–106 [Portuguese translation of 17].

M argues that the *u* of *fui* and *fuit* showed free variation in quantity and that early Portuguese therefore had the forms *fui* (<*fūi, fŭit*) and *foi* (<*fŭi, fŭit*) arbitrarily distributed in the first and third persons preterite singular. Eventually, however, *fui* was selected for the first person, while *foi* was reserved for the third person, on the basis of previously existing alternations like *pus* < **posi* < *posuī*, with a high vowel in the first person, versus *pôs* < *posuĭt*, with a mid vowel in the third person.

[19] Sôbre a classificação das palavras. *Boletim de Filologia* (Rio) 2 (1947): 87–91. On the relationship of determiners and pronouns; essentially expository, with a view toward modernization of school grammars.

[20] Morfologia e sintaxe. *Jornal de Filologia* 3 (1955): 177–82.

[21] Sur la neutralisation morphologique. *Travaux de l'Institut de Linguistique* (Paris) 2 (1957): 76–77. Answer to a questionnaire of André Martinet.

[22] A locução *a olhos vistos*. In *Miscelânea Filológica em honra à memória do professor Clóvis Monteiro*, edited by Leodegário A. de Azevedo Filho, pp. 103–105. Rio de Janeiro: Editôra do Professor, 1965.

The expression *a olhos vistos*, which may be translated freely by 'plain as day', consists of the plural noun *olhos* 'eyes' and the participle *vistos* 'seen'. The participle agrees in the masculine plural with the noun. M rejects previous speculations on the origin of the expression and suggests that this usage of the participle is perfectly analogous to that in *pessoa viajada* 'well-traveled person', *os viajantes chegados ontem* 'the travelers who arrived yesterday', etc.

[23] À propos d'un vulgarisme du portugais du Brésil. *Omagiu lui Alexandru Rosetti*, pp. 534–45. Bucharest: Editura Academiei Republicii Socialiste România, 1965. Discusses popular *viemos* for standard *vimos* 'we come', first-person plural present of *vir* 'to come'.

General Works

[24] *The Portuguese Language: History and Structure.* Translated by Anthony J. Naro. Chicago: University of Chicago Press, 1972.

[25] A língua literária. *A Literatura no Brasil*, edited by Afrânio Coutinho, pp. 101–11. Rio de Janeiro: Editorial Sul Americana, 1956.

[26] A língua literária. *A Literatura no Brasil*, 2d ed., pp. 63–70. Rio de Janeiro: Editorial Sul Americana, 1968 [reprint of item no. 25].

Traces the attitudes of various schools of Brazilian literature toward the relationship of the literary to the popular language and also the relationship between the literary languages of Brazil and Portugal. Particularly striking is the observation that nearly all schools of Brazilian poetry, even the so-called parnasianos, maintain a close connection with the sounds of the Brazilian 'living language' despite a tendency to follow European usage in other parts of the grammar.

[27] Erros de escolares como sintomas de tendências lingüísticas no português de Rio de Janeiro. *Romanistisches Jahrbuch* 8 (1957): 279–86.

An examination of linguistic 'errors' committed by eleven to thirteen-year-olds on a high school admissions exam. The subjects are all from upper class families in the *Zona Sul* of Rio. Thirteen phonetic, three morphological, and four syntactic features are discussed, but the results are perhaps somewhat overstated and a true historical perspective is lacking. For example, cited errors like *acustumado* for *acostumado* ($o > u$ before u in the next syllable), *sintiu-se* for *sentiu-se* ($e > i$ under analogous conditions), *traisueiro* for *traiçoeiro* (mid to high vowel in hiatus) can be found in Portuguese texts as early as the thirteenth century and do not show the loss of the mid-high distinction in pre-tonic position. To show this one would have to exhibit instances of the type **trucar* for *trocar* or **rular* for *rolar*, where the earlier conditioning factors are not present. Nonetheless, it is clear that the empirical data provided by this article will be of inestimable value to future historians of the Portuguese language in Brazil.

[28] Europäische Sprachen in Übersee: das brasilianische Portugiesisch. *Archiv für das studium der neueren Sprachen und Literatur* 200 (1963): 322–37 [paper read at the University of Bonn].

[29] Línguas européias de ultramar: o português do Brasil. *Revista do Livro* 8 (1965): 107–18 [Portuguese translation of item no. 28]. See chap. 1 of the present book.

[30] História externa da língua portuguêsa. *Revista de Cultura* (Rio) 242 (1956) [* reference in *Bibliographie linguistique de l'année 1957*, p. 143. Utrecht-Anvers: Spectrum, 1959].

II. Stylistic Studies in Portuguese

General Works

[31] *Contribuição à estilística portuguêsa*. Coleção Rex. Rio de Janeiro: Edição da Organização Simões, 1953 [second revised edition of 32].

[32] *Contribuicão para uma estilística da língua portuguêsa*. Rio de Janeiro, 1952 [thesis for the title 'Livre Docente' in Portuguese, Faculdade Nacional de Filosofia].

Review [31]: Maria de Lourdes Belchior in *Boletim de Filologia* (Lisboa) 15 (1954–55): 204–7.

The book is divided into two main parts—a very brief introduction to general stylistics as that study had developed up to approximately 1950, followed by a keenly insightful listing of the main features of Portuguese style. The latter are treated under the three subheadings of phonological, lexical, and syntactic stylistics. Among the topics discussed are: tone; stress; length; stylistic effect of given classes of sounds in view of the doctrine of the arbitrariness of the sign; feelings associated with words either because of the nature of that designated or for some other reason; stylistic effect of certain suffixes; personal versus impersonal infinitives; placement of clitic particles.

[33] Considerações sôbre o estilo. *Vozes* 55 (1961): 823–29.

[34] Para uma estilística estrutural. *Lengua, Literatura, Folklore: Estudios Dedicados a Rodolfo Oroz*, edited by Gastón Carrillo Herrera, pp. 291–99. Santiago: Facultad de Filosofía y Educación, 1967.

These two articles, which are essentially based on 'A coroa de Rubião' (1957, item no. 40), modify and to some extent improve upon the definition of stylistics given in sections 5–10 of part I of *Contribuição* (items nos. 31 and 32). They insist much more strongly on the ternary partition of Bühler, assigning grammar and *langue* to *Darstellung* (representation) while reserving to stylistics the deformation of *langue* brought about by *Appel* (appeal to another person) and *Kundgabe* (psychological manifestation).

[35] Um caso de colocação. *Estudos Filológicos: Homenagem a Serafim de Silva Neto*, edited by Leodegário A. de Azevedo Filho, pp. 101–6. Rio de Janeiro: Edições Tempo Brasileiro, 1967.

An analysis of the sonnet "A Cavalgada" by Raimundo Correia in terms of the principle of maximum information content of the last word of an utterance.

Machado de Assis

[36] *Ensaios machadianos: língua e estilo*. Rio de Janeiro: Livraria Acadêmica, 1962.

Reviews [36]: Zdeněk Hampejs in *Philologica Pragensia* 6 (1963): 436; Sol Saporta in *Language* 39 (1963): 545–546; Benjamin M. Woodbridge in *Romance Philology* 17 (1963): 522–523; M. de Jong in *Lingua* 16 (1966): 334–336.

Contains a preface and eleven essays, ten of which are revised versions of earlier articles. The essays are:

[36.1] *Cão e Cachorro no Quincas Borba*. pp. 9–24.
[37] *Cão e Cachorro no Quincas Borba*. *Revista de Cultura*, numbers 174, 175, 176 (1941) [* reference given in item no. 31].

In Brazil *cão* and *cachorro* 'dog' are roughly synonymous, but the second is a popular word learned during childhood while the first is learned later and is felt to be a higher or more scientific level of expression. M shows that Machado was sensitive to this stylistic distinction and analyzes his usage in *Quincas Borba*, where the plot revolves about a dog.

[36.2] O discurso indireto livre em Machado de Assis. pp. 25–41.
[38] O estilo indireto livre em Machado de Assis. In *Miscelânea de estudos em honra de Antenor Nascentes*. Rio de Janeiro, 1941 [* reference in bibliography of item no. 31 and n. 15, p. 41, of item no. 36].

Discurso direto consists of a verb of saying followed by a direct quotation; *discurso indireto* similarly has a verb of saying but a tighter connection to the embedded sentence is established by *que* 'that', the first person is shifted to the third person, sequence of tense rules apply, and so on. *Discurso indireto livre* is a sort of compromise in which there is no verb of saying and no *que*, but most other features of *discurso indireto* are present. According to M, Machado uses the intermediate style (1) as a bridge between a passage in indirect style and a passage in direct style, and (2) to communicate somewhat imprecise thoughts of a character. He states that Machado does not use the compromise style as a means of establishing a psychological link with the characters of the novel, contrary to a hypothesis of Bally.

[36.3] Da Mofina Mendes ao Padre Mendes. pp. 43–51.
[39] Da Mofina Mendes ao Padre Mendes. *Verbum* (Rio) 10 (1953): 503–6.

Basing his speculations on Gil Vicente's use of the name *Mendes* for the title character of the play *Mofina Mendes*, M offers an explanation for Machado's use of the same name for a non-existent priest.

[36.4] A coroa de Rubião. pp. 54–61.

[40] A coroa de Rubião. *Revista do Livro* 2 (1957): 105–9. See item no. 33 and n. 6, chap. 10, of the present work.

[36.5] Machado de Assis e as referências ao leitor. pp. 63–79.

[41] Machado de Assis e as suas referências ao leitor. *Boletim de Filologia* (Rio) 1 (1946): 75–86.

An insightful analysis of Machado's use of forms for 'you' (*tu, vos, o senhor*, a noun such as *o leitor* 'the reader', verb in the second or third person with no expressed subject). Particularly impressive are the disparate and seemingly inconsistent uses of *tu*.

[36.6] O coloquialismo de Machado de Assis. pp. 81–94.

[42] O coloquialismo em Machado de Assis. *Revista Brasileira de Filologia* 6 (1961): 1–33.

M attempts to show that one of Machado's goals in writing was to remain as close as possible to the spoken language in order to lend naturalness and spontaneity to his narrative.

[36.7] Quincas Borba e o humitanismo. pp. 95–107.

[43] Quincas Borba e o humitanismo. *Boletim de Filologia* (Rio) 2 (1947): 131–38.

Discusses the relationship of the doctrine of 'humânitas' with the thought of Comte, Nietzsche, Schopenhauer, and others. See also the second part of item no. 36.10.

[36.8] Machado de Assis e 'O Corvo' de Edgar Poe. pp. 109–24.

[44] Machado de Assis e 'O Corvo' de Edgar Poe. *Revista do Livro* 11 (1958): 101–9.

An appreciation of Machado's translation of Poe's *The Raven*. According to M, the brilliance of Machado's translation lies in such factors as: (1) abandonment of the English sixteen-syllable verse in favor of Portuguese verses of eight, ten, and twelve syllables because the former is simply inappropriate for Portuguese; (2) use of a rhyme scheme that suggests repeated somber beats, as in the English; and (3) alternation of normal and archaic forms to suggest a conflict of the level of everyday reality with that of the supernatural.

[36.9] Um sonêto de Machado de Assis. pp. 125–33.

[45] Um sonêto de Machado de Assis. *Revista do Livro* 2 (1957): 69–73. On the structure of the sonnet "A Carolina."

[36.10] A gíria em Machado de Assis. pp. 135–43. Analyzes, in two concrete cases, the very subtle ways in which Machado makes use of slang for purposes of indirect suggestion.

[36.11] Um caso de regência. pp. 145–73.

[46] Um caso de regência. *Miscelânea de estudos em honra de Manuel Said Ali,* pp. 49–59. Rio de Janeiro, 1938 [* reference in n. 1 of item no. 47].

[47] Um caso de regênica. *Revista de Cultura* (Rio) 36 (1944): 25–34.

For the European dialect M traces the origin of the expression *morar à rua* . . . instead of *morar na rua* . . . 'to live on . . . street' to the influence of Castilian in the sixteenth-century court, but he insists that the corresponding construction in Brazil dates only from the last quarter of the nineteenth century and has no relation to the Continental usage. In Brazil, according to M, *a* replaced *em* in *morar em* by hypercorrection from a tendency to do likewise in such expressions as *estar na janela* 'to be at the window'. This, in turn, was based on analogy to *estar junto à janela* 'to be near the window'. Concluding the essay, M provides an analysis of Machado's use of these prepositions with *morar*. He finds that Machado used *a* only for purposes of irony.

The reviewers generally agree in praising the extremely perceptive nature of M's work on Machado, although some of them noticed that the essays that compose the collection do not adhere to form a whole.

III. Linguistic Studies in Indigenous Languages of Brazil

Theoretical Works

[48] Lingüística e etnografia. *Revista do Museu Nacional* 1 (1944): 27–31 [lecture given to the Sociedade Brasileira de Antropologia, June 18, 1943].

This article deals with the place of linguistics within the study of anthropology. M discusses the necessity for anthropological fieldworkers to have good linguistic training, especially in phonetics and phonology, in order to be able to perceive non-native sounds accurately and analyze their function correctly. They will also need linguistic understanding in order to view objectively exotic languages, the structure of which is so different from their own.

[49] Língua e cultura. *Letras* (Curitiba), no. 4 (1955), pp. 51–59 [summary of a talk given to the Curso de Aperfeiçoamento de Antropologia Cultural, Secção de Estudos, Serviço de Proteção aos Indios].

In this article, M analyzes the position of language within its cultural setting. He points out that while in one sense a language is a microcosm of the culture in which it is located, nevertheless it has an autonomous structure of its own. This structure is independent of the culture, and should be studied independently.

[50] Classificação das línguas indígenas do Brasil. *Letras* (Curitiba), no. 10 (1959), pp. 56–66 [report to the fourth Reunião Brasileira de Antropologia, Curitiba, 15–18 July 1959].

M surveys the kinds of linguistic classifications that have been done in the past, and concludes that the most promising is a genetic classification, based on the theories of lexicostatistic dating as developed in the United States.

Applications

[51] *Alguns radicais jê*. Publicações Avulsas no. 28. Rio de Janeiro: Museu Nacional, 1959.

[52] Do estudo tipológico em listas de vocábulos indigenas brasileiras. *Revista de Antropologia* (São Paulo) 7 (1959): 23–30.

Review [52]: R. F. Mansur Guérios in *Letras* (Curitiba), no. 12 (1961), pp. 171–74.

Item 52 contains a detailed discussion of the technique employed in 51, which is a thorough analysis of a small and selected sample of source materials for one family of indigenous Brazilian languages.

The bulk of this source material available in 1959 consisted of a large number of vocabulary lists, collected by researchers, most of whom were not linguists or grammarians. Many in fact were amateurs. Generally, the words are listed as given by the native informant and usually include various unidentified morphological affixes. Also, each researcher tended to invent *ad hoc* a phonetic transcription system in accord with the spelling conventions of his own native language. As they stand then, the lists are not directly utilizable for linguistic research. It was M's aim to isolate cognate root morphemes from these lists for purposes of comparative studies.

Drawing from the theory of glottochronology, M establishes a list of thirty words taken from Swadesh's list, for which glosses are available in twelve Jê languages. By comparing forms, both within each language and across the whole language family, he is able to isolate and list the affixes (pp. 7–8) and the phonological changes that the forms undergo (pp. 10–12).

In the text, under each of the thirty words from the Swadesh list, he lists the gloss as it is given by the source; his morphological analysis of the gloss; a proposed, reconstructed proto-form; alternate glosses where they occur; and finally the phonological variations each form shows. At the end of the book, M gives his proposed analysis of the genetic relationships obtaining among the twelve languages.

IV. Reference and Bibliography

Dictionary

[53] *Dicionário de filologia e gramática referente à língua portuguêsa*. 3d ed. rev. Rio de Janeiro: J. Ozon, 1968 [definitive version].

[54] *Dicionário de fatos gramaticais*. Rio de Janeiro: Casa de Rui Barbosa, 1956 [first edition of preceding item].

[55] *Dicionário de filologia e gramática referente à língua portuguêsa*. 2d ed. rev. Rio de Janeiro: J. Ozon, 1964.

Reviews: [54]: Silveira Bueno in *Jornal de Filologia* 4 (1956): 70–73; R. F. Mansur Guérios in *Letras* (Curitiba) 5–6 (1956): 193–94; J. H. D. Allen, Jr., in *Language* 33 (1957): 193–95; R. A. Hall, Jr., in *Romance Philology* 12 (1958–59): 163–70. [55]: F. Gomes de Matos in *Hispania* 49 (1966): 181–82.

The title of the first edition of this dictionary reflects the author's declared purpose to produce neither a handbook of terminology nor a dictionary for the whole of linguistics:

. . . the object was to give grammatical notions in alphabetical order, for consultation when necessary, as a basis for the structural, functional, and historical understanding of the Portuguese language (Explicação Preliminar, *Dicionário* 1st ed., p. 11).

The book then is intended as a simple guide, in the form of a dictionary, to concepts involved in the study of language.

Each entry usually begins with a definition of the term in question, followed by an explanation that may range from a single sentence to several paragraphs of detailed discussion and exemplification. Alternate terminology is often given, and there are many cross-references, both as separate entries and within the text. Examples are almost exclusively drawn from Modern or Archaic Portuguese.

That the book is intended for use by specialists and nonspecialists alike is shown by the range of entries included, the terminology used by M in his explanations, and the nature of the explanations themselves. While these do reflect the focus of M's own work—structural linguistics of a Praguean sort on the one hand, and an interest in stylistics and literary language on the other— they do not represent a doctrinaire *prise de position*. There is a good distribution of terms of phonetics, most referring to articulatory phonetics; there are many terms pertaining to structural linguistic analysis, particularly of Sapirian and Jakobsonian inspiration; there are terms familiar to traditional grammar and traditional philology; there are many familiar terms of stylistics; and there are also some terms of a very general nature, such as *fraseologia*, *escola*, *literatura*, and *folclore*. The terminology M uses is generally conservative for a structuralist writing in the mid-fifties, and the explanations and definitions, especially in the first edition, are very often the traditional ones.

The second edition is an expanded and revised version of the first, with the emphasis much more clearly on structural analysis. Many new entries are added, most of which refer to fundamental structuralist concepts, such as *oposição*, *neutralização*, *morfofonema*, *sândi*, and *grafema*. Many of the old entries are expanded, often by means of a further analysis in structuralist terms. The bibliography in the second edition is split into two lists—one literary, the other linguistic—and many of the additions to the latter are books and articles by linguists—Abercrombie, Boas, Hjelmslev, Joos, Rosetti, and Jakobson—that were not unavailable at the time of the first edition.

This change in emphasis in the second edition seems to reflect a growing acceptance on the part of the Brazilian public of modern linguistic works. In the 'Advertência para a 2.a edição' (p. 5), M states:

. . . now, in 1963, I find that I have evolved somewhat in comparison with what I dared to say in 1956 and that I am more sure of my ideas and less afraid to state them openly. Those who share these ideas with me will consider this good; those who disagree with them will consider it bad.

The third edition has a few new entries added, and some old ones corrected, but remains essentially identical to the second edition.

Of the reviewers, Silveira Bueno complains that M has not sufficiently taken into account Silveira Bueno's own writings, nor indeed those of any of the São Paulo group. Mansur Guérios considers that a dictionary of linguistics, purified of all the literary, traditional grammatical, and stylistic terminology, would have been more useful. Hall's fundamental objection is that the book does not reflect the linguistic philosophy prevalent in the United States in the fifties, an approach to linguistic analysis that Hall terms 'operational'. He considers highly questionable linguistic insights and grammatical 'facts' arrived at by any other approach. In somewhat the same vein, Allen sees a major weakness in the fact that the book has no systematic explanation of the 'allo-' and '-emic' concepts. On the other hand, the fact that there is likewise no explicit treatment of neutralization, given the (in Allen's view) linguistically unsophisticated public for whom the book is intended, may in fact be to its advantage. Gomes de Matos, reviewing the second revised edition, points out its considerably changed character, and finds it eminently successful.

Despite the author's declared intention in the preface, the reviewers of the first edition fail to understand what kind of book M intended to write and the probable diversity of the public for whom he was writing, or they are so committed to their own brands of linguistics that they cannot recognize the value of work done with a different theoretical orientation.

Bibliographical Essays

[56] Filologia. *Manual Bibliográfico de Estudos Brasileiros*, edited by Rubens Borba de Moraes and William Berrien, pp. 257–84. Rio de Janeiro: Gráfica Editora Souza, 1949.

[57] Brazilian linguistics. *Current Trends in Linguistics*, edited by Thomas A. Sebeok, 4:229–47. The Hague: Mouton, 1968.

[58] Contemporary Brazilian studies in Portuguese linguistics. *Portugal and Brazil in Transition*, edited by Raymond S. Sayers, pp. 56–69. Minneapolis: University of Minnesota Press, 1968.

Commentary [58]: Brian F. Head in *Portugal and Brazil in Transition*, edited by Raymond S. Sayers, pp. 69–70. Minneapolis: University of Minnesota Press, 1968.

M's contribution to the *Manual* consists of an introductory statement followed by a selective list of approximately 250 items dealing with all aspects of Brazilian Portuguese. Works are listed alphabetically by author (not restricted to Brazilians) and each one is provided with an analytical comment. The listing even includes page references to passing comments on Brazilian Portuguese in more general works.

The two listings of 1968 are more discursive in character than the earlier one and include, for the most part, only major contributions by Brazilians. The *Current Trends* article refers to approximately 75 items, while the *Transition* article refers to only about 30. The former covers all subfields of linguistics, while the latter concentrates on the Portuguese language in Brazil. Both treatments are somewhat more critical than the earlier listing in points of concrete detail, and the *Current Trends* article is particularly valuable for M's comments on his own work.

[59] *A obra lingüística de Curt Nimuendaju.* Publicações Avulsas do Museu Nacional, No. 29. Rio de Janeiro, 1959.

A bibliography, with commentary, of the linguistic work of Carl Unkel (1883–1945). Thirty items dealing with indigenous languages of Brazil are listed.

V. Commentary and Discussion

Linguists

[60] Otto Jespersen. *Boletim de Filologia* (Rio de Janeiro) 1 (1946): 149–52.
[61] Crônica lingüística: Roman Jakobson. *Revista Brasileira de Filologia* 2 (1956): 55–64.
[62] A teoria sintagmática de Mikus. *Revista Brasileira de Filologia* 2 (1956): 245–59.
[63] Gonçalves Viana and the phonic sciences. *For Roman Jakobson*, edited by Morris Halle, Horace G. Lunt, Hugh McLean, and Cornelis H. Van Schooneveld, pp. 328–31. The Hague: Mouton, 1956 [based on chap. 2 of M's doctoral dissertation, Universidade do Brasil, 1949].
[64] As idéias gramaticais de João Ribeiro. *Letras* (Curitiba), no. 12 (1961), pp. 22–35.
[65] Said Ali e a língua portuguêsa. *Vozes* (Petrópolis) 55 (1961): 415–16.
[66] Antenor Nascentes e a filologia brasileira. *Vozes* (Petrópolis) 60 (1966): 459–62.
[67] Maurício Swadesh (1909–1967). *Estudos Lingüísticos* 2 (1967): 112–15.

Each of these articles is a comprehensive summary of the contributions of the linguist in question, with an evaluation of his work both in terms of his contemporaries and in terms of the subsequent development of the study of language. Particular attention is paid to those aspects of his work that in M's view have been of greatest significance to the development of modern linguistics.

Language and Linguistics

[68] A pronúncia do latim. *Revista de Cultura* (Rio de Janeiro) 31 (1942): 264–66. A plea for historical accuracy in the teaching of Latin pronunciation in the revised curriculum of Brazilian schools.

[69] Notas gramaticais de sânscrito. *Revista de Cultura* (Rio de Janeiro) 37 (1945): 114–18, 137–41, 237–42. A brief introductory account of the phonology of Sanskrit, written in a traditional style.

[70] *Os estudos lingüísticos nos Estados Unidos da América do Norte.* Publicações Avulsas, no. 1. Rio de Janeiro: Museu Nacional, 1945. Written after M's

one-year stay in the United States, this book is an account of American activity in classical philology and linguistics.

Review: [70]: A. Gomes Ferreira in *Humanitas* (Coimbra) 2 (1948–1949): 522–525.

[71] O ensino de língua na América do Norte. *Boletim de Filologia* (Rio de Janeiro) 1 (1946): 145–48. A report of the flurry of activity in foreign-language teaching that took place in the United States during the Second World War.

[72] Os estudos lingüísticos regionais. *Boletim de Filologia* (Rio de Janeiro) 2 (1947): 3–17. M presents the theoretical framework he considers necessary for any future work in Brazilian Portuguese dialects.

[73] A conferência de Indiana entre antropólogos e lingüistas. *Revista Brasileira de Filologia* 1 (1955): 187.

[74] O Sexto Congresso Internacional de Lingüistas. *Revista Brasileira de Filologia* 1 (1955): 53.

[75] Primeira Reunião de Antropologia. *Revista Brasileira de Filologia* 1 (1955): 251–60. These three conference reports include references both to papers given and to comments made by participants, and include as well commentary by M.

[76] Crônica lingüística: glotocronologia e estatística léxica. *Revista Brasileira de Filologia* 5 (1959–60): 209–15. A description and critical evaluation of the theory of glottochronology, or lexicostatistic dating, as developed in the United States.

[77] Nomenclatura gramatical. *Letras* (Curitiba), no. 11 (1960), pp. 1–16. A discussion of grammatical terminology and linguistic principles, with particular reference to the *Nomenclatura Gramatical Brasileira* (Rio de Janeiro: Ministério da Educação e Cultura, 1958).

[78] Comentário do co-relator J. Mattoso Câmara Jr. ao relatório (parte geral) do prof. Aryón dall'Igna Rodrigues. *Revista de Antropologia* (São Paulo) 11 (1963): 17–19. In this report, M points out several encouraging signs of the growing field of indigenous linguistics in Brazil.

[79] O espanhol no Brasil e a conexão entre o português e o espanhol na América do Norte. *Presente y Futuro de la Lengua Española*, 1: 337–43. Madrid: Oficina Internacional de Información y Observación del Español, 1964.

This article is concerned with the cultural isolation of Brazil in Latin America and the inferior rôle played by the Portuguese language in Latin American studies in North America. M's proposed solutions to these problems are cast in terms of suggested curriculum revisions for schools in both Latin America and North America.

[80] Os estudos da língua portuguêsa em Portugal e no Brasil. *El Simposio de Bloomington: agosto de 1964: actas, informes y comunicaciones.* Programa

Interamericano de Lingüística y Enseñanza de Idiomas, pp. 154–65. Bogotá: Instituto Caro y Cuervo, 1967. A critique of methods of teaching Portuguese in Brazilian and Portuguese schools, together with specific recommendations for improving the situation.

[81] Panorama da evolução da linguística nos Estados Unidos da América. *El Simposio de Cartagena: agosto de 1963: informes y comunicaciones.* Programa Interamericano de Lingüística y Enseñanza de Idiomas, pp. 199–229. Bogotá: Instituto Caro y Cuervo, 1965. A comprehensive account of the growth and development of American linguistic theories.

[82] O estruturalismo lingüístico. *Tempo Brasileiro* 15–16 (1967): 5–43 [slightly revised version of a paper given at the first Seminário de Lingüística, 15–19 August 1966, Marília, Brazil]. M establishes a philosophical definition of structuralism and relates it to the theoretical positions of a wide variety of schools of linguistic thought, both ancient and modern.

[83] Carta ao professor Sílvio Elia. *Revista de Cultura* 32 (1942): 60–61.

[84] Carta dos Estados Unidos. *Revista de Cultura* 35 (1944): 66–67. Of interest for a study of the development of M's thought.

VI. Reviews

[85] Académie de la République Populaire Roumaine. *Mélanges linguistiques, publiés à l'occasion du VIIIe congrès international des linguistes à Oslo du 5 au 9 août 1957.* Bucharest: Éditions de l'Académie de la R.P.R. In *Romance Philology* 17 (1963): 449–53.

[86] Amaral, Amadeu. *O dialeto Caipira.* São Paulo: Editora Anhembi, 1955. In *Revista de Antropologia* (São Paulo) 3 (1955): 143–45.

[87] Catalán Menéndez-Pidal, Diego. *La escuela lingüística española.* Madrid: Editorial Gredos, 1955. In *Revista Brasileira de Filologia* 2 (1956): 261–64.

[88] Faria, Ernesto. *O latim e a cultura contemporânea.* Rio de Janeiro: F. Briguiet et Cia, 1941. In *Revista de Filología Hispánica* 3 (1941): 395–96.

[89] van Ginneken, Jacques. *La reconstruction typologique des langues archaïques de l'humanité.* Amsterdam, 1940. In *Boletim de Filologia* (Rio) 1 (1946): 47–51.

[90] Gorski, D. P., ed. *Pensamiento y lenguaje.* Translated by Augusto Vidal Roget. Montevideo: Ediciones Pueblos Unidos. In *Revista Brasileira de Filologia* 5 (1959–60): 217–20.

[91] Herculano de Carvalho, José G. C. *Fonologia Mirandesa.* Coimbra, 1958. In *Letras* (Curitiba), no. 10 (1959), pp. 143–45.

[92] Herculano de Carvalho, José G. C. *Teoria da linguagem.* Volume 1. Coimbra: Atlântida Editora, 1967. In *Language* 45 (1969): 117–19.

[93] von Humboldt, Wilhelm. *Schriften zur Sprachphilosophie.* Stuttgart: J. G. Cotta'sche Buchhandlung, 1963. In *Linguistics*, no. 33 (1967), pp 101–3.

[94] Hymes, Dell, ed. *A Reader in Linguistics and Anthropology.* New York: Harper and Row, 1964. In *Linguistics*, no. 28 (1966), pp. 106–11.

[95] Jakobson, Roman. *Kindersprache, Aphasie und allgemeine Lautgesetze.* Uppsala, 1941. In *Boletim de Filologia* (Rio) 1 (1946): 37–40.

[96] Jakobson, Roman. *Selected Writings I: Phonological Studies.* The Hague: Mouton, 1962. In *Word* 20 (1964) 79–89. Also appears in Portuguese translation under the title *Os estudos fonológicos de Roman Jakobson* as an appendix to item no. 126.

[97] Kainz, Friedrich. *Psychologie der Sprache.* Stuttgart, 1941. In *Boletim de Filologia* (Rio) 1 (1946): 186–89.

[98] Lapa, M. Rodrigues. *Estilística da língua portuguesa.* Lisbon, 1945. In *Boletim de Filologia* 1 (1946): 233–36.

[99] Lenneberg, Eric H. *New Directions in the Study of Language.* Cambridge, Mass.: MIT Press, 1964. In *Linguistics*, no. 44 (1968), pp. 96–97.

[100] Lopes, J. Simões. *Contos Gauchescos e Lendas do Sul.* Edited by Aurélio Buarque de Holanda. Rio de Janeiro: Editôra Glôbo, 1949. In *Boletim de Filologia* 3 (1949): 123–27.

[101] Neto, Serafim da Silva. *Manual de gramática histórica.* In *Revista de Cultura* (Rio) 31 (1942): 327.

[102] Nidermann, J. *Kultur, Werden und Wandlungen des Begriffs.* In *Revista Brasileira de Filologia* 1 (1955): 61.

[103] Paiva Boléo, Manuel de. *Introdução ao estudo da filologia portuguêsa.* Lisbon: Edição da Revista de Portugal, 1946. In *Boletim de Filologia* (Rio) 2 (1947): 113–16.

[104] Paiva Boléo, Manuel de. Algumas tendências e perspectivas da lingüística moderna. Separata from *Revista Portuguêsa de Filologia* 13 (1964–65). In *Estudos Lingüísticos*, vol. 1, no. 1, (1966), pp. 41–42.

[105] Read, William A. *Louisiana French.* Rev. ed. Louisiana State University Press, 1963. In *Archiv für das Studium der neueren Sprachen und Literatur* 202 (1965–66): 474–75.

[106] Rocha Lima, Henrique. *Anotações a textos errados.* In *Revista de Cultura* (Rio) 33 (1943): 140.

[107] Sturtevant, Edgar H. *An Introduction to Linguistic Science.* In *Revista Brasileira de Filologia* 1 (1955): 64.

[108] Sturtevant, Edgar H. *The Indo-Hittite Laryngeals.* Linguistic Society of America, 1942. In *Boletim de Filologia* (Rio) 2 (1947): 116–17.

[109] Swadesh, Morris. *La nueva filología.* México: El Nacional, 1941. In *Boletim de Filologia* (Rio) 1 (1946): 40–47.

[110] Terracini, A. Benvenuto. *¿Qué es la lingüística?* Tucumán: Universidad Nacional de Tucumán, 1942. In *Boletim de Filologia* (Rio) 2 (1948): 249–51.

[111] Trubetzkoy, N. S. *Grundzüge der Phonologie.* Travaux du Cercle Linguistique de Prague, 7. Prague, 1939. In *Boletim de Filologia* (Rio) 1 (1946): 97–107.

[112] Trubetzkoy, N. S. *Principes de Phonologie.* Translated by J. Cantineau. Paris: Librairie Klienksieck, 1949. In *Boletim de Filologia* (Rio) 2 (1949): 53–54.

[113] Zamora Vicente, Alonso. *Las Sonatas de Valle Inclán.* Madrid: Editorial Gredos, 1955. In *Revista Brasileira de Filologia* 2 (1956): 102–6.

VII. Texts

[114] *Princípios de lingüística geral como introdução aos estudos superiores da língua portuguêsa.* 4th ed., rev. Biblioteca Brasileira de Filologia. Rio de Janeiro: Livraria Acadêmica, 1965.

[115] Lições de lingüística geral. *Revista de Cultura* (Rio de Janeiro) 25 (1939): 99–104, 183–89, 216–22, 279–84; 26 (1939): 43–47, 81–86, 177–85; 27 (1940): 21–27, 83–88, 141–46, 202–8; 28 (1940): 11–17.

[116] *Princípios de lingüística geral como fundamento para os estudos superiores da língua portuguesa.* Rio de Janeiro: F. Briguet, 1942.

[117] *Princípios de lingüística geral como introdução aos estudos superiores da língua portuguêsa.* 2d ed., rev. Biblioteca Brasileira de Filologia No. 5. Rio de Janeiro: Livraria Acadêmica, 1954.

[118] *Princípios de lingüística geral como introdução aos estudos superiores da língua portuguêsa.* 3d ed., rev. Biblioteca Brasileira de Filologia no. 5. Rio de Janeiro: Livraria Acadêmica, 1959.

Reviews [115]: Sousa da Silveira in *Revista de Cultura* (Rio de Janeiro) 34: 230. [116]: Vincenzo Cocco in *Revista Portuguesa de Filologia* 1:528–30. See also correction in *Revista Portuguesa de Filologia* 2:537–38. [117]: Júlio García Morejón in *Paideia* (Sorocaba) 1:128 [*cited in Pinto's review of *Princípios* in *Revista de Letras* (Assis) 1:239–42]; R. F. Mansur Guérios in *Letras* (Curitiba), no. 2 (1954), pp. 127–29. [118]: R. F. Mansur Guérios in *Letras* (Curitiba), no. 10 (1959), pp. 148–49; Rolando Morel Pinto in *Revista de Letras* (Assis) 1 (1960):239–42; J. G. Herculano de Carvalho in *Revista Portuguesa de Filologia* 10 (1960): 285–86; Sol Saporta in *Language* 36 (1960): 89–97; E. Alarcos Llorach in *Romance Philology* 15 (1962): 335–38. [114]: Arnold von Buggenhagen in *Revista de Antropologia* (São Paulo) 14 (1966): 134–35; Leodegário. A. de Azevedo in *Revista de Portugal* 31 (1966): 135–48.

From the first to the fourth editions of the *Princípios*, many revisions and expansions were made in the text and bibliography, but the book's basic orientation and coverage remained essentially the same.

This text was written, as M points out in his Nota Prévia in the second edition (pp. 7–8), not as a comprehensive guide to the whole of general linguistics, but rather in order to 'establish those principles that can be called valid in the science of language'. It contains chapters on the scope of linguistics, the phonological, morphological and syntactic structure of language, grammatical categories, historical linguistics, the nature of linguistic loans, and language classification. These fundamental divisions, and the theoretical positions taken on each of them remain the same throughout the succeeding editions, although they were slightly rearranged in the third edition.

Generous additions were, however, made in each new edition. These generally include a fuller discussion of various aspects of each topic, added examples, and, most importantly, many additional bibliographical references. The discussion of phonology, for example, which in the first edition is based primarily on Sapir and Trubetzkoy, includes in the fourth edition references to Harris' simultaneous components, Pike's distinction between 'emic' and 'etic' levels of analysis, a much fuller discussion of the Prague school theories, Jakobson's acoustic distinctive features, and examples of phonological neutralization. The discussion of experimental phonetics includes references to technological innovations that simply did not exist in 1942, such as the sound spectrograph. In the fourth edition the discussion of phoneme types is much more complete, including, for example, clicks and coarticulated stops. But M's basic view of phonological theory remains unchanged.

While the new bibliographic entries added to each edition do not reflect any fundamental change in the text itself, they do broaden its scope significantly since references to them are constantly made in the text. The net result in the fourth edition is a very comprehensive introduction to general linguistics.

The bibliographical additions are of course a direct reflection of the kind of reading M was doing (Nota Prévia in *Princípios*, 2d ed. pp. 7–8) and, as such, are a reasonable guide to the development of his thought. In the first edition, his orientation is heavily French, great stress being laid on Saussure, Grammont, Vendryes, and Meillet in particular. Also, Sapir, Jespersen, and Trubetzkoy are central at this time. M's visit to the United States is reflected in the second edition where a wide variety of American entries predominate. The Italian neolinguists and areal linguists are mentioned for the first time, perhaps in direct response to Cocco's review, which criticized the first edition on this point. Scandinavians (including Hjelmslev), Germans, and many works dealing with Indo-European historical linguistics and with semantics are also mentioned. In the third edition there are many new references to American descriptive linguistics, and in the fourth edition there are for the first time references to Rumanians as well as many more works dealing in some way with semantics. References to works on non-Indo-European are added to every edition.

[119] *Manual de transcrição fonética.* Manuais do Museu Nacional, Série A, no. 2. Rio de Janeiro: Museu Nacional, 1957.

This manual is intended as a practical guide to field work in phonetics, but is brief and has some surprising innovations. It contains a short discussion of narrow and wide phonetic transcriptions, and identifies the latter with a phonemic transcription. The discussion of the varieties of speech sound is based entirely on articulatory descriptions. A system of symbols for phonetic transcription is proposed that has little connection with the IPA. The symbols /e./, /e/ and /e:/ represent low mid, mid, and high mid vowels respectively. Portuguese nasalization is represented by /(n)/, placed after the vowel. The symbols /l₁/ and /r₁/ represent the velar varieties of /l/ and /r/, and /a/ is classified, surprisingly, as a front vowel.

Examples of wide and narrow transcriptions of Portuguese words are given (i.e., /be(n)/ as opposed to /beⁱ(n)/), but a wide transcription by M's definition is phonemic, while the narrow transcriptions he gives are not in fact very detailed.

[120] *Problemas de lingüística descritiva.* Petrópolis: Editôra Vozes, 1969 [first appeared in serialized form in *Vozes* (Petrópolis) 61–62 (1967–68)].

This text consists mainly of a demonstration of the techniques of structural analysis applied to Portuguese. There is a brief introduction to linguistics, a phonemic analysis of the Portuguese vowels, a discussion of syllable types and Portuguese phonotactics, and of what constitutes a phonological word in Portuguese. In the chapter on morphology, M notes that the purpose of diachronic analysis will yield different results from those arrived at by strict attention to the exigencies of synchronic analysis. Examples of morphophonemic alternations are given, and there is a discussion of the differences between inflectional and derivational morphological patterns. Finally, there are two chapters giving a detailed analysis of the most important inflectional and derivational patterns found in the Portuguese nominal and verbal paradigms.

[121] *Introdução às línguas indígenas brasileiras.* 2d ed. rev. Rio de Janeiro: Livraria Acadêmica, 1965 [series of lectures given at the Museu Nacional in 1960. We have seen no reference to a first edition].
[122] Da natureza das línguas indígenas. Separata from *Revista de Letras* (Assis) 3 (1962): 17–29 [reprint of chapter 5 of the preceding item].
Review [121]: Aryón dall'Igna Rodrigues in *Estudos Lingüísticos* 1 (1966): 67–70.

The first five chapters of this book are an introduction to general linguistics, very similar in nature to certain chapters of M's *Princípios*. Chapters 6–8, however, contain a very interesting survey of work done on Brazilian indigenous languages. In Chapter 6, devoted to Tupi studies, M makes a case for the traditional view taken in Brazil that the pidginization of the *língua geral* was primarily the deliberate work of missionaries. Their goal in their work in indigenous languages has always been, M claims, the practical one of communication, rather than the study of the languages themselves. In his review, however, Rodrigues offers arguments against this theory.

Chapters 7 and 8 contain bibliographical sketches of past and present researchers of other indigenous languages. M analyzes the shortcomings of previous research, and discusses the directions new research should take. This text was written specifically to provide the kind of background in linguistics that M feels is necessary for reliable research in indigenous languages. He discusses in this context the valuable work of such contemporaries as Oiticica, Mansur Guérios, Jules Henry, Olive Shell, and Buell Quain, and the important influence of the Summer Institute of Linguistics.

Chapters 9 and 10 contain a discussion of the problems and methods of language classification, including especially references to theories of genetic classification and glottochronology. These chapters are again very similar to parts of the *Princípios*.

The second section of the book is a supplement on research techniques by Sarah Gudschinsky of the Summer Institute of Linguistics.

[123] *Manual de expressão oral e escrita.* Rio de Janeiro: J. Ozon, 1961 [expanded version of lectures given at the Escola de Comando e Estado Maior da Aeronáutica].
Reviews [123]: R. F. Mansur Guérios in *Letras* (Curitiba), no. 12 (1961), pp. 178–80; Lyrio Neotti in *Vozes* (Petrópolis) 56 (1962): 158–59; Sol Saporta in *Romance Philology* 16 (1963): 476–77.

The topics covered in this manual of style include elocution, exposition, composition, sentence structure, spelling, correct usage, purism, choice of words, and figurative speech. Each chapter contains a theoretical discussion of the point in question, followed by a few illustrative examples. As a practical guide to usage it is brief, but nevertheless presents a balanced introduction to the problems involved in saying or writing clearly what one means, particularly for the lay audience for which it was first intended.

M's position throughout is intermediate between that of a purist, for whom the literary language is the only acceptable model, and the view taken by so many linguists that usage is defined simply by what occurs in speech. According to M, the purpose of language is to communicate, so one's primary aim should be simply to avoid disturbing the communication process. On the other hand, all languages recognize a norm, and adherence to this norm is a socially conditioned requirement. Imitation of literary language is not always appropriate, nor is the indiscriminate use of popular speech. 'A língua culta' lies between these two extremes of style, and is the kind of norm most situations require.

VIII. Translations

[124] Sapir, Edward. *A linguagem: introdução ao estudo da fala.* Rio de Janeiro: Instituto Nacional do Livro, 1954. Contains a translator's preface, pp. 7–16.
Reviews [124]: B(ueno), (Francisco da) S(ilveira) in *Jornal de Filologia* 3 (1955): 155–59; N(eto), S(erafim) S(ilva) in *Revista Brasileira de Filologia* 1 (1955): 79–81.

[125] Sapir, Edward. *Lingüística como ciência.* Rio de Janeiro: Livraria Acadêmica, 1961. A selection of articles by Sapir, translated and provided with notes. Contains a translator's preface ('Do tradutor para o leitor'), pp. 7–15.
Review [125]: Lyrio Neotti in *Vozes* 56 (1962): 157–58.

[126] Jakobson, Roman. *Fonema e fonologia.* Rio de Janeiro: Livraria Acadêmica, 1967. A selection of articles from Jakobson's *Selected Writings I: Phonological Studies*, translated and provided with notes. Contains a Portuguese translation of item no. 96.

Index by Date of Publication

Index of Reviewers

Indexes

The Latin and Portuguese word lists included here are by no means exhaustive, and some explanation is needed of the criteria used in choice of the items to be indexed. The words chosen all have some bearing on one of the following topics: structure of Latin, structure of Portuguese, diachronic changes from Latin to Portuguese, and the structure of the lexicon. The numbers refer to pages, and the following abbreviations have been used to indicate, insofar as possible, the context in which the word is discussed.

s–synchronic
d–diachronic
v–vocalism
c–consonantism
st–stress

m–morphophonemics
syl–syllabification
g–gender
n–number
l–lexicon

The underlined items are the immediate topic of discussion, and the few double underlined items are those that I felt to be especially interesting because of some particular problem that they contain.

Kimball L. Robinson

LATIN WORD LIST

acetum 41 d c
actum 53 d v, 47 d c, d syl
ad 46 d c, d syl
afflare 41 d c, 168 l
ager 38 s c
agger 38 s c
agnum 42 d c
amat 46 d c, d syl
annus 167 l, 38 s c
anus 38 s c
apícŭla 24 s st, 25 d v, 168 l
apis 168 l
aratrum 167 l
ars 45 s c
articulum 170 l
attingo 38 s c
audio 133 d c
auiolum 25 s st, 56 d v, 168 l
auum 168 l

battuere 56 d v
bene 51 d c
bona 41 d c
bonum 51 d c, 39 d c
bouem 167 l
bŭcca 38 s c, 168 l
buxum 41 d c

*caballu 168 l
caelum 53 d v
canem 167 l
canere 168 l
cantare 168 l
capio 134 d c, d v
capitia 168 l
caput 168 l, 169 l
carum 39 d c
casa 168 l
caseum 56 d c, 41 d c
Castella 61 d g
causa 167 l
Cepta 47 d c, d syl
cera 40 d c
cĕras 30 s v
cĕras 30 s v
ciconia 56 d v
cíto 40 d c
clamare 41 d c

collína 24 s st
comedere 168 l
complētum 170 d v
conceptum 47 d c, d syl
consul 50 d c
cotidie 45 s c
crus 168 l
cum 46 d c, d syl

dare 39 d c
dedi 53 d v
deus 53 d v
díco 30 s v, 133 d c
díco 30 s v
diem 168 l
digitum 167 l, 41 d c
domus 168 l

edere 168 l
equus 168 l
et 46 d c, d syl

faba 39 d c, 41 d c
*fabulare 168 l
facio 133 d c
filium 167 l
finem 51 d c
focum 167 l
folia 61 d g
fui 53 d v
fuit 53 d v
funis 168 l
fŭrnum 65 d m

gestum 40 d c
grŏssum 65 d m
gutta 39 d c

habeam 133 d c
habere 134 d
hodie 56 d c
horā 30 s v
horă 30 s v

in 46 d c, d syl
integrum 46 s c
inuenire 168 l
iter 169 l
iustum 40 d c

PORTUGUESE WORD LIST

a 46 d c, d syl
abelha 25 d v, 168 l
abrir 49 s syl
absoluto 48 s syl
acaju 173 l
acará 173 l
acougue 173 l
açoute 35 s v
achar 41 d c, 168 l
açu 173 l
admitir 48 s syl
ado(p)ção 34 s v
advogado 48 s syl
águia 43 d c
albufeira 173 l
alcaçuz 173 l
alcaide 173 l
alcova 173 l
aldeia 173 l
alemã 70 s m
alemães 70 s m
alemao 70 s m
alface 43 d c, 173 l
alfageme 173 l
alfaiate 43 d c, 173 l
alfazêma 173 l
alferes 173 l
alfinete 173 l
alforge 173 l
algodão 173 l
alizar 173 l
almocadém 173 l
almotacé 173 l
alto 44 s c v, 49 s syl
amara 26 s st
amará 26 s st
amásseis 53 d v
amaveis 66 s m
amável 67 s m
amplo 42 s c
anho 42 d c
anil 67 s m
animais 49 s syl
animal 67 s m
ano 167 l
anum 173 l
anzol 67 s m
aquarela 174 l
arado 167 l
argênteo 171 l
armazém 173 l
arpejo 174 l
arroba 173 l
arroio 172 l
arroz 173 l

arrue 55 s v
arte 49 s syl
artigo 170 l
aspecto 48 s syl
atue 55 s v
áureo 52 s v, 171 l
auto 44 s c, s v, 47 d c, d syl, 53 d v
avelã 168 l
avô 25 s st, 56 d v, 70 s m, 168 l
azêdo 41 d c
azeite 173 l
azenha 173 l
azinhaga 173 l
azuis 54 s v
azul 67 s m

bairro 173 l
balsa 172 l
ba(p)tismo 34 s v
bater 56 d v
batuque 173 l
beijar 169 l
bela 70 s m
bem 51 d c
bengala 175 l
bezerro 172 l
bloco 49 s syl
boa 41 d c, 70 s m
bôca 168 l
boi 167 l
bom 39 d c, 51 d c, 70 s m
bonzo 175 l
bretão 70 s m
bretoa 70 s m
bretões 70 s m
bússola 174 l
buxo 41 d c

cabeça 168 l
caber 133 d v
cachorro 172 l
cada 36 v
cadente 172 l
caipora 173 l
calunia 171 l
caminho 169 l
camisa 169 l
campo 49 s syl
canja 175 l
cantar 168 l
cão 167 l
capilar 171 l
capim 173 l
cara 169 l
caro 39 d c

SUBJECT INDEX

PORTUGALLIÆ
ET
ALGARBIÆ
REGNA
cu confin:Hispan:Prov:
simul vero pecul:Mappa
BRASILIÆ REGN:
in America Merid:
ujus ora marit:Reg Portu:
Domin: veneratur
t Primog:Regio Infanti
prope dicata flore t
recentina de linea
Cura et Studio
M. SEUTTER
S.C.M.G.
Aug V

OCCIDENTALIS sive ATLANTICUS

OCEANUS

BRASILIA

BRASILIÆ
REGNUM
in America
Meridio
Cum Gir:et Priv:
S.R.I.Vicar:

BAR

BARO

RUAM

MARE

DEL

NORT

Circulus seu Linea Æquinoctialis

Tropicus Capricorni

Septentr.

Meridies

Occidens

Mill. Germanica
Mill. Hispanica
Milliaria Gallica

Scala
Milliaria German:
Milliaria His:
Milliaria Ga: